Endorsements

I am a raving fan of Micky Blackwell, who was a major player in starting our Lead Like Jesus ministry. Micky is a servant leader through and through. Read Enterprise Servant Leadership *to learn about Micky's leadership philosophy and how to be "the best of the best," just like Micky.*

Ken Blanchard, Co-Author,
The New One Minute Manager
and *Lead Like Jesus*

What is unique about this book is that the author uses the real-world experience of James "Micky" Blackwell, a former member of Lockheed Martin's senior leadership team, as a role model for describing how to practice servant leadership before it became popular. Using Micky's experience as an example, he makes a major contribution to the literature. He also gives Micky the credit he so richly deserves.

I met and worked with Micky when I was the Commander-in-Chief of the US Transportation Command, Commander of Air Mobility Command, and later as the Chief of Staff of the United States Air Force. I was unaware of the uniqueness of his leadership philosophy. I only knew he was a gentleman and member of a defense company who made good on his promises to me and to the combat effectiveness of the US Air Force.

Having read this book and learned about Micky's approach to leadership, I now understand why he was so good — and what makes this book so special.

Ron Fogleman, General, USAF, Retired
15th Chief of Staff
United States Air Force

Micky Blackwell is a servant leader in the best sense of the word. I have known Micky for over 50 years both as a leader of business and in our Methodist church. He distinguished himself in business and was an outstanding Sunday School teacher. I highly recommend Enterprise Servant Leadership *as a blueprint for business and a pattern for life.*

Former Georgia Governor Roy E. Barnes
Attorney, Barnes Law Group, LLC
Marietta, Georgia

Enterprise Servant Leadership is a full-blown celebration of the timeless principles of servant leadership and its power to guide a life, transform an organization, and deliver spectacular results. This book blends an engaging personal testimony, a detailed case study, and road map for others to follow into a high value resource.

The story of Micky's journey to become a leader of great influence is inspiring and candid. Micky is quick to pay tribute to the people who helped along the way. Special credit is given to growing up in a Christian family and being joined in his journey by his beloved wife Billie. The lessons he learned along the way are a special gift.

Materna's case study documents the influence of one man who was committed to applying servant leadership to transform an organization resulting in a product that became the F-22 Stealth Fighter. The stakes were high for his organization and his country. The competition was fierce, and the standards of excellence were absolute. The servant leader organization, and the thinking behind it, is clearly presented in a well-organized way.

The core principle of servant leadership "to serve rather than be served" is not new. But as Micky Blackwell demonstrated and Robert Materna celebrates, it is as powerful and effective today as it was when the greatest servant leader of all time established it as a mandate.

"Not so with you but whoever wants to be great among you, let him be your servant…Just as the son of Man came to serve rather than be served" (Matthew 20:27-28 NIV).

Read it and be inspired. Live it and inspire others.

Phil Hodges, Co-Founder,
The Center for Faithwalk Leadership
dba *Lead Like Jesus*

Dr. Robert Materna's excellent book tells the story of Micky Blackwell from his youth into retirement. As head of development and manufacturing of the F-22 Raptor at Lockheed and later as the president and COO of the Lockheed Martin Aeronautical Sector, Blackwell developed a style of management called "Enterprise Servant Leadership." Blackwell's approach was to lead like Jesus, totally devoted to serving his staff as well as other stakeholders. In the process, he inspired employees to turn the Raptor into a stealth fighter aircraft that could keep America safe. The book explains how Micky changed the way management systems could be modified — from traditional functional management to one based on teams and concurrent engineering.

Micky Blackwell used the Bible as a guide and service to others as a model. As a result of these efforts, Micky will forever stand tall in business, as well as in life.

Neely Young, Emeritus Editor
Georgia Trend Magazine

Enterprise Servant Leadership

a new way of doing business to
Be the Best of the Best

Based on Lessons Learned from the Life and Work of
James "Micky" Blackwell
Leader of the F-22 Stealth Fighter
and Lockheed Martin's Aeronautics Sector

ROBERT MATERNA, PH.D.

United Writers Press
Asheville, N.C.

ISBN: 978-1-961813-54-0 (Casebound)
ISBN: 978-1-961813-55-7 (Paperback)
ISBN: 978-1-961813-56-4 (ePub)

Published by:
United Writers Press
Asheville, N.C.
www.UWPnew.com
828-505-1037

Where scriptural verses have been included within, the Bible translation from which they were taken is noted with the verses themselves. They include the *English Standard Version (ESV)*, the *New King James Version (NKJV)*, the *King James Version (KJV)*, the *New American Standard Bible (NAS)*, *the New International Version (NIV)*, *The Living Bible (TLB)*, and *the Modern English Version (MEV)*.

Cover Photograph:

Fast pass: Maj. Josh Gunderson, F-22 Raptor Demonstration Team pilot and commander, performs a high-speed pass during the Wings Over Houston Airshow at Ellington Airport in Houston, Oct. 10, 2021. The high-speed pass reaches speeds up to 94 percent of the speed of sound, which is only a fraction of the aircraft's speed capability. (US Air Force photo by Staff Sgt. Don Hudson)

Skunk Works® is a registered trademark of the Lockheed Martin Corporation.

Printed in the USA.

To my wife Sharyn

Whose unwavering spirit and years of support made this book possible.
You are the love of my life. Thank you for never giving up on me.

Contents

Part II: Servant Leadership of Integrated Product Teams 51

List of Acronyms and Abbreviations

AAF	Army Air Force
AEW	Airborne Early Warning
AFRL	Air Force Research Laboratories
AFSC	Air Force Systems Command
AIAA	American Institute of Aeronautics and Astronautics
AMDC	Aviation Museum and Discovery Center
AMRAAM	Advanced Medium Range Air-to-Air Missile
ASD	Aeronautical Systems Division
ASG	Aeronautical Systems Group
ASW	Anti-submarine Warfare
ATF	Advanced Tactical Fighter
BRAC	Base Realignment and Closure
CBO	Congressional Budget Office
CEO	Chief Executive Officer
CIP	Common Integrated Processor
CONUS	Continental United States
COO	Chief Operating Officer
CPFR	Collaborative Planning, Forecasting, and Replenishment
CRS	Congressional Research Service
CTOL	Conventional Takeoff and Landing
DARPA	Defense Advanced Research Projects Agency
DEM/VAL	Demonstration and Validation
DOD	Department of Defense
ECM	Electronic Countermeasures
EMD	Engineering and Management Development
ERP	Enterprise Resource Planning
ESL	Enterprise Servant Leadership
ESLMM	Enterprise Servant Leadership Management Model
EVP	Executive Vice President
EW	Electronic Warfare
FAA	Federal Aviation Administration
G&A	General and Administrative
GAO	General Accountability Office
GD	General Dynamics
HPO	High Performing Organization
HPP	High Performing Partnership

HQ	USAF Headquarters United States Air Force
HUD	Housing and Urban Development
ICIM	Integrated Corporate Infrastructure Management
IOC	Initial Operating Capability
IPDT	Integrated Product Development Team
IPT	Integrated Product Team
IR&D	Internal Research and Development
IRIS	Integrated Resource and Infrastructure Solutions
JIT	Just in Time
JSF	Joint Strike Fighter
LAAC	Lockheed Advanced Aeronautics Company
LASC	Lockheed Aeronautical Systems Company
LCC	Lifecycle Cost
LM	Lockheed Martin
LPPD	Lean Product and Process Development
MFUMC	Marietta First United Methodist Church
MOD	Ministry of Defense
MRC	Marietta Redevelopment Corporation
MRO	Maintenance, Repair, and Overhaul
MTBF	Mean Time Between Failures
MTTR	Mean Time to Repair
NASA	National Aeronautics & Space Administration
NATF	Navy Advanced Tactical Fighter
OEM	Original Equipment Manufacturer
OSD	Office of Secretary of Defense
R&D	Research and Development
R&M	Reliability and Maintainability
R&R	Rest and Recuperation
RAAF	Royal Australian Air Force
RCS	Radar Cross Section
RDT&E	Research Development Test and Evaluation
RFP	Request for Proposal
SAF	Secretary of the Air Force
SDD	System Development and Demonstration
SECDEF	Secretary of Defense
SPO	System Program Office
SRA	Strategically Relevant Activities
STEM	Science, Technology, Engineering, and Mathematics

STOL	Short Takeoff and Landing
TAC	Tactical Air Command
TARP	Troubled Asset Relief Program
TQM	Total Quality Management
TPO	Team Project Office
UAV	Unmanned Aerial Vehicle
UK	United Kingdom
UTC	United Technology Corporation
V/STOL	Vertical Short Takeoff and Landing
WBS	Work Breakdown Structure

List of Figures

Figure 1. The first F-22 was unveiled on April 9, 1997, at Lockheed Martin's facilities in Marietta, Georgia. This initial fifth-generation fighter was called the Spirit of America. During the unveiling, it was given its official nickname—Raptor. (Photo by John Rossino, Lockheed Martin).	1
Figure 2. The figure above represents the flow of information in this book that describes the transformation of the Traditional Functional Management Model into the Enterprise Servant Leadership Management Model.	7
Figure 3. Micky at 10 in Jasper, Alabama. (Photo courtesy of Micky Blackwell)	13
Figure 4. Micky and Billie's wedding reception. (Photo courtesy of Micky Blackwell)	14
Figure 5. Micky's supervisor at NASA Langley, Dr. Richard "Dick" Whitcomb. (NASA Photo)	19
FIgure 6. Royal Saudi Air Force C-130 Hercules. (Public Domain)	23
Figure 7. Evolution of the F-22 Raptor.	35
Figure 8. The Lockheed/Boeing/General Dynamics YF-22 fires an AIM-120 missile over the Pacific. (Lockheed Martin Photo)	35
Figure 9. The Northrop-McDonnell Douglas YF-23 in flight. (USAF photo)	35
Figure 10. Memo Announcing Micky's Assignment as Vice President and Assistant General Manager of the F-22. (Image provided by Micky Blackwell)	37
Figure 11. Micky's personal notes from the F-22 "We Won!" speech.	43
Figure 12. The Five Levels of Servant Leadership.	59
Figure 13. The SR-71 is an example of what the Skunk Works does best. Unofficially known as the "Blackbird," it was a long-range, advanced, strategic reconnaissance aircraft, now retired. (US Air Force photo by Tech. Sgt. Michael Haggerty)	68
Figure 14. Micky's Steps for Developing and Using Integrated Product Teams.	88
Figure 15. Servant-Led Business Model.	113
Figure 16. Innovation icon.	119
Figure 17. Define the Business Model for a New Business Opportunity.	126
Figure 18. Conduct a Capabilities Assessment.	127
Figure 19. Prioritize the Gaps.	128
Figure 20. Select and Place People.	128
Figure 21. Add Value for Stakeholders.	129
Figure 22. The Elements of the Enterprise Servant Leadership Management Model.	132
Figure 23. Memo Announcing Micky's Promotion to president, Lockheed Aeronautical Systems Company. (Image courtesy of Micky Blackwell)	152
Figure 24. A C-5M Super Galaxy assigned to the 60th Air Mobility Wing, Travis Air Force Base, Calif. sits on the flight line at Yokota Air Base, Japan, Sept. 14, 2021. Airmen from the 730th Air Mobility Squadron participated in different training exercises including maintenance, inspections and loading capabilities in order to maintain mission readiness. (Photo courtesy of the USAF)	153
Figure 25. Micky discussing issues with Gen. Ron Fogleman. (Photo courtesy of Micky Blackwell)	155
Figure 26. Micky with Prince Philip at an Air Tattoo Show in England. (Photo courtesy of Micky Blackwell)	155
Figure 27. Micky with Prince Sultan in tent in Saudi Arabia. (Photo courtesy of Micky Blackwell)	157
Figure 28. Micky with King and Queen of Jordan at an International Air Tattoo in England.	158
Figure 29. Micky recognized as AIAA Fellow. (Courtesy of Bill Petros)	158
Figure 30. Micky (right) at lunch with Ken Cannestra (left) and Donald Rumsfeld (center). (Photo courtesy of Micky Blackwell)	159
Figure 31. Invitation to event acknowledging Micky as a "Captain of Industry."	159
Figure 32. Billie and Micky at a black-tie event in Washington, D.C. (Photo courtesy of Micky Blackwell)	159
Figure 33. Lockheed Martin Sales by Sector, 1994.	164
Figure 34 a, b, and c. Preparing for First Flight of the Raptor. (Photos courtesy of Micky Blackwell)	166
Figure 35. Micky with Dan Goldin, Director of NASA, on Space Day, 1997. (Photo courtesy of Micky Blackwell)	168

The Seed, The Sower
— and —
The F-22 Raptor

This book is dedicated to the one who taught in parables.

It is a real-life example of the parable of the sower.

The story is about a seed that was sown on good ground.

The seed grew up in a family where he knew he was loved.

His parents took him to church and taught him the Word.

The Word shaped the man's heart and everything he did.

He taught us how to love, and he taught us how to serve.

God blessed him mightily and then blessed him more.

The seed grew into a man

who became a servant leader.

That gentle leader became

the spirit of the F-22 Raptor.

Foreword

It is a privilege for me to recommend this book. It is about a man who used servant leadership to build the F-22 Raptor. His name is James "Micky" Blackwell, and he is a paragon of leadership in a world starved for excellence. He embodies the qualities defined by Jesus Christ in the Bible: humility, perseverance, integrity, and forgiveness. He used those qualities to accomplish what many said was impossible. My hope is that you will also use the lessons in this book to achieve something remarkable—something wholesome and good that adds value to our world.

Servant leadership was barely known when Micky implemented it on the Raptor. It was one of our country's finest achievements, yet few know much about it. Micky was in charge during the development and manufacturing stage of an aircraft that was so sophisticated it could not be exported. Twenty years ago, it stunned the world with its stealth qualities. Today, it still provides our Air Force with first-look, first-shoot, first-kill capabilities. It can fly at more than the speed of sound without engaging afterburners, and our enemies cannot see it because it is still stealthy.

The US Air Force gave the name "Raptor" to the F-22 when it was introduced in 1997. The name is derived from the word "rapio," which means to take by force. Today, the Merriam-Webster Dictionary says "raptor" refers to a bird with sharp eyes and long claws—a predator that can kill others before they know what hit them. It is clear the Air Force did a great job naming this fighter. The naming of the aircraft could not be better.

The development of the Raptor was highly visible and important to our county. It was visible because of its cost, and important because of the need for the United States to maintain air superiority. Our enemies were beginning to threaten us, and our ability to defend ourselves was being challenged. America needed help, and needed it fast, before our enemies could close the fighter performance gap. There were not many options for maintaining our lead in aerospace, but that is exactly what Micky did when he led the development of this remarkable aircraft.

Micky's achievements are legion, but one stands out—how he applied servant leadership to design and produce this state-of-the-art fighter. Today, people realize servant leadership motivates people. People need to be recognized, and they want to be respected. That is part ofthe culture Micky built into the F-22 program. When barriers are broken, innovation takes over, and innovation is the hallmark of the F-22 Raptor. More ideas create more value, and the cycle continues. This book is rich with examples that illustrate how this works. It is also very personal as it reveals what Micky learned from his failures.

After a lifetime of serving others, Micky knows how to inspire people. Part of inspiring people comes from trusting them to do what is right. Doing what is right leads to a free and fulfilling life. Such a life makes one realize the value of service—as servant leaders submit themselves to the one who created the earth.

This book is a tribute to James "Micky" Blackwell. It also presents new information about being a servant leader. If you find these words encouraging, I urge you to read this book.

Tom Gray
Senior Pastor, Mars Hill Community Church

Introduction

The business of servant leadership is bigger than all of us.

Gen. David Goldfein
Chief of Staff, United States Air Force
Address at the USAF Academy
22 February 2019

The Right Stuff

In 1979, Tom Wolfe published a novel about test pilots and astronauts. The title was *The Right Stuff,* and it was an overnight success. Thanks to Wolfe's book and the movie that followed, people now know what it took to be the world's best test pilot or one of the first astronauts to orbit the earth. They were the best America had to offer. Some say they were the best of the best.

This book addresses a different, but similar, question. What kind of stuff does it take for a leader to build the world's best air superiority fighter,[1] the F-22 (see Figure 1), propel Lockheed Martin[2] to the top of the aeronautical defense industry, and build a servant-led enterprise that produces superior value for customers? This story is not about test pilots or astronauts, but it is about a leader who had that same passion to be the best of the best. His name is James A. Blackwell, Jr., known by his nickname, "Micky." As you read this book, you can be the judge of whether "Micky" had the "right stuff."

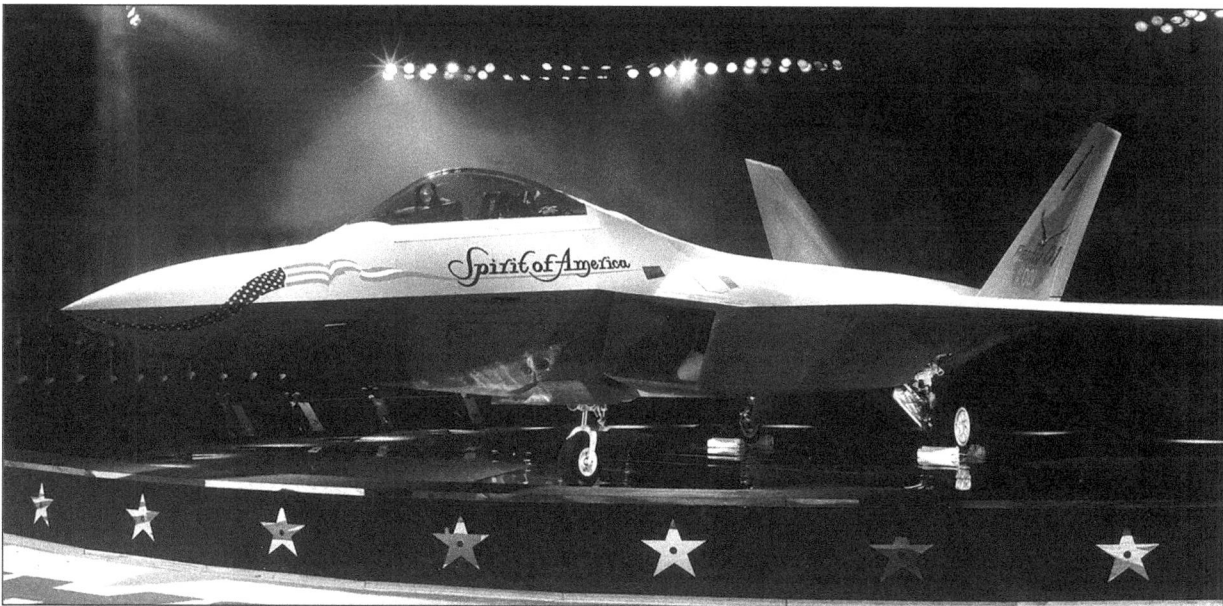

Figure 1. The first F-22 was unveiled on April 9, 1997, at Lockheed Martin's facilities in Marietta, Georgia. This initial fifth-generation fighter was called the Spirit of America. During the unveiling, it was given its official nickname—Raptor.
(Photo by John Rossino, Lockheed Martin).

I came to know Micky in 1995, when my wife and I purchased his home in Marietta, Georgia. Micky was in the process of moving to Washington, D.C. to be president and COO of the Lockheed Martin Aeronautics Sector.[3] In this role, he would lead all of Lockheed Martin's aeronautical business around the world. Later, when Micky retired and moved back to Marietta, we struck up a friendship. We participated together in a weekly Bible study and often played golf together. As a Christian, former Air Force pilot, and former professor of business at Embry-Riddle Aeronautical University–Worldwide, I became intrigued with what Micky had accomplished and how he had done it.

When I looked deeper into Micky's life and work, I saw that he had led the creation of a new **Enterprise Servant Leader Management Model** that was superior to any management model that had existed before. He used **Servant Leaders** to successfully lead small projects, the development of the F-22 Raptor, and the reengineering of very large Lockheed Martin enterprises. I felt it was important to pass on to others what Micky and his teams had created and used successfully, so that others could benefit from his work.

*A **management model** summarizes the behavior demonstrated by managers.*

A servant leader is "one who is totally devoted to serving others and totally committed to achieving their personal or professional goals." — Micky Blackwell

---

Like any good book, there are always many parts to a story. In this case, the story isn't just about Micky's many achievements. The real story is about how Micky evolved as a servant leader and changed the way the world's largest defense contractor managed their entire enterprise. This change moved Lockheed Martin from producing very good products and services to producing the best of the best.

You can talk about servant leaders all day long, but ultimately people need to see them in action, producing superior value, before they change their behavior and adopt the core values of a servant leader. That is why I tell the story about Micky Blackwell as a servant leader in considerable detail. I want you to see that servant leadership is *real* and produces superior results.

In today's world, future leaders need real role models to pattern their lives after. Seeing and studying the lives of successful servant leaders is simply the best way to communicate how a servant leader is to behave and not to behave. Servant leaders give themselves to the people they lead. They live with their people, work with them, love them, suffer with them, rejoice with them, and demonstrate, by example, how a servant leader should lead.

Where can these role models be found? Leading and serving others within many faith traditions but also in a secular life. As we will see, Micky's servant leader role model is Jesus, whom he considers to be the greatest servant leader of all time, and he believes that the best version of a servant leader is one who lives their life following the core values found in the Bible.

Micky Blackwell's Story

Micky Blackwell retired from Lockheed Martin in 2000, more than 20 years before this book was written. Even though he is well known as Vice President and General Manager of the F-22 stealth fighter, few know about his rise to become president and chief operating officer of the Aeronautics Sector at Lockheed Martin Corporation—and even fewer know about his many public service achievements.

The key to Micky's success wasn't his keen intellect or charismatic nature. What made him so effective was his commitment to people. He was committed to those he worked for and a servant to those he led. He loved and respected his people. He had a servant leader's heart. His passion was to always be the best of the best.

This is a story about a young man who grew up on a farm in Alabama, became a Christian at age 13, evolved into a man, and captured the spirit of a servant leader. In the process, he, introduced multifunctional integrated product teams, led the development of the world's most advanced air superiority fighter (the F-22), and implemented world-class process improvements in the organizations he led—increasing quality, reducing costs, and enhancing supportability. Later, he became president of the Lockheed Aeronautical Systems Company in Marietta, Georgia and led the Lockheed Martin Corporation's Aeronautics Sector as president and COO. After he retired, he worked to improve the quality of life for people in his home city of Marietta and in his home state of Georgia using the same servant leadership concepts, business skills, and processes he used during his professional career.

Micky Blackwell and the Raptor play a key part in this book, not because they were good, but because they were the best. It was Lockheed Martin's desire to win the Advanced Tactical Fighter program that provided the motivation to re-engineer all its business processes to become a **lean enterprise.**

Even though Micky poured his heart and soul into the F-22 program, he will be the first to say that many people deserve credit for its success. From the time it was conceived to the time it was operational, many hands touched the Raptor before it was deployed. Some are mentioned in this book, but others are not. It is not because they don't deserve it, but because the focus of this book is on Micky's servant leadership style, organizational innovations, and lean business processes that he successfully implemented.

*A **lean enterprise** is an organization that is focused on value creation for the end customer with minimal waste and processes.*

During Micky's retirement ceremony, the CEO of Lockheed Martin called him the "Father of the Raptor," a title not readily given to many aerospace engineers who lead programs. It is a mark of Micky's humility that he does not accept this title. In Micky's opinion, designing and then building the F-22 was a total team effort led by many outstanding leaders.

Years later, the F-22 won the Collier Trophy for the greatest aeronautical achievement in America for 2006.[4] Not only did the F-22 exceed expectations, but Micky's stellar leadership set new thresholds for excellence.

Years after retirement, Micky continues to amaze us. The breadth and depth of his knowledge is remarkable and, as an engineer, he had few equals. Captains of industry rarely rest on their laurels, and Micky is no exception. He served on the boards of large universities and corporations and chaired the Military Affairs Committee for two governors of Georgia. He is active in his community and led the city-wide Redevelopment Task Force for the mayor of Marietta, Georgia. He participates and teaches in a weekly Bible study and is active as a leader in his church. He has written a book on "corporate prayer"[5] and recently published a memoir of his and his wife's lives, *All the Days of our Lives: The Heritage and History of Billie and James Blackwell.*[6]

For those who may be thinking this sounds like a lot of spin, this story is not just about Micky's successes as a servant leader, it is also about what he learned from some of his most painful and public failures.

Micky is intelligent, well spoken, and has a naturally commanding presence, but it is what people don't see that makes him so special. When asked where he learned about servant leadership, Micky's response was straightforward: "All I know about servant leadership came from Jesus, the best servant leader to ever walk the earth."

All I know about leadership came from Jesus,
the best servant leader to ever walk the earth. – Micky Blackwell

---

New Management Model and Business Systems Needed for the F-22

The importance of Lockheed (now Lockheed Martin) winning the Advanced Tactical Fighter (ATF) contract (which became the F-22 program) cannot be overstated. In the late 1980s, all the aircraft production programs within Lockheed, with one exception, were ending. *The ATF was a must-win for Lockheed!*

The US Air Force badly needed the ATF to replace the aging F-15 Eagle Fighter. Based on the aircraft industry's poor track record of remaining under budget in the 1980s, the United States Air Force was worried about major cost overruns on the program. As a result, in their ATF Request for Proposal (RFP), the Air Force signaled their willingness to change how they did business. The ATF RFP required teams to create and implement a new management model that emphasized **concurrent engineering**.

A major turning point in Micky's professional life came on January 19, 1989, when he was appointed Vice President and Assistant General Manager (VP & Asst. GM) of the ATF program.

Concurrent engineering is a work approach to product design and development that emphasizes performing design engineering, manufacturing engineering, and other work functions concurrently and collaboratively in teams.

He recognized that leading the internal Lockheed portion of the ATF was going to be a major challenge. He also knew there had to be drastic changes if Lockheed and its team, which included Boeing and General Dynamics, were to have a chance of winning the ATF program.

Using traditional management models, the ATF design and development would be complex to manage, and perhaps, most important, would be very costly to produce. It was clear that "business-as-usual" would no longer work. Traditional design and manufacturing approaches could not produce an aircraft at a price the government could afford. Nor could it produce an aircraft fast enough to meet the demand needed.

The "traditional management model" used in the aircraft industry in the late 1980s was organized around "functional stovepipes." This model inhibited communication and collaboration. It also resulted in major cost increases when a design could not be manufactured or supported and had to be redesigned. The stovepipe model encouraged managers to micromanage their organizations and give directions from the top down without collaborating with their employees or with sister functional organizations. This reduced the willingness of employees to innovate and to take risks.

The stovepipe model had to be replaced with one that promoted integrated teams using concurrent engineering and servant leadership. Collaborative engineering was needed to execute the ATF program successfully.

Most of the business systems in the aircraft industry in the late 1980s were in dire need of being updated to provide timely management data. Timely data was needed to enable the use of lean enterprise processes (creating needed value with fewer resources and less waste). Manufacturing systems had to be shifted from batch processing to one-piece flow to reduce waste and cost. Manufacturing times had to be shortened and quality processes, such as 6-Sigma (methodologies and tools used to improve business processes by reducing defects and errors, minimizing variation, and increasing quality and efficiency) had to be implemented. In short, a new management model was needed to create superior value for Lockheed's customers. Because the ATF was a must win for the Corporation, the Lockheed leadership was willing to invest in the new organizational and management process changes that were needed to be successful.

Just prior to the announcement that Lockheed Martin and its partners had won the AFT competition, Lockheed named Micky to lead the F-22 team. As a result, Micky knew that when Lockheed won the award for the ATF program, it would be his responsibility to design and implement the management and business process changes.

When the Air Force announced that the Lockheed team was the ATF winner (and the jet would be designated F-22), Micky and Col. James A. Fain,[7] the Air Force System Program Office (SPO) Director, immediately began to work on a more collaborative approach toward building the airplane. Colonel Fain was willing to walk away from the military's arms-length procurement practices if a "better management model could be created. The Air Force was also very supportive of implementing new business systems and lean enterprise processes that would lower cost and improve the quality of the F-22.

Enterprise Servant Leadership Management Model

Working with the Air Force Systems Program Office, a new management model emerged out of the design and production of the F-22 stealth fighter. The new model was further developed through the subsequent reengineering of the Lockheed Aeronautical Systems Company and the Lockheed Martin Aeronautics Sector.

To distinguish the new model from the traditional management paradigm, I have named the new model the **"Enterprise Servant Leadership Management Model."** This new model is based on using servant leaders to transform the traditional management model by organizing around collaborative multifunctional integrated product teams that implement new world-class lean enterprise systems and processes that maximize value for the end customer.

Enterprise Servant Leaders *lead collaborative multifunctional integrated product teams that implement world-class lean enterprise processes to create maximum value for the end customer.*

Leaders in this new model are called **"Enterprise Servant Leaders."** The term "Enterprise" is used because it denotes the ability to accomplish something difficult that involves the entire organization. The term **"Servant Leaders"** is used to describe the collaborative way people maximize organizational performance, minimize cost, and serve the best interests of the organization and the people in it.

Purpose of Book

The purpose of this book is to describe in detail a new way of doing business called the "Enterprise Servant Leadership Management Model" (ESLMM) that is superior to traditional management models. The ESLMM is based on the life and work of James "Micky" Blackwell and his teams. Specifically, I would like to show how this new model:

- **Helps future leaders and their organizations become the best of the best.**
- **Creates maximum value for their customers.**
- **Fully engages company employees to attain maximum performance in every area of the business enterprise.**

Overview of Book

In the chapters that follow, we will address, from Micky's life and work, enterprise servant leader implementation guidelines; new enterprise management processes, systems, and models that produce superior value; and new development tools that improve quality, cut costs, and reduce time to market. The information from each of these topics flows together as illustrated in Figure 2 to transform the "Traditional Functional Management Model" that describes the way managers have traditionally behaved into an **"Enterprise Servant Leader Management Model"** that describes how the managers of the future will behave.

The Enterprise Servant Leadership Management Model presented in this book is based on Christian core values. Select verses from scripture are inserted in the text to help the reader better understand these core values and how they apply to the Enterprise Servant Leader Management Model described in this book.

The book is divided into four parts followed by concluding remarks:

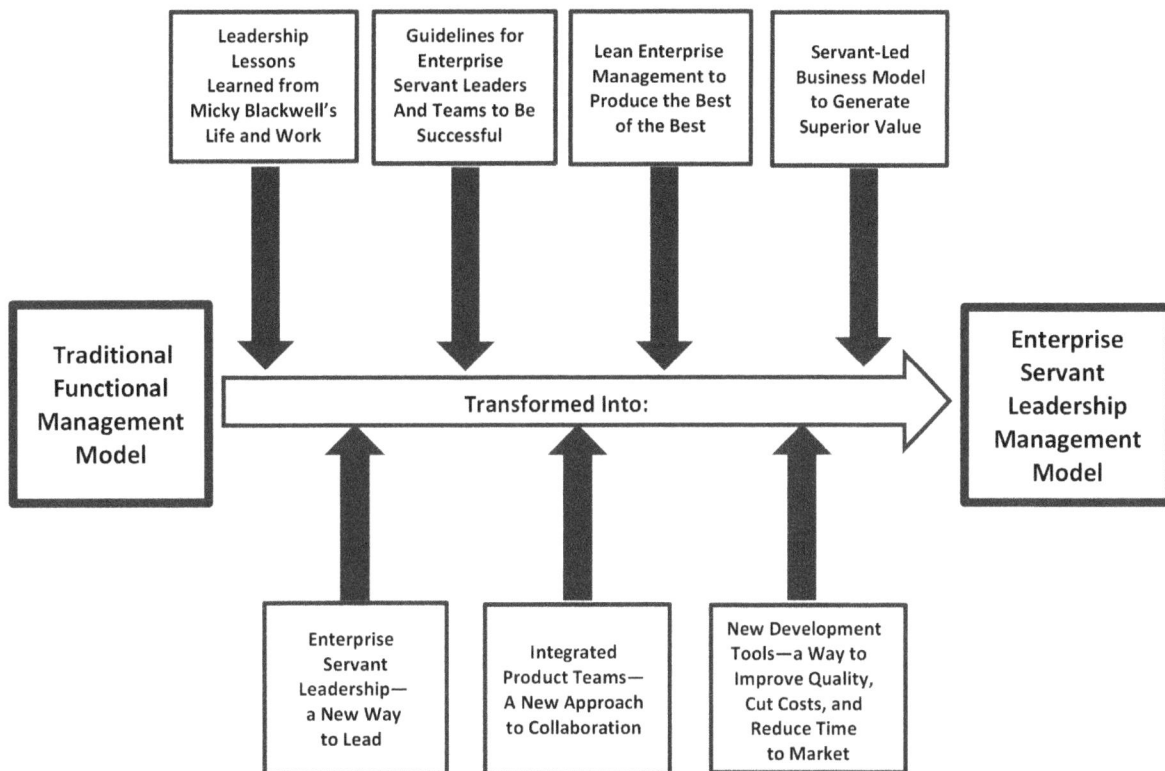

Figure 2. The figure above represents the flow of information in this book that describes the transformation of the Traditional Functional Management Model into the Enterprise Servant Leadership Management Model.

Part I: Learning to Be a Servant Leader (Chapters 1 to 4). The story begins by describing Micky's journey to learn about Servant Leadership. Micky's early years are covered where he was just learning about servant leadership. It includes seven years working at NASA Langley Research Center in Virginia that developed his engineering skills and showed him how to operate in a large organization. That was followed by his moves to Lockheed in Marietta, Georgia and Burbank, California that provided his first opportunity to lead and absorb greater responsibilities.

Part II: Servant Leadership of Integrated Product Teams (Chapters 5 to 7). These chapters show how enterprise servant leadership can make a positive difference in managing major programs. It presents guidelines for helping enterprise servant leaders be successful and outlines how to organize collaborative multifunctional, high-performance integrated product teams.

Part III: A New Enterprise Servant Leadership Model (Chapters 8 to 10). This part of the book describes the use of enterprise management development tools such as Lean, Enterprise Resource Planning, Kaizen, 6-Sigma, 6S, and other Total Quality Management processes to improve quality, reduce man-hours, reduce labor costs, reduce overhead expenses, and lower material costs. A new servant-led business model is also presented that can be used to create superior value for end customers. Finally, a map for the reader is provided so they can implement the Enterprise Servant Leader Management Model in various ways and venues.

Part IV: Using the Enterprise Servant Leadership Model to Become the Best of the best (Chapters 11 to 14). These chapters present examples of how the use of Enterprise Servant Leaders, integrated product teams, lean enterprise management, integrated business systems, and lean enterprise development tools were used under Micky's leadership at the Lockheed Aeronautical Systems Company, the Lockheed Martin Aeronautics Sector, and in the private sector after he retired from Lockheed Martin in pursuit of becoming the best of the best.

Concluding Remarks: In the final chapter of the book, I offer some concluding remarks. Specifically, I will talk about how Servant Leadership is different from most management philosophies. I also address how this book expands the body of knowledge on servant leadership for readers.

The Power of What Is Possible

As this book was assembled, it began to paint a picture. The picture is not complete, but one thing is certain. If the American people knew the whole story, they would forever be thankful to James "Micky" Blackwell. While the F-22 made us safer, what he taught us was more important. He showed us the power of what's possible when we put our fellow man first.

Commit to being the best you can be in every facet of your life. Your good name is your most important asset. Once you lose it, you can almost never get it back.
— Micky Blackwell

Chapter Notes

1 The Lockheed, Boeing, and General Dynamics aircraft in the USAF Advanced Tactical Fighter competition, the YF-22, which was later designated the F-22 and named Raptor.

2 The Lockheed Corporation merged with the Martin Marietta Corporation in 1995 to become the Lockheed Martin Corporation.

3 Micky's title of "Lockheed Martin Corporation president and COO of the Aeronautics Sector" was later renamed to "Lockheed Martin Corporation Executive Vice President of the Aeronautical Systems Business Area." To avoid confusion, I have continued with the first title throughout the book.

4 Lockheed Martin News Room. n.d. Lockheed Martin F-22 Named Collier Trophy Winner. PRNewswire-FirstCall, Orlando, Florida. Retrieved March 16, 2022 https://news.lockheedmartin.com/2007-02-08-Lockheed-Martin-F-22-Named-Collier-Trophy-Winner

5 James "Micky" Blackwell. 2009. *When Two or More are Gathered in Prayer: How Praying Together can Change our World.* Asheville, N.C.: United Writers Press.

6 James "Micky" Blackwell. 2021. *All the Days of our Lives: The Heritage and History of Billie and James Blackwell.* Asheville, N.C.: United Writers Press.

7 Col. James A. Fain, the Air Force System Program Office Director was subsequently promoted to major general while leading the F-22 program. He retired in 1995 as a lieutenant general serving as Assistant Vice Chief of Staff, Headquarters, US Air Force at the Pentagon.

Part I:
Learning to Be a Servant Leader

Chapter 1
Getting Ready to Serve

The first thing the F-22 will kill is the enemy's appetite for war.

Micky Blackwell
President & COO Aeronautics Sector (Retired)
Lockheed Martin Corporation

In Part I of the book, Micky's journey to become an Enterprise Servant Leader is described. We begin by presenting in Chapter 1 a description of his early years where he was just learning about servant leadership and God was preparing him to serve others.

The Formative Years

James A. Blackwell, Jr. was born in Memphis, Tennessee, on December 22, 1940. Micky's father's full name was James Augusta Blackwell Sr., but his friends called him "Jim" or "Jimmy." His mother was Bonnie Jean Blackwell. When their new son was born, he was named after his father. However, there was an issue. His parents didn't want to call their newborn "James," "Jim," or "Jimmy." A nickname was needed. Someone suggested "Micky" and everyone seemed to like it. From that day forward, James Augusta Blackwell Jr. was simply called "Micky."[1]

In June 1943, during World War II, his father went to work for the Army Air Force (AAF) in Gadsden, Alabama where he worked at the Goodyear Tire and Rubber Company. He was "Inspector in Charge" for the AAF where he was responsible for overseeing the inspection of tires and self-sealing fuel tanks for multiple types of military aircraft. He remained in the job until January 1945, not long after the arrival of Micky's younger brother Doug.

The AAF then transferred Micky's father to Bristol, Virginia where he continued his work as chief inspector of fuel cells for the B-24 and B-29 bombers. In late 1945, he was involuntarily separated from the Army Air Force due to a reduction-in-force at the end of the war. Micky and his family then moved back to Memphis, where his dad held various jobs in the chemical industry.

In January 1950, Micky's family moved from Memphis to his father's childhood home near Jasper, Alabama, where Micky's father bought most of his father's farm.[2] Later that year, Micky's family moved into a new home, just down the road from where his grandfather lived. It was a modest two-bedroom home, with one bath, a kitchen, den, living room, and dining room. Telephone party lines were common, and the water had a slight taste of sulfur. Micky helped his father grow cotton, corn, and hay on their new family farm. They also raised cows and kept a vegetable garden to furnish them with plenty of healthy food.

Great Parents, Small Stature, and a Desire to be the Best

Micky's father then took a job with Alabama Power Company in Gorgas, Alabama, working in water treatment. He enjoyed working with chemicals and loved to farm and his schedule at the power company gave him time to farm in the evenings. He also farmed on Saturdays, but that is where he drew the line. He never worked on Sundays. That was family time. Micky's mother, who worked for Sears in Memphis before she married Micky's father, was able to continue working in the Sears catalogue store in Jasper.

The closest community to the farm, was Townley, Alabama. That's where Micky went to school, and the family joined a small church. At one time, Townley had a bank, a movie theater, a small number of stores, and a jail. Underground coal mines brought prosperity to Townley, but when the mines closed, almost everything else left as well. As a result, Townley became a ghost town with only a few churches, a post office, and small grocery stores remaining. However, several stately homes continued to be occupied. That is how it was when Micky arrived in Townley.

The name of their place of worship was Townley First Baptist Church. That might sound convenient, but it wasn't exactly like it sounds. Their home was located four miles from a paved road. Getting to church twice on Sunday and once on Wednesday wasn't hard, but as Micky himself will tell you, it wasn't always easy either.

When asked about his mother and father, Micky said he could not have had better parents. They loved him without measure and made sure he went to church. They taught him good manners, and to treat everyone with respect. They also taught him to always do your best.

One of Micky's fondest memories occurred every night before he and his brother went to bed. His father would read the two boys stories from the Bible. He would then pray for each of his sons before they fell asleep. Micky thought his father set a great example for the kids—he was a great role model for how a father should treat his children.

The influence of his parents and the training he received during his youth gave Micky a foundation of faith that has lasted for life.

In addition to having parents of faith with good family values, Micky was fortunate to have Sunday school teachers who knew the Bible. Little did they know that the young man they were teaching would grow up to become a brilliant engineer and extraordinary leader. They would also be pleased to know that he continued what they started. Micky is still active in church and a highly respected Sunday School teacher.

Starting School

Micky started school at the age of five. By the time he turned ten, he was one of the smallest boys in his grammar school class. Figure 3 is a picture of Micky helping in the construction of his family's new home. Because of his size, he was almost always the last to be selected for pickup games in sports. After years of being rejected, he channeled his anger into something positive—a determination to be the "best of the best."

Figure 3. Micky at 10 in Jasper, Alabama. (Photo courtesy of Micky Blackwell)

Becoming a Christian

When Micky was twelve, his pastor asked him if he would like to accept Jesus as his personal Savior. Micky said "yes" and invited Him into his life.

The day after he accepted Christ, a bully at school who was much bigger than he was, started picking on Micky. Micky reacted with newfound boldness and faced the bully down. The lesson Micky learned was that if you face your problems squarely and rely on God's strength, your issues will almost always resolve themselves, sometimes without a fight.

God's Plans for Micky

As Micky entered high school, he liked math, science, and fast cars. Except for his eighth-grade heartthrob, who later became his wife, he was not comfortable being around girls. There is no other way to say it—most kids today would have considered Micky a "nerd." Fortunately, most of Micky's friends were nerds as well—good in math and science, but shy around girls.

God has plans for those who know Him, and He certainly had plans for Micky. Evidence of Micky's leadership began to appear in his adolescent years. He graduated from junior high school with the highest grades in his class. He earned all "A's" in high school, except for one "B." He was elected to the Beta Club, an organization that promotes student leaders who are interested in community involvement. He was active in the Student Council and a member of the National Honor Society.

What was even more important to Micky, however, was that he was no longer the last to be selected for pick-up games like basketball. By the time Micky finished high school, he was six feet tall and still growing. It was an exciting time for Micky. He was ready to go to college.

Making Wise Choices

When I was still in high school, a group of us went to the prom. We were standing around talking when someone asked me what my major was going to be in college.

The question caught me off guard until I remembered that Russia had just launched Sputnik. Even though the US was behind Russia in space, the US was entering the race with all it had to win. Inspired by the thought, I told them I was going into aerospace.

Shortly thereafter, I enrolled in aerospace engineering in the only college that mattered — the University of Alabama, home to new football coach Bear Bryant.

— Micky Blackwell

College, Marriage, and Difficult Decisions

Micky attended the University of Alabama from 1958 to 1962 with the goal of obtaining his bachelor of science in Aerospace Engineering. As an engineering student, Micky excelled in almost every course he took. By the time he was ready to graduate, he was invited to join three prestigious institutions: Tau Beta Pi, the oldest engineering honor society in the country; Sigma Gamma Tau, which recognizes excellence in aeronautics and astronautics; and Pi Mu Epsilon, a society that promotes scholarly work in mathematics.

Figure 4. Micky and Billie's wedding reception. (Photo courtesy of Micky Blackwell)

Between his junior and senior year in college, Micky married his eighth-grade sweetheart (see Figure 4). Her name was Billie Guthrie. As of this writing, they have been married 63 years.[3] Being married increased Micky's focus on his studies, and he finished very near the top of his engineering class. His grades and letters of reference got the attention of potential employers.

In early 1962, he interviewed with several companies for aerospace engineering positions. Some were with the federal government, but most were with private companies. It wasn't long before Micky's hard work in school paid off. He had offers from two highly respected firms and one well-known government agency: Lockheed-Georgia Company in Marietta, Georgia; the Convair Division of General Dynamics in Fort Worth, Texas; and the NASA Langley Research Center in Hampton, Virginia.

Micky found himself facing a difficult choice. He had three good offers, and each promised interesting work. After weighing his options, Micky accepted the position at NASA. The tiebreaker was their offer to pay part of Micky's expenses for graduate school at the University of Virginia. It was an appealing incentive for the young man from Alabama. In the early 1960s, not many organizations offered new employees the opportunity to attend graduate school at their expense. It was indicative of what people saw in Micky—a talented young leader with a positive attitude, who knew what he wanted to do, and he knew how to do it.

Power of Prayer Revealed

Micky recalls, with fondness, Wednesday night services at his church in Townley. These gatherings were different from other church meetings. At this service, people in the community gathered to pray. They prayed out of concern for their neighbors because they knew their needs. They prayed for state and national officials, as well as world leaders. They also prayed for people around the world who were suffering from disasters.

Nevertheless, as Micky notes in his book *When Two or More are Gathered…in Prayer,* somewhere along the way, those pleasant mid-week nights at church became part of a fading past. Fortunately, for Micky and the people who later worked for him, the Wednesday night meetings had already accomplished their purpose. At an early age, Micky had already seen the good things that happen when two or more people gather to pray.

Seeds of Servant Leadership Planted

Micky first heard about servant leadership while he was still in high school. He was attending a chapel service when the visiting minister spoke about Jesus taking the role of a servant and washing his disciple's feet (John 13) telling them that if they want to be great, they must follow his example and be a servant to others (Mark 10:43-45). In addition, the minister talked about Robert Greenleaf's research on "servant leadership." Greenleaf spent almost four decades at AT&T, where he ultimately became the Director of Management Development. During this time, he honed many of his servant leader ideas on his colleagues and future leaders. He retired from AT&T in 1964 and started the Greenleaf Center. This allowed him to continue his research on servant leadership.[4]

In 1970, Greenleaf published his first essay on servant leadership. It was contrary to what was being taught at the time, and it turned many leadership theories on their head.[5] The visiting minister in Micky's high school and Robert Greenleaf arrived at the same conclusion—the best leaders in the world serve their people first. The minister went on to say, the highest calling of leadership was to be a servant leader that leads like Jesus.

The concept of servant leadership touched something deep in Micky's soul. From that point on, he was committed to learn more about the mystery of how a parent, a business leader, or a church leader could be a servant leader.

Servant Leadership Options

For some aspiring leaders, servant leadership may be optional – one of many tools they may use to help them deal with certain situations. That was never the case with Micky, because Micky knew his scriptures.

For Micky, it was never an option. As found in Mark 10:45, it was a clearly stated command from the One who created the earth.[6]

> *For even the Son of Man did not come to be served, but to serve, and to give His life a ransom for many.*
>
> — Mark 10:45 (NKJV)

Developing a Servant Leader's Mindset

As Micky matured, he thought more about his own plans. He soon realized he needed a framework to turn his plans into goals and his goals into actions. Some ideas came from the farm; some came from friends; others from basketball; but most came from his family and from studying the Bible. Over time, these ideas evolved into an action-oriented mindset. Whenever he confronted a problem, he would remember his personal checklist:

- **Be a servant first.**
- **When you have an opportunity, seize it.**
- **Whatever you choose to do, do it to win, and do it with confidence.**
- **Be prepared.**
- **Always go first to set the standard others must follow.**

Over time, Micky learned that self-confidence comes with experience, and experience comes from hard work. From competing in sports, to competing for the future of the company, only later did Micky realize how important these steps would become. They became part of his character that defined how he acted in class, in his personal life, and, most certainly, in his profession. The thoughts behind the checklist helped Micky and his team win one of biggest contracts ever—the contract to build the world's most sophisticated air superiority fighter, the F-22.

Lesson in Strategic Thinking

Learning how to study during the first year in college, was my first lesson in learning how to think out of the box. In this case, the "box" was my college dorm room. I knew the day I started the noise level was unacceptable. I also knew at once I had to do something about it.

To solve this problem, I created a new plan. The plan was to have supper and go directly to bed. I would get up at midnight and study till 4:00 in the morning. I would then crawl back in bed and get up before classes. My roommate was my best friend from high school and my new plan almost drove him crazy. However, learning how to make it work taught me an important lesson—if your strategy isn't working, you better change your thinking.

— Micky Blackwell

Lessons Learned and Important Points

Lessons learned and important points presented in this chapter include:

- Micky was exposed to servant leadership as a teenager in high school.
- His interest in servant leadership grew in college and evolved during his adult years.
- He was intrigued by the possibility that one man could be both a leader and a servant.
- He knew he wanted to be a servant leader. There was never any doubt.
- Micky's view of servant leadership was greatly influenced by what he learned from scripture.
- Over time, his ideas evolved into a framework that could be used professionally and personally.
- That mindset became the foundation for practicing Enterprise Servant Leadership.
- Micky attended the University of Alabama and married his junior-high-school sweetheart between his junior and senior years in college.

Chapter Notes

1 James "Micky" Blackwell. 2021. *All the Days of Our Lives. The Heritage and History of Billie and James Blackwell.* Asheville, NC: United Writers Press, p. 27.

2 Micky's grandfather bought the land from Micky's great-grandfather. Micky's great-grandfather purchased the land through a land grant program implemented following the relocation of the Cherokee tribe to Oklahoma. The forced relocation of the Cherokee is one of the low points in US history. The *Trail of Tears* memorializes the routes used to remove the Cherokee from their long-held ancestral lands. According to the National Park Service, the relocation took place between 1838 and 1839. For more information, click on http://alabamanews center.com/2016/12/16/trail-of-tears-memorializes-removal-of-cherokee-from-alabama-southeast/

3 Everyone agrees that Micky and Billie are well suited for each other. Billie supported Micky through many moves and a long career. Micky looked to Billie to take care of things at home. They have two daughters, Kaye and Kelley; one granddaughter, Cecilia; and three grandsons: Garrett, Ethan, and Matthew.

4 Don M. Frick. n.d. *Robert K. Greenleaf Biography, Robert K. Greenleaf Center for Servant Leadership.* Accessed February 26, 2018. https://www.greenleaf.org/about-us/robert-k-greenleaf-biography/.

5 Robert K. Greenleaf. 1970. *The Servant as Leader.* Robert K. Greenleaf Publishing. For more information click on https://www.greenleaf.org/what-is-servant-leadership/

6 Blanchard and Hodges note that servant leadership is not voluntary; it is a mandate for Christians and not an option. See Ken Blanchard and Phil Hodges. 2005. *Lead Like Jesus: Lessons from the Greatest Leadership Role Model of All Time.* Nashville, Tenn.: Thomas Nelson, Inc., p. 12.

Chapter 2
Seven Years at NASA Langley

This chapter discusses Micky's first job, a job that was both humbling and rewarding. What Micky learned at NASA Langley helped turn his early work in aerospace into successes throughout his life.

In 1962, when Micky reported for work at NASA's Langley Research Center at Hampton, Virginia he was both surprised and disappointed to find he didn't get to work in the engineering specialty he wanted—aerostructures. He was assigned to the 8-Foot Transonic Wind Tunnel Branch. His disappointment increased when he learned about having to work nights and weekends. An occasional weekend was okay, but he really didn't want to work nights away from his wife, Billie. However, this was just the beginning for the young man who had recently graduated from college. Micky still had much to learn about being a humble servant.

A Lesson in Humility

After arriving at NASA Langley, his first job was to test a small inflatable parachute at transonic speeds. The parachute was called a "ballute," and it was being developed for emergency recovery of the astronauts in the Gemini space program. Micky was still learning how to use the Transonic Wind Tunnel. When he increased the speed, the recovery system became unstable. As the system began to falter, it broke the tether holding the ballute. Debris from the failed parachute damaged some of the fan blades in the tunnel. The now inoperable tunnel took several weeks to repair.[1] It was not a good start for the young engineer from Alabama. NASA wasn't happy, but still had faith in Micky—and Micky was quite pleased when he heard about his next assignment.

An Extraordinary Assignment

Not long after the incident in the NASA wind tunnel, Micky was given another opportunity to display his talent. His new job was to develop drawings for a model of a supersonic passenger aircraft. This was more aligned with Micky's skills, but what really made it interesting was the name of his new boss. Micky's new supervisor was Dr. Richard (Dick) Whitcomb (see Figure 5), one of the world's foremost aerodynamicists and winner of the prestigious Collier Trophy awarded yearly for the greatest achievement in American aviation.[2]

At first, their relationship was distant. Micky recognized Dr. Whitcomb's brilliance, but there was an issue they had to work through. Dr. Whitcomb would rush into Micky's office and tell him to "draw a curve from here to there." After doing this several times, Micky pushed back and said, "I don't mind drawing lines, but I would really appreciate your telling me why." Their relationship immediately changed and changed for the better. From that day forward, when Dr. Whitcomb told Micky to draw a line, he always told him why.

Figure 5. Micky's supervisor at NASA Langley, Dr. Richard "Dick" Whitcomb. (NASA Photo)

Dr. Whitcomb took Micky under his wing, and over time he taught him what he had learned about modern aerodynamics. Most of what he taught wasn't published in articles or books. That steady transfer of knowledge was invaluable to Micky—and it showed the young engineer the value of a good mentor.

While Micky was still under Dr. Whitcomb's supervision, he worked with him on multiple NASA projects. One of these involved the development of supercritical airfoils for transport aircraft wings—a design that delays the onset of wave drag in the transonic speed range. This was a major contribution to the advancement of aeronautics since it allowed commercial passenger and military transport aircraft to fly efficiently near the speed of sound. The invention of supercritical airfoil technology belongs to Whitcomb, but Micky did the theoretical work and contributed to the design of the airfoil. Later, when he was a lead engineer, he applied supercritical technology to other aerospace vehicles, such as helicopters.

Whitcomb and Micky also collaborated on the invention of winglets to reduce drag on aircraft wings. Again, Whitcomb did the experimental work, and Micky did the theoretical studies. Micky's engineering studies helped engineers understand how winglets helped improve fuel efficiency and aircraft performance.[3] Other contributions included work on missile aerodynamics, Reynolds number effects (a dimensionless quantity that helps predict flow patterns in different situations by measuring the ratio between inertial and viscous forces) on transonic aerodynamics, and new wall designs for transonic wind tunnels.

As previously noted, Micky had completed his Master of Science degree in Aerospace Engineering at the University of Virginia under NASA sponsorship. Micky returned the favor by doing research on a topic that was important to NASA. The title of his thesis was, "Numerical Method for the Design of Warped Surfaces for Subsonic Wings with Arbitrary Planform."

His last project and paper while at NASA focused on a topic that only an aerospace engineer could appreciate: "Developing Techniques at a Low Reynolds Number that Could Get Air to React like it was Operating at a High Reynolds Number."

Strong Publication Record

During his seven years at NASA Langley, Micky made many significant contributions that would be documented in professional scientific reports and journal articles. These reports and articles provide insight into the work Micky was doing. Almost forty publications describing his work at NASA and Lockheed are listed in chronological order in Appendix A.

Seeds Planted for the Future

There were other reasons why Micky's time at NASA Langley was beneficial. The longer he stayed, the more he became aware of the enormous capabilities NASA had in its networks. Micky leveraged that knowledge later when he used NASA to conduct various tests on Lockheed aircraft like the Lockheed C-130, C-141, C-5, F-22, and F-35.

In 1991, Micky went out of his way to thank NASA Langley for the work they performed on the F-22. In a letter of appreciation to the Langley Center Director, Richard H. Peterson, Micky thanked Mr. Petersen and his staff for the accuracy of their wind-tunnel predictions. Because of their performance, Lockheed Martin continues to use NASA Langley as a resource for testing to this day.[4]

Young Lions Must Keep Moving

After seven years at NASA Langley, Micky knew it was time to consider moving. With a growing list of accomplishments, Micky was ready to expand his boundaries. He decided to apply for work on the private side of aerospace—an industry he knew well, and which he also knew could be volatile. He created a professional resume. The Lockheed-Georgia Company in Marietta, Georgia was at the top of his list of potential employers.[5] The engineering expertise he learned while at NASA was directly applicable to research being done at Lockheed. Also, Marietta was much closer to Jasper, Alabama and his and Billie's parents.

If Micky could connect with Lockheed-Georgia, he was ready to make a move. That happened in early 1969 at a technical symposium in Georgia, where he ran into Ted Dansby, head of the Lockheed-Georgia Advanced Design Aerodynamics Department. When Dansby jokingly asked him, "When are you going to come work for me?" Micky handed him a copy of the resume he had already prepared. Micky had been praying that God would open a door. What Micky didn't know, was that God was waiting to bless him, much like He blessed Jabez in the Bible.[6]

Lessons Learned and Important Points

The job at NASA Langley was a godsend or, as some might say, an act of divine providence. It was the perfect opportunity for Micky to practice his engineering skills, while learning how large organizations operate. Some of the lessons learned and important points from Micky's time at Langley include:

- **There is nothing like experience. Servant leaders need it too.**
- **Humility is a good thing, and there are good reasons to have it.**
- **Mentoring isn't just for children. There are times when employees also need mentors.**
- **Looking back at his years at NASA Langley, Micky made many significant engineering contributions which were documented in professional scientific reports and journals.**
- **Relationships with people are important in life and may be more important in business.**
- **Teaching Sunday School in his Hampton, Virginia, church as a young adult reinforced his core values and gave Micky the confidence to speak anywhere, and at any time, for the rest of his life.**

Chapter Notes

1 James "Micky" Blackwell. 2021. *All the Days of Our Lives. The Heritage and History of Billie and James Blackwell*. Asheville, NC: United Writers Press, p. 70.

2 The Collier Trophy is the highest award for achievement in aviation. See *Flight Global* citing *Flight International*, 2000. *"My View: Micky Blackwell, Former president of Lockheed Martin's Aeronautics Sector,"* December 31, 1999. *https://www.flightglobal.com/my-view-micky-blackwell-former-president-of-lockheed-martins-aeronautical-sector/30039.article. Accessed July 22, 2024.*

3 NASA. n.d. "Richard T. Whitcomb." *https://www.nasa.gov/centers-and-facilities/langley/richard-t-whitcomb/. Accessed July 22, 2024.*

4 For a nice summary of work done by the NASA Langley Research Center, see Joseph R. Chambers. 2000. *Partners in Freedom: Contributions of the Langley Research Center to U.S. Military Aircraft of the 1990s*. Washington D.C.: National Aeronautics and Space Administration.

5 Lockheed-Georgia was a division of Lockheed Corporation. Lockheed merged with Martin Marietta to become Lockheed Martin Corporation in 1995.

6 Jabez is mentioned only briefly in the Bible, but the reason he is mentioned is because he set a good example. Jabez asked God to bless him, grow his territory, keep him from evil, and cause no pain. God honored Jabez's request. See 1 Chronicles 4:10, NKJV.

Chapter 3
Moving to Lockheed and Moving up the Ladder

Servant leadership works. It works in the home; it works at church; and as we demonstrated at Lockheed Martin, it also works at work.

Micky Blackwell
President & COO Aeronautics Sector (Retired)
Lockheed Martin Corporation

This chapter begins by describing the early work and difficult times Micky first experienced at Lockheed-Georgia. He then starts to move up the management ladder and is promoted to lead the Lockheed-Georgia Transonic Research Group; the Lockheed-Georgia Special Projects as Chief Engineer; Research and Technology for the Lockheed Advanced Aeronautics Company as Director; Engineering for Lockheed-Georgia as Vice President; and Engineering for the Lockheed Aeronautical Systems Company as Vice President and Assistant General Manager for Research, Technology, and Engineering.

Micky moved to his new job at Lockheed-Georgia in Marietta, Georgia on July 20, 1969. He arrived in Marietta the same day astronaut Neil Armstrong first set foot on the moon.

Early Work and Difficult Times

When Micky reported to work in Georgia, he was assigned to the Lockheed Advanced Design Aerodynamics Department. His first official job was to help bring online a new in-house High Reynolds Number Transonic wind tunnel. The unique facility was key to Lockheed obtaining supercritical airfoil aerodynamic testing contracts from NASA. He also participated in Internal Research on developing advanced aerodynamic concepts for transonic transport aircraft.

All was going well until a series of unfortunate events occurred. Things happened so fast they nearly caused Lockheed's collapse. First, the Lockheed L-1011 Tristar commercial airliner ran into trouble when its engine supplier, Rolls-Royce, announced it would not be able to deliver engines to Lockheed. Much to the embarrassment of Rolls-Royce and the British government, development costs for the Tristar engine began to soar beyond what was budgeted. With no way to recover, Rolls-Royce declared bankruptcy in 1971.[1]

Lockheed had designed one of the world's most elegant widebody jets but, as it had no engines to power it, many of Lockheed's customers switched to the McDonnell Douglas DC-10. The delay in deliveries of the L-1011 allowed McDonnell Douglas to capture the early adopters. Lockheed seemed destined to fail until the US government stepped in. Many would later say it was the beginning of the "too big to fail" philosophy. At $250 million, it was the largest US bank loan guarantee in history. The administrative fees for the guarantee were fully paid by Lockheed ahead of schedule, and the guarantee was never needed. It was just what Lockheed needed to prevent a financial collapse and enable them to start producing the TriStar.[2]

By the end of the 1970s, McDonnell Douglas' share of the wide-body market was 31 percent, and Lockheed's share topped out at less than 18 percent.[3] After years of battling McDonnell Douglas,

Boeing, Airbus, and the economy, neither the DC-10 nor the L-1011 were profitable, and both programs were ended.[4]

At about the same time the L-1011 was having problems, the huge C-5A Galaxy military cargo transport built by Lockheed ran into serious cost overruns. The Galaxy was the world's largest military cargo aircraft, designed to move oversized equipment such as tanks and transportable bridges anywhere in the world. Not long after it was deployed, the Air Force directed Lockheed to redesign the center wing box (main wing) to reduce weight-related cracks and solve other potential problems.[5] After considerable review and numerous remedial actions, the C-5A production ended in 1973.

In addition to problems with the L-1011 and the C-5A, there were also cash-draining problems with Lockheed's shipbuilding business and the Army's AH-56 Cheyenne attack helicopter program. The shipyard was closed and the AH-56 was cancelled. Lockheed-Georgia cut its work force in Marietta from 34,000 to 10,000, closed several buildings, and consolidated employees—including Micky—into the Air Force-owned part of the facility. Amid all the turmoil, Micky felt fortunate to still have a job. Money was so tight at Lockheed that some highly skilled workers were told they could continue to function, but only if they took turns doing janitorial work.[6]

Figure 6. Royal Saudi Air Force C-130 Hercules. (Public Domain)

Lockheed eventually survived the bankruptcy crisis. Much of the revenue during this period came from international sales of the C-130 Hercules (see Figure 6). Saudi Arabia's decision to buy the Hercules was especially helpful and timely.

By the mid-1970s, the Royal Saudi Air Force had acquired more than 50 C-130s, making it the world's largest fleet behind the US and Britain. The scale of the program was significant. It involved more than 800 people and continued for 20 years.[7]

Head of Transonic Research Group

After a few years, things began to return to normal. Micky and other engineers moved back to the Lockheed-Georgia Research Center. Micky was put in charge of a small engineering group doing advanced aerodynamics research. It was his first job as a workforce manager and leader.

Funding was austere in the mid-1970s. To win new contracts, Lockheed needed to have the best aerodynamic technology available. Most of Lockheed's technology development money came from contracts with the US government. The rest came from Lockheed's internal research and development (IR&D) account.

One of Micky's colleagues in acoustics research developed a process for hiring Ph.D.'s from other countries as contract consultants to work on Lockheed projects. The idea was to reduce manpower costs, while maintaining a competitive edge. Micky followed his friend's lead and found that he could do the same. He was able to hire highly qualified foreign Ph.D.'s at half the cost of their US counterparts.

Employing international experts worked well for Micky and Lockheed. Lockheed became nationally recognized as one of the leaders in computational 3-D aircraft design, 3-D boundary layer computations, laminar flow control, induced drag minimization, supercritical airfoil design, and high Reynolds number effects on supercritical airfoil aerodynamics. Micky became recognized for his ability to win contracts.

Hiring good people is critical to an organization's success, and Micky was able to hire some of the world's best engineers and scientists. Many of them already had established technical reputations, and all his new hires had successful careers in aerospace. One of these was Ken Johnson, from the US Air Force Research Laboratory (AFRL) at Wright-Patterson AFB, near Dayton, Ohio.[8] Ken once told Micky that when he got up in the morning, he was so excited about his job at Lockheed, he couldn't wait to get to work. Ken was an expert in transonic computational fluid dynamics and went on to become an executive with Lockheed Martin.

Another example was Dr. Andrew Thomas. Andy was an Australian-born aerospace engineer who joined Micky's research team. During his time at Lockheed, he conducted advanced aerodynamics research. Dr. Thomas later became manager of Lockheed's Flight Sciences Division.[9] When he became an American citizen, he joined NASA's astronaut program. He completed four Space Shuttle missions, one of which included time on the Russian space station, Mir.

These two incredible co-workers were typical of the people Micky was able to hire and develop. It was, indeed, a remarkable group. Over time, Micky and his colleagues became known as the "Group of 12." They had a well-earned reputation for doing groundbreaking aerodynamics work.

The group also developed several unique aerodynamic test facilities. In addition to the High Reynolds Number Transonic Facility already mentioned, they built a low-speed, low-turbulence wind tunnel for laminar flow studies that was unique in the industry. This was complemented by the development of a large water tunnel in which they did aerodynamic flow visualization studies.

Lockheed-Georgia already had one of the world's largest low-speed wind tunnels. Using this large low-speed wind tunnel, one of Micky's new hires, Dr. Loren Lemmerman, was able to make some of the first large-scale 3-D boundary layer measurements on an aircraft wing. This allowed the development of a more robust boundary layer turbulence model to enhance theoretical aerodynamic calculations on aircraft wings.

Although he didn't realize it until sometime later, putting the research group together and providing them with resources was when Micky first started applying servant leadership in practice. He had discovered the power of serving others and personally observed the results. Micky's leadership skills were still evolving, but he already knew that servant leadership worked.

Doctoral Work or Managing People?

After building a team of multinational Ph.D. research scientists, it occurred to Micky that he might want to pursue his own terminal degree. After reviewing curricula at several universities, Micky enrolled in a doctoral program at the Georgia Institute of Technology (Georgia Tech). For years he had thought he would enjoy teaching and research, and his growing list of publications was evidence of his scholarly abilities. He successfully completed two advanced aerodynamic graduate courses. Even though he enjoyed theory-building and the work behind it, he began to realize that what he enjoyed most was managing the people and research he was already doing at Lockheed.

With these thoughts in mind, Micky decided to explore the possibility of moving into engineering management at Lockheed-Georgia. Micky found an opportunity to speak to the chief engineer in his chain of command. Micky told him that he really loved what he was doing, but he would like to be considered for a management position if an opening became available.

It wasn't long before Lockheed Engineering needed someone to fill a temporary management position in design aerodynamics. When the chief engineer asked Micky if he would like the job, Micky seized the opportunity and performed well beyond what was expected.

Micky learned two important lessons from this experience: (1) do not assume your good work will speak for itself and (2) do not assume your bosses know what you would like to do in the future. However, if you tell your bosses about your aspirations in a non-threatening manner, they will almost always remember you when the next opportunity arises.

Staff Aerodynamicist

After his temporary engineering management assignment was finished, Lockheed-Georgia's Chief Engineer asked Micky to join his staff. His role would be to supervise IR&D projects for the engineering branch. The goal of his assignment was to improve the grades assigned by the Air Force to each IR&D project. Higher grades meant more money for Lockheed-Georgia. From where Micky stood, it looked like a job with a lot of potential.

He agreed to take the job and was given the title of Staff Aerodynamicist. Micky's friends, however, weren't so certain about the opportunity he had been given. They told him it was a dead-end job, and he shouldn't accept the offer. Two years later, when Micky moved to a new position, people fought to take over his old job supervising IR&D. Not surprisingly, Micky improved the process and instituted standards for submitting research and development reports to the United States Air Force. A short time later, the Air Force grades on Lockheed's IR&D projects started trending upward.

Review of Shuttle Data for NASA

In 1981, the United States was anticipating the first launch of the Space Shuttle Columbia. At the time, the Engineering Vice President at Lockheed-Georgia was Dr. Joe Cornish. Cornish was asked by NASA to serve on a blue-ribbon space shuttle committee to review launch and recovery data for the new Space Shuttle. NASA had some concerns they wanted industry experts from around the country to evaluate prior to launch.

Dr. Cornish looked for an engineer to help him review the concerns and to make recommendations that might enhance the program's safety and success. Micky was selected to help him. Even though Micky relished the assignment, he knew the job would be a challenge. Cornish seemed to promote conflict among those who worked for him. He was not the kind of leader Micky wanted to work for—he was a self-serving leader.[10]

As it turned out, Micky's recommendations made both Cornish and Lockheed look good to the officials at NASA. Micky spent time reviewing the shuttle data and identified several areas of concern. He shared these with Cornish who, in turn, briefed NASA executives on what he had found.

Cornish was elated with Micky's performance. Micky had taken to heart what Lockheed's Chairman and CEO, Larry Kitchen, had once said about work: "No matter what kind of a boss you have, your job is to make him, or her, look like a hero." He made Cornish look like a hero to his peers. As a result of Micky's work for NASA and on other projects, Cornish arranged for Micky to be assigned to him permanently to lead a special projects organization.

No matter what kind of a boss you have, your job is to make him, or her, look like a hero.
— Lawrence O. Kitchen, Chairman and CEO, Lockheed Corporation

---

Chief Engineer for Special Projects

One of the first special projects undertaken by Micky's new organization was to assemble a team to develop the technology for a stealthy aircraft to be used by the US Army. The role of the stealthy aircraft was to insert Special Forces covertly into high-threat areas.

To develop a stealthy aircraft, the special projects team needed low-cost methods for quantifying the radar cross-section (RCS) of an aircraft. This included determining the RCS of an aircraft shape both through experimental RCS tests and analytical RCS calculations.

The RCS experts said small-scale testing of aircraft shapes could not be done. Undaunted by what the experts said, Micky's special projects team continued to look for low-cost RCS testing methods for different kinds of aircraft. To assist them in exploring alternatives, Micky hired a brilliant young electronics engineer who had recently graduated from Georgia Tech. His name was Larry Pellet. With Micky's encouragement and Larry's positive attitude, the team eventually developed a compact RCS test range that worked.

To develop stealthy aircraft, the team also needed access to RCS analytical codes to predict the radar cross-section of various aircraft shapes. The Lockheed Skunk Works had the famous ECHO radar cross-section software, but because the work that Micky's group was doing was not yet classified, they could not get access to the Lockheed classified RCS codes they needed. However, they were granted access to RCS codes developed by AFRL.[11]

With a growing workload, Micky went to Lockheed-Georgia's director of engineering to ask for more engineers. He told the director that he had been charged by the vice president of engineering to develop a stealthy aircraft for the US Army, and he needed additional engineers assigned to special projects to create preliminary aircraft designs. The director declined Micky's request and told him that most of his engineers were already assigned to other projects. Nevertheless, he was able to offer Micky a few engineers who were slated for layoffs. Micky took what he could get, and as some people like to say, the rest of the story is history.

As the RCS engineers began to work with aerodynamicists, the special projects team began to make progress. Up to that time, aircraft surfaces and wing shapes were designed with flat panels (facets) like those on the F-117 Nighthawk. Ken Burgess, an aerodynamicist, worked with Larry Pellet, the low RCS specialist, to develop a low RCS transport wing using curved surfaces that were stealthy and that would give aircraft aerodynamic performance equal to or better than existing aircraft.

Despite the naysayers, Ken and Larry succeeded. They developed a low RCS wing with curved surfaces that met the design requirements. The RCS performance of the wing was verified on the large-scale RCS range operated by the Lockheed Skunk Works. The wing was also thoroughly tested aerodynamically in Lockheed's wind-tunnels. It should be noted that this team's low RCS curved surface work had a significant impact on the design of the ATF that eventually became the F-22.

Lockheed-Georgia eventually received classification authority in the stealth arena from the Air Force. This, in turn, meant that the corporation was able to share its classified technology with Micky and his colleagues. It was a great day for Lockheed-Georgia when one of the inventors of stealth from the Lockheed Skunk Works came to Marietta to talk about their latest advancements. It was an acknowledgement of what the team had achieved, and everyone at Lockheed knew it.

If you give people a vision, while caring for them with a servant's heart, they can accomplish almost anything, which is exactly what they did. — Micky Blackwell

---

Over time, the group became known and respected for their work. Many of their ideas are still in use today on Unmanned Aerial Vehicles (UAVs), the F-22, and the F-35, as well as other aircraft we may never hear about. Their work spoke for itself, and the organization expanded.

When Micky went back to the director of engineering to ask for yet more people, the response was, "You can't have anymore, you already have all the best engineers." That was good and bad news for Micky. The good news was that the engineers that were previously scheduled to be laid off were now considered some of Lockheed's finest. The bad news was that the team still needed more engineers. It was an important lesson for Micky: if you give people a vision, while caring for them with a servant's heart, they can accomplish almost anything. That is exactly what they did.[12] All they needed was someone who believed in them and was willing to give them a chance.

Lockheed-Georgia was a subcontractor to a sister Lockheed Company for the Research and Development (R&D) of a classified project. The classified project was canceled by the US government in 1982. The residual work from the canceled project was combined with Micky's other special projects work into a new organization called "Special Projects." The additional staff from the cancelled program helped solve some of their manpower problems.[13] On March 4, 1983, Micky was officially named Chief Engineer of Special Projects—a unit that was very important to Lockheed's future.

The Lockheed-Georgia Special Projects organization was created to be an East Coast counterpart to the Skunk Works in California (see insert below). The operation was called the "Possum Works." It was also called the "Black Hole" because many of the people who went to work there dropped out of sight. That was due, in large part, to the nature of work they were doing—developing and testing classified products for the US government. During the next two years, Micky's team generated a $40 million backlog of government contracts on classified stealth-related projects.

The Lockheed Skunk Works®: A High Performing Organization

The Skunk Works has a history of pushing the boundaries of aircraft design. It began with the development of with the P-80 Shooting Star fighter in the late stages of World War II. Between then and now, the Skunk Works has produced or participated to some degree in the development of a host of an amazing variety of aircraft. Some of these include the F-94 Starfire all weather interceptor, AQM-60 Kingfisher drone, the P2V Neptune and later, the P-3 Orion maritime patrol aircraft, the C-130 Hercules tactical transport, the F-104 Starfighter, the U-2 Dragon Lady high altitude reconnaissance, the Jetstar executive transport, the A-12 Oxcart and SR-71 Blackbird Mach 3+, high altitude reconnaissance aircraft, the F-117 Nighthawk stealth attack aircraft, the F-22 Raptor, the F-35 Lightning II prototype, and the first Agena D upper stage booster rockets.

The following three examples illustrate the Skunk Work's outstanding achievements:

- *The P-80 was the first American plane to fly over 500 miles per hour. Developed in just 143 days, it had a 40-year lifespan.*
- *The U-2 was developed in eight months for a very special purpose—to take high-resolution photographs at altitudes above 60,000 feet over enemy territory. Basically a powered glider, the thin wings required unique tandem landing gear.*
- *The SR-71 was made from titanium supplied in a roundabout way by the Soviet Union. Fuel leaked all over, and the aircraft required the use of two Buick V-8 engines to turn the turbines but none of that mattered, it could accomplish its objective. The aircraft could cruise faster than a bullet (Mach 3.2+) at altitudes well over 85,000 feet.*

Although these were impressive aircraft, one of the reasons the Skunk Works was so successful was the work policies established by its original director, Clarence "Kelly" Johnson. The policies were created to allow designers, mechanics, and production workers to communicate directly, avoiding the bureaucracy that often slows down complex projects. As we will see later, Kelly Johnson's policies were instrumental in helping develop what became known as "Integrated Product Teams" on the F-22. These policies are captured in Johnson's 14 Rules. For convenience, they are presented in Appendix B.

Lockheed Advanced Aeronautics Company

In 1984, Lockheed decided to consolidate all its aircraft companies into one organization. The consolidation included Lockheed California, Lockheed-Georgia, Lockheed Aircraft Services, plus the Lockheed Skunk Works, formally known as Advanced Development Projects. With the government's cutbacks in defense, there was simply not enough work for all the Lockheed companies. The Vice Presidents of Engineering for each company were asked by the Lockheed Corporation to recommend a new operating model for Lockheed—one that would be more efficient while maximizing their capabilities.

The consolidation, unfortunately, resulted in a "double-humped management camel." The first hump was called the Aeronautical Systems Group (ASG). Within ASG, the aircraft company presidents reported to a new group president. The second hump became the Lockheed Advanced Aeronautics

Company (LAAC). The mission of LAAC was to coordinate all internal aircraft R&D throughout the ASG and initiate all new aircraft programs, similar to what is now called a "business incubator."

Dr. Joe Cornish was asked to go to Rye Canyon, California to be the head of engineering for LAAC. Ben Rich, of the Skunk Works, became president of LAAC. Both the ASG and LAAC headquarters were in Rye Canyon near Newhall, California. Rye Canyon was the site of Lockheed California's major aeronautical test facilities.

Cornish asked Micky to join him in California as the Director of Research and Technology for LAAC. Micky accepted the offer, but it was a somewhat awkward situation. The new Lockheed Advanced Aeronautics Company had to be built from scratch, but since the new company did not have an existing business base, it was not set up to accept contracts. LAAC ended up performing a coordinating role among the other Lockheed companies. Unfortunately, it created more overhead for everyone involved.

Micky's position at LAAC evolved into a role that coordinated all IR&D throughout the ASG. There was some resistance by the aircraft companies to taking direction from the LAAC staff, so it required a lot of smooth talking and selling to accomplish what had to be done. It was a frustrating job, but it gave Micky another opportunity to practice what he preached—always do your best, regardless of the circumstances.

Back to School for a Season

In 1986, Micky's boss sent him to the Advanced Management Program at Harvard Business School in Boston, Massachusetts. The program was a three-month "beauty school" where he learned a lot about business and how successful companies were run. It was a great experience for Micky, and it helped him throughout his career. It gave him new ideas for how to deal with issues as he rose through the executive ranks at Lockheed. Micky graduated from the respected program in May 1986.

Disappointment, Then Delight

Since the Lockheed Advanced Aeronautics Company was a bad idea from the start, the Lockheed corporate fathers in mid-1986 decided to abandon their attempt at consolidation. As the decision was being made, Lockheed California had an opening for Vice President of Engineering. Micky interviewed for the job but wasn't selected.

Micky was disappointed when he didn't get the engineering job. With the disestablishment of LAAC, he didn't know where he would end up. He and his wife, Billie, took their Datsun 280Z and drove up the coast of California for some well-earned rest and recreation. They were in Carmel when Micky received a call from Ken Cannestra, the newly appointed president of Lockheed-Georgia. Ken offered Micky the job as the VP of Engineering for the Lockheed-Georgia Company in Marietta. Micky was elated and Billie could not have been happier.

By the time Micky returned to Los Angeles, he had decided to accept the Lockheed-Georgia job. However, he also had to get a release from the current Lockheed ASG president, John Brizendine. In Micky's discussions with Brizendine, he could tell that Brizendine did not want him to go back to Georgia. Micky rashly promised him that if he needed him in California that he would come back.

John finally gave Micky the okay to go to Georgia, but he cashed in on Micky's promise to get him back to California just a few years later.

Micky's former boss, Bill Lassiter, had been serving as Vice President of Engineering and Advanced Programs. When President Cannestra decided to separate "Advanced Programs" from "Engineering," he named Bill Lassiter as the head of Advanced Programs and Micky as the head of engineering. It was a stroke of genius. As a result of the increased focus on new business, Lockheed-Georgia began to develop many new business opportunities.

New Initiatives and Recognition

Micky started his new job in Marietta in September 1986. During Micky's time as Vice President of Engineering at Lockheed-Georgia, the company made great progress in applying new technologies to the C-130 transport. Each of the new technologies was demonstrated in flight on the C-130 High Technology Test Bed (HTTB). This work later formed the baseline for the new C-130J.

One of the great honors that Lockheed-Georgia received while Micky was Vice President of Engineering was winning the 1987 Collier Trophy, the most prestigious award in the aeronautics industry, for the development of the Propfan Technology Assessment program, a testbed for advanced turboprop propulsion concepts. Lockheed-Georgia engineers led the NASA/Industry team.

Micky used servant leadership to manage several initiatives during this time, and the results were beginning to show up in Lockheed's bottom line. By treating people fairly and putting others first, Micky created an environment where people enjoyed their work.

> **Lesson Learned on the Golf Course**
>
> *Just before I started my job as Vice President of Engineering in Marietta, Georgia, a friend from California was visiting and talked me into a round of golf. Since there were only two of us, the course starter asked us to play with two others.*
>
> *They were impressive young men who could hit the ball a mile. After several holes, I asked one of them what type of work he did. He said, "I am an engineer for Lockheed-Georgia." I didn't say a thing, but after we played several holes, the young engineer asked me, "Who are you, and what do you do?"*
>
> *I will never forget the look on the young engineer's face when I told him "My name is Micky Blackwell. I am your new boss!"*
>
> *By the time I got to the office on my first day of work, the story was all over Lockheed-Georgia. They now knew a new sheriff was in town, but they also knew he couldn't play golf!*
>
> *— Micky Blackwell*

Advisor at Mercer

In 1986, Micky received another surprise. Ken Cannestra wanted Micky to join the Advisory Board of the new College of Engineering at Mercer University in Macon, Georgia. Since it would be several years before Mercer would produce any engineers Lockheed could hire, he told Ken that he was not really interested. Then Ken explained that Sam Nunn, the US senator from Georgia and Chairman of the Senate Armed Services Committee asked for Micky, specifically, to be appointed to the Advisory Board at the College of Engineering. That settled that.

Micky really enjoyed his time on the Mercer Engineering Board. He served on the Advisory Board until 1993. The State of Georgia needed another engineering school since, at the time, Georgia Tech was the only school granting full engineering college degrees in Georgia. Fortunately, Mercer focused on graduating engineers that could be immediately employed at Lockheed.

Consolidation of Aeronautics

In January 1986, Lockheed Chairman and CEO, Roy Anderson, retired. Larry Kitchen who had previously been Executive Vice President of Lockheed became CEO. In 1987, Mr. Kitchen decided he wanted to finish the consolidation that had been halted two years before. He formed a committee made up of the aircraft company presidents and staff. Ken Cannestra, president of Lockheed-Georgia, asked Micky to help him since he had been involved in the previous consolidation effort.

Each president and their staff had to present their ideas for aeronautics consolidation to the committee. As one might imagine, they argued over everything—from management philosophy to the location of the company headquarters. Everything was disputed including who would be in charge.

In September 1987, Lockheed announced the plan for the consolidation of their aeronautics companies. The new name of the firm was Lockheed Aeronautical Systems Company (LASC) with John Brizendine as president. The Lockheed-Georgia Company, the Lockheed-California Company, the Skunk Works, and the Lockheed Air Services Company were all disestablished.

All engineering personnel and activities from the companies would be consolidated at Lockheed's facilities in Burbank, California. It also became clear that the Marietta location would become a manufacturing plant. Micky knew this was a poor organizational concept. He knew from personal experience that it was important for engineers to be located close to manufacturing. This became more important later when he brought *"Lean Thinking"* into Lockheed's plants and operations. Lean Thinking will be discussed in more detail in later chapters.

John Brizendine promoted the number two person at the Skunk Works, Bart Krawetz, to be vice president of Engineering and general manager of the combined aircraft companies. In the new organization, Bob Ray and Micky reported directly to Bart Krawetz. Micky's new title would be vice president and assistant general manager for Research and Technology. Essentially, they took the engineering staff from the four aircraft companies and split the responsibility between the two of them down functional lines. Micky took advanced aircraft design, electronics, low observables, and fight sciences. Bob Ray became vice president and assistant general manager for Engineering Support—all programs, structures, materials, test facilities, system engineering and flight testing.

Micky's primary job following the consolidation was to facilitate the movement of engineers from Marietta, Georgia to Burbank, California. Micky rated the process as moderately successful. Since many had to move anyway, some considered and accepted offers from other companies. In addition, some who had deep roots in Marietta were just not going to move. As a result of the move from Marietta to Burbank, Lockheed lost some very good people who went to work for its competitors.

Micky learned some valuable lessons during the moving process. They were especially helpful when a few years later the Lockheed Aeronautical Systems Company reversed what they had done and moved people from Burbank back to Marietta to work on the F-22.

Lessons Learned and Important Points

Some of the lessons learned and important points from this chapter are:

- In the mid 1970s, Micky began his first leadership role as head of a Transonic Research Group. In this position, he assembled a top team of engineers to do cutting edge research. He learned that it always pays to hire the best people you can get.
- Working directly for the Lockheed-Georgia Vice President of Engineering, Micky successfully led several major projects resulting in his promotion to Chief Engineer of a new Special Projects organization called the "Possum Works." He learned that if you give people a vision, while caring for them with a servant's heart, they can accomplish almost anything.
- In 1984, Micky was asked to help start a new company called Lockheed Advanced Aeronautics Company which lasted until mid-1986. He was Director of Engineering for Research and Technology. Although a frustrating job, it gave Micky the opportunity to practice what he preached—always do your best, regardless of the circumstances.
- In 1986, Lockheed sent Micky to the Advanced Management Program at Harvard. The program was a three-month "beauty school" where he learned a lot about business and how successful companies were run.
- In mid-1986, Ken Cannestra, president of Lockheed-Georgia, offered Micky a job as Vice President of Engineering. In this role he learned that if you treat people fairly and put others first, you will create an environment where people enjoy their work and become high performers.
- One of the great honors that Lockheed-Georgia Engineering received while Micky was Vice President of Engineering, was winning the 1987 Collier Trophy for the development of advanced turboprop propulsion concepts.
- In 1987, the Lockheed Corporation completed the consolidation of its aeronautics companies into one company—the Lockheed Aeronautical Systems Company. Micky became Vice President and Assistant General Manager of Research, Technology, and Engineering.

Chapter Notes

1 John M. Lee. "Rolls-Royce is Bankrupt; Blames Lockheed Project." *New York Time Archives*. February 5, 1971. https://www.nytimes.com/1971/02/05/archives/rollsroyce-is-bankrupt-blames-lockheed-project-rollsroyce-enters.html. Accessed July 22, 2024.

2 "Lockheed Loan Backed." September 8, 1972. https://www.nytimes.com/1972/09/08/archives/lockheed-loan-backed-rail-loans-voted-by-senate-body.html. Accessed July 22, 2024. Note that the guarantee was never needed because the administrative fees were fully paid ahead of schedule.

3 Barry Bluestone, Peter Jordan, and Mark Sullivan. 1981. *Aircraft Industry Dynamics: An Analysis of Competition, Capital, and Labor.* Boston, Massachusetts: Auburn House Publishing Company, pp. 57-60.

4 In August 1971, the U.S. Government provided $250,000,000 in emergency loan guarantees to Lockheed Aircraft Corporation. Micky likes to remind people that the government got a good deal. Lockheed eventually paid the U.S. Treasury a $112 million fee (in 2008 dollars) for the loans it received. See Timothy Noah. 2009. "The government's record on industry bailouts." March 31. https://slate.com/news-and-politics/2009/03/the-government-s-record-on-industry-bailouts.html. Accessed July 22, 2024.

5 General Accounting Office. March 22, 1982. *C-5A Wing Modification: A Case Study Illustrating Problems in The Defense Weapons Acquisition Process*. Washington, D.C.: U.S. Government Printing Office.

6 James "Micky" Blackwell. 2021. *All the Days of Our Lives. The Heritage and History of Billie and James Blackwell*. Asheville, N.C.: United Writers Press, p. 85.

7 Lockheed Martin. n.d. *Lockheed Aircraft Service Company: The Beginning of a Global Lockheed Martin*. Accessed January 25, 2018. https://www.lockheedmartin.com/us/news/ features/2015/151110-lockheed-aircraft-service-company.html.

8 The Air Force Research Laboratory (AFRL) is a global technical enterprise, leading the discovery, development, and integration of affordable warfighting technologies for air, space, and cyberspace forces. See https://www.afrl.af.mil/.

9 NASA Biography. n.d. "Andrew S. W. Thomas, Ph.D. and Former NASA Astronaut." https://www.nasa.gov/wp-content/uploads/2016/01/thomas_andrew.pdf. Accessed July 22, 2024.

10 Dr. Joseph Cornish III was an engineering executive at Lockheed Martin Corporation. He became Micky's personal mentor and sponsor. He obtained a B.S. in Mechanical Engineering from Louisiana State University and earned his M.S. and Ph.D. in Aeronautical Engineering from Mississippi State University. Joe was an entrepreneurial inventor, an intellectual, a forward thinker, and a member of Mensa. See James A. Blackwell. 2021. *All the Days of Our Lives*, p. 87-88.

11 The commander who approved their request was Col. Bart Krawetz. Following retirement from the military, he accepted a position at Lockheed. Krawetz had years of experience managing aerospace-related research. He had a bachelor of science in Electrical Engineering from MIT; a master of science in Space Physics from the Air Force Institute of Technology; and a doctorate in Applied Science from the University of California. Lockheed was able to leverage Dr. Krawetz's knowledge and experience.

12 Once again, this is consistent with what the scripture says, "Where there is no vision, the people perish." Proverbs 29:18 KJV.

13 Being promoted to chief engineer of Special Projects in March 1983 brought a lot of perks. Micky was invited to have lunch every day with the president of Lockheed-Georgia. He was also eligible for a year-end bonus and Lockheed stock options. These perks had a significant positive effect on the Blackwell family's lifestyle.

Chapter 4
Next Stage of Leadership

These features ... have made the F-22 into the aircraft that fighter pilots have been asking for since the jet age began.

John Tirpak
Senior Editor, *Air Force* magazine
Writing about the F-22 Raptor

In this chapter, we will continue the journey of Micky to be an Enterprise Servant Leader as he helped win the Advanced Tactical Aircraft program and prepared to lead the F-22 Engineering and Manufacturing Development (EMD), or what was formerly referred to as Full Scale Development Program, for the Lockheed team. We will highlight the things he learned about using servant leadership, building a lean enterprise, and implementing integrated product development teams.

New Threats Emerging and Increasing Cost Pressures

In the 1980s, new enemy threats and increasing cost pressures were causing changes to the US military acquisition process. Conditions were so tenuous, the *Yale Journal on Regulation* summarized the situation as follows, "Attaining an adequate level of defense at an acceptable cost is as vital and elusive a goal as any the United States has pursued since World War II."[1]

New enemy threats were emerging while US fighter aircraft were getting older—many had already exceeded 50 percent of their service life. To maintain its air superiority into the 21st century, the Air Force and Navy needed to start development of a new generation of military fighter aircraft as soon as possible. By the time a new generation of combat aircraft would enter service, America's front-line fighters (the Air Force's F-15 Eagle built by McDonnell Douglas and the Navy's F-14 Tomcat built by Grumman) would be roughly 25 years old. The Soviets had fighters comparable to those of the US, and the Europeans were expected to start producing a new generation of advanced fighter aircraft soon. In addition to the threats posed by advanced enemy aircraft, non-friendly countries were developing more advanced surface-to-air missiles.[2]

Given the trends in military spending and the possibility of additional military force reductions, Congress, the Department of Defense, and other agencies of the government were looking at how they could meet the military's needs and future threats while controlling costs.[3]

Birth of the Raptor

Based on the need to start the development of a new generation of fighters, the US Air Force in 1983 invited aerospace manufacturers to submit proposals for developing an Advanced Tactical Fighter (ATF). Seven aircraft companies received contracts. Three years later, the Air Force asked the seven aircraft companies to submit proposals to launch an ATF demonstration and evaluation (Dem/Val) process to develop and fly full-scale prototype aircraft (see Figure 7). The Air Force selected Lockheed and Northrop to be the prime contractors. Boeing and General Dynamics joined the Lockheed YF-22 team (see Figure 8); and McDonnell-Douglas joined the Northrop YF-23 team (see Figure 9). There would be two versions—the ATF for the U.S Air Force and the Naval ATF, or NATF, for the US Navy.

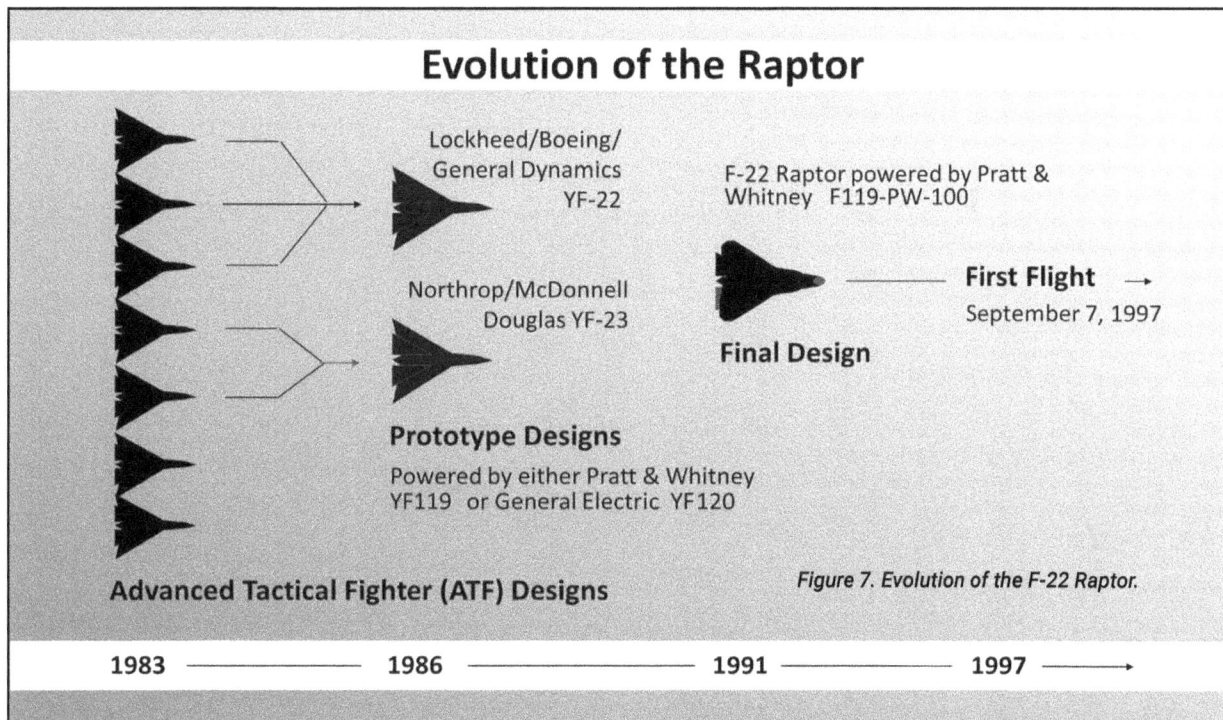

Evolution of the Raptor

Lockheed/Boeing/
General Dynamics
YF-22

F-22 Raptor powered by Pratt &
Whitney F119-PW-100

Northrop/McDonnell
Douglas YF-23

First Flight →
September 7, 1997

Final Design

Prototype Designs

Powered by either Pratt & Whitney
YF119 or General Electric YF120

Advanced Tactical Fighter (ATF) Designs

Figure 7. Evolution of the F-22 Raptor.

1983 ——— 1986 ——————— 1991 ——— 1997 ——→

Figure 8. The Lockheed/Boeing/General Dynamics YF-22 fires an AIM-120 missile over the Pacific. (Lockheed Martin Photo)

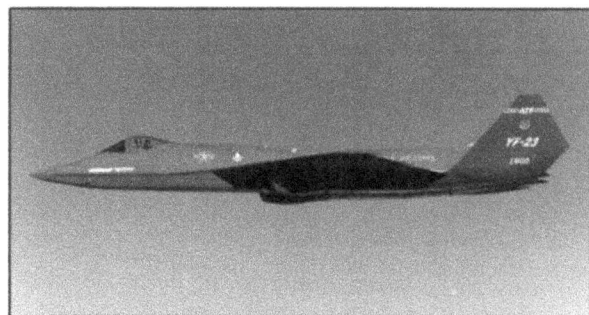

Figure 9. The Northrop-McDonnell Douglas YF-23 in flight. (USAF photo)

The work on each ATF team was shared equally among the team members based on the dollar value of work performed. As lead contractor for the Lockheed/Boeing/General Dynamics team, Lockheed's responsibilities included overall program management. The YF-22's supply base included 650 subcontractors across 32 states.[4] Pratt & Whitney (Pratt & Whitney) and General Electric (GE) competed separately for the right to produce engines for the Advanced Tactical Fighter.

In December of 1986, Colonel James Fain, Jr. was selected by the US Air Force to lead the ATF program. Fortunately, the Air Force did something wise that was virtually unheard of. They left Fain and his team untouched during the next four years of the program. The stability was invaluable. It allowed the Air Force and its contractors to focus on what they were there for—to build and fly prototypes of the Advanced Tactical Fighter.[5]

Vice President & Assistant GM Research, Technology, and Engineering

As noted in the last chapter, Micky was promoted to vice president and assistant general manager for Research, Technology, and Engineering for the new Lockheed Advanced Aeronautics Company in December of 1987. As a result, he and his family relocated from Marietta, Georgia to Newhall, California. His Lockheed office was in Burbank, California.

Most of the work done by Micky's engineering staff was in support of company funded IR&D, support for ongoing aircraft development programs, and support for aircraft production contracts. The three major aircraft development programs that demanded the most support from Engineering were the new US Navy maritime patrol aircraft dubbed the P-7, a major update to the C-130H tactical transport designated the C-130J, and the ATF Dem/Val contract.

For the ATF program, Micky's engineering functional managers were responsible to the ATF for (1) providing engineering personnel to the program with the required skills and experience, (2) supporting all functional engineering systems that were being used on the program, and (3) supplying cutting-edge test facilities to be used by the program. All engineering personnel were hard lined to the ATF program management to eliminate engineers having two bosses. The engineering functional managers had no input into the day-to-day decisions made on the ATF program. This form of organization greatly reduced confusion and improved decision-making.

Growing Pains

When Lockheed won one of the ATF Dem/Val contracts in October 1986, Dick Heppe headed the Lockheed ATF program team. In July 1987, after reviewing the Lockheed team design for the YF-22, he realized that the existing prototype design was not going to win. Heppe was a superb engineer. Heppe then made a bold "bet the future of your company" decision—he directed the Lockheed team to come up with a new design for the ATF Dem/Val competition.

With the time remaining on the contract, this meant that everything on the program had to go perfectly for the Lockheed team to be able to develop a new design, build the ATF prototypes, and still meet the Full Scale Development proposal submission deadline established by the Air Force. The schedule was ultimately extended by six months since both the Lockheed and Northrop teams needed more time to complete work on their prototypes.[6]

By October 1987, the YF-22 had been redesigned and fully analyzed for combat mission performance. Lockheed believed it now had a winner. The decision to redesign the YF-22 could have deep-sixed the entire Lockheed ATF program, but in fact it produced the design that became the winning aircraft.

On January 1, 1989, Dan Tellep was appointed Chairman and CEO of Lockheed Corporation.[7] Tellep recognized the importance of the ATF program. It was a "must win" for Lockheed. Many Lockheed aircraft production programs (with the exception of the C-130H) were coming to an end. Production of the C-130H would also end if money was not spent to make it more desirable for customers.[8]

Shortly after being appointed Chairman and CEO of Lockheed, Tellep launched an in-house review of the ATF program. The report from the review indicated the ATF program was struggling.

From his engineering perspective, Micky had concluded that the Lockheed ATF team needed a lot of miracles to make the YF-22 the winner. At that point, there was not anything more he could do other than give maximum support to his ATF colleagues.

Within a few days of the corporation completing the in-house ATF review, Micky was summoned to meet with Ken Cannestra, who had been promoted to president of Lockheed Aeronautical Systems Company. Much to Micky's surprise, Ken told Micky that he wanted him to leave engineering and take over as Lockheed vice president and assistant general manager (VP & Asst. GM) for the internal Lockheed portion of the ATF program. In this capacity, he would be reporting to Sherm Mullin, the vice president and general manager (VP & GM) of the Lockheed ATF Team who had replaced Heppe who had retired. Sherm was the former program manager of the F-117 Nighthawk stealth fighter program.

Vice President and Assistant GM of the F-22 ATF Program

Micky's new appointment was announced on January 19, 1989. His new title was Lockheed Vice President and Assistant General Manager of the F-22 ATF Program (see Figure 10). He took over the day-to-day program management duties of the internal Lockheed portion of the three-company program and would serve as deputy program director for the Lockheed/Boeing/General Dynamics Team. On July 24, 1989, Ken Cannestra announced that Micky would also report to the office of president on the internal LASC portion of the ATF program.

Starting from the time Micky joined the F-22 ATF program, the team now had less than two years to get everything done.

The three-company management team for the ATF program going forward now included

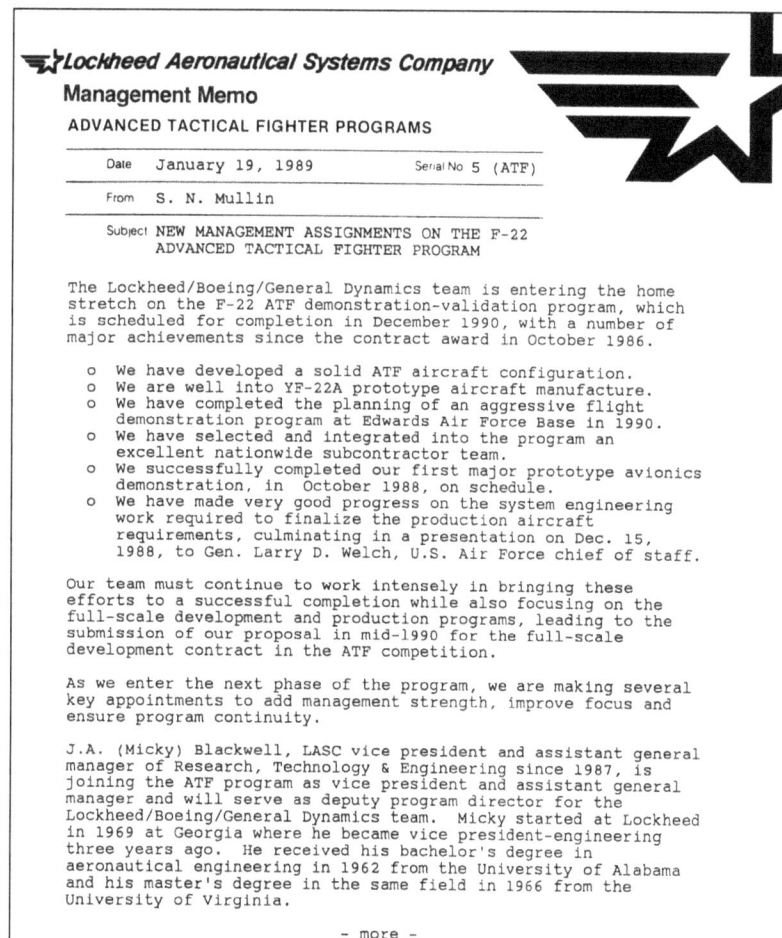

Lockheed Aeronautical Systems Company
Management Memo
ADVANCED TACTICAL FIGHTER PROGRAMS

| Date | January 19, 1989 | Serial No 5 (ATF) |
| From | S. N. Mullin | |

Subject NEW MANAGEMENT ASSIGNMENTS ON THE F-22 ADVANCED TACTICAL FIGHTER PROGRAM

The Lockheed/Boeing/General Dynamics team is entering the home stretch on the F-22 ATF demonstration-validation program, which is scheduled for completion in December 1990, with a number of major achievements since the contract award in October 1986.

o We have developed a solid ATF aircraft configuration.
o We are well into YF-22A prototype aircraft manufacture.
o We have completed the planning of an aggressive flight demonstration program at Edwards Air Force Base in 1990.
o We have selected and integrated into the program an excellent nationwide subcontractor team.
o We successfully completed our first major prototype avionics demonstration, in October 1988, on schedule.
o We have made very good progress on the system engineering work required to finalize the production aircraft requirements, culminating in a presentation on Dec. 15, 1988, to Gen. Larry D. Welch, U.S. Air Force chief of staff.

Our team must continue to work intensely in bringing these efforts to a successful completion while also focusing on the full-scale development and production programs, leading to the submission of our proposal in mid-1990 for the full-scale development contract in the ATF competition.

As we enter the next phase of the program, we are making several key appointments to add management strength, improve focus and ensure program continuity.

J.A. (Micky) Blackwell, LASC vice president and assistant general manager of Research, Technology & Engineering since 1987, is joining the ATF program as vice president and assistant general manager and will serve as deputy program director for the Lockheed/Boeing/General Dynamics team. Micky started at Lockheed in 1969 at Georgia where he became vice president-engineering three years ago. He received his bachelor's degree in aeronautical engineering in 1962 from the University of Alabama and his master's degree in the same field in 1966 from the University of Virginia.

- more -

Figure 10. Memo Announcing Micky's Assignment as Vice President and Assistant General Manager of the F-22. (Image provided by Micky Blackwell)

Sherm Mullin as the head of the ATF Team Project Office, and a Vice President supporting him from each of the three team companies: Lockheed, General Dynamics, and Boeing.

Sherm, as head of the Team Project Office, continued to lead the total program but shifted his focus to setting the team's strategy; working on three-company team interface issues; kicking off the F-22 Engineering and Management Development (EMD) proposal; and starting the planning and preparation for executing the EMD phase of the program. Sherm attacked his new Team Project Office role with vigor, and the program took a major leap forward.

Sherm Mullin was the best overall program manager that Micky was ever associated with. He was great working with the Air Force, Navy, and Department of Defense (DOD) customers. He was able to blend the three-company ATF industry team together to accomplish the program objectives, and he also developed an incredibly good strategy for winning the F-22 program.

> **Air Dominance in the 21st Century**
>
> *Air dominance in the 21st Century is often described as a first look, first shot, first kill capability.*
>
> *Gen. Richard E. Hawley, Commander of Air Combat Command, used the words of a Russian pilot to describe air dominance as follows: a prolonged capability the enemy cannot counter. It includes a high degree of stealth, high-speed supercruise, dominant situational awareness, and the capability to deliver weapons deep into enemy territory.*
>
> *What the Russian described was the F-22.*
>
> Source: Harper, Bob. 1997. "General Richard E. Hawley." Sky Power, The F-22: Air Dominance for the 21st Century, Spring: 20.

Manufacturing Decision

In May 1990, Dan Tellep asked Sherm Mullen where the F-22 should be manufactured. Several years earlier, most Lockheed aeronautical executives would have said Burbank, California. The manufacturing facilities in Marietta and Palmdale were good, but the manufacturing facilities in Burbank were not. Sherm told Dan Tellep that Lockheed's portion of the F-22 should be designed and built in Marietta, Georgia.

Tellep made it official on May 9, 1990. Assuming a win, the F-22 would be designed, manufactured, and assembled in Marietta. This meant the entire F-22 program would have to move to Marietta as soon as the government announced Lockheed as the winner—not just some people or parts of the program. The Lockheed Burbank facilities would close, and the Lockheed Skunk Works would move to more modern facilities at Plant 10 in Palmdale, California. Dan Tellep also told Micky that he would be responsible for ensuring a successful move of the program to Marietta.

Obstacles to Overcome

As Micky has often said, to meet the December 31, 1990, deadline to submit the EMD team proposal, the team needed "several miracles" to make it happen. There was no question that the F-22 would be far superior to anything ever built before it, but meeting the government's requirements in the time remaining would be a remarkable achievement.

The reader can be the judge of whether the following developments were "miracles" or not. For Micky, who was now directing Lockheed's day-to-day operations on the F-22, they will always be "miracles," because he knew what had to happen to finish the Dem/Val program on time and to meet program objectives. To get one or two items to work would have been impressive by itself, but to get all of them working together was highly improbable. From Micky's point of view, making it all work would take lots of hard work and more than a little divine help.

Miracle #1: The Wing

The first miracle needed was the design of a wing that could meet the aircraft weight requirements while, at the same time, handling the heat and stress of supersonic speeds. Prior to the ATF, fighter aircraft wings were primarily made of steel, titanium, and aluminum. Lockheed team engineers agreed that making the wings out of composite materials was the answer.

Thermoplastic composite materials were selected for the prototype wings to meet the prototype manufacturing schedule. The thermoplastic wing in the prototype met the strength requirements and could withstand the heat generated, but it was difficult to manufacture and had environmental problems.

The alternate material for manufacturing the wing was thermoset composite materials, but thermosets were not quite ready to use on the prototype. Nevertheless, the team felt that with a little more time, they could develop a thermoset composite wing that would meet or exceed the customer's requirements and have it ready for EMD after the Lockheed team won the contract—and they were successful.

Miracle #2: The Radar

The second miracle needed was the development of an advanced stealthy radar along with a stealthy nose radome. The radar would have to be compatible with the low-observable fighter design that the Lockheed team was building. Although the YF-22 prototype didn't have a radar, the Northrop Grumman/Texas Instruments team was chosen to be the F-22 radar supplier, and they developed a phenomenal radar system that met all requirements. One key Lockheed IR&D project that supported this development was the development by the Skunk Works of the low RCS radome.

Miracle #3: Low RCS with no Loss of Aerodynamic Performance

The third miracle needed for success was the development of a low RCS aircraft shape that had equal to or better aerodynamic performance than existing fighter aircraft. To meet both requirements, the external shape of the ATF had to be designed for low RCS and had to be aerodynamically smooth to achieve the aerodynamic performance requirements. This was a huge challenge for the team.

A full-scale, low observable model of the F-22 was tested at the Skunk Works' radar test range at Hellendale, California. The results were impressive and confirmed that all stealth requirements had been met. Similarly, wind tunnel tests confirmed that aerodynamic performance requirements were met.

Miracle #4: Flying at Supercruise

The fourth miracle needed was an ATF aircraft design that could fly at sustained supersonic speeds without afterburner (supercruise). This would be the first fighter to ever achieve this goal—and achieve it they did. As described by Pratt & Whitney:[9]

> *"The F119 turbofan engine is the world's first fifth-generation fighter engine. The F119 combines stealth technologies and vectored thrust performance to provide unprecedented maneuverability and survivability with a high thrust-to-weight ratio. The ability of the F-22 to supercruise gives exceptional combat performance without compromising mission range."*

Miracle #5: New Levels of Reliability and Supportability

The fifth miracle needed was the development of an aircraft that was substantially more reliable and maintainable than current fighters. The F-22 was designed to have no layering of subsystems and be accessible from the bottom and sides of the airplane. It was also designed with no safety wire on the entire airplane. All systems and subsystems were designed and tested so that the crews knew they would meet the Air Force's Mean-Time-Between-Failure (MTBF) and Mean-Time-to-Repair (MTTR) targets.

Miracle #6: The Common Integrated Processor

The sixth major miracle needed was the successful development of the Common Integrated Processor (CIP). The CIP provided the computing power for all aircraft systems. On previous fighters, each aircraft system had its own computer processor. The F-22 could not afford the weight of every system having its own computer. Many naysayers said the development of a CIP could not be done. Hughes did incredible work and successfully developed and demonstrated the CIP. The CIP has computing power equivalent to several Cray supercomputers.

In the end, all the miracles needed to push the YF-22 prototype and make the F-22 EMD proposal a success were achieved by the Lockheed/Boeing/General Dynamics team, their subcontractors, and Air Force Systems Command personnel.

Testing the Raptor

The formal rollout of the first YF-22A prototype occurred on August 29, 1990. Rollout occurred at the Skunk Works in Palmdale, California. The prototype's first flight took place in Palmdale one month later. It was an emotional time for Micky. To see the YF-22 prototype's first flight was one of the great moments of his life. The maiden flight of the second prototype occurred on October 30, 1990. The team had twelve weeks after the first flight to accumulate, validate, and insert flight data from the two prototypes into the EMD proposal. The Lockheed team completed the YF-22 flight test program at Edwards AFB, California on December 28, 1990. Key dates in the YF-22 Dem/Val Flight Test are summarized in Appendix D.

The Lockheed team demonstrated in flight the YF-22's agility, supercruise capability, thrust vectoring, aerial refueling, live missile firing, high angle-of-attack controlled maneuvering, and speeds in excess of Mach 2. It was the most tested prototype aircraft in the history of aviation. Although the Lockheed-led team started flight tests a month later than the Northrop team, the F-22 flight tests generated 40 percent more flight hours and demonstrated more advanced technology than the YF-23.

When the flight tests were complete, Dick Abrams, director of Flight Testing at the Lockheed Skunk Works, made the following comment, "From first flight of a new aircraft design to a cleared demonstration envelope in 91 days is an unequaled achievement in the modern history of aviation."[10] A number of lessons were learned from this phase of testing. Details on each lesson can be found in a report written by Mr. Abrams. The title of the report is the *YF-22A Prototype Advanced Tactical Fighter Demonstration/Validation Flight Test Program Overview.*[11]

In addition to meeting all aerodynamic and low-observable stealth requirements, the F-22 team had to demonstrate it could meet all the Air Force's avionics requirements. Testing was done on the Boeing F-22 Avionics Testbed Aircraft (a highly modified Boeing 757). The radar, the integrated processor, and all other avionics met or exceeded required performance thresholds.

The YF-22 was the most tested aircraft in the history of aviation. – Dick Abrams

Engineering and Manufacturing Development Proposal Submitted

With the help of results from a few "miracles," successful aerodynamics tests, low observable tests, and avionics tests, the Lockheed team completed their EMD proposal on December 30, 1990, one day before the Air Force's mandatory completion date. Copies of the proposal volumes were flown to the ATF SPO at Wright-Patterson AFB, Ohio. The 30,000 page, seven-volume, classified proposal was delivered on schedule and under guard December 31, 1990.[12]

Implementing Integrated Product Teams

One of the unique concepts proposed by Lockheed for the EMD phase of acquisition was the use of Integrated Product Development Teams (IPDTs). The name was later simplified to Integrated Product Teams (IPTs). IPTs were based on the principles of servant leadership and Kelly Johnson's 14 Rules (Appendix B). IPTs were the Lockheed Team's proposed approach to implement the USAF requirement to use concurrent engineering on the EMD F-22 program. The IPT concept was developed by Rudolph "Rudy" Burch who led the writing of the F-22 EMD Proposal Management Volume.

According to Graham Warwick at *Flight International* magazine, IPT managers were assigned to the four major elements of the program: air vehicle (Lockheed); training (Boeing); support (General Dynamics); and test (Boeing).[13] Each major element was broken down into sub-IPTs with each package being the responsibility of a mini-program manager. Each sub-IPT had the funding and resources to bring together design, finance, manufacturing, as well as "customers." Having Air Force personnel as an integral part of the integrated product teams was a radical departure from the way programs had operated in the past. In fact, "they have never had a customer shift from being an evaluator to being part of the process."[14]

Bringing the IPT team concept to reality wasn't necessarily easy. The F-22 program was a joint venture between three companies and many subcontractors. Each had to turn their organizational structures into team-oriented approaches for decision-making. More detail on Integrated product teams (IPT's) is presented later in the book. Suffice it to say at this point that the use of IPT's was incredibly successful and a big win for the Air Force and the Lockheed team.

Full Responsibility for the F-22 Program

On January 1, 1991, Sherm Mullin was named president of Lockheed's Advanced Development Company (the Skunk Works) succeeding Ben Rich who retired on December 31, 1990. Micky was named vice president and general manager of the F-22 Team Project Office. He would assume full responsibility for the F-22 EMD if the Lockheed team was selected to build the ATF. On January 3, 1991, Lockheed presented a verbal summary of its EMD proposal to the Air Force. Sherm Mullin led the F-22 team in delivering the presentation, and Micky briefed the team's management portion to the Air Force.

ATF Winner Announced

To win the ATF EMD program, Lockheed's marketing strategy was based on selling the superior attributes of the F-22—stealth, supercruise, supportability, and agility. The only one of these attributes that was not a requirement in the Request for Proposal was "agility." Thus, Lockheed's media strategy was to hammer agility, agility, agility! More control surfaces, combined with thrust vectoring, resulted in more controllability. This appealed to the pilots who wanted an aircraft that was highly maneuverable. The F-22 also had more useable internal volume than the F-23 would have had.

The Lockheed team was notified that the ATF source selection authority for the USAF would be the Secretary of the Air Force, Donald Rice. He would announce the winner of the ATF competition on April 23, 1991. Dan Tellep went to Washington D.C. to be in attendance when the announcement was made. Micky was at a television studio in Washington D.C. Micky's job was to wait for Dan Tellep to call, and then relay the decision, by closed circuit TV, to the Lockheed team in Burbank and Marietta and their team partners in Fort Worth and Seattle.

Micky showed up at the studio at 3:00 p.m. He went on the air live to make some introductory remarks at five minutes after 4:00 p.m. People who knew Micky were convinced Lockheed had lost. When the viewers saw Micky, he did not look well.

At 4:20 p.m., the Secretary of the Air Force announced the winner of the ATF competition. He stated that "the Lockheed/General Dynamics/Boeing team had won because the F-22 had more 'agility' than the F-23." He also announced that Pratt & Whitney had won the engine competition and would supply F119 turbofans to the winner of the aircraft competition.

Immediately after Secretary Rice made the announcement, Dan Tellep called Micky to tell him the good news. Micky broke into a huge grin and went live on closed circuit TV to relay Tellep's message to audiences all over the United States that were holding their breath. When Micky started to speak, he choked up, but finally got it out.

"We won!" Micky exclaimed, as Lockheed and their partners exploded in celebration. It was a great day for Lockheed and is etched in Micky's memory.[15] A copy of Micky's personal notes from his "We Won!" speech can be seen in Figure 11. A copy of the EMD contract is included in Appendix C.

When the story appeared in the *Wall Street Journal* the next day, Secretary Rice said the Lockheed-led team had an "edge over the rest of the aerospace industry by providing the opportunity to field a state-of-the-art aircraft combining stealth, speed, and agility."[16] Based on the Secretary's comments, it appears the Lockheed strategy was successful.

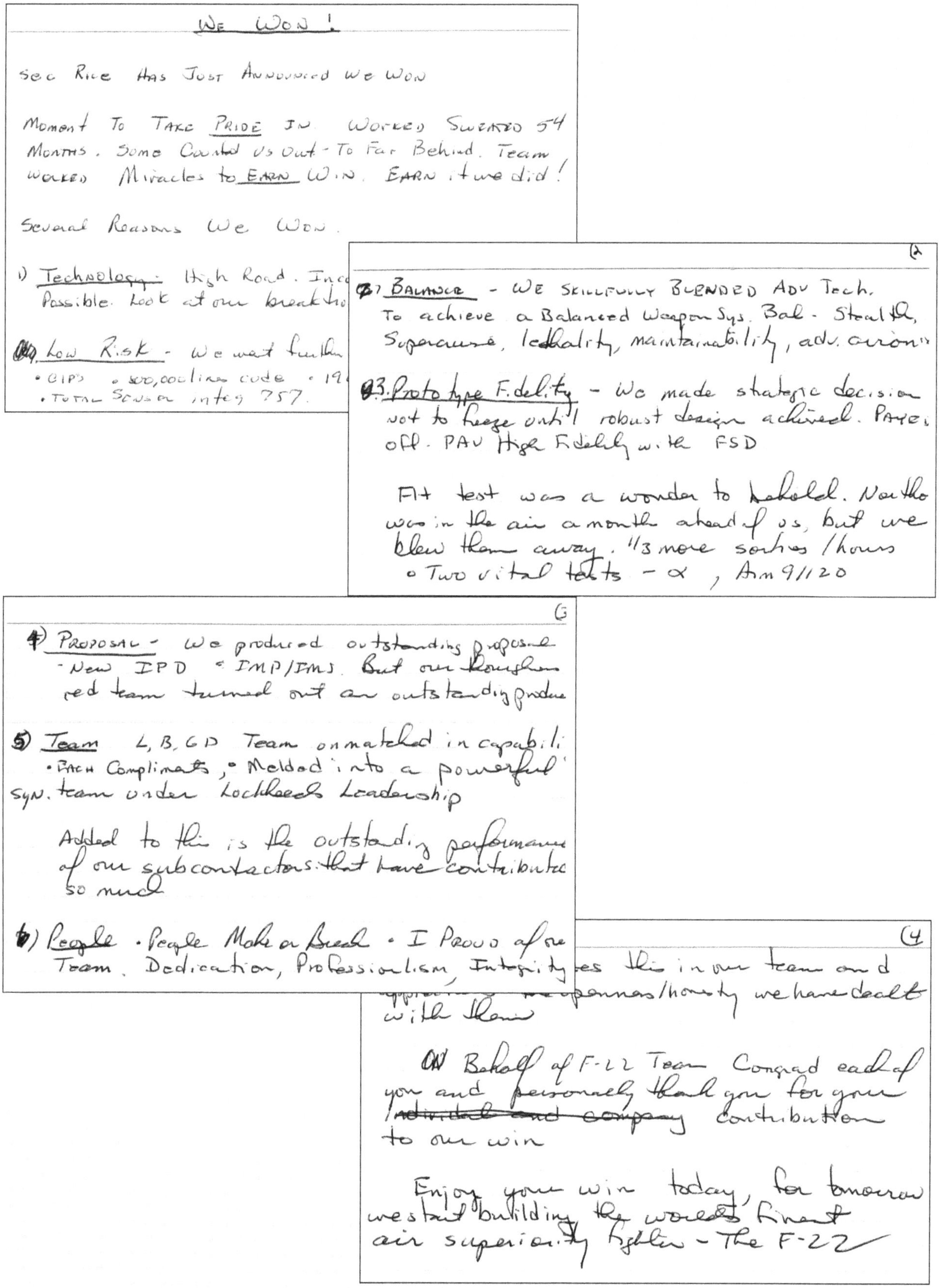

WE WON!

SEC RICE HAS JUST ANNOUNCED WE WON

MOMENT TO TAKE PRIDE IN. WORKED SWEATED 54
MONTHS. SOME COUNTED US OUT - TO FAR BEHIND. TEAM
WORKED MIRACLES TO EARN WIN. EARN IT WE DID!

SEVERAL REASONS WE WON.

1) Technology - High Road. Inc[...]
Possible. Look at our breakthro[...]

2) Low Risk - We met furth[...]
• CIPS • 800,000 lines code • 19[...]
• TOTAL SENSOR INTEG 757.

2) BALANCE - WE SKILLFULLY BLENDED ADV TECH.
TO achieve a Balanced Weapon Sys. Bal. Stealth,
Supercruise, lethality, maintainability, adv. avion[...]

3) Prototype Fidelity - We made strategic decision
not to freeze until robust design achieved. Paye[...]
off. PAV High Fidelity with FSD

Flt test was a wonder to behold. Northa
was in the air a month ahead of us, but we
blew them away. "3 more sorties/hours
• Two vital tests - α , Aim 9/120

4) PROPOSAL - We produced outstanding proposal
- New IPD • IMP/IMS. But our thoughts [...]
red team turned out an outstanding produ[...]

5) Team L, B, GD Team unmatched in capabili[...]
• EACH Compliments • Melded into a powerful
syn. team under Lockheed Leadership

Added to this is the outstanding performance
of our subcontractors that have contribute[...]
so much

6) People • People Make or Break • I Proud of our
Team. Dedication, Professionalism, Integrity [...]es this in our team and
[...]openness/honesty we have dealt
with them

On Behalf of F-22 Team Congrad each of
you and personally thank you for your
[...] and company contribution
to our win

Enjoy your win today, for tomorrow
we start building the worlds finest
air superiority fighter - The F-22

Figure 11. Micky's personal notes from the F-22 "We Won!" speech.

The Lockheed ATF team was the closest thing to a very "high-performance team" that Micky had experienced during his entire working career. They were a team in every sense of the word. They had strong leaders and communication was great. People looked out for each other, and no one cared about who took credit for the work. Everybody pulled together for the success of the team. In a word, they had melded together and become a "family." When you become a family and act like a family, it is unbelievable what can be done. Once again, Enterprise Servant Leadership paid off with an incredible win for Lockheed.

Move to Marietta, Georgia

Now, the real work began. Lockheed had to move their portion of the three-company team from Burbank to Marietta, negotiate the EMD contract with the Air Force, and get ready to start the F-22 program. Almost immediately after the Secretary announced that Lockheed had won the contract, the relocation of people from Burbank to Marietta was approved, and F-22 program activities began to ramp up in Marietta, Georgia.

Moving the F-22 staff and their families to Georgia was not like building an airplane, but it did require planning, commitment, and considerable attention. In fact, it required all the planning, project management skills, and persuasion Micky could muster. It was yet one more test of his ability to lead while helping the employees decide whether to stay or leave. Many of Lockheed's employees had grown up in California and thought the only good thing about the South was fried chicken and college football. Lower-cost housing did not hurt either.

To help the people decide whether they wanted to make the move, Lockheed arranged for all F-22 salaried employees to spend a week in Marietta with their spouses. The purpose was to allow the employees to see the area, look at housing, and assess the schools. The people of Marietta went out of their way to be good hosts. Signs popped up everywhere in Marietta welcoming the Lockheed F-22 employees from Burbank. As indicated by the following story, their hospitality must have worked.[17]

> One engineer came to Micky and said, "I cannot possibly move to Marietta." What he wanted was a transfer to the Skunk Works at their new location in Palmdale, California. Micky told the man he still had to take the trip, but if he didn't want to go after he returned from Georgia, he would personally arrange his transfer to the Skunk Works in Palmdale. The man, and his wife, immediately went to Marietta. Several days later, the man from California once again called Micky. The engineer, who so badly wanted a transfer to Palmdale, now had a different and possibly bigger problem to deal with. He said, "Micky, I am in trouble. My wife just bought a new house not far from the plant in Marietta, but I don't have an official offer to move to Georgia yet. Can you help?"

About 85 percent of the F-22 staff agreed to move permanently and others accepted temporary assignments to help get the program started. In the end, Micky personally worked with several hundred F-22 staff members to facilitate their moves to Marietta.

Standing Up the F-22 Program in Marietta, Georgia

Moving the F-22 program from Burbank to Marietta required numerous facility upgrades and additions, additional personnel, new financial and manufacturing systems, implementation of new systems to further improve quality, and actions to reduce the cost of the F-22.

Acquiring Office Space

Additional classified office space to house the F-22 program had to be acquired at the Lockheed facility in Marietta. Large temporary buildings were leased to add to the existing classified space to accommodate the program's needs.

In early 1991, the F-22 prefabricated temporary office buildings were brought in and the migration of staff from Burbank to Marietta was begun. The construction of a new three-story L-22 office building to house the F-22 program was approved, and the F-22 program moved into the new L-22 building near the end of 1992. The new building contained the latest in three-way classified video communication and computer technology, which allowed Lockheed's partners and subcontractors all over the US to communicate securely.

Adding ATF Program Personnel

Even with all the ATF personnel who moved from California to Marietta, one of Micky's biggest challenges was to add qualified people to man the program. Fortunately, Micky knew where to get most of the people he needed within Lockheed. However, some with special skills had to be hired from outside the company.

Lockheed was especially fortunate to obtain engineers who had worked on the Northrop/McDonnell Douglas YF-23 program; engineers from a cancelled RAH-66 Army armed reconaissance helicopter program; and engineers from the cancelled McDonnell Douglas/General Dynamics A-12 Avenger II Navy stealth strike aircraft program. These people became available just as the F-22 program needed them. In a relatively short period of time, Lockheed was able to add a substantial amount of outstanding talent to the F-22 team.

Upgrading Manufacturing Facilities

Once the Lockheed team had been selected to build the F-22, the Air Force and Lockheed agreed that they needed to upgrade the manufacturing facilities in Marietta. Since the facilities were owned by the US Air Force, the government provided most of the funds that were needed to make the necessary improvements.

The newest and largest facility to be built for the F-22 was the RCS verification building. Another new structure built at the Marietta plant for the F-22 was a robotic coating facility which included a large bay where the aircraft would have stealth material coatings applied.

Upgrading Financial and Manufacturing Systems

The financial and manufacturing systems in Marietta needed to be upgraded to provide F-22 decision-makers with the timely information they needed to manage. Micky later expanded the modernization to include a new Enterprise Resource Planning (ERP) system.

Implementing TQM

One of President Ken Cannestra's most successful initiatives in Marietta was implementing Total Quality Management (TQM) across the Lockheed Aeronautics Company. This effort was well underway when the F-22 program was moved to Marietta. The initial TQM focus was on reducing waste and improving quality. This effort was later overshadowed by what Micky accomplished by implementing Lean and Six Sigma—topics that are covered later in the book.

Reducing Overhead Costs

Another issue that quickly arose after the program moved to Marietta was the need to reduce the overhead rates of the three companies involved. Even though their existing rates had been approved by the Air Force, the overhead rates still needed to be reduced to keep F-22 costs under budget.

Because of Micky's persistence on this issue, Ken Cannestra put him in charge of Lockheed's company-wide overhead cost reduction task force. Micky took on the role with vengeance and ended up taking drastic measures—including forcing staff to make direct charges to programs; consolidating warehouses; closing underutilized buildings; negotiating new food service contracts; cutting health insurance costs; and eliminating unneeded services. All of these actions were effective in reducing the F-22 overhead costs.

Cost Impact from Reducing Number of Aircraft to Be Purchased

During the announcement of the winner of the ATF competition, Secretary Rice noted that the Lockheed and Pratt & Whitney design "clearly offered better capability at lower costs, thereby providing the Air Force with a true best value." When the ATF was conceived, the planned number of planes to be bought was 1,200 for the US Air Force and 1,000 for the US Navy.

By the time the Dem/Val contracts were awarded, the number of airplanes had been trimmed to 750 for the Air Force and 546 for the Navy. Unfortunately, before the EMD contract was signed, the number of USAF F-22s to be purchased was cut to 648 due to Air Force budget problems. Further reductions in the number of F-22s to be produced were made to 339 in 1997, to 277 in 2003, and to 187 in 2008. In addition, the US Navy cancelled the Naval ATF (NATF) version, which further reduced the total by another 546 airplanes. Finally, in another cost-cutting move, the Air Force eliminated the two-seat trainer version of the F-22 that would have been designated F-22B.

Each time the government cut the number of aircraft to be built, the Lockheed led team, and all its subcontractors, had to submit new cost proposals. This was deadly for the program, since any contractor or team partner that was in trouble was given an opportunity to increase their cost quote.

Enormous effort was required by all three team partners to try to limit cost increases. Even if one could hold EMD costs constant, when that cost is amortized across a smaller number of aircraft, the average cost of each airplane goes up. In addition, the aircraft that were removed from the DOD budget were the cheapest that would be bought, because they were the lowest on the "learning curve" where many of the production issues had been worked out. This again caused the average cost of each aircraft to go up.

The result was that even if the Lockheed team came in on budget, the F-22 average unit cost was going to increase substantially due to the drastically reduced purchase of airplanes. The newspapers gave the impression that the aircraft average unit cost increases were mostly the contractor's fault. This falsehood was repeated over-and-over in the press. Unfortunately, facts would not change how the newspapers reported the cost increases.

By and large, the F-22 design and development moved along smoothly. There were technical and manufacturing challenges that had to be worked out, but nothing that the team could not deal with on a relatively routine basis. The basic dimensions and general characteristics of the final F-22 configuration are shown in Appendix E.

Lockheed Acquires General Dynamics, Fort Worth

On March 15, 1993, the Lockheed Corporation purchased the Fort Worth Division of the General Dynamics Corporation for $1.5 billion. The purchase was a brilliant move by Lockheed Chairman and CEO Dan Tellep. Following the purchase, Lockheed now owned 67 percent of the F-22 by dollar value and Boeing owned the remaining 33 percent. But perhaps best of all, the popular F-16 Fighting Falcon multi-role fighter now belonged to Lockheed. The F-16 fighter was still selling well around the world and generated substantial cash flow and profit for Lockheed. This money was needed to undergird the F-22 development, the development of the C-130J Super Hercules, and later the bid for the F-35 Joint Strike Fighter.

With the General Dynamics Fort Worth acquisition, Lockheed decided to form a new Lockheed Aeronautical Systems Group (ASG) with Ken Cannestra as president. The ASG included the Lockheed Tactical Systems Company in Fort Worth, Texas; the Lockheed Air Services Company in Ontario, California; the Skunk Works in Palmdale, California; and the Lockheed Aeronautical Systems Company in Marietta, Georgia.

General Dynamics's Gordon England became president of the Lockheed Tactical Systems Company. Sherm Mullin became president of the Lockheed Advanced Development Company. Skip Bowling became president of Lockheed Air Services Company. Ken Cannestra was double-hatted as the Aeronautics Group president and Lockheed Aeronautical Systems Company president.

Lessons Learned and Important Points

This chapter described Micky's activities in taking over the F-22 Raptor. Lessons learned and important points include:

- Dick Heppe as head of the Lockheed ATF team recognized in July 1987 that the current Lockheed team ATF design was not a winner and ordered a complete redesign that became the winning design.
- In early 1989, Dan Tellep recognized the importance of the ATF program to the future of Lockheed. He launched an in-house review of the program. The review found that the Lockheed ATF team was struggling.
- Shortly after the review was concluded, Micky was promoted to Lockheed Vice President & Assistant General Manager to lead the internal Lockheed portion of the ATF Program.
- The Lockheed YF-22 was the most tested prototype aircraft in the history of aviation.
- The Lockheed ATF team was able to develop a number of new revolutionary technologies, apply them to the design of the F-22, and successfully demonstrate they worked.
- Micky liked being innovative, and he liked working with teams led by servant leaders. Integrated product teams were a good fit, and he knew how to use them.
- The Lockheed team completed the EMD proposal on December 30, 1990, and delivered it to the Air Force on schedule at Wright Patterson AFB on December 31, 1990.
- On January 3, 1991, Lockheed presented a verbal summary of its EMD proposal to the Air Force.
- The Secretary of the Air Force announced Lockheed as the winner of the ATF competition on April 23, 1991.
- Micky built a culture for the F-22 program that motivated and cared for people. Caring for people resulted in the successful move of the F-22 program and its employees from Burbank, California to Lockheed facilities in Marietta, Georgia.
- The Lockheed Corporation purchased the Fort Worth Division of the General Dynamics Corporation on March 15, 1993 for $1.5 billion. This gave Lockheed 2/3 of the F-22 program and the very successful F-16 fighter program.

Chapter Notes

1 William B. Burnett and William E. Kovacic. 1989. "Reform of United States Weapon System Acquisition Policy: Competition, Teaming Agreements, and Dual-Sourcing." *Yale Journal on Regulation* 6 (2), pp. 249-317.

2 Christopher Bolkcom. 2002. "F-22 Raptor Aircraft Program." *CRS Issue Brief for Congress, Foreign Affairs, Defense, and Trade Division.* Washington, D.C.: Congressional Research Service, p. 8.

3 Ibid.

4 Richard Abrams and Jay Miller. 1992. *Lockheed/General Dynamics/Boeing F-22: Advanced Tactical Fighter Unveiled!* Aerofax Extra 5, Arlington, Texas: Aerofax Inc., p. 3-4.

5 Sherman N. Mullin, 2012. *Winning the ATF.* Mitchell Paper 9, Arlington, Virginia: Mitchell Institute Press, pp. 37-38.

6 James "Micky" Blackwell. 2021. *All the Days of Our Lives. The Heritage and History of Billie and James Blackwell.* Asheville, NC: United Writers Press, p. 109.

7 Ibid. Micky's notes make it clear what he thought about the new CEO when he wrote, "Dan Tellep was the most outstanding and capable boss for which I ever worked...He was a unique individual who excelled at being both a chief operating officer and a chief executive officer at the corporate level." James Micky Blackwell. 2021. *All the Days of Our Lives,* p. 108.

8 Ibid, p. 109.

9 Pratt & Whitney: a United Technology Company. 2018. *F119-PW-100 Turbofan Engine.* Website Report, Hartford, CT: Pratt & Whitney.

10 Richard Abrams. 1991. *YF-22A Prototype Advanced Tactical Fighter Demonstration/Validation Flight Test Program Overview.* Palmdale, California: Lockheed Advanced Development Company, p. 21.

11 Ibid, 17-20.

12 Sherman N. Mullin, 2012. *Winning the ATF.* Mitchell Paper 9, Arlington, Virginia: Mitchell Institute Press, p. 48.

13 Graham Warwick. 1991. "Team Player." *Flight International.* 27 November – 3 December, p.21.

14 Richard W. Stevenson. 1991. "New in Defense: Teamwork." *The New York Times.* December 22, Section 3, p. 3.

15 James "Micky" Blackwell. 2021. *All the Days of Our Lives,* p. 113.

16 Rick Wartzman and Andy Pasztor. April 24, 1991. "Lockheed Team Gets Air Force Contract to Build Next-Generation Fighter Plane." *The Wall Street Journal,* A3.

17 James "Micky" Blackwell. 2021. *All the Days of Our Lives,* p. 112.

Part II: Servant Leadership of Integrated Product Teams

Levels of Servant Leadership

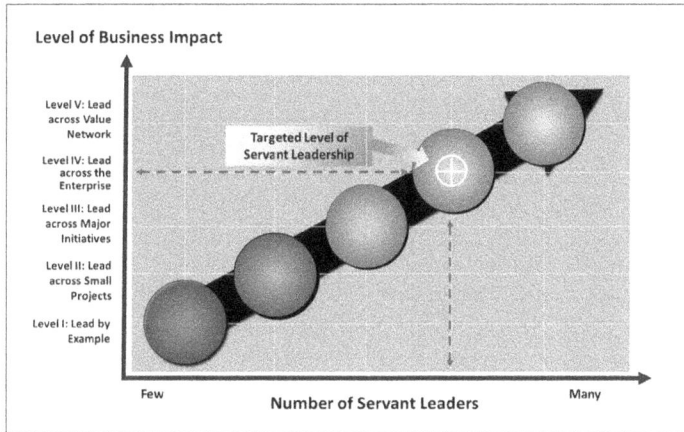

Level of Business Impact

Level V: Lead across Value Network
Level IV: Lead across the Enterprise
Level III: Lead across Major Initiatives
Level II: Lead across Small Projects
Level I: Lead by Example

Targeted Level of Servant Leadership

Few — Number of Servant Leaders — Many

Guidelines for Helping Enterprise Servant Leaders

GUIDELINE 1:

Remember your Creator; there is a reason you are the leader. Pray for the wisdom to make wise decisions; you were chosen for a purpose.

Developing and Using Integrated Product Teams

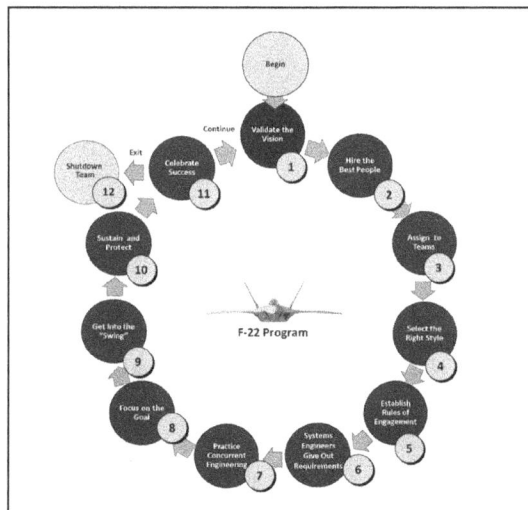

Begin

1. Validate the Vision
2. Hire the Best People
3. Assign to Teams
4. Select the Right Style
5. Establish Rules of Engagement
6. Systems Engineers Give Out Requirements
7. Practice Concurrent Engineering
8. Focus on the Goal
9. Get into the "Swing"
10. Sustain and Protect
11. Celebrate Success
12. Shutdown Team

Continue — Exit

F-22 Program

Chapter 5

Enterprise Servant Leadership and Why it Matters

Yet to truly understand the servant as leader is to unlock a secret source of energy...
legitimate power...

Dennis L. Tarr
The Strategic Toughness of Servant-Leadership

As discussed in the Introduction, the Air Force and Lockheed recognized that a new management model using "Enterprise Servant Leaders" was needed for successfully developing the F-22.

In Part II, we will describe how enterprise servant leaders can make a positive difference in managing major programs, present guidelines for helping enterprise servant leaders be successful, and outline how to organize high-performance integrated product teams.

In this chapter, we will describe the use of enterprise servant leaders and why it matters.

The Transformation Process

When the F-22 program was started in 1986, it was not totally clear what management model they were following. Authoritative management was required and some disliked taking on additional responsibilities.[1] Even though employees did the best they could with what they had, it could generally be stated that: [2]

- Organizations were not structured to maximize interdisciplinary teamwork.
- Compartmentalization impeded teamwork and communication was one-way.
- Process management was still evolving, and inefficiencies were everywhere.
- Workers were trapped in processes that were full of unnecessary steps and errors.
- Building cost-efficient designs, as well as manufacturing and support systems, were not a key focus of the organization.
- All these problems reduced creativity and innovation, and a great deal had to change for Lockheed to successfully build and field the F-22.

To address these problems, Micky believed that servant leadership applied throughout the entire business enterprise was the key to making a new management model work and would transform the way Lockheed Martin did business.

Why Servant Leadership Matters

Not long after Micky started his new job at Lockheed in 1969, Robert Greenleaf published his first essay on the topic. The title of the paper was The Servant as Leader, and one of the challenges he faced was explaining how one person could be both. The answer to that question sparked a change in leadership thinking. It changed people's ideas about the legitimacy of the servant leadership model.[3]

Today, the website for the Robert K. Greenleaf Center for Servant Leadership defines servant leadership this way:

> *"Servant leadership is a philosophy and set of practices that*
> *enriches the lives of individuals, builds better organizations and*
> *ultimately creates a more just and caring world."*[4]

One of the central themes of Greenleaf's proposal was that in order to be a leader, one must be seen as a servant first.[5]

Over thirty years later, Ken Blanchard and Phil Hodges published a book with a similar title. The title was *The Servant Leader,* and the focus was on transforming one's heart, head, hands, and habits into those of a servant leader. Their work was based on examples of how Jesus served people. This concept is embedded in the following quote from Jesus in the book of Matthew from the Bible:

> *But Jesus called them to Himself and said, "You know that the rulers of the Gentiles*
> *lord it over them, and those who are great exercise authority over them. Yet it shall*
> *not be so among you; but whoever desires to become great among you, let him be*
> *your servant. And whoever desires to be first among you, let him be your slave.*
> *Matthew 20:25-27 (NKJV)*

To put Jesus's words into practice, Blanchard and Hodges created a method for classifying people: those who desire to serve others, and those who desire to be served. They subsequently called these groups "servant leaders" and "self–serving leaders."[6] Blanchard and Hodges define servant leaders as:

> *"Those who focus on others rather than trying to acquire*
> *power, wealth, and fame for themselves."*[7]

This was consistent with Micky's experience, and he really liked what he read. However, Micky also believes that people should not be restricted to the two categories. Most people live on a spectrum between the two extremes.

Kathleen Patterson, another author, believes that servant leaders are:

> *"Those who focus on serving their followers, where the followers are the*
> *primary concern, and the organizational concerns are peripheral."*[8]

Bernie Brown, Retired CEO of WellStar Health System, observes:

> *"God's definition of a leader is our definition of a servant."*

Wikipedia defines servant leadership as:

> *Servant leadership is a leadership philosophy in which the goal of the leader is to serve. This is different from traditional leadership where the leader's main focus is the thriving of their company or organizations. A servant leader shares power, puts the needs of the employees first and helps people develop and perform as highly as possible. Instead of the people working to serve the leader, the leader exists to serve the people.*[9]

Micky defines a servant leader as:

> *"One who leads like Jesus in every aspect of their lives, who is totally devoted to serving others, and who is totally committed to achieving their personal or professional goals."*[10]

Even though these definitions of servant leadership are different, they all have much to offer. However, they fall short of describing what a servant leader actually *does*.

This new style of leadership shifted management's thinking. Relationships are no longer limited to lines drawn on paper—they are forged in teams working together for a common purpose.[11]

As Micky thought about the type of organization he wanted, he realized he would need to think about the type of people he hired. After discussing this with colleagues and reviewing literature on the topic, Micky's realized there were many views of what makes a servant leader effective.

Larry Spears, who once served as president and CEO of the Robert K. Greenleaf Center for Servant Leadership, lists ten characteristics of effective, caring leaders.[12] Ken Jennings and John Stahl-Wert proposed "five powerful actions that will transform your team, your business, and your community."[13] Dirk van Dierendonck, a European professor, uses six criteria to describe servant leader attributes.[14]

Micky did not think a particular number was important, so he did his own analysis. He went through the literature and created a list that resonated with his experience.[15] In Micky's opinion, servant leaders should:

- **Have a desire to lead but serve others first.**
- **Have a clear sense of purpose and a compelling business vision.**
- **Build a culture that cares for people and encourages innovation.**

> **Reality Check**
>
> *Before we get too excited about Lockheed's progress with Servant Leadership on the F-22, it is important to remember exactly how the program began.*
>
> - *When the F-22 started, the management model was developed on the fly.*
> - *They would probably have continued to muddle on through until the USAF made concurrent engineering mandatory.*
> - *This required Lockheed to totally review how they were going to manage the program.*
> - *Servant Leadership came in because I felt it was the right thing to do. Its implementation was not deduced in a rational sense.*
>
> *Micky Blackwell*

- **Be responsible stewards who know how to manage budgets and other resources.**
- **Use ethics to guide their choices, and core values to determine what is right.**
- **Empower subordinates and encourage them to empower others but hold them accountable.**
- **Be authentic, humble, and inspire workers to do their best.**
- **Be transparent when necessary and vulnerable when appropriate.**
- **Ask questions and listen carefully.**
- **Be situationally aware and discerning.**
- **Be positive and enthusiastic because a leader's mindset can be contagious.**[16]

Ultimately, the goal of an organization is to increase shareholder wealth, but in a servant- led firm, it is *how* it is done that makes a difference. Making good products in an enjoyable environment is a good start, but servant leadership goes far beyond that. It is a practical and effective model for all organizations and for all people.[17]

Servant Leaders Create a Culture for Being a Good Leader

Servant leaders possess the right skills to care for people. Some people might call it a cultural dimension. Others might call it a Christian dimension. Regardless of what it is called, servant leadership has a spiritual aspect to it. This dimension is captured on the following pages.

Fraker tells us that the first thing the CEO must do when building his or her organization is to internalize the belief that "people are first."[18] Tom Peters said the same thing in the 1980s when he told us that successful companies have a "bone deep belief" in the dignity and potential of everyone in the company.[19]

Servant leaders have a clear sense of purpose and a compelling business vision. They also have a need to recognize others.[20] They need to empower subordinates and encourage them to empower others. People like to be recognized and know that someone cares. Employees respond in kind when they know they are being treated fairly. Empathy, listening, awareness and community building are all part of the contagion servant leaders bring to the table. Their primary need, however, is to serve people first.[21] Christian servant leaders create a culture that motivates those working with them to work hard to achieve a common goal. Perhaps Ed Stetzer says it best in his book about Christian leadership:

Christian leadership is a process of influencing a community to use their God-given gifts toward a goal and purpose as led by the Holy Spirit.[22]

Servant Leaders Have the Authority to Develop Their People

Servant leaders focus on the growth and well-being of employees. They seek to help the people they serve by providing them with the tools and ideas they need to be successful. By exposing employees to new roles and situations, you help them grow and develop as a person. In essence, "the servant leader engages in respectful conversation which demonstrates trust in the employee to make the needed adjustments."[23]

Let's take two examples. First, consider the employee that has a new idea. In your opinion, you are not sure it is quite right. Instead of criticizing what you don't like, you focus on what you do like. Instead of criticizing the person with mean-spirited comments, you develop the person by telling them what you like about their idea. The second example relates to Jesus and his followers. The story is about preparing the disciples to achieve their full potential. Jesus was not just focused on commanding the disciples to get ready when he sent them out into the towns and villages. He was concerned about equipping them to be effective servant leaders.

However, we should remember that constructive criticism only comes when someone wants to become wise. A fool thinks he doesn't look smart when you correct him. A wise person thinks you are right and will become a little bit wiser because of it.[24]

Servant Leaders Know How to Use Teams to Solve Problems

One of the signs of someone who is wise is that they leverage everyone else's skills. When it comes to solving problems, good servant leaders know how to use teams to solve problems. To solve big problems, servant leaders empower teams to learn, grow, and innovate.[25]

Over the years, servant leadership has been used more frequently to solve problems. Solving problems is not a one-size-fits-all approach. It requires emotional intelligence, and the flexibility to know when to use it. It also requires situational awareness and the ability to adapt quickly.[26]

To apply servant leadership to teams, Dr. Justin Irving and Dr. Gail Longbotham "found that if leaders who followed the servant leadership methodology applied these themes to their workgroup, there was a significant increase in overall effectiveness." The six themes are as follows:[27]

- **Provide accountability.**
- **Support and resource.**
- **Engage in honest self-evaluation.**
- **Foster collaboration.**
- **Communicate with clarity.**
- **Value and appreciate.**

These six themes can be used to measure the effectiveness of teams in problem solving and the performance of teams in general.

Servant Leaders Are Responsible Stewards

Servant leaders know how to be responsible stewards. Merriam-Webster defines stewardship as, "The careful and responsible management of something entrusted to one's care." One organization uses the following guidelines to help their people deal with the issue of stewardship:[28]

- Take responsibility for your leadership.
- Take responsibility for your constituents.
- Take responsibility for your organization and its actions.
- Hold yourself and others accountable.

Most realize that they also need to learn more about budgets and how value is created. Once they understand that, a big part of their job is to communicate how they meet customer expectations. On the F-22 program, for example, the team knew they would have to please their primary customer, the United States Air Force, while, at the same time, be responsible stewards to Lockheed Martin and other stakeholders. We need to be good stewards in the Biblical sense:

> *Moreover, it is required in stewards, that a man be found faithful.*
> *1 Corinthians 4:2 (NKJV)*

The Relationship Between Servant Leadership and Organizational Performance

For years, scholars have suspected that servant leadership and organizational performance are correlated. Recent research suggests that it may indeed be true. Several studies have shown that there is a positive relationship between servant leadership, creativity, and innovation in organizations.[29] Another study found that "project managers who embrace servant leaders' behaviors are more likely to contribute towards successful project outcomes."[30] One 2013 study focused specifically on the aerospace industry. It explored the relationship between servant leadership and project success. The analysis revealed a positive correlation between project success and eight servant leader factors. The eight factors include empowerment, authenticity, humility, accountability, forgiveness, courage, standing back, and stewardship. Further analysis indicated that empowerment and authenticity were significant predictors of project success."[31]

The Five Levels of Servant Leadership

What started as a simple concept turned into a powerful management model—a model that was based on deep respect and love for people. There are five levels of servant leadership that determine the appropriate business impact and the resources needed (*See* Figure 12).

Level I: Lead by Example

As mentioned previously, this is the way servant leadership is introduced to many organizations. This is what Micky did and it worked well for him. Although he had no" formal" training on servant leadership, he did his best to set a good example. Bethel notes that many leaders do this naturally, because they are already out in front. Everything they do sends a message to their followers. This means that actions are as important as words, and values direct their actions.[32]

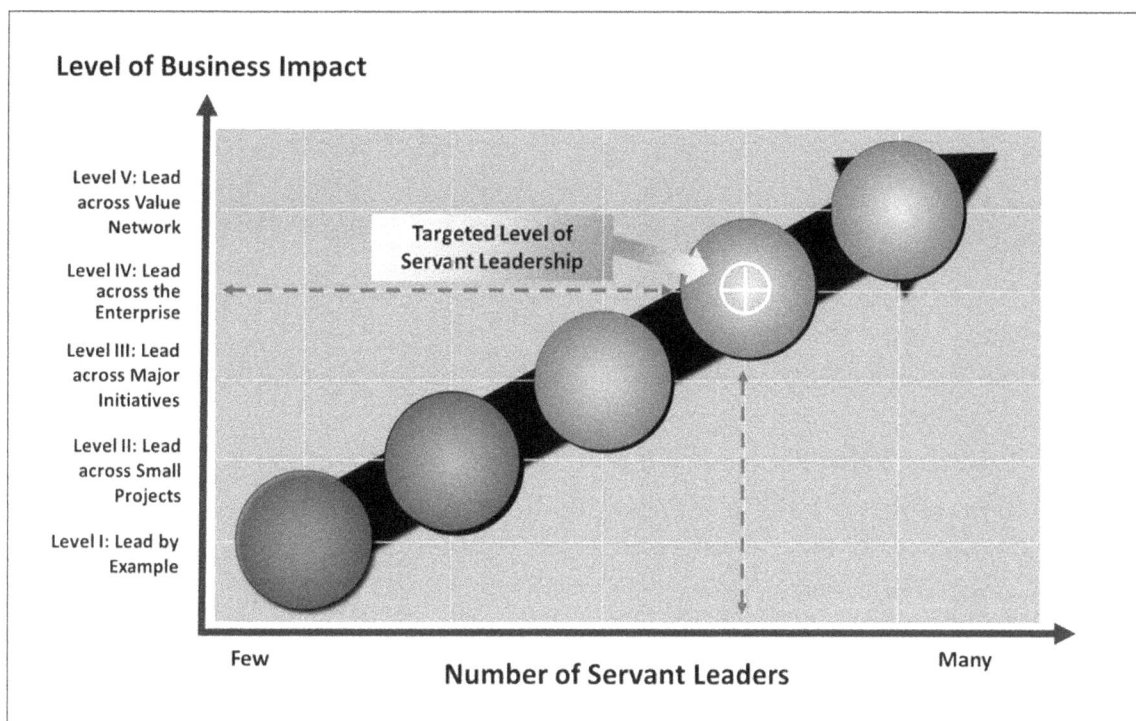

Figure 12. The Five Levels of Servant Leadership.

Level II: Lead Across Small Projects

This step involves applying servant leadership to one or more small projects. A single leader can often manage a small number of projects, but depending on the time and resources required, the leader may want to train or hire someone to assist him or her.

Some projects can be independent, while others may be linked to multiple activities. While each project has its own purpose and objectives, as the number of projects grows and more servant leaders are involved, a common set of guidelines may provide some level of standardization and quality (*See* Servant Leader Guidelines, Chapter 6).

Level III: Lead Across Major Initiatives

Major initiatives are larger and more complex projects. They often involve more business functions and require more attention than Level II projects. Even though they require more time and resources than Level II projects, servant leaders are usually worth the effort because they tend to create more value.

Level IV: Lead Across the Enterprise

Applying servant leadership throughout the enterprise requires significant planning and coordination across activities. That is why I call Level IV servant leaders "**Enterprise Servant Leaders.**" The distinguishing feature of this level of servant leadership is that numerous business function IPTs throughout the enterprise are needed to create value in a unique or distinctive manner.

Even though using servant leaders across the enterprise requires planning and coordination, it also creates a broader view of the full spectrum of opportunities. Part of what is required is asking the right questions. As senior leaders bring new people in, the people being hired must have the right traits and qualifications.

Level V: Lead Across the Value Network

This refers to using servant leaders to influence one or more organizations to join the firm's "value network"—a business network that creates value like what Porter calls the "value system." Such relationships cannot be forced, but they can be influenced—which is one of the key roles of a good servant leader.

This form of servant leadership is based on what many successful firms are already doing. They have transformed themselves and their supply chain partners into value networks so that they can proactively deliver parts when and where needed or Just in Time (JIT). In supply chain management, this is called Collaborative Planning, Forecasting, and Replenishment (CPFR).

Research suggests that differences between how two or more partners perform can influence the effectiveness of the entire value generation network. In other words, the low performance of one partner can negatively impact the performance of the other. At the same time, improvements in the performance of one partner can foster improvements across that entire network. To enjoy these benefits, it is important that partners collaborate in their continuous improvement efforts. It also means that each partner's practices must be of the highest caliber. Thus, it is not enough for all parties in the Servant-led Business Model (*see* Chapter 9) to become High Performing Organizations (HPOs); the links between the partners need to support High Performing Partnerships (HPPs). HPPs require every partner in the network to do their part.[33]

When Micky was promoted to president and COO of the Aeronautics Sector, he encouraged other programs to move in this direction. Before leaving this topic, however, it is important to remember that there are really no bounds that limit the use of servant leaders. Servant leadership can be applied enterprise wide across a "network of networks," just like what was done on the development of the F-22 Raptor.

Business Impact

Money only measures one element of value—profit. Some say the real measure should be long-term satisfaction over immediate gratification.[34] Other metrics can be used for other measures such as market share, on-time deliveries, defect rates, employee attitudes, and so on. Thus, to consider the full spectrum of enterprise servant leadership, we should be looking at a broader set of values named "business impact."[35] The values assigned to meet the needs of this metric can be adjusted, as necessary, to address what is required.

In Figure 12, there is an item called "Targeted Level of Servant Leadership." It refers to one of the decisions a Program Manager must make. In this case, it is aligned with Level IV Lead Across the Enterprise. This means that servant leadership must be implemented across all IPTs in the Enterprise.

For a large program, this can mean a significant commitment of time and other resources. It also means that the business impact should be relatively high.

Alternatively, one can start by specifying the desired level of business impact and work backwards through the model to determine the level of servant leaders required.

Robert Vanourck states that, "there is no doubt in my mind that this value system is enormously helpful in guiding people in their daily decisions. And the guiding principles are based on creating value for people…"[36]

ESL models are based on a relationship where people grow "by becoming healthier, wiser, freer, more autonomous, and more likely to become servant leaders themselves."[37] The journey may not be easy, or the path smooth, but ESL provides a foundation for managing programs that is balanced and true.[38]

Vanourck continues by stating, "The more I learn, the more I realize that serving is the highest form of leadership and achievement."[39] The bottom line is "…if people are working effectively with an attitude of serving," that is their reward, and we are not going to change it.[40]

Lessons Learned and Important Points

Enterprise Servant Leadership is highlighted in this chapter. Lessons learned and important points include:

- **Traditional functional management can be transformed into Enterprise Servant Leadership management.**
- **A servant leader serves first. He influences others and puts others before self.**
- **A servant leader provides employees with development opportunities.**
- **Servant leadership is a philosophy that enriches the lives of people.**
- **Blanchard and Hodges created a method for classifying people: those who desire to serve others, and those who desire to be served.**
- **The goal of an organization is to increase shareholder wealth; but in a servant-led firm, it is how it is done that makes a difference.**
- **A servant-led culture leads to more revenue and greater profits.**
- **Servant leaders have the authority for developing their people.**
- **Servant leaders create a culture for being a good leader.**
- **Servant leaders are responsible stewards.**
- **Servant leaders use teams to solve problems.**
- **Scholars have suspected that servant leadership and organizational performance are correlated. Research supports this.**
- **Value can be created by servant leaders at various levels of implementation ranging from "Leading by Example" to "Leading Across the Value Network."**
- **When servant leaders lead across an enterprise or value network, I refer to them as "Enterprise Servant Leaders."**

- Servant-led collaboration can leverage the value created. The performance of one partner can foster improvements across the entire network.
- Money only measures one element of value—profit. Some say the real measure should be long-term satisfaction over immediate gratification.

Chapter Notes

1 "Theory X and Theory Y." n.d. *MSG Management Study Guide.* Accessed April 12, 2021. https://www. managementstudyguide.com/theory-x-y-motivation.htm

2 "Six Indicators of Inefficient Work Management." n.d. *Workfront.* Accessed May 7, 2018. https://www. workfront.com/blog/six-indicators-of-inefficient-work- management#:~:text=Six%20Indicators%20 of%20Inefficient%20Work%20Management.%201%20Continually,6%20Burnt%20out%2C%20 frustrated%2C%20and%20disengaged%20employees.%20

3 According to Greenleaf, the concept of servant-leadership was inspired by Hermann Hesse in his popular novel, Journey to the East. See Robert K. Greenleaf in "The Servant as Leader," Robert K. Greenleaf Essays. 2002. *Servant Leadership: A Journey into the Nature of Legitimate Power and Greatness 25th Anniversary Edition.* Edited by Larry C. Spears. New York/Mahwah, New Jersey: Paulist Press, p. 21.

4 See the website for the Robert K. Greenleaf Center for Servant Leadership where it poses the question: What is Servant-Leadership? Accessed March 20, 2019. https://www.greenleaf.org/what-is-servant-leadership/

5 Robert K. Greenleaf. "The Servant as Leader," p. 21.

6 Ken Blanchard and Phil Hodges. 2003. *The Servant Leader.* Nashville, TN: Thomas Nelson, Inc., pp. 17-18.

7 This definition is a slightly modified version of a definition attributed to Kent Keith, president of Pacific Rim Christian University and past CEO of the Robert K. Greenleaf Center for Servant Leadership. The Center's website can be accessed by clicking on https://www.greenleaf.org/

8 Robert S. Dennis, and Mihai Bocarnea. 2005. "Development of the servant leadership assessment instrument." *Leadership & Organization Development Journal,* 26 (8), p. 601.

9 "Servant Leadership." n.d. *Wikipedia.* Accessed September 18, 2021. https://en.wikipedia.org/wiki/ Servant_leadership

10 James "Micky" Blackwell. 2014. "Learning to lead like Jesus: Part I," p. 5.

11 Jennings and Hyde capture the spirit of this in their book, *The Greater Goal.* See Kenneth R. Jennings and Heather Hyde. 2012. *The Greater Goal: Connecting Purpose and Performance.* Oakland, CA: Berrett-Koehler.

12 Larry C. Spears. 2010. "Character and Servant Leadership: Ten Characteristics of Effective, Caring Leaders." *The Journal of Virtues & Leadership,* 1 (1), pp. 25-30.

13 Kenneth R. Jennings and John Stahl-Wert. 2004. *The Serving Leader: Five Powerful Actions That Will Transform Your Team, Your Business, and Your Community.* Oakland, CA: Berrett-Koehler.

14 Dirk Van Dierendonck. 2011. 6 Key Servant Leadership Attributes." *IEDP Developing Leaders.* September 26. Accessed February 1, 2018. https://www.iedp.com/articles/six-key- servant-leadership-attributes/

15 Subsequent studies have used scientific tools, such as regression analysis and factor analysis, to uncover relationships between large numbers of servant leadership variables. See, for example, Robert S. Dennis and Mihai Bocarnea. 2005. "Development of the servant leadership assessment instrument." *Leadership & Organization Development,* Journal 26 (8), pp. 600-615.

16 Micky borrowed this thought from the U.S. Air Force. For more on this topic see John Schaeufele. 2004. *Enthusiasm: definitely a force multiplier.* October 5. Accessed March 26, 2019. https://www. af.mil/News/Commentaries/Display/Article/142275/enthusiasm- definitely-a-force-multiplier/.

17 Ken Blanchard and Phil Hodges. 2005. *Lead Like Jesus.* Nashville, TN: Thomas Nelson, Inc., p. XIII.

18 Larry C. Spears, ed. 1995. *Reflections on Leadership: How Robert K. Greenleaf's Theory of Servant Leadership Influenced Today's Top Management Thinkers.* New York: John Wiley & Sons, p. 46.

19 Ibid, p. 81.

20 Robert A. Vanourck. 1995. "Servant Leadership and the Future" in Larry C. Spears, ed. 1995. *Reflections on Leadership: How Robert K. Greenleaf's Theory of Servant Leadership Influenced Today's Top Management Thinkers.* New York: John Wiley & Sons, pp. 301- 302.

21 Ibid.

22 Ed Stetzer. 2019. "Defining Leadership: What Is It and Why Does It Matter in Church?" *Christianity Today.* https://www.christianitytoday.com/edstetzer/2019/september/defining-leadership-christian-serving-god-empower-people.html

23 Mark Tarallo. May 17, 2018. "The Art of Servant Leadership." *SHRM.* Accessed August 20, 2021. https://www.shrm.org/ResourcesAndTools/hr-topics/organizational-and- employee-development/Pages/The-Art-of-Servant-Leadership.aspx

24 Derek Hill. n.d. *What Does the Bible Say About Criticism? A Christian Study. What Christians Want to Know.* Accessed February 21, 2021. https://www.whatchristianswanttoknow.com/what-does-the-bible-say-about-criticism- a-christian-study/

25 Renita Kalhorn. September 2, 2020. "The Hidden Pitfalls of Servant Leadership." *Forbes.* Accessed September 1, 2021. https://www.forbes.com/sites/renitakalhorn/2020/09/02/the-hidden-pitfalls-of-servant-leadership/

26 Ibid.

27 Jason Weber. n.d. "Improving Team Effectiveness through Servant Leadership." *Leadership: Training Industry.* Accessed September 2, 2021. https://trainingindustry.com/magazine/mar-apr-2018/improving-team-effectiveness- through-servant-leadership/

28 "4 Ways to Build Stewardship as a Servant Leader." n.d. *Career Cert.* Accessed September 1, 2021. https://www.careercert.com/blog/ems/4-ways-to-build-stewardship-as-a- servant-leader/

29 There have been several studies that have explored the relationship between Servant Leadership and organizational performance. Examples include: Jin Yang, Hefu Liu, and Jibao Gu. 2017. "A multi-level study of servant leadership on creativity: The roles of self- efficacy and power distance." *Leadership & Organization Development Journal*, 38 (5): pp. 610-629; and Mustafa Kemal Topcu; Ali Gursoy; and Poyraz Gurson. 2015. "The Role of the Servant Leadership on the Relation between Ethical Climate Perception and Innovative Work." *European Research Studies*; Anixis 18 (1), pp. 67-79.

30 Kenneth N. Thompson. 2010. *Servant Leadership: An Effective Model for Project Management.* Doctoral Dissertation, Capella University, p. 97.

31 Michael T. Dominik. 2013. *Servant leadership behaviors of aerospace and defense project managers and their relation to project success.* Doctoral Dissertation, Philadelphia, PA: Eastern University.

32 Sheila Murray Bethel. 1995. "Servant-Leadership and Corporate Risk Taking: When Risk Taking Makes a Difference," p. 140.

33 André de Waal, Ruben Orij and Simon van der Veer. May 2010. "The High-Performance Partnership Framework as Value Chain Enhancer." *The HPO Center*, The Netherlands.

34 Michael Kelley. 1995. "The New Leadership," in Larry C. Spears, ed. 1995. *Reflections on Leadership: How Robert K. Greenleaf's Theory of Servant Leadership Influenced Today's Top Management Thinkers.* New York: John Wiley & Sons, p. 194.

35 Business impact includes whatever needs to be there. Market share, on-time deliveries, defect rates, employee attitudes, attrition, are just some of the multiple metrics that can be defined by the term.

36 Robert A. Vanourck. 1995. "Servant Leadership and the Future," p. 305.

37 Tina Rasmussen. 1995. "Creating a Culture of Servant Leadership: a Real Life Story," p. 287.

38 James B. Tatum. 1995. "Meditations on Servant Leadership" in Larry C. Spears, ed. 1995. *Reflections on Leadership: How Robert K. Greenleaf's Theory of Servant Leadership Influenced Today's Top Management Thinkers*. New York: John Wiley & Sons, p. 309.

39 Robert A. Vanourck. 1995. "Servant Leadership and the Future," p. 307.

40 Don M. Frick. 1995. "Pyramids, Circles, and Gardens: Stories of Implementing Servant Leadership," in Larry C. Spears, ed. 1995. *Reflections on Leadership: How Robert K. Greenleaf's Theory of Servant Leadership Influenced Today's Top Management Thinkers*. New York: John Wiley & Sons, p. 269.

Chapter 6

Guidelines for Helping Enterprise Servant Leaders

How the leader leads makes a difference in the organization's destiny.

Micky Blackwell
President and COO Aeronautics Sector (Retired)
Lockheed Martin Corporation

This chapter presents guidelines for helping Enterprise Servant Leaders. Since Micky was one of the first to put servant leadership into practice, he did not have the benefit of all the guidance and advice that exists today. Some of the guidelines he used are original and evolved through trial and error. Others are not original and are cited where appropriate.

Reflecting on his life and work experiences allowed Micky to correct some ideas that didn't work and adjust others that worked better than expected. Over time, these concepts provided the foundation for the ideas presented here. Collectively, they advance our thinking of how to practice enterprise servant leadership.

Leadership can be both simple and complex. In its simplest form, it is about the ability to influence people. At the other extreme, it has the power to transform businesses, nations, and ideas. After considerable reflection about what he had learned, Micky turned his experience into guidelines with plenty of examples. Specifically, guidelines to make servant leaders, integrated product teams, and communication throughout the enterprise more effective are included.

Guidelines for Servant Leaders

This section includes "Enterprise Servant Leader guidelines" and examples of their use derived primarily from Micky's leadership of the F-22 program. Some of these ideas were known, articulated, and practiced on the program. Others were applied in principle, but not always well documented.

A few guidelines are based on Micky's leadership roles after he was promoted into positions of larger leadership that will be discussed in later chapters. Some guidelines are general in nature based on Micky's life and work experience. Collectively, the servant leader guidelines represent a comprehensive set of suggestions that Micky thought might be useful for others with similar mindsets.[1]

Except for the first guideline, the order in which they are listed is incidental. The first guideline is vital and should probably remain first; however, all other guidelines should be treated with equal importance.

GUIDELINE 1:	**Remember your Creator; there is a reason you are the leader. Pray for the wisdom to make wise decisions; you were chosen for a purpose.**

When you think about what this guideline says, you may need to stop what you are doing and thank God for His provision. Blanchard and Hodges remind us that, "staying the course means frequently checking where you are and where you are headed and making necessary course corrections."[2] In their book, they provide tools to help leaders deal with fear, temptation, pride, values, and repentance; plus, they provide a checklist to ensure that their heart, head, hands, and habits are pointing in the right direction.[3]

> *Leadership is a gift from a higher authority. It should be exercised with much care and with a noble purpose.*
> — *Bernard J. Brown, Jr., CEO (Retired), WellStar Health System*

Checking his direction and making continuous corrections became part of Micky's routine that continues to this day. Micky knew the importance of prayer in making wise decisions, but when he ran the F-22 program and later, as president of Lockheed Aeronautical Systems Company, it seemed like the need for humility and reflection grew along with increased responsibility. It reached a peak when he became head of the Aeronautics Sector at Lockheed Martin. At that point, he was fully aware that there was a reason he was the leader, and how important it was to stay in contact with the Creator.

GUIDELINE 2:	**Commit to the vision and build strategies to support it.**

The importance of vision cannot be overemphasized. Scripture makes it clear when it says, "Where there is no vision, the people perish…"[4]

The need for vision is true for individuals, and it is true for nations. It is also true for the people who design and build advanced aircraft. Once you have a vision for what you need to do, commit to it with all your heart and mind.

The ATF was developed to deliver a first look, first shoot, and first kill capability, where the goal was to "achieve and maintain air superiority well into the next century."[5] As simple as it sounds, it took a decade for Air Force leadership to agree on that statement. Once the decision was made, the vision set the boundaries for the size, weight, and functionality of the aircraft. It had to be large enough to carry a pilot, along with the weapons, fuel, and sensors to have the first look, first shot, first kill capabilities.

It also had to be reliable and supportable in the field to make sure it was available when and where it was needed.[6] The initial vision for the F-22 has since been expanded. At the time the F-22 vision was written, however, it perfectly described the planned future for the Raptor.

The vision statement for this aircraft was something the Lockheed team could commit to achieving with all their heart and mind. It was bold, brief, and captured the reason for building the Raptor. It also guided the values of the people who manufactured and assembled it.[7]

From Micky's point of view, his job was to inspire others to achieve the vision for the F-22 and build strategies to make it happen. Developing strategies around changing budgets was a little more challenging.

GUIDELINE 3:   **Know the business of the business and think survival.**

Two examples illustrate the value of this guideline.

The first example involves the Skunk Works in Palmdale, California. The Skunk Works has a reputation for producing remarkable state-of-the-art aircraft. Jay Miller, author of *Lockheed's Skunk Works: The First Fifty Years*, states the Skunk Works represents an "extraordinary body of work" based on a "high level of business acumen and technology" that created the standard by which similar companies are judged.[8]

What makes the story interesting is that each major aircraft developed and produced by the Skunk Works was substantially different. They used different approaches and materials to accomplish different missions, but there is one thing they had in common. They followed the principles developed by Clarence "Kelly" Johnson.

Today, they are a good example of what can happen when an organization builds on what it does best.[9] Kelly Johnson's 14 Rules (see Appendix B) were developed to protect his teams from too much red tape, redundancy, and bureaucracy. They improved communications, and what we now call "process management." By demanding that managers be given virtually complete control of their programs and requiring strong, small, secure project offices manned by the military and industry people working in collaboration, Johnson set the standard for developing modern military aircraft.

Today, the success of the Skunk Works speaks for itself (see Figure 13). The organization has demonstrated that it knows the "business of the business." Current and future programs are still influenced by these standards. Micky did his best to comply with Johnson's 14 Rules. Delays occurred when the principles were violated.

The second example comes from when the F-22 team started implementing Lean (see Chapter 8). The team knew the first thing they had to do was get control over all its cradle-to-grave business processes. This meant that they had to radically reevaluate how each new technology and process could improve business performance. In the process of changing their thinking, they found that comparing

Figure 13. The SR-71 is an example of what the Skunk Works does best. Unofficially known as the "Blackbird," it was a long-range, advanced, strategic reconnaissance aircraft, now retired.
(US Air Force photo by Tech. Sgt. Michael Haggerty)

themselves to others was not really working. It was called "benchmarking." While benchmarking might make you better, it will not make you the best. You get better by competing with yourself, not others. Changing key processes and leveraging them with new technologies, made the processes more efficient and confirmed that they did know the "business of the business." Following this guideline led to a leaner organization and more efficient processes. Keeping the teams continually thinking "lean" led to a survival state of mind.[10]

| GUIDELINE 4: | **Lead by example.**
This will help others to see how to lead and serve better. |

Some people are natural leaders. They just know how to lead people. Others must learn how to lead by watching other leaders. Servant leaders must be prepared to teach others how to lead through their example. Leading by example is the most common way to implement servant leadership. One's influence may be limited, but even a single leader can influence many people.

Micky served as a good model for developing servant leaders. Micky had prepared himself for servant leadership since he was a junior in high school. When he worked at NASA Langley, and later at Lockheed, Micky observed that "real power" involved the ability to inspire and influence others.[11]

He tried to set a good example in everything he did. When Micky held a meeting, he was always on time. He expected the same from those who worked for him, and few were ever late. He also had rules that are now relatively common, such as always coming prepared to a meeting and never interrupting others who were speaking. His writing was superb. Among all his gifts, however, one really stood out. Micky loved his people. Of that, there was no doubt.

In most firms, senior managers set the tone for the culture of the organization.[12] Unfortunately, several managers on the ATF program tended to curse and shout at those who were under-performing. That kind of behavior did not encourage people. In fact, it usually discouraged them (see insert on "The Spirit of a Commander"). Micky knew they could do better, but he would have to set the example.

The Spirit of a Commander

On August 11, 1879, one hundred years before The Right Stuff *was published, Maj. Gen. John Schofield, the superintendent at West Point, addressed the cadets on an important topic. With the eloquence one would expect from the Superintendent and future Chief of Staff of the US Army, Schofield stated,*

> *The discipline which makes the soldiers of a free country reliable in battle, is not to be gained by harsh or tyrannical treatment. On the contrary, such treatment is far more likely to destroy than to make an army. It is possible to impart instructions and to give commands in such a manner and such a tone of voice as to inspire in the soldier no feeling but an intense desire to obey, while the opposite manner and tone of voice, cannot fail to excite strong resentment and a desire to disobey. The one mode or other of dealing with subordinates, springs from a corresponding spirit in the breast of the commander. He who feels the respect which is due others cannot fail to inspire in them respect for himself . . .*

Schofield's words are as valid today as they were in 1879. Gen. MacArthur's comments about "duty, honor, and country" will always be important, but it is "the spirit in the breast of the commander" that binds followers to their leaders.

Source: The Air Force Cadet Wing. Contrails: The Air Force Cadet Handbook, *Volume II, 1965-66. United States Air Force Academy, Colorado, 26-27.*

GUIDELINE 5:	**Hold true to your core values.** **They will help guide your actions and keep you out of trouble.**

To understand this guideline, consider what Micky had to deal with when Lockheed Aeronautical Systems Company (LASC) was charged with unethical behavior.

The unethical behavior involved the sale of C-130H transports to Egypt using an Egyptian consultant who unknown to Lockheed management had become a government employee (a member of the Egyptian Parliament). Micky had been promoted to president of LASC in April 1993, and even though the event occurred several years before he became president, Micky had to properly respond or risk losing the ability to sell aircraft to the US government.

It was a serious situation. Recently, changes had been made in US law regarding how foreign consultants could be used in response to a series of scandals. The Foreign Corrupt Practices Act (FCPA) of 1977 made it illegal for Americans to bribe foreign government officials.[13]

In response to charges that Lockheed was paying a government employee, Micky and his staff, along with corporate lawyers, developed a multi-year program that required everyone's participation. As part of the process, Micky and his ethics team developed a set of "core values." Patrick Lencioni defines core values as "the deeply ingrained principles that guide all of a company's actions; they serve as its cultural cornerstones."[14]

Micky often said: "Core values should drive behavior. They are what the firm stands for." The core values used by Micky included items such as:

- Spiritual Beliefs.
- Ethical Conduct.
- Honesty and Integrity.
- Courage.

- Loyalty.
- Trustworthiness.
- Accessibility.

These core values came into play not too long after the ethics training was complete. An international country indicated it was interested in buying the Lockheed C-130H Hercules. However, they hinted at wanting a kickback. Lockheed decided not to do business in this country. After a number of years, Lockheed eventually did business with the country but on ethical terms.

Good leaders honor their core values, but they are flexible in how they execute them. As a leader, you may have to decide between two almost identical choices. If you know who you are and have a strong sense of core values, you will know what to do when the time comes to make a decision.

> **Core Values**
> *Core values should drive behavior.*
> *They are what the firm stands for.*
>
> *–Micky Blackwell*

GUIDELINE 6:	**Be strong in your convictions.** **Raising the bar is necessary. *Failing* to raise it can be deadly.**

As the ATF team was developing their prototype, they knew they had a good plan, but also knew they did not have all the answers. As one team member put it, "if they were going to win the contract, they were going to need several miracles."

For the YF-22 aircraft prototype to perform as needed, several breakthroughs would be required—which is another way of saying the bar would have to be raised. Some of the needed breakthroughs were:

- **The composite wing was pushing the boundaries, and some questioned whether it could handle the heat and stress.**
- **The scanning array radar planned for the production aircraft was a wonder, but some wondered if it was reliable.**
- **The low RCS shape seemed promising, but it had yet to be fully tested.**
- **Supercruise claims were appealing, but there were questions about extended use.**
- **The aircraft was designed to have a low lifecycle cost. Only time would tell if it would be as reliable and supportable as expected.**
- **The Common Integrated Processor (CIP) was impressive. It managed power for the aircraft's systems. Nevertheless, there were still questions about how it would perform under combat conditions.**

As Micky and his team will tell you, miracles did happen. The YF-22 aircraft met all the requirements and Lockheed won the contract. But most importantly, the performance bar was indeed raised. As stated on the Air Force website "The F-22 cannot be matched by any known or projected fighter aircraft." Twenty years later, no enemy fighter has been able to match the Raptor.[15]

GUIDELINE 7:	**Ensure your processes are world-class and you are achieving the right outcomes.**

When Micky became the president and COO of the Lockheed Martin Aeronautics Sector (Chapter 12), he knew their engineering, financial, and manufacturing systems needed to be modernized and integrated to effectively manage the then-coming Joint Strike Fighter (JSF) program.

With competition for the JSF fully underway, the Lockheed Martin Aeronautics Sector needed a complete Enterprise Resource Plan (ERP) to produce the lowest cost and highest performing aircraft. Each individual system module used to design, manufacture, and support the JSF needed to be best-in-class, plus all the enterprise systems had to be integrated to share information efficiently. In addition, the new solution had to support the best Lean practices. After an exhaustive review, the Lockheed Martin Aeronautics Sector contracted with the SAP Corporation to install a new ERP system sector wide.

A major requirement was that SAP continuously update and maintain the Lockheed Martin ERP without LM having to develop system interfaces. To ensure they got what they wanted, LM laid out what they had to have, and worked with SAP to ensure they met Lockheed Martin's desired outcomes.[16] Since SAP's R/3 ERP system supported Lean, Micky's goal was to ensure they had a world-class integrated system substantially online by the time they won the JSF program.

GUIDELINE 8:	**Embrace risk and encourage innovation.**

When asked about his role in encouraging innovation, Micky described himself as a benevolent dictator who wanted to empower innovative people.[17] He was a leader in the sense he encouraged people to entertain risk. He was a servant when he offered them resources on how to resolve differences. If their differences could not be resolved, Micky would decide for them.

For America to maintain its lead in aerospace, Micky knew that they would have to take risks. Sherm Mullin, Micky's predecessor on the F-22, put it this way, "There is no such thing as a low-risk future program in advanced aeronautics."[18] Micky shared the same view.

As mentioned previously, in the case of the F-22, there were at least six major challenges to overcome before the program could be declared successful. Each of these challenges involved different levels of risk and risk mitigation.

Micky's view is that people are more willing to take risks when they have access to the facts. That willingness to take risks grows when they have ownership in the outcome.

Research shows that there are a range of reasons people resist risk. At one end of the spectrum, people fear failure because of criticism, loss of esteem, or termination by their boss. At the other end, some are afraid that if they do get it right, false expectations will be created that will be difficult to live up to.

Micky drew on his experience to come up with several suggestions that may help otherwise brilliant leaders overcome their aversion to risk. To encourage taking risks and to stimulate innovation, Micky knew he had to come up with an environment that accepted failure and was not a reason for termination. Some ideas were as follows.

- When screening new people, certain candidates seem predisposed to risk. "For example, some integrity tests ask candidates to state whether they like taking risks. The logic behind this is people who like risks are more likely to deviate from acceptable behavior. Yet in many instances, risk takers can be positive for organizations."[19] Integrity testing can help leaders select the right people.

- The leader needs to inspire others to want to be part of a risk-taking program. For some, this may mean a complete reversal of attitude—from wanting to avoid risk to wanting to embrace it. One of the best ways to embrace risk is to engage people in decision-making. Only then will they be responsible and accountable for the project's success.

- When testing new designs, there are times when we can learn a lot from observing how systems fail. That is why virtually everything on the F-22 was integrity tested. Some parts were tested thousands of times. Some tests were done in wind tunnels; some tests were conducted in controlled environments; and some were done in flight to ensure they could meet operational requirements. The radar underwent extraordinary testing, as did different cockpit displays, ejection seats, and other aspects involving human engineering. Radars and radomes were tested for low observability, and internal missiles were tested to determine the impact on aircraft performance and safety. Pratt & Whitney and Lockheed Martin worked together to test the F119 engine. All of these tests were necessary to define the aircraft's operational parameters. Once these parameters were established, more testing was done to continuously improve the product and manage any risk associated with the aircraft and its systems.

What is unique and transforming is how servant leaders can help managers think differently about risk. The spectrum is broad and runs from fear of failing to systemized learning where the lessons learned from failing are embedded in the process of learning. Failures can lead to new research, and new research can lead to new solutions. Thomas Edison once said, "our failures teach us that things cannot be done a certain way, but they also give us new ideas and more information."[20] Sheila Murray Bethel describes risk-taking as "building the skills for succeeding."[21]

Guidelines for Teams

In 1993, just after Micky started to implement teams on the Raptor, Katzenbach and Smith wrote a book called *The Wisdom of Teams: Creating the High-Performance Organization*.[22] (The latest edition of the book was published in 2015.) There is a reason this book was a national best seller—it stuck a nerve among senior managers who knew they needed help. One of many statements that got Micky's attention was, "Simply put, teams will be the primary building block of performance in the high-performance organization of the future."[23] Few realized at the time how important they would be.

In the early 1990s, Lockheed initiated the use of Integrated Product Teams (IPTs) on the F-22 (See Chapter 7) where IPTs resemble what are now called "high-performance teams." Not many realize it, but that marked the first time that such teams were used on a large scale outside of Lockheed's Skunk Works. Since then, they have been widely adopted as an industry best practice.

GUIDELINE 9:	Use Integrated Product Teams (IPTs) to do integrated work. There is a reason they are integrated. Let the teams do the work.

In general, teams are more effective at accomplishing tasks than individuals. Part of the reason is because teams tend to encourage more brainstorming and knowledge sharing. Teams with different skills and perspectives know how and when to leverage those differences to take advantage of their unique capabilities. This often results in more ideas and better solutions.

Following Kelly Johnson's 14 Rules, teams on the F-22 were kept small and focused. This is consistent with today's thinking, where a team is defined as "a small number of people with complementary skills who are committed to a common purpose, performance goals, and approach for which they are mutually accountable."[24] All program functions, including the customer, are represented on the IPTs. This meant that when a design was complete, it met all the needs of the customer.[25] For example, the Landing Gear IPT included the landing gear design engineers, systems engineers, supportability staff, manufacturing people, finance, materials, marketing team partners, and the Air Force customer. Each representative on the IPT had to meet their individual targets (e.g., cost and performance), but also had to approve the final design.

IPTs mirrored the government's Work Breakdown Structure (WBS) method. At each node in the WBS, the system requirements were allocated and monitored by system engineers. Each team had strong leaders and communication was superb. Teams looked out for each other, and no one cared about who got the credit. More information about the use of teams is included in the next chapter.

GUIDELINE 10:	**Select team members with care.** **Look at educational basics, track records, and experience.**

There needs to be a selection process for team members. Each candidate's position should be based on pre-defined criteria, but that is only the beginning of the final selection procedure. Criteria for selection may include the characteristics of servant leaders described earlier in the book, tailored as necessary for the program or function where they can add the most value.

Micky prefers it when the leaders participate in the hiring of those who will work for them. Always be on the lookout for exceptional talent and hire as many as you can.

A recent article in the *Wall Street Journal* reinforced the importance of selecting the right people. Based on input from 2,000,000 employees in 300,000 business units, collected over 80 years, the results of the analysis indicated that managers accounted for 70 percent of the variance in successful organizations. In other words, the data indicates that having a highly engaged and qualified manager has a huge impact on performance.[26] For Micky, the message was clear and reinforced his experience—if you want to be successful, hire the best people.

GUIDELINE 11:	**Encourage collaboration. Provide mentoring when necessary.**

Encouraging collaboration seems to be correlated with team effectiveness.[27] People like to be recognized for the good work they do, and that is particularly important when you are building a winning team. Research suggests that most bonding takes place during non-working hours, and time spent getting to know your teammates can pay dividends later. Knowing someone's strengths can improve communication. Communicating with them personally can lead to higher levels of performance. Knowing an employee's strengths can be helpful in a team environment, but when their strength is combined with others, it can boost performance even higher.[28]

The same thing can be said for mentoring employees. Blanchard and Hodges remind us that Jesus invested most of his time training and equipping the disciples. Servant leaders should also look beyond themselves to "prepare the next generation of leaders."[29]

Team members or team leaders may also need a mentor. In many cases they may not realize it or just don't know who to ask. In retrospect, Micky often reflects on how NASA's Dr. Richard Whitcomb took the time to teach him what he had learned when he was a young engineer. This was a great example for Micky on how important it is to invest in others. Today, some people refer to this as the practice of "paying it forward." This is another form of servant leadership, where the leader is doing something for one or more employees who will never be able to return the favor.

| GUIDELINE 12: | **Train your teams well.**
Excellent training can save you money. It can also boost morale. |

When Micky first started using servant leadership on the Raptor, there was little, if any, formal training available.

As discussed earlier, Micky soon realized he would have to lead by example. He also knew that a program as big and visible as the F-22 would require changes to Lockheed's command and control structure. "Viewing organizations in light of their culture is a welcome contrast to regarding them as machines designed to crank out deliverables through a process of planning and predicting, commanding and controlling."[30]

Micky relied on his direct reports to start modeling his behavior. Although it was not formal training, per se, it was enough to start changing employee behavior. Today, Micky would use highly qualified staff with plenty of materials to train people on servant leadership, but he did what he could with the resources he had at the time.

Implementing Lean was a different story altogether. The principles were well documented in a book called *Lean Thinking*.[31] Micky hired an expert in Lean, Mike Joyce, to assist with the training. It took several years to implement Lean across the entire Aeronautics Sector. It was Micky's goal to make Lockheed Martin the "best of the best" in aerospace. To be the best of the best meant satisfied customers. It also meant employees had an enjoyable place to work.

In terms of saving money, employees were looking for major improvements of 80 percent or more. In one example, the administrative processes were fragmented with too many handoffs. As a result, they formed a team to look at a common administration organization for the whole company. The objective of their training was to create seamless, robust, administrative processes to serve their programs, IPTs, functional organizations and general managers.

Another goal was to identify a single process owner. As a result, the task force was charged with identifying "as-is" and "to-be" states for all administrative processes. The benefits include more responsive support, less cost, fewer systems to administer, fewer hand-offs, and one owner who had visibility over the entire process. After all, if you own the process, you can smooth it or streamline it to get the quantum improvements you need.[32]

Even though Micky does not have a complete list of all the ways Lean training saved time and money, there is no doubt that training helped. It also boosted morale across the Aeronautics Sector.[33]

| GUIDELINE 13: | **Include your partners in your value networks to lower costs and create more value.** |

The following examples show how employees in different companies, with the support of senior management, can work together to create more value for each other and the overall project.

Since subcontractors supplied 60 percent of the value of the F-22, even small levels of collaboration with these providers had the potential to offer significant savings. The first example occurred when Lockheed, working with Pratt & Whitney, started holding annual supplier conferences. The purpose of the conferences was to focus on supply issues. At one conference, the theme was on Lean, and subcontractors who were not already practicing it were given training and encouragement to adopt it.[34] Some suppliers kept most of the savings. Others used their savings to bring down the costs billed to Lockheed.

The second example involved digitizing manufacturing practices.[35] When Dassault Systèmes shared what they had done on the CATIA (Computer-Aided Three-Dimensional Interactive Application) design tool with Lockheed Martin and its partners, it was clear they had created a powerful new capability. Workers could now create a three-dimensional animated image of the aircraft and the assembly process. This, in turn, allowed them to enlarge areas of interest to show where parts fit. This enabled engineers to see how changes to the original part(s), could or could not require changes to other elements of the system.[36] This had a significant impact on the digital mockups of the F-22's assembly and maintainability processes and helped reduce the life-cycle costs of the program.

The third example comes from the discipline of supply chain management. This required linking Pratt & Whitney and Lockheed Martin through their supply chains, to unlock even more value between the two partners. As mentioned previously, experts in supply chain management call it Collaborative Planning, Forecasting, and Replenishment (CPFR). CPFR is a set of business processes that requires partners in the supply chain to share information to plan and build forecasts that will benefit each other.[37] This means that processes must be coordinated to avoid disruptions, and common metrics must be used to measure performance. It also means that procedures must be developed to resolve exceptions.

CPFR is essential to implementing enterprise-wide servant leadership. Using it is necessary to build more accurate forecasts. More accurate forecasts result in better execution. Better execution leads to fewer stock-outs, less inventory, and lower transportation costs—in other words, higher margins for all those involved.

Guidelines for Communication

One precept of business management is that perception is reality and managing it is important. In Micky's opinion, Lockheed did an excellent job managing perceptions with the media. When Micky spoke to people outside the walls of Lockheed, he would never sit down without his vice president of communications. According to Micky, that simple step kept a good and well-meaning engineer out of a great deal of trouble. When Micky forgot this simple step, he got in trouble.[38]

| GUIDELINE 14: | Have a well-defined strategy for communicating important messages. Know all your options and when to use them. |

Having a communication strategy for the F-22 was important given the high-risk, high-reward nature of the program.

Communication plans were managed by three groups of people: the F-22 head; the F-22 director of Business Development (that is, Marketing); and the company communications lead. The person who was responsible for developing the Raptor's communication strategy during the ATF competition was Sherm Mullin, Micky's predecessor on the F-22 program. Sherm had a lot of experience with the press and was highly regarded by those who worked with him. The marketing lead put the communication materials together, and then obtained Sherm's approval.

The overall strategy was to build messages that supported the vision—to achieve and maintain air superiority well into the next century. The key was knowing what the Air Force really wanted and building those capabilities into the design of the aircraft. Even though Sherm and Micky made most of the routine decisions, everyone realized that Lockheed Company's president had final approval over all messages.

Criteria for the design of marketing messages were the same as those associated with aircraft selection. These included stealth, supercruise, integrated avionics, supportability, and agility. Marketing did an excellent job keeping the message in front of the public, with a focus on agility which they knew the pilots coveted. Communication plans for the Raptor were continuous and supported by marketing. Micky knew them so well he rarely needed to refer to them. Following the spirit of this guideline, he spent the last six months before the proposal was submitted delivering Friday afternoon briefings to keep the F-22 workers informed.

According to Micky, being a servant leader makes a difference in how you communicate with people. Depending where a person falls on the spectrum, it can influence the nature of the message you want to send. Having said that, Micky is quick to point out that one had to look beyond whether a person was a servant leader or a self-serving leader to really understand how they thought. Choosing between one mode or the other is usually not practical. Most people fall within the two extremes defined by Blanchard and Hodges.

Toward the end of the Dem/Val phase of the program, Sherm focused on strategy and Micky focused on internal communications. People often said that Micky was a nice person, but deep in their hearts they knew they still had to deliver. They knew he recorded their commitments and would hold them accountable. Even though Micky respected and cared for his people, they knew he set high standards and expected no less than the best they could give him.

Even though Micky respected and cared for his people, they knew he had high standards and expected no less than the best they could give him.

Not long after Micky was promoted to head the F-22 program, Lockheed sent him to their communications training school for executives. The school trained Micky well. When he finished the program, he was able to take a question, no matter how difficult, and deliver an answer with a smile that always made Lockheed look good.

For a company like Lockheed/Lockheed Martin, all types of communication were needed. Types of communication included reading, writing, speaking, and listening.[39] These could be further broken down into formal and informal, as well as internal and external, to create a spectrum of solutions that could address almost any situation. Furthermore, as many communication experts will tell you, each type and approach has its own advantages and limitations. It is also helpful to know that different combinations of types and methods are better for reaching different market segments.

In addition to the usual barriers to communication, there is one relatively new barrier managers need to be aware of—the new and ever-changing threats caused by cyber-security attacks.

Many of these are significant and directed at the country's industrial base. To Micky's credit, one of the first things he did when he joined the F-22 program, was install a new communication system to ensure that communications were received and limited to those who were supposed to get them.

| GUIDELINE 15: | **Allow yourself to be vulnerable; it's OK to be human.** |

Blanchard and Hodges tell us that one of the most powerful things a servant leader can do is share their vulnerability with the people they are leading.[40]

Micky opened himself to his direct report employees, when he agreed to go through a 360-degree review program. The process was professionally managed, but it is never easy to go through. Micky made himself vulnerable when he agreed to take their feedback. These are some of the comments Micky received.

Positive comments:

- He takes time to listen, instead of focusing on his agenda.
- He is not afraid to give feedback, but he is careful not to do it in public.
- He is very methodical. He looks at the data, but never makes snap judgments.
- He is decidedly different from most of his predecessors. He is more people-oriented and his attitude conveys it.
- Micky does not let things fester. He identifies what is important and moves things forward.

Suggestions for improvement:

- He would do well to walk around more and talk to more employees.
- His office is hard to approach, and his executive assistant protects him. This can sometimes make it hard to get sensitive information to him quickly.

- His job is too large to do the day-to-day managing himself. Therefore, he must learn to rely on others to manage these things for him. He needs to be more comfortable delegating to others. He needs to build trust with his people and then delegate to them.
- Sometimes he gives out too much information. He wants to be viewed as one who keeps his group informed, but there are times when information does not need to be distributed to everybody.
- He needs to help us understand the role of the Lockheed companies better.

These are only a sample of more than 100 comments he received during the review. Some were negative and some were positive, but they demonstrated Micky's willingness to show that he is human.

GUIDELINE 16:   **Be empathetic towards employees and accessible when possible.**

This example highlights Micky's empathy for his people. As mentioned previously, Micky was responsible for planning the move of the F-22 program from Burbank to Marietta. This required moving all program personnel and their families from California to Georgia.

Micky knew the move would be difficult for many. He had already made the move twice, so he knew what to expect. Employees and their families had their own worries and troubles, so Micky was thrilled when he heard that almost 85 percent agreed to move from Burbank to Marietta. It was clear that being empathetic and accessible contributed to the higher-than-average ratio of those who made the move versus those who didn't.

Micky's personal attention meant a lot to the people. Eight hundred and fifty families is a pretty big number and interviewing all those people was a lot of work for Micky. It showed he was committed, and that was what people needed. At that point, the employees knew they were working for someone who cared for them. That largely explains the insert below about "A Thousand Points of Light."

A Thousand Points of Light

When we won the F-22 contract, we planned to close the plant in Burbank – the longtime home of Lockheed. Based on my own experience, I knew the move would be difficult for many of these long-term, highly- skilled, workers and their families. To see how we could help, I interviewed many people. When it came time to relocate, 85 percent agreed to move.

Just before we closed the plant, the staff asked me to join them out in front of the F-22 office building. They had rented a big mobile billboard and posted "helping-hand" personal thank you notes all over the sign. When I turned to see what they were looking at, I felt like I was looking at a thousand points of light. I will never forget that moment. How fortunate I was to be the leader of this extraordinary group of people. Each hand was made out of red construction paper and contained a personal note expressing "thanks" for what I had done to facilitate their move to Marietta, Georgia. The vision we shared and the work we had already done turned a mixed group of workers into a highly motivated team.

— Micky Blackwell

GUIDELINE 17:	Prevent conflict when possible but keep a resolution specialist in your pocket.

This guideline deals with the very real issue of how to manage conflict within and between organizations. It addresses how to prevent conflict when possible and how to resolve differences when necessary. Once again, Micky's own actions provide us with an excellent example.

Both the government and the contractors were concerned about delays in decision-making. Resolving conflicts can be time-consuming and expensive. The leadership knew it was better to prevent conflicts where possible. As Williams notes in his book on *Acquisition for the 21st Century*,[41] the F-22 leadership "believed in empowering all members of the team to work on issues and make decisions appropriate to their position and individual capability. For example, the leader of the cockpit team should worry about the weight and the cost of the canopy and would be responsible for making the necessary trade-offs to meet the users' needs for a canopy and the team requirement to meet cost and schedule performance requirements."

Brig. Gen. Jim Fain (he was promoted), Micky, and Pratt & Whitney's F119 program manager approved a cost target for each integrated product team, an allocation for weight, and sub-allocations for technical requirements when necessary.[42] They also approved plans for each team that included its own cost, schedule, and performance targets. The net result was that each team was developing its own product with the team leaders acting like program directors. Micky and the other leaders recognized that this level of empowerment would be a new experience for many workers. **Concurrent engineering** required teams to look at problems from a higher-level perspective.* This required a new set of tools and additional training. In retrospect, some say this was the secret to the success of the F-22 program.[43, 44]

> *Concurrent engineering required teams to look at problems from a higher-level perspective...some say this was the secret to the success of the F-22 program.*

The second example illustrates the importance of knowing how to resolve conflicts. Work- related conflict can have an enormous impact on organizations,[45] but when it threatened to affect the JSF, Lockheed Martin leaders knew they had to move quickly. In most cases, work-related conflict is caused by personality conflicts, stress, and overwhelming workloads. In this case, it was the result of the different expectations of F-35 work assignments for Lockheed Martin's facility in Fort Worth, Texas and the relocated Skunk Works in Palmdale, California.

It happened during the competition to develop the JSF. This has been described as "the most closely watched fighter competition ever."[46] For Lockheed, it was clearly a "bet-the-future-of-the-company" effort. However, Darleen Druyun, Principal Deputy Undersecretary of the Air Force for Acquisition, astutely observed that the competition was not really about the airplane, it was about who would develop the prototype and who would manufacture the final product.[47] According to one source, "To

---

* Concurrent engineering is defined as the practice of concurrently developing products and their manufacturing processes in multifunctional teams with all specialties working together from the earliest stages. It is the most effective way to develop products with challenges for functionality, cost, time-to-market, quality, satisfying customer needs, meeting all growth demands. and designing products for all aspects of manufacturability. See David M. Anderson. 2020. "Concurrent Engineering." Accessed on September 20, 2021. http://design4manufacturability.com/concurrent-engineering.htm.

win the JSF contract, Lockheed had to do more than build the better plane. It had to overcome a perception among Pentagon brass that its management was a distant second to that of Boeing ."[48]

The Pentagon had determined that if the Air Force, Navy, and Marines could consolidate their plans, they could reduce the JSF unit price to make it more affordable. But when Lockheed started to put its team together, differences between their tactical fighter plant in Fort Worth and the Skunk Works in Palmdale, became clear. According to Micky, "a small war erupted within Lockheed" over which group would lead the effort.[49] Both companies had the ability to lead the program—the question was who would do it.

To resolve the conflict between Fort Worth and the Skunk Works, Micky had to clarify who would handle what. In the end, Micky played the role of a conflict resolution specialist when he declared that the Skunk Works would build the JSF prototype; Fort Worth would lead the JSF production program.[50]

GUIDELINE 18:	**Listen to your customers and listen to your employees.** **Meet with them on a regular basis.**

Everyone knows that communication is important. This guideline addresses the importance of communicating on a regular basis—not only with customers, but also with employees.

Understanding the needs of customers is paramount. It was an important issue for Micky and something he often stressed.[51] Personal interviews, surveys, focus groups, customer satisfaction programs, and other tools were routinely used to do this.[52]

> *If any one word could sum up Micky's term as our president, it's "communication." He made it a point to be accessible to employees and customers alike, ready to answer questions and supply essential information.*
>
> **John McLellan**
> **President (Retired)**
> **Lockheed Aeronautical Systems Company**

Both salaried and union employees welcomed the implementation of IPTs, Lean, and other Quality initiatives. They resulted in a more efficient, cleaner, safer, and healthier place to work. Workers were being listened to, unnecessary steps were being eliminated, and costs were being trimmed.

In the case of the F-22, the customer went far beyond this. Based on their knowledge of trends in leadership and the benefits of teams, the Air Force mandated the use of concurrent engineering teams in the F-22 contract. This caused Lockheed Martin, Boeing, and Pratt & Whitney to do something that had never been tried before—create IPTs to manage the needs of the program. The IPTs, in turn, used Lean, Six Sigma, and other Quality-based initiatives to reduce waste and flowtimes and make other improvements based on the voice of the customer.

GUIDELINE 19: Reduce costs and improve quality by adopting practices such as IPTs, Lean, Six Sigma, and the Enterprise Servant Leadership Management Model.

See Chapters 7 through 10 for examples of how many of these concepts were implemented.

Lessons Learned and Important Points

This chapter outlined lessons learned and important points for achieving successful outcomes using Enterprise Servant Leadership. A summary of these guidelines is as follows.

Guidelines for Servant Leaders

- Remember your Creator; there is a reason you are the leader. Pray for the wisdom to make wise decisions; you were chosen for a purpose.
- Commit to the vision and build strategies to support it.
- Know the business of the business and think survival.
- Lead by example. This will help others see how to lead and serve better.
- Hold true to your core values. They will help guide your actions and keep you out of trouble.
- Be strong in your convictions. Raising the bar is necessary. *Failing* to raise it can be deadly.
- Ensure your processes are world-class and you are achieving the right outcomes.
- Embrace risk and encourage innovation.

Guidelines for Teams

- Use Integrated Product Teams (IPTs) to do integrated work. There is a reason they are integrated. Let the teams do the work.
- Select team members with care. Look at educational basics, track record, and experience.
- Encourage collaboration. Provide mentoring when necessary.
- Train your teams well. Excellent training can save you money. It can also boost morale.
- Include your partners in your value networks to lower costs and create more value.

Guidelines for Communication

- Have a well-defined strategy for communicating important messages. Know all your options and know when to use them.
- Allow yourself to be vulnerable; it's OK to be human.
- Be empathetic towards employees, and accessible when possible.
- Prevent conflict when possible but keep a resolution specialist in your pocket.
- Listen to your customers and listen to your employees. Meet with them both on a regular basis.
- Reduce costs and improve quality by adopting practices such as IPTs, Lean, Six Sigma, and the Enterprise Servant Leadership Management Model.

Chapter Notes

1 The aerospace and defense (A&D) industry is highly regulated by the US government. Although that doesn't change the role of a servant leader, it can have an impact on how a program is managed and how success is measured. For example, changes in Congressional funding and the number of aircraft produced, had a major impact on the unit cost of the F-22.

2 Ken Blanchard and Phil Hodges. 2005. *Lead Like Jesus: Lessons from the Greatest Leadership Role Model of All Time.* Nashville, TN: Thomas Nelson, Inc., pp. 217-227.

3 Ibid.

4 The Bible, of course, told us this many years ago when the author of Proverbs wrote, "where there is no vision, the people perish." See Proverbs 29:18, KJV.

5 Stanley W. Kandebo and David Hughes. 1995. "F-22 to Counter 21st Century Threats." *Aviation Week & Space Technology*, 143 (4), pp. 38-43.

6 One of many reasons the process took so long was because of the debates about how military technology was changing and what could be done to anticipate and prepare for the changes. See David C. Aronstein, Michael J. Hirschberg, and Albert C. Piccirillo. 1998. *Advanced Tactical Fighter to F-22 Raptor: Origins of the 21st Century Air Dominance Fighter.* Reston, Virginia: American Institute of Aeronautics and Astronautics.

7 For a classic article on how to build a corporate vision, see James C. Collins and Jerry I. Porras. 1996. "Building Your Company's Vision." *Harvard Business Review* 74 (5), pp. 65-77.

8 Jay Miller. 1993. *Lockheed's Skunk Works: The First Fifty Years.* Arlington, Texas: Aerofax, Inc., p. 5.

9 Kelly Johnson's 14 Rules are listed in Appendix B.

10 Ibid.

11 James "Micky" Blackwell. November 8, 2011. "Lecture on Leadership and Management." Kennesaw State University, Kennesaw, GA, p. 13.

12 Lora L. Reed, Deborah Vidaver-Cohen, and Scott R. Colwell. 2011. "A New Scale to Measure Executive Servant Leadership: Development, Analysis." *Journal of Business Ethics*, p. 416.

13 See David Boulton. 1978. *The Grease Machine: The Inside Story of Lockheed's Dollar Diplomacy.* New York, NY: Harper & Row Publishers Inc.

14 Patrick M. Lencioni. July, 2002. "Make Your Values Mean Something." *Harvard Business Review,* 80 (7), pp. 113-117.

15 U.S. Air Force. September 23, 2015. *F-22 Raptor.* Accessed October 19, 2018. https://www.af.mil/About-Us/Fact-Sheets/Display/Article/104506/f-22-raptor/.

16 Roberto Michel (Senior ed.). 1999. "Lean Meets ERP." *Manufacturing Systems.* New York, NY: Cahners Business Information, Mid-November (article reprint).

17 Ibid.

18 Sherman N. Mullin. 1992. *The Evolution of the F-22 Advanced Tactical Fighter.* 1992 Wright Brothers Lecture, American Institute of Aeronautics and Astronautics, p. 15.

19 Nikoletta Bika. n.d. *The problems with employee integrity tests.* Accessed December 31, 2020. https://resources.workable.com/stories-and-insights/employee-integrity-tests.

20 Larry C. Spears, ed. 1995. *Reflections on Leadership: How Robert K. Greenleaf's Theory of Servant Leadership Influenced Today's Top Management Thinkers.* New York, NY: John Wiley & Sons, p. 147.

21 Ibid, p. 140.

22 Jon R. Katzenbach, and Douglas K Smith. 2003. *The Wisdom of Teams: Creating the High- Performance Organization.* New York, NY: McKinsey & Company.

23 Ibid, p. 239.

24 Ibid, p. 45.

25 James Micky Blackwell. 2021. *All the Days of Our Lives*, p. 111.

26 Sam Walker. March 23-24, 2019. "One Fix for All That's Wrong: Better Managers." *The Wall Street Journal*, pp. B1-B2.

27 Justin A. Irving and Gail J. Longbotham. 2007. "Team Effectiveness and Six Essential Servant Leadership Themes: A Regression Model Based on items in the Organizational Leadership Assessment." *International Journal of Leadership Studies,* (Regents University) 2 (2), p. 107.

28 Zappos Insights. 2014. *5 Benefits of Getting to Know Your Team.* Accessed August 18, 2018. https://www.zapposinsights.com/blog/item/5-benefits-of-getting-to-know-your-team.

29 Ken Blanchard and Phil Hodges. 2003. *The Servant Leader.* Nashville, TN: Thomas Nelson Inc., p. 21.

30 Tina Rasmussen. 1995. "Creating a Culture of Servant Leadership: a Real Life Story," in Larry C. Spears, ed. 1995. *Reflections on Leadership: How Robert K. Greenleaf's Theory of Servant Leadership Influenced Today's Top Management Thinkers.* New York: John Wiley & Sons, p. 296.

31 James P. Womack and Daniel T. Jones. 2003. *Lean Thinking: Banish Waste and Create Wealth in Your Corporation.* 2nd Ed. New York, NY: Free Press.

32 Susan Miles. May 27,1993. "Blackwell: Radical changes needed to compete in the '90s marketplace." *Lockheed Aeronautical Systems Company Star,* pp. 1, 3.

33 Micky Blackwell. February 10, 1994. "Like 'Humpty Dumpy' LASC processes are too fragmented." *Star,* p. 2.

34 Stanley W. Kandebo. July 12, 1999. "Lean Thinking Prompts Line Shift for F-22." *Aviation Week & Space Technology,* 151 (2), p. 63.

35 CATIA stands for the IBM-Dassault Systèmes-designed Computer Aided, Three-Dimensional Interactive Application (CATIA).

36 Ibid.

37 Joel D. Wisner, Keah-Choon Tan, and G. Keong Leong. 2012. *Principles of Supply Chain Management: A Balanced Approach.* 3rd ed. Mason, OH: South-Western Cengage Learning, pp. 150-162.

38 For more detail on business communications, see Courtland L. Bovee, John V. Thill, and Barbara R. Schatzman. 2003. *Business Communication Today.* Upper Saddle River, NJ: Prentice Hall, pp. 7-25.

39 CNN Money. 1999. *Lockheed's $70 M Comma: Spelling error leaves defense giant in the red after military jet sale.* June 18. Accessed July 17, 2018, at https://money.cnn.com/1999/06/18/ worldbiz/ lockheed/.

40 See Lockheed Martin's website on its ethics and core values. "Ethics and Core Values. Lockheed Martin." Accessed February 11, 2000. https://www. lockheedmartin.com/en- us/who-we-are/ethics. html

41 Ken Blanchard and Phil Hodges. 2003. *The Servant Leader*, p. 105.

42 Michael D. Williams. 1999. *Acquisition for the 21st Century: The F-22 Development Program.* Washington D.C.: National Defense University Press, p. 41.

43 Ibid, pp. 41-42.

44 Ibid, p. 31.

45 When one highly respected firm commissioned a study on workplace conflict in 2008 They found that workplace-related conflict accounted for the loss of over $350 billion in paid hours based on an average hourly earnings of $17.95, or the equivalent of 385 million working days. See Brett Cooper and Evans Kerrigan. 2020. "Productive vs. Unproductive Conflict in the Workplace." *HR Daily Advisor*. October 2. Accessed December 2, 2020. https://hrdailyadvisor.blr.com/2020/10/02/productive-vs-unproductive-conflict-in-the- workplace/

46 The quotes in this paragraph are from a 2002 article in *Fast Company*. See Bill Breen. March 31, 2002. "High Stakes, Big Bets." *Fast Company*. Accessed October 11, 2019. https://www.fastcompany.com/44742/high-stakes-big-bets.

47 Ibid.

48 Ibid.

49 Ibid.

50 Ibid.

51 John McLellan. March 30, 1995. "Blackwell taught us value of open communications with employees, customers." *Lockheed Aeronautical Systems Company Star*, p. 2.

52 Cost-of-Quality concepts that reduce the cost of failure or rework leave more time to spend doing other work or non-work activities. One might conclude that this would lead to a loss of jobs because of increased efficiency. But the team was able to show that the increased efficiency would allow existing employees to make better use of their time, winning more work and increasing profits.

Chapter 7
How to Set Up and Use Integrated Product Teams

Integrated product teams were based on servant leadership principles. The product was more important than the person. Everybody wanted to win.

Micky Blackwell
President & COO Aeronautics Sector (Retired)
Lockheed Martin Corporation

The last chapter addressed guidelines that would help Enterprise Servant Leaders be successful. This chapter addresses how to set up and operate Integrated Product Teams (IPTs) using Enterprise Servant Leaders to manage the project. This will be followed by a discussion of why it is important to use IPTs.

The Lockheed team F-22 Engineering and Management Development (EMD) proposal was delivered to the Air Force on December 31, 1990. In its proposal, Lockheed proposed managing the F-22 program using a formal structure of Integrated Product Teams to respond to the Air Force's concurrent engineering requirement. The invention and use of IPTs was a natural extension of the Skunk Work's Basic Operating Rules (Appendix B).

Managing the F-22 program through IPTs was subsequently approved by the Air Force System Program Office. As a result, the F-22 weapon system was organized using integrated product development from the beginning. As stated in a *New York Times* article:

> "The three primary F-22 builders—the Lockheed Corporation, the General Dynamics Corporation, and the Boeing Company—largely abandoned the rigid prime contractor-subcontractor arrangements that have been the industry standard. Instead, they are trying to operate as a flexible team..."[1]

IPTs are defined as "a multi-disciplined team made up of members from specific disciplines working together on a project to identify, address and resolve issues to help achieve project goals and objectives."[2] As noted in Ecclesiastes 4:9-10, teams are superior to individuals in producing good results. Because of the success that came from using IPTs on the F-22, the Secretary of Defense in 1995 directed DOD to use IPTs as a preferred oversight and management approach for acquiring goods and services.[3]

Two can accomplish more than twice as much as one, for the results can be much better. If one falls, the other pulls him up; but if a man falls when he is alone, he's in trouble.

Ecclesiastes 4:9-10 (TLB)

The Lockheed team believed that by using integrated product teams to manage the program they could achieve the goals set for the F-22.[4] The productivity improvements made by the IPTs on the F-22 were astounding. The inclusion of Air Force personnel on the integrated product teams set a new standard for collaborative government/industry partnerships.

Knowledge has long been recognized as a key to competitive advantage in global aerospace markets,[5] and teams are one of the best ways to manage the distribution of knowledge. One study concluded that, "about 80 percent of new engineers and 90 percent of established engineers" worked with others to complete or solve their most important project.[6] However, all teams are not created equal. A collection of people is not a team. Some teams are more effective than others. A high-performance team yields results that are greater than the sum of the parts.

> *Knowledge has long been recognized as a key to competitive advantage… and teams are one of the best ways to manage the distribution of knowledge.*

IPTs (which play a key role in design, production, and support) simultaneously include all disciplines from the enterprise that impact the project, e.g., research, engineering, finance, marketing, procurement, support, and maintenance.[7] Management's goal for all IPTs is for them to become **high-performance teams.**

A high-performance team meets the definition of an IPT team; however, its members are also deeply committed to each other's personal growth and success, have a common purpose, and have a passion to succeed. Furthermore, those commitments usually transcend the team. A high-performance team believes they are both individually and mutually accountable for their goals. In fact, "when combined, the intense commitments to one another and their mutual cause plus their shared leadership and interchangeable skills make high-performance teams entirely self-sufficient." [8]

A collection of people is not a team, nor is it a given that a team can become a high- performance integrated product team. Katzenbach in *Wisdom of Teams* shows a team goes through a five-step process to become high-performance team:

- **They start as "working groups" who come together to just share information and delineate individual roles.**
- **A team is formed called a "pseudo team," but they are not focused on collective performance and are not really trying to achieve it.**
- **When a team recognizes a common purpose, they become a "potential team." They understand there is a real need for performance improvement; however, there is no common approach or accountability.**
- **A "real team" is one that has complimentary skills, is committed to a common goal and approach, and holds themselves accountable. There is frank and open communication. There is a core covenant.**
- **A "high-performance team" is one whose members are truly committed to one another's personal growth and success. This is when the team's effectiveness is at peak performance. The team has become a family!**

Micky instinctively knew that building high-performance IPTs led by servant leaders was not something to be taken lightly. It was important for the teams to be built right and in a consistent manner.

Figure 14 below is a summary of Micky's approach to building and using high-performance IPTs led by servant leaders. The approach consists of 12 steps.

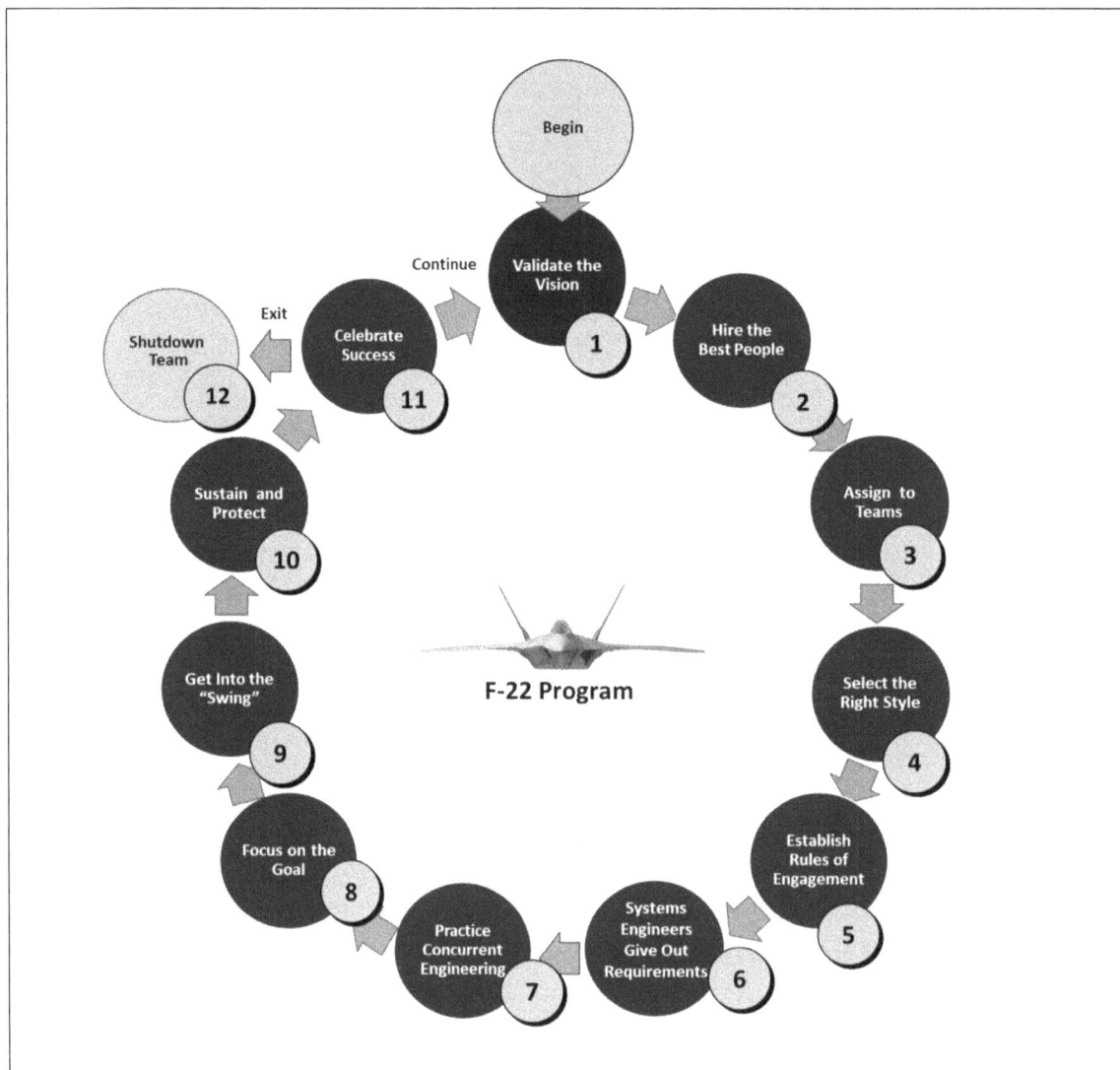

Figure 14. Micky's Steps for Developing and Using Integrated Product Teams.

Steps for Developing and Using IPTs

Step 1: Validate the Vision

The first step in building a team is to define or validate the vision. For the F-22, an important corollary was that each team's vision had to support the visions of other teams on the program, as well as the overall vision for the F-22. Doing so made it clear what each team was doing. It also ensured that all teams were pointed in the same direction.

Step 2: Hire the Best People

You always want to hire the best people, and Micky enjoyed reaching out to promising young talent as well as experienced personnel. Micky and his team were looking for people that could both lead and serve. For many aspiring leaders, it was just what they needed.[9] In fact, the ability to do both was a criterion for moving forward.[10] He always carried a yellow pad with him that he used to record names of people from organizations who impressed him. Then he would try to hire them.

Step 3: Assign People to Teams

Team leaders were designated by program managers. Team members were assigned to teams by their functional managers in negotiation with IPT team leaders. Once a person was assigned to a project, functional managers no longer had any team oversight. However, they were still responsible for the processes used by their people. This eliminated the problem of having two bosses telling one person what to do, while maintaining the standards associated with each function. In addition to its own people and those from its major partners, Lockheed Martin also included subcontractors on their IPT's along with Air Force personnel.

Step 4: Select the Right Leadership Style

In their book, *The Servant Leader*, Blanchard and Hodges define a concept called "Situational Leadership." As the title implies, it described different ways to lead under different conditions. From Micky's point of view, it complemented what he already knew. It provided leaders with additional tools for use in different situations. The four styles of leadership include: [11]

- **Directing a person (or team) that clearly needs direction.**
- **Coaching those who are moving in the right direction but still need oversight.**
- **Supporting those who are already doing well and don't need much direction.**
- **Delegating to leaders who can be trusted to make key decisions.**

It is important to understand what leadership style is needed for each team member. The servant leader can then use the appropriate style to help a person or team get started.

Step 5: Establish Rules of Engagement

The next step is to agree to the rules of engagement—a clever way of saying what is expected of team members. The F-22 was the first program to employ IPT management. According to Micky, it was exciting to watch. Each team developed its own operating rules.

Integrated product teams were set up to eliminate the need for a "stovepipe mentality" and to speed up the design and manufacturing processes. Each team brought together the personnel needed to design, produce, and maintain a particular part of the aircraft and make sure it worked with the other parts of the system. They also had to make sure it met performance requirements and the financial design-to-cost targets that were given.[12]

Teams changed the way Lockheed Martin did business. Improvements had to be substantial and radical. What they did every day had to be rethought. IPTs were introduced to the idea of "discontinuous thinking"—they could no longer look at a process in terms of continuous improvement. Process changes had to be more significant than that. They couldn't make a change that led to a 20 percent improvement—they were looking for improvements of 80 percent or more.

Focused vs. Flexible vs. Conventional Factories

The term "Focused Factory" was first used in a Harvard Business Review article in 1974. In the article, the author explains, a focused factory is designed for narrow operations that serve specific markets and niches.* The author notes that it can be a competitive weapon when it focuses on carrying out a specific task.

Because its systems and processes are built to serve narrow markets, its costs and overhead are lower than those of "Flexible" or "Conventional" plants.

"Flexible Factories," on the other hand, are those that can rapidly reconfigure themselves to produce a wide variety of products. Short changeover times are typical, and they can run across different products and markets. Other factors include the size and location of plant and capacity, choice of equipment, type of production process, type of scheduling system, etc. For these reasons, costs and overhead are usually higher than normal.

"Conventional Factories," produce multiple products for multiple customers. The result is that the plant is likely to be noncompetitive because its policies are not focused on one single manufacturing task to make it competitive.**

Sources:

* Wickham Skinner. 1974. The Focused Factories. Harvard Business Review. May-June. pp. 113-120.
** Conventional Factory. n.d. Accessed January 20, 2021. https: bing.com.

Two examples may help. First, the focused factory (see insert) ensured the right things such as labor and materials were available only when needed. The unique part about this system is that it only provides one day's worth of shop orders at a time. There is no backlog of open orders, no searching through stacks for supplies, and no manual for expediting orders. This helped the factory reduce throughput time by 77 percent.[13]

Second, the focused factory has also aided in stabilizing the work force. In the past they had recalled workers only to surplus half of them a few months later. They were striving to keep the work at a constant level to avoid that problem.

Load leveling takes the normal highs and lows of workflow and attempts to even them out over a long period of time. Since then, they have achieved something incredible for the industry—they have had the same amount of work in one shop for almost two years. Because the computer keeps the work-in-process at a constant level, the only work-in-process orders they have are the ones that need to get out that day.

Now the operators can concentrate on what they know best—assembling airplane parts the best way they can. The senior leadership of the organization has always been interested in employee involvement. Today, employees are not just talking about changes to their operations, but when necessary, actually making the changes to fulfill their requirements.

Step 6: System Engineers Allocate Requirements

Systems engineers allocate the requirements for each IPT (e.g., weight, heat, cost, etc.) and monitor the IPTs to make sure they are meeting the requirements. They also provide tradeoffs of requirements among the IPTs as necessary.

Step 7: Practice Concurrent Engineering

Even though the styles mentioned above were helpful, what management was really looking for were people who could lead and work concurrently. The teams were connected at the program level, but also worked together across different products. This meant that as each team was developing its own suite of products, they each had their own cost, schedule, and performance targets.

Even though they were separate teams, they all worked together to achieve a common purpose. What made it work was when teams developed products concurrently. In other words, what the designers created, the engineers could build, and the maintainers could service. In addition, the entire system could be built to a cost that met the budget.[14] This required people with a broader perspective. As mentioned previously, this concept was called "concurrent engineering."

Step 8: Focus on the Goals

Even though the teams had different goals at different levels, the overarching goal was to be the best of the best. Being the "best" meant more than just satisfying customers. It also meant providing an enjoyable environment in which people can work. Teams spend many hours in the factory, and there's no doubt that happy workers build better products.[15] The "6S" process was applied to the factory floor which resulted in a cleaner, safer, and more efficient work environment (see Chapter 8 for description of the 6S process). Factory workers loved the workplace environment which produced higher quality parts, at lower costs, with greater customer satisfaction.

This meant reengineering the company or starting over in some areas. The name of the game for the F-22 was affordability, affordability, affordability. The major problems that came from the Air Force really weren't technical, they were related to costs. To keep their customers happy, Lockheed Martin knew they needed to do better at controlling costs. That does not mean they had not done well historically, but it does mean that to compete in today's environment, they had to do better than anyone had anticipated in the past.

Focus creates energy.[16] Ken Jennings and Heather Hyde describe this in their book, *The Greater Goal*, where the focus is on inspiring employees to achieve a higher purpose.[17] Micky knew he needed to do this before he took over the program. He not only had to adjust his own behavior, he had to embed it into the culture of the organization. He knew it would not be easy, but that is exactly what he had trained for since he first learned about servant leadership.

To accomplish their objectives, the F-22 team established the following goals:[18]

- **Validate and focus on the new business activities.**
- **Reengineer the complete company organization.**
- **Radically overhaul all processes.**
- **Establish new management and measurement systems.**
- **Find new ways to reduce costs.**
- **Instill new values and beliefs for the company of the future.**

One of the major tools to help them accomplish their goals was metrics. Teams developed metrics for things such as return-on-assets, cash, profit margins, management ratios, sales, signups, cycle times, fixed asset requirements as well as performance, schedule, and cost in each program and functional organization. These metrics had to apply throughout the entire Lockheed Martin Aeronautics Sector.[19]

Step 9: Getting Into the Swing

As used in this book, "getting into the swing" refers to what happens when hard-working people strive together synergistically for a common purpose. When people are in the "swing," work seems effortless, sweet, smooth, and can be sustained. This, in turn, defines and yields a **High-Performance Team.**

The process of getting there, however, is often just the opposite. Like the winners in the book *The Boys in the Boat*, high performing teams know exactly what this means. The last line in the movie based on the book is: "I didn't row with eight—I rowed with one." Synergy causes the whole to be greater than the sum of its parts.[20]

That is exactly what happened to the teams working on the Raptor. The teams had real momentum. You could sense it in the air. When Micky saw what was happening, that was all the reward he needed. He knew he had succeeded as a leader serving his people.

Step 10: Sustain and Protect

Scripture tells us the enemy is always out there.[21] Many business leaders know exactly what that means. To be sure he never wavered, Micky used prayer, scripture, and accountability to sustain his momentum and guard his behavior. He knew it was important to take care of himself, his family, and his people.

The IPTs also spawned a world-class culture among teams working on the F-22. The IPTs were producing dramatic results, and Micky wanted to give them the respect they deserved. They were world-class people, and in his opinion they were the best aircraft company in the industry. Knowing that his people were making a real difference, Micky wanted them to feel satisfied in their jobs. He also wanted them to feel like they were being listened to. In other words, he wanted them to enjoy what they were doing and have a good time doing it.

Step 11: Celebrate Success

Innovation, technology, lean production, and reliable support—the F-22 team did it all, and they did it well. Vance Coffman, the CEO and president of Lockheed Martin, told Lockheed Martin employees that the F–22 flight test program was the most successful in Air Force history because of the quality of engineering and simulation that went into the design of the prototypes. He also said that their outstanding performance in producing the F-22 could only be attributed to Micky.[22]

> *The vision we shared and the work we had already done turned a mixed group of workers into a highly motivated team.*
>
> Micky Blackwell

The Lockheed Martin Aeronautics Sector was on its way to operating as a virtual company, a unified aerospace entity with unmatched capabilities to satisfy their customers.[23] By transforming the company to a lean enterprise, the company became more efficient and its people more productive. They clearly knew what they were after and were in a great position to achieve their goals.[24]

Step 12: Shut Down the Team

The final circle in the upper left-hand corner of Figure 14, indicates that the team is terminated when its mission has been fulfilled—or adjusted, if necessary, to pursue another vision and mission.

Why IPTs Are Important

IPTs are important for several reasons. First, they represent the future of acquisition in the military. The IPTs were so successful on the F-22, that they were included in DOD Directive 5000.1. This made them mandatory for all new major acquisition programs that followed. Second, IPTs are responsible for meeting all cost, schedule, performance, and supportability targets. These multifunctional teams enable concurrent engineering, which leads to faster, better, and cheaper product development.

Integrated Product Plans and Master Schedules

The F-22 EMD program pioneered the use of Integrated Master Plans (IMPs) and Integrated Master Schedules (IMSs). They provided each IPT a roadmap to do their work and ensured that all the IPTs were operating in sync with each other. They are now an established part of doing business in the DOD.

According to Wikipedia:

> "...the Integrated Master Plan (IMP) and the Integrated Master Schedule (IMS) are important program management tools that provide significant assistance in the planning and scheduling of work efforts in large and complex materiel acquisitions. The IMP is an event-driven plan that documents the significant accomplishments necessary to complete the work and ties each accomplishment to a key program event. The IMP is expanded to a time-based IMS to produce a networked and multi-layered schedule showing all detailed tasks required to accomplish the work effort contained in the IMP. The IMS flows directly from the IMP and supplements it with additional levels of detail." [25]

Both IMPs and IMSs are used to form the foundation for implementing an Earned Value Management System which is required on major government contracts.

Lessons Learned and Important Points

This chapter addressed the use of high-performance IPTs led by servant leaders and why IPTs are important. Lessons learned and important points include:

- **The F-22 was one of the first major programs to implement servant leadership with IPTs.**
- **IPTs are the future for several reasons. First, they represent the future of acquisition in the military. Second, IPTs are responsible for meeting all cost, schedule, performance, and supportability targets in the most cost-effective way possible.**
- **IPTs should be formed as early as possible on a program to identify problems with the objective of eliminating rework. Eliminating rework allows teams to save dollars or focus on other areas.**
- **Know how to leverage the skills of IPTs. Having a good vision and focusing on the goal, can help pull people together like nothing else can.**
- **Profits will be greatest when partners are part of the process. Being part of the process, means sharing your knowledge and data.**
- **IPTs should be well trained. Trained people can save money and boost morale.**
- **Because the computer keeps the work-in-process at a constant level, the only work-in-process orders employees have are the ones that need to get out that day.**
- **Synergy between IPTs causes the whole to be greater than the sum of its parts. This is exactly what happened to teams working on the Raptor.**
- **The IPTs spawned a world-class culture among teams working on the F-22.**
- **The IPTs produced dramatic results on the F-22.**
- **IMPs and IMSs are used to provide a roadmap for the IPTs and the foundations for implementing an Earned Value Management System.**

Chapter Notes

1 Office of the Inspector General, DOD. March 23, 2001. "Executive Summary: Defense Contract Audit Agency's Role in Integrated Product Teams." DoD. Report No. D-2001-6-003..

2 Program Management. n.d. Integrated Product Team (IPT). "Definition." *DAU Glossary*. Accessed April 4, 2022. https://www.dau.edu/glossary/Pages/Glossary.aspx#!both|I|27700

3 Richard W. Stevenson. December 22, 1991. "Managing; New in Defense: Teamwork." *The New York Times*, Section 3, p.23.

4 Micky Blackwell. December 17, 1992. "Challenges of 1990s Business Climate Equate to Some Drastic Changes for U.S. Defense Industry 1992-1993." *Lockheed Aeronautical Systems Company Star*, Volume 5, Number 24, p. 7.

5 To assist in analyzing and managing the findings from this work, knowledge was broken down into tacit and explicit knowledge; and further categorized into product-embodied knowledge, process knowledge, knowledge about systems integration, and management knowledge. Thomas E. Pinelli, Rebecca O. Barclay, John M. Kennedy, and Ann P. Bishop. 1997. *Knowledge Diffusion in the U.S. Aerospace Industry*. Greenwich, Conn.: Ablex Publishing Corporation, p. 25-26.

6 Ibid, p. 413.

7 Susan Miles. February 10, 1994. "Lean Production's Streamlined Processes Bring Increased Efficiency to Manufacturing Areas." *Lockheed Aeronautical Systems Company Star*. Lockheed Aeronautical Systems Company, Volume 7, Number 2, p. 4.

8 Jon R. Katzenbach and Douglas K Smith. 2003. *The Wisdom of Teams: Creating the High- Performance Organization*. New York, NY: McKinsey & Company, p. 80.

9 Vance D. Coffman, Chairman, Chief Executive Officer and president, Lockheed Martin Corporation. 2000. *Retirement speech for James A. Blackwell Jr.* Washington, D.C.: Lockheed Martin Corporation, p. 8.

10 Dirk Van Dierendonck. September 26, 2011. "6 Key Servant Leadership Attributes." *IEDP Developing Leaders*. Accessed February 1, 2018. https://www.iedp.com/articles/six-key- servant-leadership-attributes/

11 Ken Blanchard and Phil Hodges. 2003. *The Servant Leader*. Nashville, Tenn.: Thomas Nelson Inc., pp. 73-75.

12 Richard W. Stevenson. December 22,1991. "New in Defense: Teamwork." *The New York Times*. Section 3, p. 3.

13 Ibid.

14 Vickie M. Graham. 1995. "One Contractor's Viewpoint." *Airman*. February, pp. 26-29.

15 Susan Miles. January 20, 1994. "Goal in Manufacturing is to be the Best in the Business." *Lockheed Aeronautical Systems Company Star*, Volume 7, Number 1, p. 1, 4.

16 The "S-Curve" is frequently used to describe a step-level increase in performance. For more on this topic, see Paul Nunes and Tim Breene. January-February 2011. "Reinvent Your Business Before It's Too Late." *Harvard Business Review*, 89 (1/2), pp. 81-87.

17 Kenneth R. Jennings and Heather Hyde. 2012. *The Greater Goal: Connecting Purpose and Performance*. San Francisco, Ca.: Berrett-Koehler Publishers, inc.

18 Micky Blackwell. 1993. "New Column to Focus on Issues Affecting LASC Team." *Lockheed Aeronautical Systems Company Star*. Lockheed Aeronautical Systems Company, June 17, Volume 6, Number 8, p. 2.

19 Susan Miles. 1993. "Blackwell: Radical Change Needed to Compete in '90s Marketplace." *Lockheed Aeronautical Systems Company Star*. Lockheed Aeronautical Systems Company, May 27, Volume 6, Number 7, p. 1, 3.

20 This should not be surprising since, once again, the Bible reminds us that two are better than one and they will get a good reward for their labor. See NKJV Ecclesiastes 4:9.

21 See NKJV 1 Peter 5:8-10. For more information about how to fight against the rulers of darkness and spiritual wickedness, see NKJV Ephesians 6: 10-18.

22 Vance D. Coffman, Chairman, Chief Executive Officer and president, Lockheed Martin Corporation. 2000. *Retirement speech for James A. Blackwell Jr.*, p. 7.

23 Micky Blackwell. September, 1999. "Aeronautics Sector: An Overview." *Lockheed Martin Today*. Bethesda, MD: Volume 5, Number 9, p. 3, 8.

24 Donna LeFew. 1993. "Blackwell Emphasizes Dramatic Change for LASC's Future." *The Leader*. The Lockheed-Georgia Management Association. Marietta, GA: December, Volume 41, Number 12, p. 5.

25 Overview: Integrated Master Plan. nd. *Wikipedia*. Accessed January 15, 2022 at https://en.wikipedia.org/wiki/Integrated_master_plan

Part III:
A New Enterprise Servant Leadership Model

Servant-Led Business Model

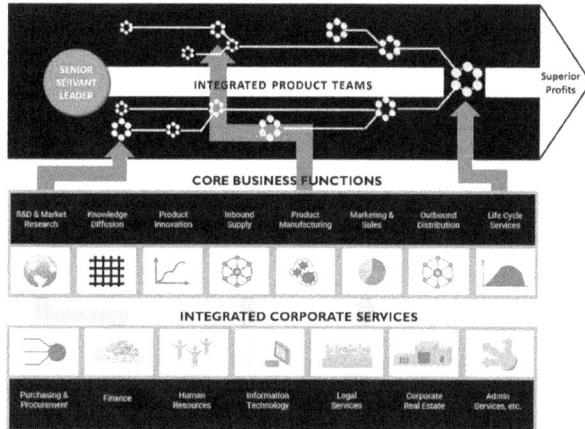

Adding Value to the System

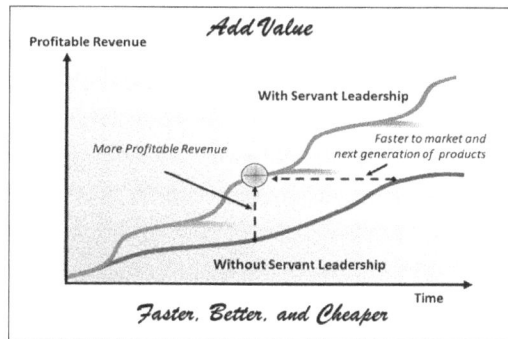

Enterprise Servant Leadership Management Model

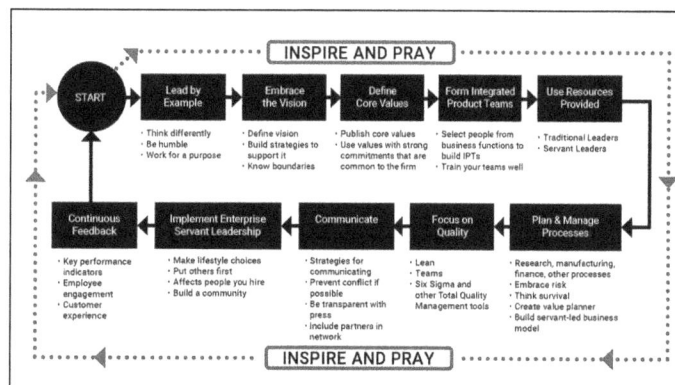

Chapter 8
Lean Enterprise Management

Being a servant leader has many rewards. One of the most important is a sense of personal satisfaction that comes from being part of a team that persevered until they won. When participating in a program like the Raptor, a great deal of comfort can also be obtained by knowing you contributed to something that will help protect you and your family.

Micky Blackwell
President & COO Aeronautics Sector (Retired)
Lockheed Martin Corporation

So far, we have described why servant leadership matters and how to build and use IPTs based on Micky Blackwell's life and work experience.

In Part III, Lean Enterprise Management and the associated development tools used for implementation will be described. A new servant-led business model will be presented that can be used to create superior value for customers using what we have learned. We will conclude Part III by describing a new Enterprise Servant Leadership Management Model (ESLMM) and showing the reader how the new ESLMM can be implemented in various ways and venues.

In the Introduction, we defined a "Lean Enterprise" as an organization that is focused on value creation for the end customer with minimal waste and processes. In this chapter, we will address the management of a Lean Enterprise using an array of new development tools. For the purposes of this book, Lean Enterprise Management includes the use of Lean Thinking, Enterprise Resource Planning, Six Sigma, Kaizen, 6S, and Total Quality Management (TQM). Each of these tools will be discussed.

Lean Enterprise Management Development Tools

Lean Thinking

Lean Thinking came to F-22 engine builder Pratt & Whitney (P&W) through Otis Elevator Company, a sister firm owned by United Technologies Corporation (UTC). The story goes that when the Japanese visited Otis Elevator, they told the Otis management that any new elevator they purchased must never fail. If Otis could not guarantee 100 percent reliability, they would buy their elevators elsewhere.

UTC asked the Japanese to tell them how to achieve 100 percent reliability. The Japanese agreed to send UTC an expert on how to do this with one proviso: they had to do whatever the Japanese expert told them to do. UTC agreed. They called it "Lean Thinking."

In simplest terms, Lean Thinking is the application of common sense. Lean was so successful at Otis Elevator, the CEO ported it over to Pratt & Whitney.

While determining how to make the F-22 program successful, several events occurred that heavily influenced Micky's thinking. The first occurred when the Air Froce invited the Lockheed F-22 Team executives to visit the Pratt & Whitney plant to see how they were applying Lean Thinking.

In the early 1980s, Pratt & Whitney was like many of its competitors. Its factories were designed to support mass production but were not configured to support small teams working on large jet engines.

When the Lockheed F-22 Team arrived at East Hartford, Connecticut, they were shocked by what they saw. Pratt & Whitney had totally transformed themselves and the way they made engines. Micky vividly remembers his reaction during their visit. "As soon as I saw Lean Thinking in action, I knew we had to have it."[1]

> When Lockheed is done with Lean, they will be #1 in the military market. They will be faster, better, and cheaper than any other airplane maker.
>
> *Micky Blackwell*

The second event came in the form of two successful business books. Soon after Micky saw what was happening with Lean at P&W, he quickly became a fan of the men who had helped them. James Womack and Daniel Jones co-authored two books that had an equally profound impact on Micky: *The Machine That Changed the World* and *Lean Thinking*. Womack and Jones were university professors who worked at P&W as consultants, so many of the examples in the book are based on their experiences there. Even today, Micky gives credit to Pratt & Whitney and Womack and Jones for helping Lockheed Martin find its own path to Lean.

A third significant factor was when Micky hired Mike Joyce as Aeronautics Sector vice president of operations. Mike, who had worked in Lean at Pratt & Whitney, was hired to implement it across the entire sector.

People in aerospace like to think that their products and processes are the best. Nevertheless, in the 1980s, many aerospace firms had not yet embraced Lean methods. Micky says that if the truth were told, many aerospace manufacturers did not really have world-class processes and practices. According to him, claims of quality, cost, and speed may have been uninformed or exaggerated by ambitious contractors.

Micky charged Joyce with hiring Lean experts for each Lockheed Martin Aeronautics company. Together, they looked for consultants to train Sector people. Each company received training in Lean, Kaizen, Kanban, 6S, and Six Sigma. Later, Mike moved to Lockheed Martin Corporate where he helped spread Lean throughout all Lockheed Martin companies.

Even though he realized that it would take several years to teach his people Lean Thinking, Micky's goal was to make the Lockheed Martin Aeronautics Sector the best of the best in aerospace.

The cost reductions that resulted from applying Lean to the Sector's processes were astonishing. As a rule of thumb, anywhere they applied Lean, they reduced their cost by at least 30 percent. As part of implementing Lean, they formed a Centralized Procurement Center for materials management for the Aeronautics Sector companies. The Center saved substantial amounts every year on a steady basis. Essentially, the Sector was buying material in volume from fewer vendors for better prices.

One might conclude that the implementation of Lean would lead to a loss of jobs because of increased efficiency. Micky sold the idea to Lockheed Martin employees that by increasing efficiency, they absolutely would win more work and would employ more people. As remarkable as it seemed, it turned out to be true.

Both salaried and union employees embraced Lean. Their talents and energies were channeled toward value and away from waste. On top of that, Lean produced a cleaner, safer, and more ergonomic place to work. Unneeded steps in every process were being eliminated, and worker suggestions were being listened to since they possessed the knowledge of how to improve the processes. As a result of implementing Lean, they saw major cost reductions in their programs. There was no doubt about it— in the Aeronautics Sector, Lean was a home run!

What is Lean?

Lean is a way of thinking about creating value with fewer resources and less waste... Lean thinking always starts with the customer. What does the customer value? Or, stated differently and in a way that invites concrete action, what problem does the customer need to solve?

Lean practice begins with the work—the actions that directly and indirectly create value for the customer—and the people doing that work. Through ongoing experimentation, workers and managers learn by innovating in their work—be it physical or knowledge work—for increasingly better quality and flow, less time and effort, and lower cost. Therefore, an organization characterized by lean practice is highly adaptive to its ever-changing environment when compared to its peers because of the systematic and continuous learning engendered by lean thinking and practice.

A lean enterprise is organized to keep understanding the customer and their context, i.e., specifying value and looking for better ways to provide it:

- *Through product and process development.*
- *During fulfillment from order through production to delivery.*
- *Through the product's and/or service's use cycle from delivery through maintenance and upgrades to recycling.*

A popular misconception is that Lean is suited only for manufacturing. Not true. Lean applies to every business and in every process. It is not a tactic or a cost reduction program, but a way of thinking and acting for an entire organization.

Source: Adapted from James P. Womack and Daniel T. Jones. "What is Lean?" Lean Enterprise Institute. Accessed on December 4, 2021. https://www.lean.org/WhatsLean/

The Three Principles of Lean

Micky acknowledged that if Lockheed wanted its products to be the best of the best, their processes needed to be the best of the best as well. Shortly thereafter, they started training people on the three principles of Lean: takt time, flow, and pull.[2]

Takt Time

"Takt" is a German word that refers to the rate at which products must be completed. It determines the pace of production in a manufacturing plant.

In the past, Lockheed bought big machines that could produce parts rapidly. They would run as many batches through as possible to justify the expense of having them. The problem was that the costs saved by machining products in big batches, were later spent waiting in line at the next machine for processing. Instead of buying machines designed to produce big lots, Lockheed shifted to machines that could meet their desired takt times.

Flow

Today, many systems are set up to optimize labor and headcount. If you want to optimize labor and headcount, that approach may make sense, but if you want to reduce total costs, you must optimize the "flow." When you're optimizing flow, you must minimize the costs associated with intra-plant transportation, unnecessary verifications, and the time products spend in the que waiting to be processed.

Furthermore, using one-piece flow, instead of batches, allows workers to detect problems faster. Feedback is immediate and people can make on-the-spot adjustments, which is better than sending an inspector to determine the cause after the fact. It is better to fix the problem quickly and keep the flow moving smoothly.

Pull

The third principle is "pull." Womack and Jones define it as: "A system of cascading production and delivery instructions from downstream to upstream activities in which nothing is produced by the upstream supplier until the downstream customer signals a need."

Pull is the process of aligning production with the needs of the customer. This is done by ensuring that the data needs of the prime are linked to the data systems of suppliers. When data moves directly from the factory floor to suppliers, the suppliers can schedule production to meet the needs of the prime and its customer.

That is what Micky wanted, and just what the program needed. See insert on next page about Lean Process and Product Development.

The Journey to Lean Begins

Lockheed's journey to Lean began in the mid-1980s with Total Quality Management (TQM) as described by Dr. W. Edwards Deming. During that time, Lockheed introduced focused–factories and advanced quality improvements. In the late 1980s, they continued to make improvements by reengineering their business processes. Lean, as described in the sidebar, was initially implemented in the late 1990s on the F-22. Supporters called it the "**Lean Enterprise.**" As mentioned earlier, the Lean Enterprise included 6S, Six Sigma, Enterprise Resource Planning and Lean. It was a catchall phrase to name all the improvements they were making.

One of the reasons to go Lean was to counter the rising cost of producing and supporting the F-22 aircraft. The original plan was to build 750 aircraft, at a total cost of a little over $99 billion.

The biggest cost increase was due to a reduction in the number of aircraft to be built. As the cost per aircraft went up, the number of aircraft to be produced went down. Some of the added costs were driven by new requirements or changed specifications. Other costs were driven using new materials and technologies. The bottom line is that the cost to develop, process, and assemble the parts, equipment, and structures for the F-22 was difficult to predict in advance.

Several "miracles," addressed earlier, were dependent on new technologies.

Lean Process and Product Development (LPPD) is Built on Six Core Principles

1. *People first: Design the innovation system to engage and challenge every individual in your organization to do and be their very best.*
2. *Understand, then execute: deeply understand your customers and their contexts and then experiment to learn and to home in on what your unique value proposition is for that specific customer before you start the detailed development work.*
3. *It's a team sport: engage everyone in the organization, including people from design, engineering, manufacturing, delivery, and installation, to collaborate to maximize value for your customer.*
4. *Synchronize workflows: ensure the coordination and collaboration of all parts of the organization throughout the creation of new products and processes, paying particular attention to handoffs from one function to another.*
5. *Build-in learning and knowledge reuse: promote and celebrate discovery at all development stages and broadly share all data, information, knowledge, and insights gained throughout the value-creation process.*
6. *Create new value streams: a focus on thinking through each step in the innovation process creates value for the customer, including the fulfillment processes of production, delivery, and installation.*

By promoting early consideration for not only what gets made but how it will be made, the LPPD process identifies and addresses potential upstream problems in the design phase, so rework in upstream stages is considerably reduced or eliminated.

Source: Product and Process Development. Adapted from "What is Lean." Lean Enterprise Institute. Accessed on December 4, 2021. https://www.lean.org/WhatsLean/

Composite wings and a stealthy radar are two examples that illustrate the point. They were both necessary for the Raptor to achieve its mission, but they both had to be developed and undergo thorough and expensive testing.

As the program continued, all the players knew it would be expensive, but no one expected the costs to be as high as they were.[3] After several reductions in the number of aircraft, the total cost for 187 Raptors turned out to be $67.3 billion.[4]

Areas of Focus on the F-22

When you ask manufacturing managers to describe Lean manufacturing, they tend to use terms like "teamwork" and "streamlined organizations."[5] In their drive to achieve Lean manufacturing on the F-22, the IPTs focused on four distinct areas: productivity, labor costs, overhead, and material costs. Combined, they created a formula that can be expressed as follows:

Best Customer Value = Reduced man-hours (due to increased productivity) X reduced labor costs X lower overhead and G&A rates + lower material costs.

Lean Manufacturing

The focus of Lean is on cutting waste. This means ending all non-value-adding activities as well as excessive inventory and wait times. It depends on the continuous measurement and improvement of processes, cross-trained and empowered workers, efficient machines and machine layouts, Just In Time (JIT) delivery, preventive maintenance, and integrated relationships with supply chain partners.

Source: James R. Evans and William M. Lindsay. (2005). *The Management and Control of Quality (6th Ed.)* Thompson Southwestern. 496-497.

To achieve its potential, Lockheed needed to make products more affordable. Making products more affordable required major changes in key processes. One of the things Micky used to say was, "Chuck Yeager broke the sound barrier. It's up to us to break the cost barrier." Senior leaders agreed. If they could do what they wanted, it would propel the industry forward.[6]

Reduce Man-hours

Several initiatives were started to reduce man-hours while Micky was the F-22 program manager. Several more were added once he became the Lockheed Martin Aeronautics Sector president. Each of these initiatives is summarized below.

- **Improved teamwork. Good things happen when good people work together, and IPTs helped the company deliver products faster, better, and cheaper.**

  Thinking in terms of survival kept the teams thinking Lean.

- **Improved software and system integration capabilities. Lockheed Martin had achieved a Software Engineering Institute (SEI) Level 3 in software engineering and was pushing hard to get to Level 4. They were proud of their ranking and told their customers – the quality of their software was high and so was their systems integration. Since Lockheed Martin's products were becoming more dependent on software, achieving higher ratings was very important.**

- **Engaged in Single Process Initiatives (SPIs). Lockheed Martin alone was responsible for about 25 percent of all DOD's SPI concept papers submitted and accounted for 40% of the savings realized through these initiatives.**

- **Became ISO 9001 certified. Lockheed Martin's plant in Fort Worth, Texas became the first aerospace facility in the US to become ISO 9001 certified. The Skunk Works in Palmdale, California and Lockheed Martin's plant in Marietta, Georgia subsequently declared their ISO 9001 certification. This was important because the JSF and other programs would use ISO 9001 as their quality standard.**

- **Initiated the use of commercial contracts. Worked with the US Air Force to start using commercial contracts to acquire military systems. The C-130J was the first major system to be acquired in this manner. It was a significant landmark in acquisition reform and senior leaders at Lockheed were proud to be involved. The new contract led to less paperwork and less time negotiating, resulting in higher productivity for everyone involved. As a result, the new C-130Js were being built in half the time it took 10 years earlier.**

- **Implemented enhanced computer-aided design process. Taking CAD/CAM at Lockheed Martin to a new level, they established a strategic alliance with Dassault Systèmes and IBM to jointly develop the next generation of CATIA design processes.**

- Eliminated the need for many physical mock-ups. Lockheed Martin invested heavily in new computer modeling and simulation processes, which they were able to use on the F-22 Raptor. This eliminated the need to build many physical mock-ups to ensure that parts fit the way they were supposed to prior to building the aircraft. These advanced tools are now used on the F-35 (formerly JSF), allowing Lockheed Martin and their partners to model the whole production process.
- Applied Lean Thinking to manufacturing processes. This was one of Lockheed Martin's major attempts to improve productivity. While military airplanes are more sophisticated than most commercial products, local supermarkets were operating more efficiently than some firms in aerospace. When the F-22s first went into production, the tail of the aircraft had to travel seven miles before it rolled off the line. After the process was re-engineered with Lean, the length of the production line was reduced to 100 yards![7]

The Priceless Minds of Production Workers

The minds of experienced production workers are invaluable. They are the key to maintaining quality and an essential source of competitive advantage. True continuous improvement requires the participation of people who have been on the manufacturing floor.

To ensure that workers know the value of their ideas, the following activities can help sustain their cooperation:

- *Robust continuous improvement training*
- *Kaizen suggestion system*
- *Recognition programs*
- *A succession planning process*

Source: Eric Bigelow. 2015. *Continuous Improvement Requires Servant Leadership.* January 20. Accessed September 24, 2018. https://www. Industryweek.com/requires-servant-leadership.

Reduce Labor Costs

The second major variable was to reduce hourly labor costs. Labor rates are generally the same across the industry. Lockheed Martin must pay competitive salaries and wages, but at the same time control costs to ensure their products remain competitive. Like other firms, Lockheed Martin could not afford to pay high rates for people with low skills. If they couldn't afford the rates, such tasks were usually outsourced.

Lower Overhead and G&A Expenses

The third major cost that was minimized in their "Journey to Lean" was to lower overhead costs and general and administrative (G&A) expenses. The following examples describe how this was done.

- Flattened the management structure. This improved communication and helped people focus on their responsibilities.
- Lowered costs of delivering personnel benefits. The costs of delivering benefits were reduced by increasing competition, while simultaneously maintaining the high quality and range of benefits that employees value.
- Reduced personnel costs. By moving indirect personnel to a direct charge, personnel costs were reduced when program managers had to pay for them.

- Reduced taxes and utilities. Negotiated reduced taxes and lower utility rates in the municipalities where they operated.
- Renegotiated food service contracts in company cafeterias and ended up with better food at lower costs.
- Implemented new non-smoking policies. In one of Lockheed's companies, they adjusted policies to not hire people who smoked resulting in lower health costs and higher productivity.
- Reduced real estate costs. Eliminated excess capacity by closing more than 20 facilities.
- Disposed of other assets. Removed outdated equipment and some that were kept "just in case" you might need it. These were removed from the books, making operations leaner, but they also found that by removing these excess machines, they improved the flow through the factory.

Lower Material Costs

The last action in the equation is to "lower material costs." Lockheed Martin lowered material costs by moving to centralized procurement. At Lockheed Martin, this was called the "Aeronautics Materials Management Center." The Center was based in Fort Worth, Texas, and bought everything from office supplies to production materials.

Some of their results:

> **Attack, Attack, Attack**
>
> - *Attack inventory: you don't want to see it and you don't want it in your plant. You just want to know that it will be there when you need it.**
> - *Attack doing it over: time is precious, and resources are expensive. You don't want to do it over; you just want to do it right the first time.*
> - *Attack labor: labor is expensive, and you don't want to waste it. The market is large and competition is strong — that gives us an advantage in teaching them how to do it.***
>
> Sources:
>
> *Luke Johnson. 1994. Blackwell working on surviving. *Marietta Daily Journal*. Marietta, Georgia, February 27. 4B-5B
> **Dwyer Gunn. 2018. What caused the decline of unions in America? *Pacific Standard*. Accessed May 8, 2020, at https://psmag.com/

- Negotiated better deals. Used the scale of the sector to negotiate better deals over longer periods. These longer-term agreements allowed their suppliers to be more consistent in their planning, resulting in a win-win situation for both parties.
- Reviewed and reduced supplier base. Selected the most reliable suppliers to deliver quality products at the best value. In just two years, they reduced the number of suppliers by 28%; from 12,500 to about 9,000.
- Implemented volume pricing to get the lowest cost possible.
- Reduced excess inventory. One of the most insidious material costs is inventory, a natural enemy of Lean. In one situation, they wanted to implement Just in Time (JIT) in work cells, but found that before they could do that, they had to wait months because they had so much inventory.
- Collectively these changes resulted in $400 million in savings over a three-year period, and an additional $100 million each year after that.[8]

Enterprise Resource Planning

With the competition for the JSF fully underway, there was a need to modernize Lockheed Martin's Financial and Manufacturing Systems as well as other Sector-wide processes. They needed to drive down costs by improving efficiency as well as the way they communicated within the Sector and with their industrial partners.

Micky organized an Aeronautics Sector-wide team to determine the approach the Sector should follow. It was decided that a full Enterprise Resource Plan (ERP) should be implemented that would encompass every process in the organization. For each individual system, they wanted the best-in-class. Plus, they wanted all the enterprise systems to be integrated so they could talk to each other. In addition, the new ERP had to support all Lean practices. Finally, Micky wanted a solution that did not require them to keep updating the system with Lockheed Martin money. They wanted other companies to keep the system updated with new code or applications that would seamlessly support the new integrated ERP system.

The sector-wide Aeronautics team selected SAP to provide the new ERP software. Micky appointed Gene Elmore, an engineering executive, to initially lead the new ERP organization. It turned out that Gene, who was well versed in finance and manufacturing systems was the ideal choice.

Lockheed Martin Aeronautics' implementation of an integrated ERP system was the largest in the aerospace industry at that time. The goal was to make the Aeronautics Sector the standard of excellence for ERP in the aerospace industry. The Sector experienced the usual resistance to change, and a few threats and personnel changes were needed to move it along. In general, however, the implementation proceeded quite well. The ERP solution performed as promised and gave them the tools they needed to create a truly Lean enterprise.

Six Sigma

Lockheed saw Six Sigma demonstrated at GE. Six Sigma is a framework for managing the quality of a process or operation. The term is based on a measure that is equal to 3.4 or fewer defects per million, which is another way of saying 99.999 percent of the readings are within specifications. The goal is to ensure that all processes are operating at this level or better. The purpose is to reduce variance and eliminate rework.

Between 1997 and 1999, Lockheed Martin implemented over 100 Six Sigma projects to improve quality on the F-22. What started with five people ended up with 25 full-time employees, exploring manufacturing issues such as fastener flushness variances. After changing the specifications and manufacturing processes, employees reported a 75 percent decline in non-value-added rework compared to the first aircraft.[9, 10]

Kaizen

Like Lean and Six Sigma, "Kaizen is a Lean manufacturing tool that improves quality, productivity, safety, and workplace culture."[11] Kaizen first appeared in Japan after World War II when US consultants were working with the Japanese. The purpose was to improve their manufacturing skills, and their work resulted in a concept called Kaizen.

"Kaizen refers to activities that continuously improve all functions and involve all employees from the CEO to the assembly line workers."[12]

Kaizen's strength comes from workers making suggestions to improve the business. But the purpose of Kaizen goes beyond productivity improvements.

"When done correctly, the process humanizes the workplace, eliminates overly hard work, and teaches people how to spot and eliminate waste in business processes... Although improvements under Kaizen are small and incremental, the process brings about dramatic results over time. Additionally, Kaizen is a low-risk and an inexpensive approach. It involves process improvements that do not require a large capital investment." [13,14]

As a result, the program encourages workers to experiment with new ideas. If Kaizen does not work, the changes can be reversed at relatively low cost.[15]

6S

Another contribution of Lean to business improvement has been a tool that anyone can use to improve work places and work processes. The tool, called 6S, addresses this situation. Most people think of 6S as tool for use with manufacturing, but it is just as applicable in an office environment. The following labels are similar to what was used on the F-22.[16]

- **Sort:** Distinguish between what is necessary and what is unnecessary and dispose of the latter.
- **Stabilize:** Enforce a place for everything and put everything in its place.
- **Shine:** Clean up the workplace and look for ways to keep it clean.
- **Standardize:** Maintain and monitor improvement to the first three Ss.
- **Sustain:** Follow the rules to properly maintain the correct 6S procedure.
- **Safety:** Ensures safety throughout the entire process and eliminate hazards.

As suggested, 6S is about eliminating waste and maximizing value. "To this end, 6S uses its process to create and maintain an organized, clean, safe, and efficient setting that enables the highest level of value-added performance."[17]

Total Quality Management

For those who have not followed the Quality revolution, it can sometimes seem confusing. J. Edwards Deming may have started it with his work in Japan, but when it was finally embraced in the United States, scholars and practitioners continued to build on the foundation Deming started. Today, Lean and Six Sigma can operate on their own, but are often included in a broader set of tools called TQM. Today, TQM includes a broad range of initiatives, which all have a place in improving product and service quality.

Some of the concepts included in TQM included business process redesign or process reengineering; ISO 9000 and related programs; Kaizen; Lean; Six-Sigma; cost-of Quality; Quality function deployment; Statistical Process Control; and the use of flowcharts, control charts, histograms, Pareto diagrams, scatter diagrams, cause and effect diagrams, and other Quality-related tools.[18] All of these techniques are used at Lockheed Martin, but many of them got a boost when Micky implemented Lean and Six Sigma.

Impact of Lean, Six Sigma, Kaizen, 6S, and TQM
On Other Functions and Programs

As these changes started to transform how work was done on the F-22, they also had an impact on other aeronautics programs and functions. Lean and Six Sigma saved time and eliminated rework. In addition to manufacturing, Lean, Six Sigma, Kaizen, 6S, and other Quality programs, made their way into engineering and business functions such as finance, development, procurement, operations, human resources, cash management, and contracting.

Lessons Learned and Important Points

This chapter addressed Lean Enterprise Management. Lessons learned and important points include:

- **When the Lockheed F-22 Team arrived at Pratt & Whitney (P&W), they were shocked by what they saw. The firm had transformed itself and the way they made engines.**
- **Soon after Micky saw what was happening at P&W, he quickly became a fan of the men who had helped the company.**
- **James Womack and Daniel Jones co-authored two books that had a profound impact on Micky: *The Machine That Changed the World* and *Lean Thinking*.**
- **Micky hired a vice president of operations, Mike Joyce, who had worked in Lean at Pratt Whitney, to implement Lean across the entire Lockheed Martin Aeronautics Sector.**
- **Micky sold the idea to Lockheed Martin that by increasing efficiency, they could win more work and would employ more people.**
- **Lean is a way of thinking about creating value with fewer resources and less waste.**
- **The three principles of Lean include *takt time, flow,* and *pull*.**

- One of the reasons to go Lean was to counter the rising cost to produce and support the F-22.
- Major innovations such as Lean Thinking, Enterprise Resource Planning, Six Sigma, 6S, Kaizen, and TQM were implemented throughout Lockheed Martin producing superior value for the company and for its customers.
- Areas of focus on the F-22 included reduced man-hours, reduced labor costs, lower overhead and G&A expenses, and lower material costs.
- Lean and Six Sigma saved time and eliminated rework. As these changes started to transform how work was done on the Raptor, they also had an impact on other programs and functions at Lockheed Martin Aeronautics Sector.

Chapter Notes

1 James "Micky" Blackwell. 2021. *All the Days of Our Lives. The Heritage and History of Billie and James Blackwell*. Asheville, NC: United Writers Press, p. 139.

2 Principles based on material from Womack and Jones. See James P. Womack, and Daniel T. Jones. 2003. *Lean Thinking: Banish Waste and Create Wealth in Your Corporation*. 2nd ed. New York, N.Y.: Free Press.

3 The services had originally planned to buy 750 Air Force F-22s plus 618 Navy ATF versions. The Navy, however, withdrew from the program, citing the expense of NATF, its weight, and schedule delays. Cold War cuts reduced planned Air Force production from 750 to 648 at a cost of $86.6 billion. After further review in 1993, the planned quantity of F- 22s was reduced to 442 at an estimated cost of $71.6 billion. In 2009, the program was cut to 187 aircraft due to high costs, perceived lack of a mission, a ban on exports, and development of the F-35.

4 Brendan McGarry. April 19, 2013. "House Lawmakers Want Air Force to Study Restarting F- 22 Production." *Military.com*. Accessed February 3, 2020. https://www.military.com/daily-news/2016/04/19/house-lawmakers-air-force-study- restarting-f22-production.html

5 Susan Miles. February 10, 1994. "Lean Production's streamlined processes bring increased efficiency to Manufacturing areas." *Lockheed Aeronautical Systems Company Star*, p. 4.

6 Propelling the industry forward, required applying the three principles of Lean. The three principles of Lean are takt time, flow, and pull.

7 Lockheed Martin. 1998. "Lean Thinking is Real Too." *Newsline Daily, Farnborough International*. London, England: Lockheed Martin International, p. 4.

8 Ibid.

9 Stanley W. Kandebo. July 12, 1999. "Lean Thinking Prompts Line Shift for F-22." *Aviation Week & Space Technology*, 51 (2) p. 63.

10 Several years later, Six Sigma is still paying off. By re-examining space allocations, the company was able to reduce costs by over 20%. Six Sigma has also improved the efficiency by reducing water use and carbon emissions by 20%. They have also achieved a 36% decrease in landfill materials, while energy costs have been reduced by another 12 %. Stacy Zell. June 20, 2014. "Lockheed Martin, Six Sigma and Corporate Sustainability." *Six Sigma Daily*. Accessed October 7, 2020. https://www. sixsigmadaily.com/six-sigma-guides-lockheed-martin-sustainability goals/#:~:text=Six%20Sigma%20 Guides%20Lockheed%20Martin%20Toward%20Corp orate%20Sustainability,begun%20applying%20 these%20strategies%20toward%20cor porate%20sustainability%20goals.

11 This section on Kaizen is based on Doanh Do. August 5, 2017. "What is Continuous Improvement (Kaizen)?" *The Lean Way Blog.* Accessed November 20, 2020. https://www.linkedin.com/pulse/what-continuous-improvement-kaizen-doanh-do.

12 Ibid.

13 Ibid.

14 Ibid.

15 Ibid.

16 Based, in part, on Laura McAndrews. 2009. "6S Leads to AMC Success." *U.S. Air Force.* Accessed February 2, 2021. https://www.af.mil/News/Article- Display/Article/120482/6s-leads-to-amc-success/

17 Ibid.

18 For one example of a text that addresses most quality programs, see, James R. Evans and William M. Lindsay. 2005. *The Management and Control of Quality* (6th ed.). Mason, OH: Thompson Southwestern.

Chapter 9

A Servant-Led Business Model for Generating Superior Value

High performance comes from creating as much value as possible...from managing value in a superior fashion.

Tom Copeland, Time Koller, and Jack Murrin
"Valuation: Measuring and Managing the Value of Companies"
McKinsey & Company, Inc.

The previous chapter described how a servant-led organization creates and delivers value through Lean Enterprise Management. In this chapter, a new servant-led business model will be described along with the full range of business activities needed to create a product or service.

In general, **a business model** describes the rationale for how an organization creates and delivers value. The "value chain" is one version of a business model that has been popular in recent years. According to Michael Porter, the creator of the concept, the value chain disaggregates a firm into its Strategically Relevant Activities (SRAs) to understand costs and sources of differentiation.[1]

> *A business model describes the rationale for how an organization creates and delivers value.*

The new model is called the **Servant-Led Business Model** to differentiate it from Porter's "Value Chain." The Servant-Led Business Model also looks at SRAs across the entire enterprise, but it does so in a way that is different than a value chain.

Description of a Servant-Led Business Model

The Servant-Led Business Model is displayed in Figure 15. It shows those activities that an organization carries out to create value for its customers. What is most different from Porter's model are the IPTs ( ) that appear at the top of the figure. The big dot on the left represents the senior Servant Leader/Program Manager. This person is highlighted because he or she is the key to motivating and managing people. The broad white arrow moving to the right from the left symbolizes the value created by the IPTs.

The white and black rows of boxes directly under the IPTs are similar to what Porter calls the firm's primary value creating activities. However, the mix of activities that appear in these rows is different. Similarly, the two rows at the bottom refer to the firm's value creating support activities. However, the way these are managed is also different from what Porter envisioned.

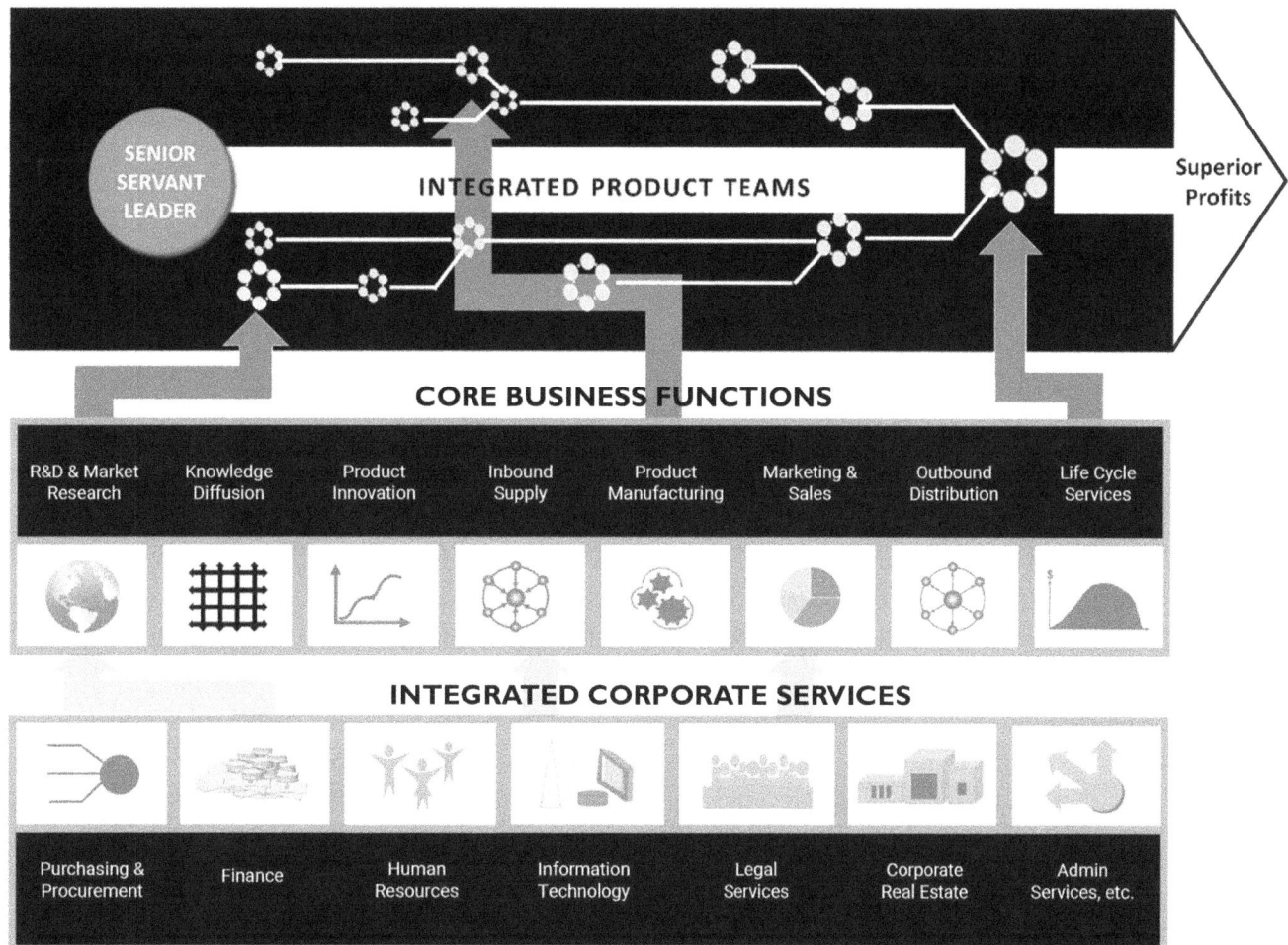

Figure 15. Servant-Led Business Model.

The arrows pointing up from the Core Business Functions indicate that they are providing permanent resources to the IPTs. The arrows pointing up from the Integrated Corporate Services show that resources are being provided to the Core Business Functions on a temporary basis.

Like Porter's value chain, value is created in a servant-led organization by calculating the value of Strategically Relevant Activities (SRAs).* Porter claims that these activities are "the discrete building blocks of competitive advantage.[2] ... A firm gains competitive advantage by performing these strategically important activities more cheaply or better than its competitors.[3] ... When SRAs are calculated, they determine whether a firm is high or low on costs or other features that lead to differentiation or focus.[4] The firm can then be viewed as a collection of interdependent activities, and the way they are linked determines competitive advantage.[5]

In the case of the Servant-led Business Model, the SRAs are located inside the Core Business Functions and Integrated Product Teams. The costs or differentiation associated with the SRAs are based on the people, material, and time associated with building the product or performing a service. The people who are located on an IPT are Team Members from the Core Business Functions who are "hardlined" to their Team Leaders. Having them hardlined to their Team Leaders avoids several

---

* For more information on calculating the value of an SRA inside a value chain, the reader is encouraged to read Michael E. Porter. 1985. *Competitive Advantage: Creating and Sustaining Superior Performance.* New York: NY: The Free Press.

problems. First, it eliminates the problem of having someone reporting to two bosses. Second it eliminates paying for extra overhead which is always an issue. The people from the Core Business Functions assigned to an IPT are relatively permanent, highly responsive, and represent all costs associated with the IPT's operation.

The people in Integrated Corporate Services, on the other hand, are responsive but not permanent. With only a few exceptions, their services tend to be temporary, and their time is charged to overhead.

For example, an IPT needs a software engineer. The program person with the need would first go back to his home organization. If the software function had the person that was needed, they would hardline him or her directly into the IPT. If the functional manager, working on behalf of the IPT, did not have a person who can fulfill the requirement, they would go to Human Resources who would begin a search for a person with the right credentials. Once they find a person, HR would submit his or her resume to the functional head as well as to the program person. In most cases they would agree on the person to be hired, and if the person is suitable, they would be assigned directly to the Integrated Product Team.

It should also be noted that a senior functional manager who is not on a team can provide input on work quality or processes but cannot provide direction to the program itself.

How each activity is performed determines how a firm differentiates itself. Comparing the business models of competitors "exposes differences that determine competitive advantage."[6]

The Servant-Led Business Model consists of value activities and margins. Value activities are those activities a firm performs in designing, manufacturing, and supporting a product. The margins are the difference between revenues and the cost of performing those services.

Collectively, they represent a firm's source of competitive advantage.

Operating Principles

As stated earlier, servant leadership is a philosophy, not a checklist, and it is all about people.[7] Scattered among the IPTs are leaders serving others to make the program work. Such people are critical in a servant-led enterprise and how well they do their jobs makes a big difference.

There are a couple of important principles that guide the relationship between the Core Business Functions, Integrated Corporate Services, and Integrated Product Teams.

- **First, IPTs always work through the functional organizations to obtain the people, tools, and quality control they need.**
- **Second, IPT's rarely independently hire people or build tools themselves. As a result, IPT's have people on their teams that interface back to their functional home to resolve people, tools, and quality problems.**
- **Third, functional people do not in any way manage work on the project. However, senior functional people are often called on to do quality checks or help solve technical problems.**
- **Fourth, people in areas such as legal, finance, administration and IT are assigned to the program as support personnel on an as needed basis.**

Organizational Roles in the Servant-Led Business Model

The three main organizational groupings in the Servant-Led Business Model that generate superior value for the customer are shown in Figure 15. In this section, the role of each of the main organizational groupings will be discussed in detail:

- **Role of Integrated Product Teams.**
- **Role of Core Business Functions.**
- **Role of Integrated Corporate Services.**

Role of Integrated Product Teams in a Servant-Led Business Model

Chapter 7 addressed how IPTs were constructed. This portion discusses how IPTs operate in practice. Prior to the F-22, aircraft were designed along functional lines. If a new landing gear was needed, it was designed by engineers who worked in that function.

When the engineers designed the gear, however, they often did so without knowing what was required to manufacture or support the product. They were good engineers that had just never been trained to think about interdependencies. When the engineers were done, they sent their design to manufacturing. Manufacturing, in turn, produced a plan that may or may not have been manufacturable. The manufacturing plan was then sent to supportability to figure out the best way to support the product. If the people in manufacturing or supportability found a problem, the whole design was sent back to engineering for redesign.

Redesigns are expensive. They take time and cost money. Even after getting approval at each stage in the process, all work could be for naught if costs went over budget. The part would have to be redesigned until it met manufacturing and supportability requirements.

Defense officials knew that costly redesigns had to stop. They also knew that integrated teams were part of the solution. The new solution involved concurrent engineering. Concurrent engineering, coupled with joint decision-making, enabled the teams to move forward with approval from all disciplines.[8] Putting integrated product teams into the EMD proposal, made it mandatory for the F-22. To make it official, the Department of Defense Revised DOD Directive 5000[1] making the new directive requiring IPTs mandatory for all major new weapon systems.

Fortunately, for Lockheed, this gave them a leg up on the competition. Following Kelly Johnson's lead, the Lockheed Skunk Works had already developed a process for meeting multiple requirements simultaneously. Based on their experience, Lockheed proposed that the F-22 teams should be designed using Integrated Product Teams (IPTs).

As head of the F-22 Team Project Office, Micky was responsible for leading the Lockheed-led team in negotiations with the Air Force on the Engineering and Manufacturing Development Contract. The F-22 SPO director at that time was Brig. Gen. James A. Fain, Jr. Fain was told by his superiors to "bring a standard of excellence to military procurement." No more was said. The general knew exactly what they meant.[9]

On August 2, 1991, the Air Force and Lockheed signed a $9.55 billion contract (see Appendix C) for Engineering and Manufacturing Development (EMD). Gen. Fain created a parallel structure within the SPO that mirrored Lockheed Martin's IPT structure. The IPTs were structured to align with the project's Work Breakdown Structure.[10]

> *Creating value is not just about new technologies and processes. Value creation also depends on how teams manage knowledge to create superior products.*

Integrated product team leaders were assigned by F-22 Program Managers. IPT members were assigned by the Core Business Functions. The Core Business Functions were responsible for ensuring that the processes used on the contract were executed correctly and not misused. Once the core functions assigned a person to a project, they no longer had any oversight over that person's work assignments. Finance, legal, administration, and other support functions were matrixed in only when their services were needed.

Lockheed team leaders filled the teams with people from Lockheed, Boeing, General Dynamics, Pratt & Whitney, and their subcontractors. Gen. Fain then assigned one or more people from the SPO to each IPT.[11] The IPTs were structured around the Air Vehicle, Engine, Training System, and Support Systems. Each of these were broken down into sub-IPTS. The Air Vehicle IPT, for example, included the Armaments, Propulsion System, Airframe, Avionics, Cockpit, Utilities and Subsystems, and Vehicle Management System sub-IPTs. Each of the remaining IPTs were broken down into sub-IPTs in a similar manner. In the end, more than 80 IPTs, or sub-IPTs, were involved in the design and manufacture of the aircraft.[12]

One of the things that made an IPT successful was that each IPT was given specific cost, weight, interface, and performance goals for their product. Using the principles of concurrent engineering, each IPT had to recycle their designs until they had met all their requirements. This insured that that they would meet all the cost, schedule, performance, and supportability goals at each level of design before the IPT passed their product to the next level of integration.

Role of Core Business Functions in a Servant-Led Business Model

Value is created though the IPTs with the help of the Core Business Functions. The role of the Core Business Functions is similar to what Porter calls the primary value creating activities.

The term "Core Business Functions" was preferred to "primary activities." He also adjusted what the functions represent. The following pages describe the role of each function in creating value, and why some are different from Porter's thinking on the subject.

The core functions involved with the design and development of an aircraft include research and development, market research, knowledge diffusion, product innovation, product design, product development,

> *Part of what makes servant leadership so effective is the name itself. It doesn't sound authoritative, but hidden behind the name is a leader who cares about people.*

inbound supply chain management, product manufacturing and, occasionally, life cycle services. Each of these core functions are described below.

Engineering R&D and Market Research

For this book, the first function includes two types of research: engineering R&D and market research.

Engineering R&D

R&D engineers develop new products, redesign existing products, and perform research and testing on product concepts.[13] In most corporations, engineering R&D is broken down into (a) basic or applied research and further divided into (b) internal or external research. Basic research is usually driven by scientific curiosity. It is often carried out without testable research objectives. Basic research results in knowledge that may help answer important questions but may or may not be able to solve the problems that are interesting to customers. Applied research, on the other hand, is used to investigate specific questions that could lead directly to the development of new products and sales.

Internal R&D projects are those conducted within the boundaries of the organization. Such projects are usually accomplished using internal funds that have been budgeted for specific reasons. External R&D funds are enormously important to firms that build products for the US Department of Defense. For companies like Lockheed Martin, these funds are necessary for the firm to maintain its competitive edge.

Big questions in R&D include how does the firm know it is investing in the right research topics? Are they using the right techniques to analyze different opportunities? How are they dealing with different levels of risk and uncertainty? Are the new materials or designs reliable, maintainable, and sustainable over the system's life cycle?

Market Research

In many organizations, market research is part of marketing, but there is a reason why it is where it is in the diagram. It was put up front to emphasize the fact that servant leader organizations are known for their creativity and innovation. When communication barriers go down, the number of ideas goes up. Over time, that becomes a sign of a well-run organization.

Market research should be engaged in identifying markets for new products and determining what features, functions, and price will attract the most consumers. The activities in this function involve

> *When communication barriers go down, the number of ideas goes up. Over time, that becomes a sign of a well-run organization.*

collecting and analyzing primary and secondary information on products and services. The scope of services varies greatly, depending on the industry and organization. Market research addresses topics such as the effectiveness of advertising; short and long-term forecasts of demand in different markets; studies on desired features; as well as brand recognition in different countries and regions. Many firms also use market research to collect information on competitors.

Some companies have large staffs and do a lot of research internally, while others hire specialists who do most work externally. For example, some firms may want to conduct in- person or telephone surveys of key customers themselves but outsource the development of surveys to firms that do so on a regular basis. In other situations, companies may hire firms that specialize in specific areas, such as running focus groups on new products in high-tech manufacturing.

Market research can be relatively simple, such as gathering data from newspapers or journals; or extraordinarily complex using multivariate statistics to analyze the results. Some of the information obtained through market research, may also lead to new R&D projects. Key activities in this area include, but are not be limited to, brand awareness, product development, customer satisfaction, and competitive analysis. As ideas are collected and prioritized, they are distributed across the firm using knowledge diffusion procedures.

⊞ Knowledge Diffusion

In 1997, Pinelli, Barclay, Kennedy and Bishop published a book called ***Knowledge Diffusion in the US Aerospace Industry***. The authors acknowledge that knowledge is a source of competitive advantage, and that knowledge management is necessary to compete in today's global economy.[14] The authors then address four different types of knowledge: product-embodied knowledge; process knowledge; systems integration knowledge; and management knowledge. Knowledge in each category can be promoted or controlled according to how it is used. For example, access to product-embodied, process, or systems integration knowledge is often a good reason for entering into joint ventures, licensing, or coproduction agreements. In commercial aviation, such knowledge can often be spun-off and used in other industries as well.[15]

Knowledge diffusion is particularly important in servant-led organizations. That is because knowledge sharing is higher in organizations with lower communication barriers. More ideas are generated and sharing them is important. Finding an artifact that was discovered a decade ago, may be just as important as tracking some little-known, but critical, trend in consumer behavior. That is why knowledge management is important and part of the function. Being able to access knowledge, identify relationships, and test specific hypotheses is an important part of the scientific method.

Not all knowledge diffuses equally, and there are times when an "idea evangelist" may need to be called in. They call all their contacts and use all their networks to do whatever they can do to get their ideas heard.[16]

Unfortunately, some types of knowledge can be used against you. As a result, such property must be closely held and protected. This was the case with the F-22. Despite intense pressure from America's closest allies, the F-22 has always been on the US export control list. This example speaks volumes about the importance of knowledge management and how well-managed knowledge can lead to the next level of innovation.

Product Innovation

Innovation is the offspring of Knowledge Diffusion. The success of the F-22 was dependent on research-led breakthroughs. Solving these breakthroughs led to the design and development of the 5th generation fighter. Some people describe the F-22 in terms of "S" curves. Such curves capture the spirit of why innovation is important (see Figure 16).

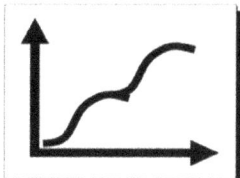

The innovation icon is an attempt to illustrate how the "S" curve works. The lower line in the figure represents the performance of the previous air-superiority fighter, while the upper line represents the performance of the F-22 with all its innovation. No single breakthrough can account for the F-22's performance but putting them all together created the "first look, first shot, first kill" capability. Nunes and Breene point out that "jumping the S-curve requires frequent injections of new blood and a continual shake-up of the top team."[17] This was certainly true with the F-22. At least five managers were given the opportunity to lead through the critical years of design and development, including Micky. The reason both lines drop from the level of peak performance is because of fatigue and increased maintenance as aircraft get older. Both lines can be extended by changes in technology but for the purposes of this book, these curves illustrate what typically occurs.

Figure 16. Innovation icon.

This function ensures that the firm has the right suppliers to support manufacturing. This raises strategic questions about where the firm sources materials that go into production. It also raises questions about the importance of shared trust, the right designs, and a common vision.

Do potential suppliers have the knowledge, experience, and desire to support Lean and Six Sigma? How do they handle Material Requirements Planning? What is the accuracy of their demand forecasts? Is the firm capable of Collaborative Planning, Forecasting, and Replenishment? Do they have the technology, software, and processes that will allow them to seamlessly integrate materials and parts into the manufacturer's systems?

How do they track parts from different sources around the world? What types of inventory models do they use? How do they determine their reorder point and ensure it will align the needs of manufacturing? Do they use the same, or compatible, metrics to evaluate performance? Do they possess any type of Enterprise Resource Planning solution? If inbound suppliers do not have these capabilities, disconnects can occur between suppliers and manufacturers.

Sourcing, demand forecasting, tracking, inventory management, operations planning, material management, capacity planning, continuous improvement, reverse logistics, security, and customer relationship management are all important activities in inbound supply chain management. Reverse logistics refers to the movement and processing of returned goods or damaged parts. Many firms hire third party logistics providers that specialize in this practice to ensure that such items are handled correctly.[18]

⬡ Inbound Supply Chain Management

This function ensures that the firm has the right suppliers to support manufacturing. This raises strategic questions about where the firm sources materials that go into production. It also raises questions about the importance of shared trust, the right designs, and a common vision.

Do potential suppliers have the knowledge, experience, and desire to support Lean and Six Sigma? How do they handle Material Requirements Planning? What is the accuracy of their demand forecasts? Is the firm capable of Collaborative Planning, Forecasting, and Replenishment? Do they have the technology, software, and processes that will allow them to seamlessly integrate materials and parts into the manufacturer's systems?

How do they track parts from different sources around the world? What types of inventory models do they use? How do they determine their reorder point and ensure it will align with the needs of manufacturing? Do they use the same, or compatible, metrics to evaluate performance? Do they possess any type of Enterprise Resource Planning solution? If inbound suppliers do not have these capabilities, disconnects can occur between suppliers and manufacturers.

Sourcing, demand forecasting, tracking, inventory management, operations planning, material management, capacity planning, continuous improvement, reverse logistics, security, and customer relationship management are all important activities in inbound supply chain management. Reverse logistics refers to the movement and processing of returned goods or damaged parts. Many firms hire third party logistics providers that specialize in this practice to ensure that such items are handled correctly.

⬡ Product Manufacturing

Aircraft manufacturing is a major driver of the US economy, so economists and business leaders are concerned about wages and employment. Both commercial and military aircraft depend on state-of-the-art manufacturing and all manufacturers are searching for new ways to improve production. A knowledge-based company like Lockheed Martin is always seeking new and innovative materials. Today, Lockheed Martin's areas of focus include additive manufacturing, next-generation electronics, advanced polymers, nanomaterials, composites, and lightweight metals as well as others.

People in manufacturing know that one of the best ways to boost productivity is to have accurate demand planning. Accurate demand planning allows managers to develop good designs and apply Lean manufacturing to produce aircraft efficiently. Processes must be updated and enabled with technology, and manufacturing software must be linked to the firm's customers and suppliers.

Being world class in the aerospace industry today, means having the right resources when and where needed. Building such capabilities, however, is capital intensive. This often means betting the future of the company on one or two products that meet customer demand. This was the case with the ATF. Lockheed bet its future on the F-22 Raptor.

Key activities in aircraft production include, but are not limited to, design, development, testing, lean assembly, lean manufacturing, systems integration, quality assurance, and other activities intended to increase connectivity across multinational clusters. Many of these rely on computer-aided design, manufacturing, and simulation software to provide executives with the tools they need to make more effective decisions. Self-diagnostics, software agents, and various levels of artificial intelligence are increasingly being used in advanced aircraft manufacturing. Maintenance, Repair, and Overhaul (MRO) are also included in this function.

Marketing and Sales

This function develops plans for marketing and selling the product. Such plans should be aligned with the company's mission and vision and ensure strategies are in-place with measurable objectives. Each objective, in turn, must have milestones and budgets for which someone is accountable.

In addition to gathering information about trends in target markets, marketing collects and analyzes data on the marketing mix for the product: i.e., product features and functions; pricing alternatives; packaging and promotion; as well as thoughts about how the product should be distributed.

Plans for handling customer returns are also important, as is customer satisfaction, which must be routinely captured and tracked. Unexpected deviations should immediately be corrected. Good customers will tell you when sales are improving; your best customers will tell you why sales are declining.

International markets are a good way of extending a product's lifecycle. This is often done for pre-owned or leased military and commercial aircraft. As mentioned previously, this was not possible for the F-22, due to the sensitive nature of its extraordinary capabilities.

Outbound Distribution Management

Being a reliable and efficient distributor can be a challenging task. Like inbound supply management, linking production schedules to those of the customer, coupled with modern tracking technologies, adjustments to demands can be made faster and cheaper.

In addition to having the right tracking capabilities, the firm must establish a reliable transportation network. The best modes of transportation should be selected for the markets it serves and distribution centers should be located to optimize order fulfillment. The firm should consider whether to manage distribution itself or consider using third party logistics (3PL) providers that have already invested in many of these capabilities. The firm should also consider the value of reverse logistics and how it should handle this less visible, but important, part of the distribution function.

Key activities include, but are not limited to, determining the best location for a strategic distribution center, forms and modes of transportation, regulatory compliance, security, pricing, customer relations, performance management, and maintaining technologies that anticipate customer demands.

Life Cycle Services

This category can include a wide number of services from scheduled and unscheduled maintenance to the return and disposal of hard-to-get-rid-of items. Parts supply, manuals, maintenance training, and other services can also be included.

Although it is often overlooked as a significant source of revenue, for products that break frequently or need routine maintenance, reverse logistics can be a nice stream of revenue for the original equipment manufacturer (OEM) or others.

Role of Integrated Corporate Services in a Servant-Led Business Model

As used in this book, the term Integrated Corporate Services generally includes what Porter calls the firm's support activities. Typically, these include procurement, human resources, information technology, corporate real estate, finance, legal, administrative support, and other non-core activities. In many firms, there is a trend toward managing these in a more integrated fashion to minimize costs for a project or organization. Many labels have been tried, but most people call it Integrated Corporate Infrastructure Management (ICIM) or Integrated Resource and Infrastructure Solutions (IRIS). Over a number of years, a nonprofit studied this topic. At the

> *Although it is often overlooked as a significant source of revenue, for products that break frequently or need routine maintenance...reverse logistics can be a nice stream of revenue for the OEM or others.*

end of their research, they reported that several firms were trying to optimize the way they managed their infrastructure resources.[19] In their opinion, a more systems-oriented approach may lead to a smaller, more efficient, and better-balanced footprint in many organizations.

When applied to a program as complex as an airplane, the impact on resources can be relatively substantial. Consider the following examples. When new technology is combined with process reengineering, many firms claim a 30 to 40 percent savings. These savings provide firms with the option to do the same with less cost or increase output holding the factors of production constant. Similarly,

> *A more systems-oriented approach...may lead to a smaller, more efficient, and better-balanced footprint in many organizations.*

technology is changing the footprint of firms. Large factories and multiple warehouses are being replaced with strategically located distribution centers. When new machinery is combined with lean manufacturing, inventory goes down when finished products match demand. This means less people, equipment, real estate, and insurance.

And then there is the workplace. Leading architectural firms have teamed up with progressive furniture makers to redefine the workplace and how, when, and where people work. When services are tailored to meet the demands of an integrated team, costs go down and customer satisfaction goes up.

Purchasing and Procurement

Purchasing and procurement are often used interchangeably, However, procurement generally deals with the sourcing and selection of products and purchasing refers to how goods and services are ordered and paid for.

Procurement is more strategic and should reflect the needs of the company. In many cases it involves setting goals, attending trade shows, identifying foreign and domestic sources, selecting and evaluating vendors, creating and negotiating contracts, and defining terms of payment. It also involves selecting software, defining workflows, and maintaining standards of quality.

Purchasing is a subset of procurement. It is more operational and involves day-to-day buying, receiving, recording invoices, and paying for goods and services.

Finance

The finance function is an important management responsibility that deals with the procurement and administration of funds and achieving the firm's objectives.[20] People on IPTs should understand the need for financing and the role of the financial manager in dealing with markets and issues.

They should understand design-to-cost issues and that 60-70 percent of a product's life cycle costs are committed based on decisions made during concept development.[21] They should know how to calculate the present value of a stream of earnings, and make wise investments based on net present value. They should understand the cost of capital and the rate of return on investments. They also need to understand the basics of portfolio selection. Capital budgeting is important and managing risk is necessary; diversification can help but is not always sufficient.

Understanding how cost overruns can jeopardize a program is imperative. Using financial ratios to prevent them is even better. Decision trees can help determine what happens to investments under different conditions. Using real options to make decisions when risk and uncertainty are present, can change the decision about whether to invest or not.

Common activities in managing a company's finances include knowing how to use cash and working capital, as well as how to lend or borrow money if necessary. Choosing between investments when resources are limited is common but knowing the cost of capital and using financial ratios can be helpful. Some knowledge of international finance is often expected, and financial planning is essential to grow and manage the business. All these topics, and more, are important. People should know where to go if they need financial assistance.

Human Resources

For large programs like the F-22, Human Resources (HR) must confirm there are funds in the budget to support people's training. HR should update its team profiles and have job descriptions ready for the positions it is trying to fill. HR should develop training for all team members and ensure that the training aligns with the vision the teams are pursuing.

Does HR have metrics to ensure they are meeting their functional objectives? HR activities include teaching employees about the company's mission, vision, and values. Company policies on compensation, savings, retirement, and other benefits are also important. Other topics include career planning, project management, performance reviews and labor laws. For people employed internationally, training on how to do business overseas and the Foreign Corrupt Practices Act are also important. If training will be outsourced, who will do the training? When and where will it be done?

For people that work on projects like the F-22, teamwork and collaboration are also at the top of the list. It is also important to note that HR fills positions in core functions, not projects involving IPTs. Training people about servant leadership is also important. Helping staff the program with high quality people is always commendable and can help the firm become the "best of the best."

Information Technology

How does the firm know if teams have the technology they need? Do they understand the role of technology in business process reengineering? Are the systems in-place to support the firm's work-at-home people? Does the firm have published policies that explain work-at-home expectations? Is IT training available for those who need it? Do people understand how technology can help reduce the cost-of-quality? What about data protection and cyber- security? How is data backed up and does the firm have remote servers that are protected against viruses and hacking? Does IT use any type of benchmarking? If so, who does it, how often, and what types of benchmarks are being used?

Common IT responsibilities include defining the firm's IT architecture, hardware, software, and networks. Ordering, programming, deploying, and upgrading computers are also important.

Managing the firm's website, employee training, preventive maintenance, and technical support are all part of IT services in large organizations.

Legal Services

Each firm is different and so are their supporting infrastructures. Some firms have their own legal department, while others choose to outsource their legal needs to teams of outside providers. Both approaches have their pro and cons. They way each firm operates depends on its experience, preferences, and culture.

Corporate Real Estate

How does the firm know they have optimized their real estate and facilities portfolio? What is the firm doing to maximize the value of its real estate in a networked world? How are employees reacting to the furniture and workspace that were intended to improve productivity? Are the firm's facilities designed to support Lean? If the firm recognizes the strategic role of real estate, what metrics should be used to measure its performance? What tools are used to track and run real estate operations? Does the firm have the right people managing its real estate and facilities portfolio? Or should they outsource the management to one or more of their service-provider partners?

Activities that are common in corporate real estate management include leasing, buying, or disposing of property. Other roles involve site selection, workplace design, facility management, and managing service providers. More recent activities include the integrated management of human resources, corporate real estate, information technology, and other services to meet the needs of the Business Units and IPTs.

Administrative Services and Other Needs

Some companies choose to build large administrative offices, while others choose to hire a professional employer organization (PEO). The same is true for other corporate services.

After putting these components together, i.e., the IPTs, the Core Business Functions, and Integrated Corporate Services, Micky had the answer he was looking for—a business model for generating superior value.

Building and Implementing a Servant-Led Business Model

The process for creating a Servant-Led Business Model can be broken down into six steps:

Step 1: Identify the Firm's Best Customers

The first step involves identifying the firm's best customers—this is where superior value comes from, i.e., recognizing and supporting the firm's best customers. People need to focus on the right customers and new prospects. A Pareto analysis can help find the most profitable customers. The firm should then endeavor to learn everything it can about these people— including why they purchase from you and why they do it so frequently. An effort should also be made to detect any features that make their purchase unique.

Once you know who your best customers are, ask them what they would like to see improved. Once you know what they would like to see improved, develop and implement strategies to make the changes happen. Then focus your marketing on attracting more new customers. These actions will lead to more revenue and superior profits.[22]

Step 2: Build the Servant-Led Business Model

The second step involves building a servant-led business model. Value, according to Michael Porter, "is the amount buyers are willing to pay for what a firm provides them."[23] The step involves defining what should be included in the servant-led business model. This may involve going through each item in Chapters 5 through 9 of this book.

In addition to being the prime motivator on the overall team, in a servant-led organization, value generation usually begins with the senior servant leader. This is where new ideas enter the system. The servant leader directs the diffusion of new ideas into the program and many of these ideas lead to innovative products and services.

In a 2007 article in the *Harvard Business Review*, Hansen and Birkinshaw describe "The Innovation Value Chain."[24] Not surprisingly, the process starts with new idea generation. Some of these ideas are converted into innovative products. Innovative products are then diffused throughout the organization. Idea generation, conversion, and diffusion levels may vary with each product, but can all be adjusted to support what is appropriate for the organization. These are almost identical to the first three steps in the Servant-Led Business Model, which prepares them for determining what level of support will be required from each Core Business Function throughout the business cycle.

At the same time the IPTs consider what will be required from the Core Business Functions, the teams should be considering what level of temporary support will be required from Integrated Corporate Services. With the teams fully supported, the team leaders should ensure that their teams are ready to go. The teams use concurrent engineering to make all decisions and ensure that all disciplines are represented on the IPTs. A product cannot move forward unless all IPT members have signed off on the project, and a project cannot be signed off without a 2-level, team leader and team member, value check.

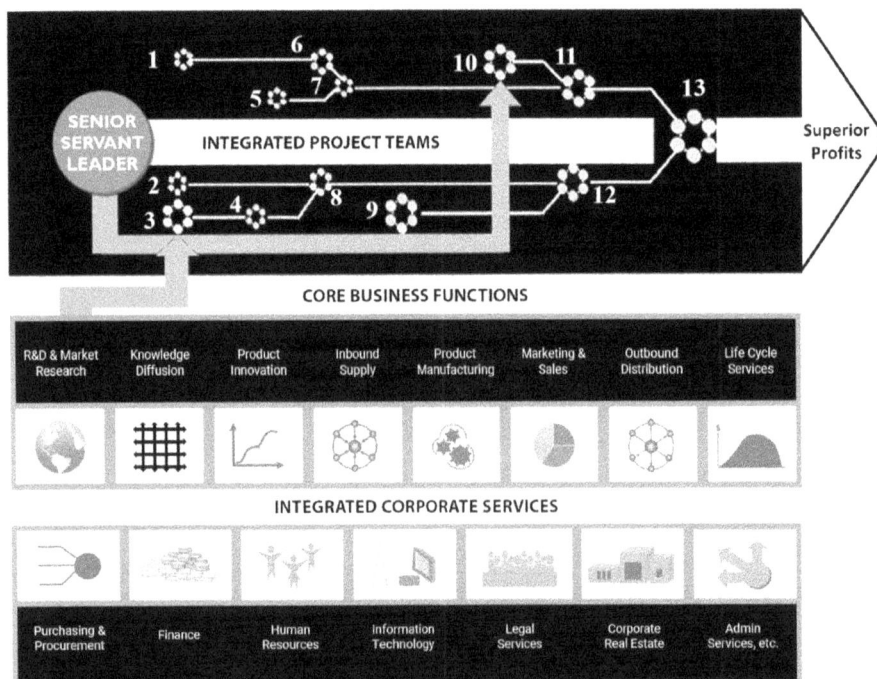

Figure 17. Define the Business Model for a New Business Opportunity.

The numbers appearing next to each IPT in Figure 17 indicate the number associated with that IPT. In short, value planning reviews the role and purpose of each IPT and how it adds value to the product. It also deepens our understanding of the risks that may impact a project and can be useful for highlighting a manager's strategies for meeting his or her objectives.

Figure 17 represents an image of a generic Value Planner. Once the needs are known, Step 3 involves conducting a capabilities assessment. These are triggered by some event such as the need to hire a new IPT Leader or the need to replace a member of a Core Business Function. It is well known that using a good capabilities assessment can substantially increase the probability of your employing more competent people. The following section describes how these assessments are used.

Step 3: Conduct a Capabilities Assessment

The purpose of assessments is to identify gaps in critical positions. Good leaders already know who is strong and who is weak but going through the process can be useful and has other benefits.[25] Porter talks extensively about Strategically Relevant Activitiess. In Figure 18, SRAs exist in an IPT and a Core Business Function.

Naming the SRAs requires knowledge of how they create value. Porter reminds us that whatever labels are chosen should provide insight into the business.[26] SRAs for the Core Business Function, Market Research, IPT 3, for example, might include brand awareness, new product development, customer satisfaction, and competitive analysis.

SRAs for a Team Leader Assessment might include making sure that the team includes all relevant stakeholders, and that all stakeholders agree to the final

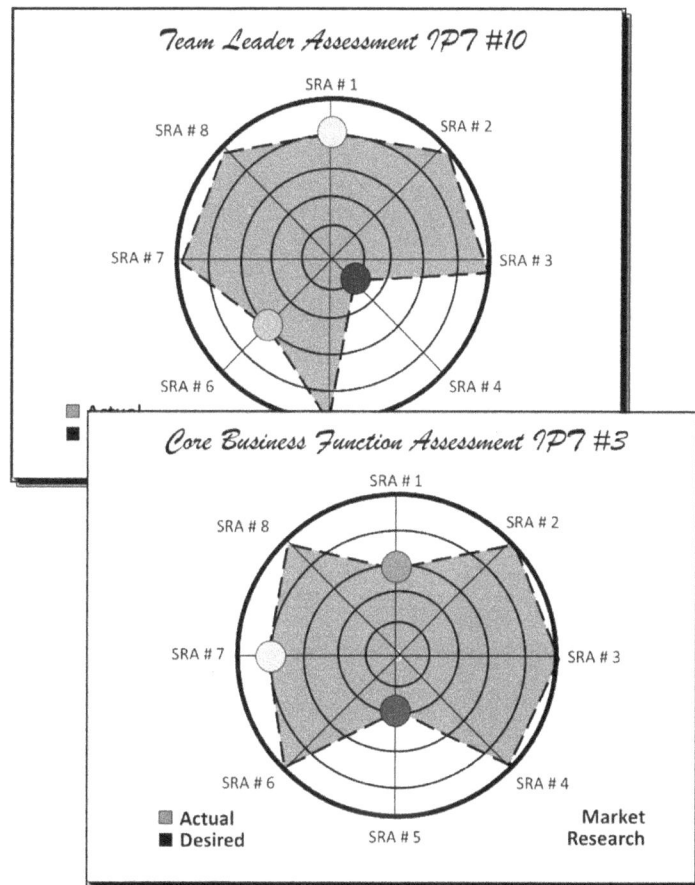

Figure 18. Conduct a Capabilities Assessment.

design. The Leader must also be sure that everyone has a common vision, and that the product is more important than someone's personal agenda. Finally, IPT Leaders should be certain that team members support one another and want to win at all costs. As can be seen in Figure 18, activities can be ranked in order of importance by gap. On the Team Leader Assessment for IPT 10, SRA #4 is ranked more important than SRA #6 or activity #1.

On the Core Business Function Assessment for Market Research for IPT 3, SRA #5 is more important than SRA #1 or SRA #7. All other SRAs meet the desired level of performance.

These assessments require two rating levels—an operational level (Core Business Function), and a more strategic level (Team Leader). Capability assessments must be developed for each Core Business Function. An assessment must also be developed for every IPT. Business Function assessments are reviewed by their respective Team Leaders. Team Leader assessments are reviewed by the Program Manager.

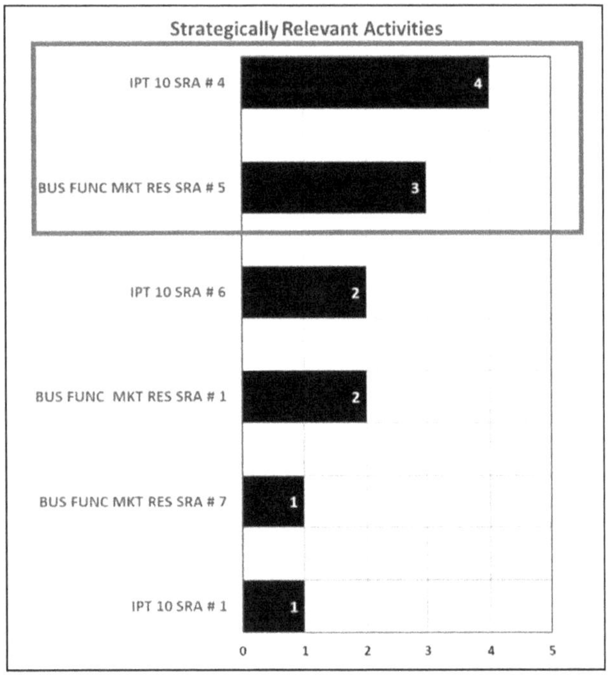

Figure 19. Prioritize the Gaps.

Step 4: Prioritize the Gaps

This step deals with prioritizing the gaps and determining what type of training would serve employees the best (see Figure 19). In this case, the greatest gap appears in IPT 10 SRA #4. A high-level gap also appears in IPT 3 Core Business Function for Marketing Research SRA #5.

These results suggest that team members in Market Research and IPTs should receive remedial training in those strategic areas that indicate a need for improvement. For people that need training, the buck stops here. They are returned to their teams, after training, to continue to develop the product.

For teams that are recruiting new members, the assessments can be used to build job descriptions if necessary. Each SRA represents a distinct knowledge activity for a position in a Core Business Function or an IPT.

The box at the top of Figure 19 indicates that the program has the resources to train people for two SRAs: IPT 10 SRA # 4 and IPT 3 Core Business Function Market Research SRA # 5. Each of these can be broken down into more detail if necessary.

Step 5: Select and Place People

For teams that are recruiting, the next step involves selecting and placing the people where they can create the most value. In the situation shown in Figure 20, two people with experience or an interest in servant leadership would be selected based on the best match of their backgrounds with the needs in the assessments.

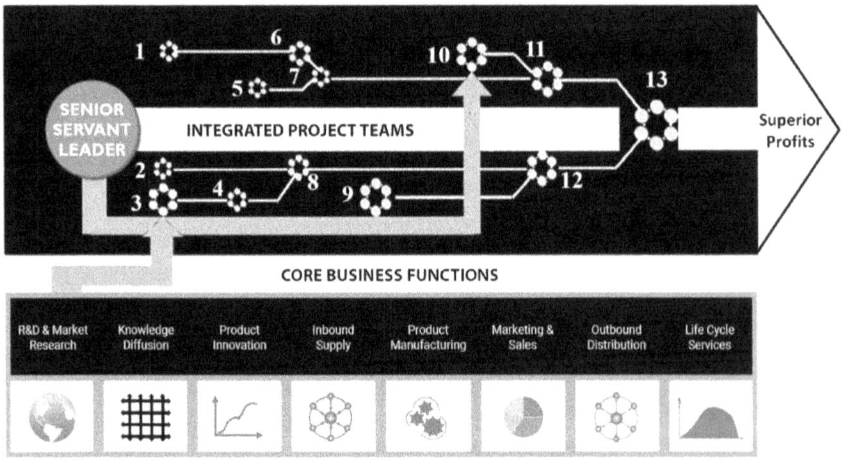

The light grey line between the Senior Servant Lader and IPT 10 indicates that a Team Leader was selected and placed on a team by the

Figure 20. Select and Place People.

overall program manager. The light grey line flowing between Market Research and IPT 3, indicates the selection and placement of a member from the Market Research Core Business Function.

Step 6: Add Value for Stakeholders

Value creation takes place in Step 6, when the teams find ways to reduce costs, differentiate the product, or achieve some type of cost or differentiation focus (see Figure 21):

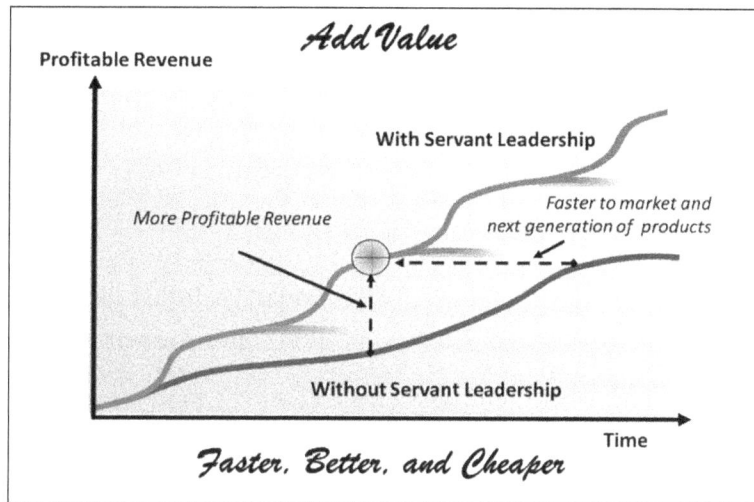

Figure 21. Add Value for Stakeholders.

- **Cost leadership refers to a set of policies that are directed at reducing costs.**
- **Differentiation occurs when something unique and valuable is added.**
- **Cost or differentiation focus represents some combination of the two directed at a particular strategic target.**[27]

Regardless of where the breakthrough occurs, the key to creating value lies in how to motivate people. Assuming the appropriate systems and processes have been installed, and that the resources are available when and where needed, the idea of putting servant leaders in key positions has profound implications on the probability of success for all IPTs and the overall program.

The level of value generated depends on the leader's knowledge, personality, and leadership skills; plus, the number of servant leaders participating on IPTs. As a result, more motivated people managing more strategic activities have the potential to create more profitable revenue than a single leader on a small project.

For Micky, the impact of this revelation was like discovering the keys to the universe. What better way to ensure success than by building servant leaders into IPTs? The amount of value generated by doing this depends on where and when servant leaders are added. Micky quickly discerned that creating value through servant leaders on IPTs, was like other design principles—hire or train as many servant leaders as you can and put them into key positions as early as possible.[28] For the F-22, the result was better performance, lower costs, and higher margins throughout the program.

Three Reasons Why Servant Leaders Will Always Outperform Others

Programs managed by Servant Leaders will always outperform others. The reasons are straight forward and should not be surprising.

- *The first reason is because people enjoy working in a Servant Leader environment. They know they are respected and like being nurtured. People want to be part of it—it is part of who they are.*
- *The second reason is because they like to be part of a winning team. Teams become winners when they share new ideas.*
- *The third reason is because people like knowing they are not working alone. They know they are part of a team that will never let them down. They also know that someone higher up is looking after them. Some call it luck. Some call it providence.*

Lessons Learned and Important Points

This chapter addresses how to create a servant-led business model utilizing integrated product teams, core business functions, and integrated corporate services. Points to remember include:

- Value is created in a servant-led organization by calculating the value of Strategically Relevant Activities (SRAs).
- A new paradigm called the "Servant-Led Business Model" was developed to promote teamwork around small IPTs which included the customer.
- IPTs work successfully and can eliminate rework. Every requirement is met and approved at the lowest level.
- IPTs should be formed as early as possible. Solving problems early minimizes design costs and leads to lower life cycle costs. Delays create uncertainty and, almost always, higher costs.
- Training is important. The F-22 was the first to implement IPTs, so employees had to learn how to make them work.
- Servant leadership creates a culture that makes IPTs work. IPTs work best when they exist in a culture of innovation.
- The role of IPTs is an important one. Redesigns are expensive, and they take time and cost money. Even after getting approval at each step in the process, all work could be for nothing if the cost is over budget.
- Knowledge diffusion is an important part of knowing how the process works. Ideas are passed to the IPTs which discard them or use them.
- Concurrent engineering requires teams to look at problems from a higher level, resulting in new ways to solve problems by servant-led teams.
- Core Business Functions supply IPTs with personnel and systems.
- Integrated Corporate Services supply Core Business Functions, on an as needed basis.
- The Servant-Led Business Model generates superior value for the customer.

Chapter Notes

1 Michael E. Porter. 1985. *Competitive Advantage: Creating and Sustaining Superior Performance.* New York: The Free Press. p. 33.

2 Ibid, p. 38.

3 Ibid, pp. 33-34.

4 Ibid, pp. 38-39.

5 Ibid, p. 48.

6 Ibid, p. 39.

7 Sameer Dholakia. May 24, 2018. *Servant Leadership Is a Philosophy, Not a Checklist.* Accessed May 28, 2018. https://www.entrepreneur.com/article/313475.

8 Gary F. Wagner and Randall White. 1993. *An Investigation of Integrated Product Development Teams on the F-22 Program.* Wright-Patterson Air Force Base, Ohio: Air Force Institute of Technology, pp. 1-2.

9 Stephanie Lopez. 1994. *An Investigation of Integrated Product Development: A Case Study of an F-22 Prime Contractor.* Wright-Patterson Air Force Base, Ohio: Air Force Institute of Technology, pp. 8-9.

10 A Work Breakdown Structure (WBS) is tool used in Project Management. It is developed to establish a common understanding of a project's scope. "It is a hierarchical description of the work that must be done to complete the deliverables of a project. Each descending level in the WBS represents an increasingly detailed description of the project deliverables," and all "deliverables must be identified, estimated, scheduled, and budgeted." See Visual Paradigm. "What is Work Breakdown Structure?" Accessed August 1, 2021. https://www.visual-paradigm.com/guide/project-management/what-is- work-breakdownstructure/#:~:text=What%20is%20Work%20Breakdown%20Structure%3F%201%20Work%20 Breakdown,5%20Other%20Use%20Cases%20of%20Breakdown%20Structure.%20

11 James "Micky" Blackwell. 2021. *All the Days of Our Lives. The Heritage and History of Billie and James Blackwell.* Asheville, North Carolina: United Writers Press, p. 120.

12 Global Security.org, n.d. *F-22 Raptor Contractors.* Accessed August 18, 2019. https://www.globalsecurity.org/military/systems/aircraft/f-22-contract.htm

13 "R&D Engineer Job Description." Job Hero. Accessed June 21, 2021. https://www.jobhero.com/job-description/examples/engineering/r-d-engineer#:~:text=R%26D%20Engineer%20Job%20 Description%20R%26D%20engineers% 2C%20or%20research,and%20perform%20research%20and%20 testing%20on%20product%20concepts.

14 Thomas E. Pinelli, Rebecca O. Barclay, John M. Kennedy, and Ann P. Bishop. 1997. *Knowledge Diffusion in the U.S. Aerospace Industry: Managing Knowledge for Competitive Advantage.* Greenwich, Conn.: Ablex Publishing Company, p. xi.

15 Ibid, 24-29.

16 Morton T. Hansen and Julian Birkinshaw. June, 2007. "The Innovation Value Chain." Boston, MA: *Harvard Business Review*, (85) 6, p. 128.

17 Paul Nunes and Tom Breene. January-February 2011. "Reinvent Your Business Before It's Too Late." Boston, MA: *Harvard Business Review*, (89) 1/2, pp. 80-87.

18 Joel D. Wisner, Keah-Choon Tan, and G. Keong Leong. 2012. *Principles of Supply Chain Management: A Balanced Approach. 3rd ed.* Mason, Ohio: South-Western Cengage Learning, pp. 336-337.

19 Karen Ellzey and Steve Valenziano. 2004. *Corporate Real Estate 2010: Integrated Resource and Infrastructure Solutions.* Atlanta, Georgia: CoreNet Global.

20 "Managing the Finance Function in Engineering." *Course Hero.* Accessed June 21, 2021. https://www.coursehero.com/file/97642722/MANAGING-THE-FINANCE-FUNCTION-IN- ENGINEERING-1docx/

21 "Achieving Design-to-Cost Objectives." n.d. *NPD Solutions.* Accessed June 21, 2021. https://www.npd-solutions.com/dtc.html#:~:text=A%20design%20to%20cost%20approach%20consists%2 0of%20 the,development%20budgets%20and%20target%20costs%3B%20More%20item s...%20

22 Elizabeth Harris. n.d. "4 Steps to Profitable Revenue Growth." *Resultist Consulting.* Accessed November 30, 2019. https://www.resultist.com/blog/bid/256549/4-Steps-to-Profitable- Revenue-Growth

23 Michael Porter. n.d. *The Value Chain from Competitive Advantage.* Accessed January 10, 2021. http://people.tamu.edu/~v-buenger/466/Value_Chain.pdf, 1.

24 Morton T. Hansen and Julian Birkinshaw. June 2007. *The Innovation Value Chain*, pp. 121-130.

25 For example, a weak assessment can be used to remove or replace a manager. They can also be helpful when a new person is assigned to lead an activity.

26 Michael E. Porter. 1980. *Competitive Strategy*, pp. 34-41.

27 Ibid.

28 Blanchard addresses this when he talks about "including life-cycle considerations in the decision-making process from the beginning is critical" and the greatest impact on life-cycle cost..."can be realized during the early phases of system design and development." Benjamin S. Blanchard. 2004. *Logistics Engineering and Management (6th ed.).* Upper Saddle River, New Jersey: Pearson Prentice Hall, pp. 24-26.

Chapter 10
Putting it all Together:
The Enterprise Servant Leadership Management Model

Programs like the F-22 don't just happen. They are fed by the fertile minds of employees working together.

Micky Blackwell
President & COO, Aeronautics Sector (Retired)
Lockheed Martin Corporation

In the Introduction, it was stated that the purpose of a "management model" was to summarize the behavior demonstrated by managers. In this chapter, we will describe a new management model that evolved on the F-22 Raptor program in response to the need to produce the best aircraft possible, reduce program costs, and create an enjoyable work environment.

This new management model is called the **Enterprise Servant Leadership Management Model** (ESLMM). The ESLMM summarizes the behavior of the F-22 management as they sought to successfully complete the F-22 EMD contract with a new management approach, new development tools, and new processes.

The major elements of the Enterprise Servant Leadership Management Model consist of the management actions described in Figure 22. To appreciate how the model produces increased value, each of the elements in the model will be described. The discussion includes the ten management actions "Lead by Example" through "Continuous Feedback" which are connected by the solid line in Figure 22. We will conclude by talking about the element "Inspire and Pray," which is represented by the dotted line surrounding all the other elements of the Enterprise Servant Leadership Management Model.

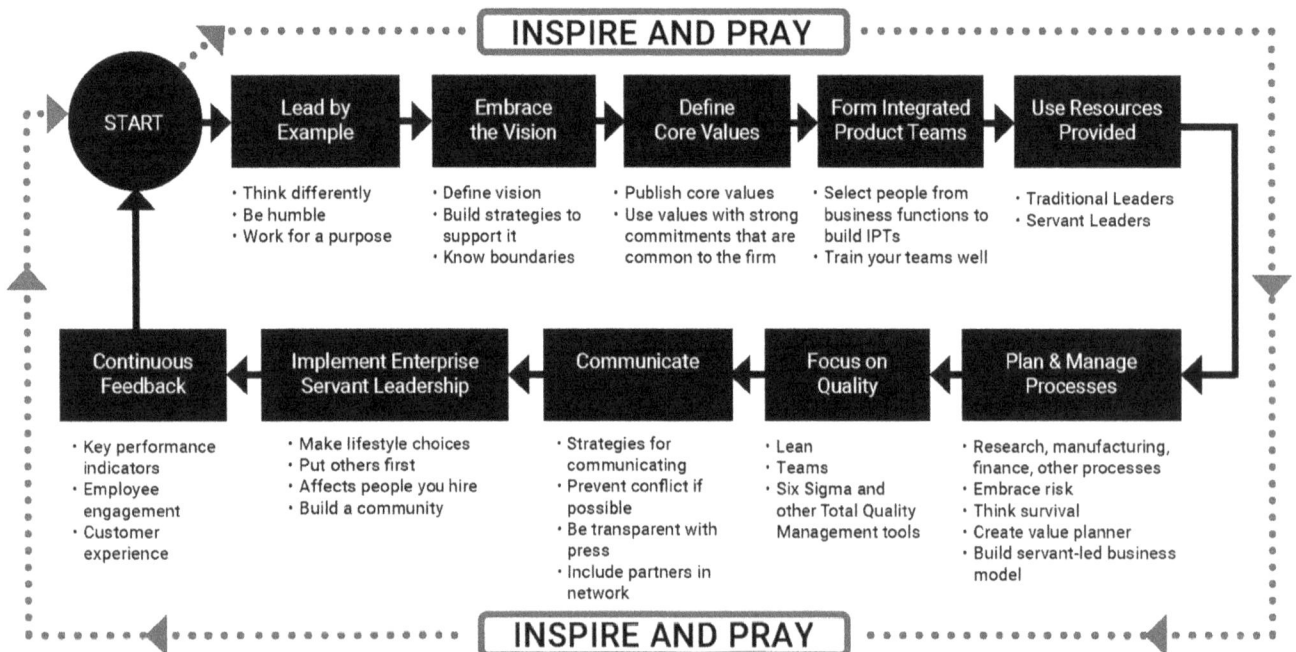

Figure 22. The Elements of the Enterprise Servant Leadership Management Model.

Lead by Example

Think Differently

Servant leaders possess a mindset that is unique. Because they think differently, they often lead by example. They are humble, authentic, and concerned about the needs of people. They break down barriers to foster new ideas. New ideas lead to new products, and new products lead to new sales.

Be Humble

Steven Covey, in his management books, reminds us that "sacrifice is the essence of moral authority, and humility is the foundational attribute of sacrifice."[1] Covey continues by stating, "Power and moral supremacy emerge from humility, where the greatest becomes the servant of all."[2] Indeed, "humility binds leaders and followers together."[3] Paul tells us to associate with the humble (Romans 12:16).

> *Do not set your mind on high things, but associate with the humble.*
> Romans 12:16 (NKJV)

Work for a Purpose

Leading by example includes working for a purpose. Working for a purpose is what motivates people. Purpose-driven people result in higher levels of retention. As stated by management experts Jennings and Hyde, "An organization aligned, individual-by-individual and team-by-team, to a shared Greater Goal is one of the most powerful for good on the earth."[4] As servant leaders, we should work with a purpose for good not only for ourselves but for our entire team (1 Corinthians 10:24).

> *Let no one seek his own good, but the good of his neighbor.*
> 1 Corinthians 10:24 (EVS)

Embrace Vision and Strategies

Define the Vision

For people like Micky, the vison for the F-22 was already well established. His job was to embrace it and move the ball forward. For all other program managers, the job is to define and embrace the vision. The vision provides the framework for making plans and commitments. By creating a compelling vision and enabling the right culture, ideas will spring forth that will lead to the right plans and resources. If there had not been a vision for the F-22, the program would not have been successful (Proverbs 29:18).

> *Where there is no vision, the people perish.*
> Proverbs 29:18 (KJV)

Develop Your Plans

Plans and commitments must be made to achieve and enhance the vision. Some may be long-term, others may be short-term, but all managers must have the flexibility to respond to changes in requirements. Furthermore, business plans will not be achieved "without sharing the load and responsibility."[5] Servant leaders are enablers. That is part of their work.

Build Strategies and Goals to Support Each Plan

Strategies should be built to support each plan. Each plan should have goals that are specific, measurable, and relevant. Milestones should be developed so their progress can be tracked.[6] Interdependencies should be analyzed so there are no surprises.

Know the Business of the Business

Kelly Johnson's 14 Rules (see Appendix B) helped set the boundaries for building military aircraft (and almost everything else) is a good example of what happens when a company knows and follows what it does best. By specifying how teams were to operate, he reduced regulations and red tape. He also set expectations on timelines for manufacturing the product.

Define Your Core Values

Importance of Core Values

Many people don't realize the importance of core values. The reason they are important is because they "set the company apart."[7] As defined earlier in the book, they are "the deeply ingrained principles that guide all of a company's actions."[8] Core values impact the culture, and the culture impacts the productivity, creativity, and growth of the firm.[9] Hence, it is important for them to be known, published, and established.

Having core values can:

- **Educate customers who don't know what you stand for.**
- **Remind employees of who they are and what they stand for.**
- **Sustain values that are authentic and important to the enterprise.**
- **Improve decision-making by using values that are common to the firm.**
- **Make better decisions when investments are not quantifiable.**

Be Strong in Your Convictions

Having a strong vision with the conviction to get things done, helps overcome obstacles with the energy to make them happen.[10] Servant leaders use ethics driven by Christian principles to guide their choices and core values to determine what is right. Ethics exist when you do the right thing when no one is looking.[11] Ethical people trust their morals and are open to new ideas.

As stated by Maria Connolly in a recent webpost, when you're strongly convinced that what you say and do matters, "your energy shifts and you become more attractive and persuasive."[12] Belinda John said it well when she stated, "the most successful leaders are moved and motivated by conviction. Their messages seem to have a pulse, and their words carry life."[13] They are strong and courageous because of their belief in God (Joshua 1:9).

> *Have I not commanded you? Be strong and courageous. Do not be frightened, and do not be dismayed, for the Lord your God is with you wherever you go.*
>
> Joshua 1:9 (NIV)

Form Integrated Product Teams (IPTs)

Select and Build Teams

Servant leaders and IPTs work together to create value, so selecting and building teams is a critical next step. The reason it is so important is because this is where the real work gets done. Selecting the right Team Leaders is essential and so is the selection of team members. Team leaders are appointed by the overall program manager. Team members work with IPT leaders to assign people from the Core Business Functions. According to Hecker:

> "The process of how IPTs are formed is as important as the make-up of the teams themselves. It all starts with a set of common program objectives, goals, requirements, and their allocation. It is imperative that the customer and contractor collaborate to identify, document, internalize and communicate the overall program objectives, goals, strategies and key performance parameters very early in the program and sustain this communication throughout the program life cycle."[14]

Furthermore, Hecker states:

> "Although it may be a functional organization's responsibility to hire, train, place, and replace people in an organization, it is the program manager's and each IPT leader's job to assure the right people are on the right teams to help assure success."[15]

Most people think teams can make value chains more efficient. While true, few seem to have thought through how servant leaders can do that. The real issue is how they use their role as servant leaders to influence the actions of teams whose choices will increase or decrease the value of the product. A breakthrough occurred in a flash of insight when someone realized the key to creating value is not just about new technologies and processes, but also depends on how servant leaders use IPTs to manage knowledge.

Typical characteristics of an IPT leader include confidence, trustworthiness, achievement and a results orientation. IPT leaders are organizationally aware and can influence, communicate, manage conflict, and adapt to changes. They don't just manage; they are force multipliers.[16]

Train Your Teams Well

Teams, working together, shared a common vision for the Raptor. Teams working in the "swing" caused the Raptor to happen.

Good training brings out the best in teams. On the F-22, teams working together shared a common vision for the Raptor. After a season of working together, teams working in the "swing" (See Chapter 7, page 92) caused the Raptor to happen. Being "in the swing" is an interesting place to be. The team is working so closely together, that time almost stops as they outperform their competitors.

Encourage Collaboration

Collaboration up, down, and across the corporation is the key to making things happen. Good servant leaders build a culture of collaboration, and collaboration is a key to advancing the mission of a successful organization.[17] Training opens people's minds so they can see what is "possible." Collaboration among teams makes the possible real.

Include Partners

At the higher levels of ESL, reaching out across boundaries enables more value to be created. Without partners, value creation is limited. With partners, it is just the opposite. Partners working together create the greatest good for the group.

Use Resources You Have Been Provided

There are two sets of tools available to servant leaders. There are tools that are used by traditional business leaders; and tools that are used by true servant leaders.

Tools for Traditional Leaders

All business leaders must compete using sound business practices. Hermanson, Kotter, Porter, Samuelson, and many others have created a rich legacy of courses that define how to do business. The curricula are broad and constantly changing and include a core set of courses that are fundamental to business. Some of these include marketing, communications, finance, accounting, economics, statistics, management, operations, supply chain management and other courses that are relevant to a particular business-oriented discipline.

However, Christensen, Davenport, Norton, Prahalad, Handy and other scholars taught us how to challenge traditional thinking with new ideas that cut across disciplines. Some of these include new ways to think about creativity and innovation, process reengineering, balanced scorecards, core competencies, and jump curves to name a few.

Tools for Servant Leaders

Servant leaders are somewhat different from traditional business leaders. In addition to being well educated, they have a special gift. Others want to follow them because they care about people. Several years ago, there were only a few books that talked about "servant leaders." Today, a quick computer search reveals hundreds of books with that term in the title. When the words "servant leadership" are used, over a thousand different titles can be added to the list. When journal articles and conference proceedings are included, it is clear there is no longer a lack of information on the topic.

In addition to the articles and books that have been written, there are a variety of organizations that offer training on the subject. Many consultants have deep experience dealing with issues related to servant leadership. Others are very good at facilitating lively discussions around subtle, but important, points. One example is The Robert K. Greenleaf Center for Servant Leadership. The mission of the

Greenleaf Center is "to advance the awareness, understanding, and practice of servant leadership by individuals and organizations."[18] In addition to training adults, the organization offers youth-oriented programs to help prepare young leaders for the future.

> *All Scripture is breathed out by God and profitable for teaching, for reproof, for correction, and for training in righteousness, that the man of God may be competent, equipped for every good work.*
>
> 2 Timothy 3:16-17 (ESV)

Tools for aspiring servant leaders are found in abundance in the Holy Bible (2 Timothy 3:16-17). Jesus was very clear as to how we are to behave to be effective in our world. If we want to be great, then we need to serve our people (Matthew 20: 26-27) and to "pray for them without ceasing."[19] "Lead Like Jesus" is one example of a nonprofit organization that inspires people to become Godly servant leaders.[20]

> *But it shall not be so among you: but whosoever will be great among you, let him be your minister; And whosoever will be chief among you, let him be your servant.*
>
> Matthew 20:26-27 (NKJV)

An increasing number of universities are offering programs for those who want to be servant leaders in a variety of formats. Some of these include Cornell University, Dallas Baptist University, Case Western University, Emory University, Georgia Institute of Technology, Gonzaga University, Liberty University, Mercer University, Mississippi College, the Massachusetts Institute of Technology, The Ohio State University, Olympic College, Purdue Global, Regent University, the University of California, the University of Dayton, the University of Georgia, the University of Michigan, the University of San Diego, the University of Texas, the University of Virginia, and the University of Wisconsin-Madison.

Plan and Manage Your Processes

Cultivate Process Owners

To be the best of the best, each process must have an owner that is worthy of the same distinction. Processes are important and must be world-class.

When processes work together, great things can be accomplished. A few words from Hammer and Champy seem relevant here. When a company reengineers its business processes, everything changes as indicated below.[21]

- **Work units change—from functional departments to process teams.**
- **Jobs change—from simple tasks to multidimensional work.**
- **People's roles change—from controlled to empowered.**
- **Job preparation changes—from training to education.**
- **Focus of performance measures and compensation shifts—from activity to results.**
- **Advancement criteria change—from performance to ability.**
- **Values change—from protective to productive.**
- **Managers change—from supervisor to coach.**
- **Organizational structures change—from hierarchical to flat.**
- **Executives change—from scorekeepers to leaders.**

Process owners should have access to knowledge that affects the end-to-end performance of the company's supply chain. Furthermore, they should have the skills, authority, technology, and other resources to make changes happen.[22] The processes should be standardized with metrics to optimize performance and make the continuous improvements necessary to maintain world-class results. Furthermore, it is important to link processes to an employee's day-to-day activities.[23]

Manage Processes

Market research, knowledge diffusion, product innovation, inbound supply chain management, product manufacturing, marketing and sales, outbound distribution, and life cycle services, are typical of the Core Business Function processes that must be managed. Human resources, finance, information technology, corporate real estate, legal services, and administration are typical of the Integrated Corporate Services used. Collectively, they represent most of the functions and services that must be managed.

Embrace Risk and Think Survival

At this point it is important to define the risk you are willing to take. Implementing servant leadership can turn an organization upside down. That is a big risk for many companies in highly competitive industries.[24] On the other hand, servant leadership can be beneficial because it engages and develops employees. As the followers' trust in their leader increases, the commitment of the team to the success of the project also increases.

It is risky to put responsibilities in the hands of people at lower levels, but service leaders believe it is acceptable to fail while employees build the skills necessary for succeeding. Servant leaders inspire people before asking them to join them in taking risk.[25] Servant-led people don't fear that if they take a risk they could get punished.[26]

Taking risks is not easy, "All risks involve change, and all change involves risk."[27] Servant leaders that are Christians inspire people to take risks and expand their comfort zone; because they have confidence that God is directing their paths (Proverbs 3:5-6). "Expecting that you can achieve 100 percent success only rewards safe bets."[28]

> *Trust in the Lord with all thine heart; and lean not unto thine own understanding. In all thy ways acknowledge him, and he shall direct thy paths.*
> Proverbs 3:5-6 (KJV)

The greater the risks of taking on an initiative, the greater the value servant leadership can provide.[29] It is also important for teams to think in terms of survival, but how this is done depends on how the servant-led business model is constructed.

Build a Servant-Led Business Model

This step is one of the most important in defining how superior value will be created. Strategically related activities in each of the IPTs must be identified where appropriate. Missing IPT people and activities must be supplemented, as necessary, by Integrated Corporate Services acting in response to requests from the Core Business Functions. Furthermore, the more servant leaders you can add to your business model, the more likely their performance will be correlated with positive results. The value created, in turn, will be based on the superior margins created and sustained by the IPTs. Concurrent engineering, practiced by the IPTs, helps avoid rework and comes up with better solutions.

Focus on Quality

Improve Quality Through Lean, 6S, Six Sigma, Kaizen, and Other TQM tools

As demonstrated on the F-22 Raptor, Lean, 6S, Six Sigma and Kaizen are each powerful tools. Together, they are unstoppable at reducing costs and improving quality.[30] Lean is about minimizing or eliminating waste. The focus of 6S is on maintaining a safe and efficient workplace. Six Sigma is about reducing variation in the process. More recently Lean and Six Sigma have been applied together in something called "Lean Six Sigma."[31] According to the *Lean Way blog*, Kaizen refers to teams taking responsibility for their work and then making improvements to enhance their working experience. "Most people want to be successful and proud of the work that they do, and Kaizen helps them to achieve this while benefitting the organization."[32]

Lean, 6S, Six Sigma, and Kaizen can be applied to services as well as manufacturing. Improvements in service include reducing costs, improving service delivery time, and expanding capacity without adding cost.[33]

Fortunately, many of these benefits can be extended to a firm's vendors as well, which is exactly what Lockheed/Lockheed Martin did on the F-22 with its multiple tiers of suppliers.

Communicate

Have a Strategy for Communicating

Effective communication is at the center of every successful servant leader.[34] In fact, the more responsibility servant leaders have, the more important communication becomes.[35] It is important to be discerning (Philippians 4:8) when learning how to communicate. Communicating in a clear manner is necessary for influencing others. Communication is also important for

> *Finally, brothers, whatever is true, whatever is honorable, whatever is just, whatever is pure, whatever is lovely, whatever is commendable, if there is any excellence, if there is anything worthy of praise, think about these things.*
> Philippians 4:8 (ESV)

teams. The traditional approach leaves each function too isolated—which is a "special danger" for a complex, interdependent product like the F-22.[36]

Communication also has many moving parts. In some organizations, withholding information is the basis for power. In a servant-led organization, information needs to be shared to know what is happening.[37]

Ask questions and listen carefully. Responsible leaders engage in responsible listening.[38] They also take learning styles into account.[39]

Servant leaders must also prepare their IPTs to communicate effectively. When possible, each team should have long-term and short-term strategies for communicating performance or identifying needs.

Examples of when the F-22 needed effective communications included:

- **Communicating with the Department of Defense, the General Accounting Office, and Congress about cost, schedule, and performance.**
- **Communicating with the public about the status of the F-22 program.**
- **Announcing the winning team of the ATF competition.**
- **Communicating among partners on the F-22.**
- **Introducing the F-22 to the public.**
- **Managing messages about safety and costs.**
- **Coordinating messages with their primary customer, the USAF.**

Prevent Conflict When Possible

A conflict arises when someone on a team tries to block another person or refuses to work together. Understanding the cause isn't always sufficient to resolve the problem. The next step is to find common ground, so that they can build trust and a relationship. Finding common ground isn't necessarily easy but understanding the group's differences can resolve many issues.[40]

A servant leader should create opportunities for people to work together (Romans 8:28), and at the same time provide a means to work together through their differences. As stated by Omar Rabbolini, management consultant and former VP of engineering for Divide (acquired by Google in 2014), "Of course, there's always the possibility that the conflicting parties won't get any closer ... This doesn't mean we need to remove either person from the team, nor that we should encourage them to leave."[41] Unless they're required to work closely with each other, it's perfectly fine for them to work apart. If that is not possible, the servant leader can arrange for someone to mediate between them.

And we know that for those who love God all things work together for good, for those who are called according to his purpose.

Romans 8:28 (ESV)

Fadi Smiley reminds us that conflict should not be considered good or bad. Rather it should be viewed as a way to build relationships between people. How the conflict is handled will determine whether or not it is productive.[42]

Conflict is inevitable in teams of any size, and that's something that servant leaders must address through communication and transparency.[43] Encourage communication and celebrate small wins until there's enough trust to solve almost anyone's problems.[44]

Some people call it "compassionate collaboration."[45] Others call it opening your mind to new and creative thinking. Think about what will work with your new ideas.[46] This can help you resolve conflicts while keeping your composure. When all else fails, hiring a conflict resolution specialist can help.

Be Transparent with Press

How servant leaders are depicted depends, to a certain extent, on their relationship with the press. It is important to be transparent, but you can't make the press trust you—that is built over time. But you can have plans and strategies for dealing with the press. When you meet with the press, always have the story you want to tell thought out in your mind. Answer the questions you are asked but use them to segue into the story you want to tell. Prepare for the unexpected or controversial. Communicating effectively can be effectively managed, even during the worst of times. Do not speak untruths. They will nearly always rise up to bite you (Colossians 3:9). The decisions

> *Do not lie to one another, seeing that you have put off the old self with its practices.*
> **Colossians 3:9 (ESV)**

leaders make, as well as how they make them, determine whether or not they are ethical leaders— which directly affects the press and how you deal with them. As a minimum, one should strive for "clarity in all communication, spoken and written, so that there are no misunderstandings" in one's relationship with the press.[47]

Include Partners in Network

Do you systematically search for opportunities to create value with your supply chain network? According to the United States Postal Service, "a flexible mindset can help businesses forecast demand, too. A future-forward approach can lead to more effective product planning and better customer experience."[48]

> *Let each of you look not only to his own interests, but also to the interests of others.*
> **Philippians 2:4 (ESV)**

The selection of the right partner is important, since changing providers takes time, is costly, and requires considerable effort. After selecting the right partner, it is important to have a solid contract in place with the right service level agreements, key performance indicators, and an account management structure, to properly manage the relationship over time (Philippians 2:4). Key criteria for developing the right partner include:[49]

- **Trust.**
- **Strategic compatibility.**
- **Cultural fit.**
- **Industry know-how.**
- **Experience.**
- **Capability and performance.**
- **Financial stability.**
- **Other factors as necessary.**

Implement Enterprise Servant Leadership

Implementing ESL requires filling in the boxes in Figure 22. The process starts with thinking about how to lead. It ends when all tasks have been completed and you have prayed for your people.

Make Lifestyle Choices

Part of the choice depends on factors such as one's personality, leadership style, knowledge, and desire to serve. ESL can be implemented at home and at work. At home, it applies to how one relates to family and friends. At work, it allows the firm to be the best of the best.

As stated by Ray Blunt, servant leaders are prepared to leave their legacy in the lives of others.[50] This does not mean you are unworthy. On the contrary, it means that you rise above yourself when you put others first.

Put Others First

In the Enterprise Servant Leadership Management Model, people truly care about each other. According to Greenleaf, "the central thought of putting others first is what drives servant leadership"[51] (Philippians 2:3). That is because people possess a serve-first mindset. They are focused on empowering and uplifting those who work for them.[52]

> *Do nothing from rivalry or conceit, but in humility count others more significant than yourselves.*
> Philippians 2:3 (EVS)

ESL Affects the People You Hire

To be sure, ESL affects the people you hire. After all, it takes the "traditional leadership model" and turns it completely on its head.[53] The discipline associated with serving others brings out the best in us—such as attention to detail, better communication, and a focus on quality.

ESL impacts every aspect of the organization—from planning and managing resources to executing team-based transactions. People serve instead of demand, show humility instead of brandishing authority, and enhance the development of staff in ways that unlock their potential and sense of purpose.[54]

As stated by John Maxwell, "People don't care how much you know until they know how much you care." Learning what is important to employees, shows them that you do.[55]

Build a Community

Community is something people do,[56] and people working together can do almost anything.[57] People want that feeling of community because they don't have it in their lives.[58] As a result of the shift from local communities to large institutions, much has been lost in terms of that "community" feeling. Servant leadership suggests that true communities can be created among those who work in businesses and other institutions.

Serving each other (Galatians 6:2) is a powerful hedge against isolation. As people bond together for a common cause, we impact ourselves and the communities that are created.[59]

> *Bear one another's burdens, and so fulfill the law of Christ.*
> Galatians 6:2 (NKJV)

"Servant leaders understand how to build a workplace where communities are valued."[60] Communities are recognized by stories, myths, rights, and rituals.[61] Respect each other's opinion and through synergy come to conclusions.[62] Consider your purpose and consider your conversations. Your conversations can help create a better shared vision.[63]

Build a culture that cares for people and encourages innovation. A leader's commitment to model the values of the organization is the most important factor in changing the organization's culture.[64]

Continuous Feedback

Building continuous feedback into the ESLMM is not necessarily difficult, but it isn't easy either. Part of providing continuous feedback includes reinforcing the habits and behaviors required to practice it.[65] This means that servant leaders should build into the model a structure and process for obtaining continuous feedback. The structure for obtaining feedback may include something like the following:[66]

- **Key performance indicators: such as sales, profitability, share price, and market share.**
- **Employee engagement: it is important to survey employees about their engagement with work, trust in leaders and co-workers, and loyalty to the company.**
- **Customer experience: servant leadership focuses on meeting customer needs by focusing on employees first. Customer surveys and product ratings can provide insight into their experience.**

There are some who suggest that servant leaders should receive feedback first, i.e., they should model how to receive feedback from those they serve.[67]

Processes should be built into the model, so that feedback can be delivered when and where needed. Regardless of what is included or how frequently it is done, it is essential to have continuous feedback built into the ESLMM.

Inspire and Pray

The final "element" of the Enterprise Servant Leadership Management Model is the all-encompassing "Inspire and Pray." The element is represented in Figure 22 by the dotted line surrounding the other elements of the ESLMM. The servant leader's actions to inspire their team by demonstrating Christian core values and to pray for their team members affects every element of the management model. [68]

For God gave us a spirit not of fear but of power and love and self-control.

2 Timothy 1:7 (EVS)

Servant leaders set the standard of behavior for how a project's activities will be conducted. Inspiring others with Christian core values learned from scripture and praying for their team demonstrates that serving others is the true motivation behind their hearts. This behavior lets team members see real servant leaders in action who can be role models for themselves and others (2 Timothy 1:7).[69]

A servant leader gives himself or herself to the people they lead. A servant leader lives with their people, works with them, loves with them, suffers with them, celebrates with them, and demonstrates by example how a servant leader should lead.

Prayer by a servant leader brings the power of God to bear on every aspect of the project or program. Praying is fundamental for most Christians, as well as for most other major religions. Christian Enterprise Servant Leaders should surround their project with prayer. They should pray that God's will be done, pray for a servant's heart, pray for successful collaboration among all players, pray for the health of their employees, pray for wisdom and knowledge to produce the best of the best, pray for help in resolving personnel conflicts, pray for the project to be successful, and pray for the resolution of any other problems that arise.

In their book *Servant Leader*, Blanchard and Hodges state that "Change is a given. It will happen. Your organization will adapt or die."[70] The best organizational changes come when those in leadership are open to praying for God's guidance.

After years of working in traditional stovepipe organizations, Micky knew he was making a difference when he applied servant leadership principles to those he led, but it wasn't easy to gauge the impact. Progress to build a high-performance organization managed by servant leaders was slow, but Micky knew it was the right thing to do.

The USAF mandated that concurrent engineering organizational concepts be used on the F-22 program. This was the catalyst for radical organizational change in how Lockheed Martin organized and managed programs. Micky saw that this change allowed the implementation of collaborative teams (IPTs) led by servant leaders.

In many projects and programs, there are shared burdens and a common vision for the entire team. For that reason alone, praying for God's guidance is a good fit for any organization that wants to bring God's will to earth (Romans 8:31).

> *What then shall we say to these things? If God is for us, who can be against us?*
>
> Romans 8:31

Prayer was of such importance to Micky that after he retired, he wrote a book on how to maximize the power of prayer. The title of the book is *When Two or More are Gathered…in Prayer.*[71]

When a servant leader prays for a team member, their heart changes, and their relationship with the team member changes. Their behavior toward the team member becomes more Christ-like. The team member usually responds in the same way. In short, they both move toward becoming a family. The result is a substantial increase in team performance.

On the F-22, teams had to meet the goals of their IPTs. Those led by servant leaders inspired their teams in the pursuit of these goals by demonstrating with their lives Christian core values based on scripture (e.g. kindness, honesty, humility, service, passion, humor, courage, and collaboration).

In general, servant leaders that pray for their team make a big difference in how people treat each other as they seek to achieve their goals. As a byproduct, servant leaders find that serving others also gives inspiration to themselves.[72]

Lessons Learned and Important Points

This chapter completes the framework for the Enterprise Servant Leadership Model. It creates a way forward for those seeking to know more about the topic. Lessons learned and important points include:

- **Lead by example.**
- **Embrace the vision and core business strategies.**
- **Define your core values and why they are important.**
- **Form Integrated Product Teams.**
- **Use the resources you have been provided.**
- **Plan and manage your processes.**
- **Build your servant-led business model.**

- **Focus on quality.**
- **Provide continuous feedback.**
- **Communicate.**
- **Implement Enterprise Servant Leadership.**
- **Inspire others with Christian core values and pray for your people.**

Chapter Notes

1 Steven R. Covey. 1977. "Forward." *Servant Leadership: A Journey into the Nature of Legitimate Power & Greatness.* Paulist Press, p. 11.

2 Ibid.

3 Joe Iarocci. n.d. 4 Reasons Humility is a Cardinal Virtue of Servant Leadership. *Cairnway.* Accessed August 2, 2021. https://serveleadnow.com/blog-4-reasons- humility/#:~:text=These%20particular%20 things%20might%20humble%20servant- leaders%2C%20of%20course%2C,than%20me.%20 Humility%20binds%20leaders%20and%20followers%20together.

4 Kenneth R. Jennings and Heather Hyde. 2012. *The Greater Goal: Connecting Purpose and Performance.* Berrett-Koehler, p. 2.

5 Ibid.

6 Together, these spell out the acronym SMART. Darrell Zahorsky. 2019. "5 Elements of a SMART Business Goal." *The Balance Small Business.* Accessed February 13, 2020. https://www.thebalancesmb.com/ elements-of-a-smart-business-goal-2951530

7 Patrick M. Lencioni. 2002, July. "Make Your Values Mean Something." *Harvard Business Review*, 80 (7), pp. 113-117.

8 Ibid.

9 Vivian Maza. 2019, March 26. The Importance of Establishing Company Core Values—And How To Define Them. *Forbes.* Accessed February 13, 2020. https://www.forbes.com/sites/ forbeshumanresourcescouncil/2019/03/26/the- importance-of-establishing-company-core-values-and-how-to-define-them/#730818849af9

10 Maria Connolly., August 17, 2016. "Strong Convictions – The Secret to Becoming an Influential Leader in Your Community." *Neways.* Accessed February 14, 2020. https://newayscenter.com/2016/08/17/ strong-convictions-secret-becoming-influential- leader-community/

11 Debbie Mason. 2017. Ethical Behavior Through Servant Leadership. *Business.* Accessed February 19, 2021, at https: //www.businessmagazinegainesville.com/ethical-behavior- through-servant-leadership/

12 Ibid.

13 Belinda John. August 15, 2016. "Conviction: The Strength of Successful Leadership." *SW.* Accessed February 14, 2020. https://www.shulamitewomen.com/conviction-the- strength-of-successful-leadership/

14 Hecker, M.L. 2000. "Setting up and managing integrated product teams." Paper presented at Project Management Institute Annual Seminars & Symposium, Houston, Tex.. Newtown Square, Penn.: Project Management Institute.

15 Ibid.

16 Ibid.

17 W. Roger Miller and Jeffrey P. Miller. n.d. "Leadership Styles for Success in Collaborative Work." *Association of Leadership Educators.* Accessed June 1, 2012. https://www.leadershipeducators.org/ Resources/Documents/Conferences/FortWorth/ Miller.pdf

18 See Our Mission and Vision. n.d. Robert K. Greenleaf Center for Servant Leadership Website. Accessed June 7, 2019. https://www.greenleaf.org/our-journey/.

19 See 1 Thessalonians 5:17 (KJV).

20 See www.LeadLike Jesus.com.

21 Michael Hammer and James Champy. 1993. *Reengineering the Corporation: a Manifesto for Business Revolution*. New York, NY: Harper Business, pp. 65-82.

22 Greg Ray. January 21, 2014. "World class processes begin with the 'right' process owners." *Industry Week*. Accessed February 16, 2020. https://www.industryweek.com/finance/cost-management-bpm/article/21965469/ worldclass-processes-begin-with-the-right-process-owners?page=1

23 Tina Rasmussen. 1995. "Creating a Culture of Servant Leadership: a Real Life Story," in Larry C. Spears, ed. 1995. *Reflections on Leadership: How Robert K. Greenleaf's Theory of Servant Leadership Influenced Today's Top Management Thinkers*. New York: John Wiley & Sons, p. 294.

24 "Challenges of Servant Leadership." n.d. *Penn State Leadership*. Accessed August 2, 2021. https://sites.psu.edu/leadership/2013/11/11/challenges-of-servant-leadership/

25 Sheila Murray Bethel. 1995. "Servant Leadership and Corporate Risk Taking: When Risk Taking Makes a Difference" in Larry Spears, ed. 1995. *Reflections on Leadership: How Robert K. Greenleaf's Theory of Servant Leadership Influenced Today's Top Management Thinkers*. New York: John Wiley & Sons, p. 140.

26 Rebecca Herman. 2020. "What is Servant Leadership?"

27 Sheila Murray Bethel. 1995. "Servant Leadership and Corporate Risk Taking: When Risk Taking Makes a Difference," pp. 136-139.

28 Lei Lei Tun. July 8, 2020. "Encouraging Innovation Through Servant Leadership." *Udacity*. Accessed June 23, 2021. https://www.udacity.com/blog/2020/07/encouraging- innovation-through-servant-leadership.html

29 Grant Avery. June 21, 2018. "Servant Leadership: Reducing the Risks of Complex Projects." *Linked In*. Accessed August 2, 2021. https://www.linkedin.com/pulse/servant- leadership-reducing-risks-complex-projects-grant-avery

30 Integrating the voice of the customer into new product designs can also be done using Quality Function Deployment.

31 In one example, a tier-one automobile supplier claimed the following benefits of Lean Six Sigma: reduced manufacturing lead time from 14 days to 2 days, increased work in process inventory turns from 23 to 67 per year, reduced manufacturing overhead and quality costs by 22 percent, increased gross profit margin from 12 percent to 19.6 percent, increased operating margins from 5.4 percent to 13.8 percent, and increased return on invested capital from 10 percent to 33 percent. See Michael L. George. 2002. *Lean Six Sigma: Combining Six Sigma Quality with Lean Speed*. The McGraw-Hill Companies. New York, NY. p. 7.

32 Doanh Do. August 5, 2017. "What is Continuous Improvement (Kaizen)?" *Lean Way Blog*. Accessed November 6, 2021 at https://theleanway.net/what-is-continuous- improvement

33 Michael L. George. 2003. *Lean Six Sigma for Service*. The McGraw-Hill Companies. New York, NY. Back cover.

34 Matt Rocco. August 5, 2020. "Why is Effective Communication Crucial to Become a Servant Leader?" *Etech*. Accessed August 3, 2021 at https://www.etechgs.com/blog/effective- communication-to-become-a-servant-leader/

35 Alvin Plexico. n.d. Leadership Communication Styles - The Pros and Cons. *Purdue University*. Accessed June 22, 2021. https://www.cla.purdue.edu/academic/communication/graduate/online/leadership-communication-styles.html

36 "Managing; General Fain, the Team Player." December 22, 1991. *The New York Times*, Section 3, p. 23.

37 Don M. Frick. 1995. "Pyramids, Circles, and Gardens: Stories of Implementing Servant Leadership," p. 267.

38 "Communication Tips for Servant Leaders: Do You Fail to Communicate Because You Fail to Listen?" n.d. Accessed June 23, 2021. http://christian-leadership.org/communication- tips-for-servant-leaders-do-you-fail-to-communicate-because-you-fail-to-listen/

39 "Communication Tips for Servant Leaders: 6 Ways That Learning Styles Help Your Listeners Hear You." n.d. Accessed June 23, 2021. http://christian-leadership.org/communication- tips-for-servant-leaders-6-ways-that-you-can-help-your-listeners-hear-you/

40 Omar Rabbolini. 2020. "How To Resolve Conflicts Like A Servant Leader," *The Startup*. Accessed February 10, 2020. https://medium.com/swlh/how-to-resolve-conflicts-like-a- servant-leader-460c73707dec

41 Ibid.

42 Fadi Smiley. 2018. "Leadership Guide to Conflict and Conflict Management." *Leadership in Healthcare and Public Health*. Columbus, OH: The Ohio State University.

43 Ibid.

44 Omar Rabbolini. 2020. "How to Resolve Conflicts Like A Servant Leader."

45 Crystal J. Davis. April 17, 2015. "Servant Leadership and Handling Conflict." *CID Consulting Solutions, LLC.* Accessed June 22, 2021. https://drcrystaldavis.wordpress.com/

46 Don M. Frick. 1995. "Pyramids, Circles, and Gardens: Stories of Implementing Servant Leadership," p. 267.

47 "Section 8: Ethical Leadership. Community Tool Box." Accessed August 20, 2021. https://ctb.ku.edu/ en/table-of-contents/leadership/leadership-ideas/ethical- leadership/main

48 "Navigate Challenges with a Resilient Business Mindset." *USPS Delivers*. Accessed August 21, 2021. https://www.uspsdelivers.com/resilient-business-start-with-flexibility/

49 BCI Global. n.d. *Logistics Partner Selection.* Accessed 28 September 2021. https://bciglobal.com/en/ logistics-partner-selection

50 Ray Blunt. "The Toughest Choices a Leader Must Make." *GovLeaders.org*. Accessed August 20, 2021. https://govleaders.org/choices.htm

51 Vantage Circle. "Servant Leadership, its Principles and Examples in the Workplace." Accessed August 20, 2021. https://blog.vantagecircle.com/servant-leadership/

52 Mark Tarallo. May 17, 2018. "The Art of Servant Leadership." SHRM. Accessed 4 April, 2022. https://www.shrm.org/ResourcesAndTools/hr-topics/organizational-and-employee- development/Pages/The-Art-of-Servant-Leadership.aspx

53 Ibid.

54 Ibid.

55 "Servant Leadership." December 16, 2020. Accessed August 22, 2021. https://www.weempowerleaders.com/servant-leadership-pros/

56 Scott Peck. 1995. "Servant Leadership Training and Discipline in Authentic Community" in Larry C. Spears, ed. 1995. *Reflections on Leadership: How Robert K. Greenleaf's Theory of Servant Leadership Influenced Today's Top Management Thinkers*. New York: John Wiley & Sons, p. 97.

57 Philip Chamberlin. 1995. "Team Building and Servant Leadership" in Larry C. Spears, ed. 1995. *Reflections on Leadership: How Robert K. Greenleaf's Theory of Servant Leadership Influenced Today's Top Management Thinkers*. New York: John Wiley & Sons, p. 170.

58 Rebecca Herman. 2020. "What is Servant Leadership?" *Purdue Global*. Accessed June 18, 2021, at https://www.purdueglobal.edu/blog/business/what-is-servant-leadership/

59 Dave Shoff. March 2, 2020. "Servant Leader Principle #10 – Community." *Leader as Servant*. Accessed August 30, 2021.https://leader-as servant.com/2020/03/02/servant-leader-principle-10-community/

60 Ibid.

61 Tina Rasmussen. 1995. "Creating a Culture of Servant Leadership: a Real Life Story," in Larry C. Spears, ed. 1995. *Reflections on Leadership: How Robert K. Greenleaf's Theory of Servant Leadership Influenced Today's Top Management Thinkers*. New York: John Wiley & Sons, p. 296.

62 Don M. Frick. 1995. "Pyramids, Circles, and Gardens: Stories of Implementing Servant Leadership" in Larry C. Spears, ed. 1995. *Reflections on Leadership: How Robert K. Greenleaf's Theory of Servant Leadership Influenced Today's Top Management Thinkers*. New York: John Wiley & Sons, p. 266.

63 Walter Kiechel. 1995. "The Leader as Servant," in Larry Spears, ed. 1995. *Reflections on Leadership: How Robert K. Greenleaf's Theory of Servant Leadership Influenced Today's Top Management Thinkers*. New York: John Wiley & Sons, p. 125.

64 Tina Rasmussen. 1995. "Creating a Culture of Servant Leadership: A Real Life Story," *Reflections on Leadership*, by Larry C. Spears, ed., 282-297. New York, NY: John Wiley & Sons, Inc., p. 295.

65 Mike Gibbons. June 4, 2020. *Servant Leadership Examples and Characteristics*. Accessed October 6, 2021. https://peoplemanagingpeople.com/articles/what-it-really-takes-to- do-servant-leadership/#measuring-success

66 Ibid.

67 Chris Thyberg. August 15, 2018. *When It Comes to Feedback, Servant-Leaders Receive First*. Robert K. Greenleaf Center for Servant Leadership. Accessed October 5, 2021. https://www.greenleaf.org/comes-feedback-servant-leaders-receive-first/

68 "All About Truth." n.d. *The Inspiration of Scripture*. Accessed June 20, 2021. https://www.allabouttruth.org/inspiration-of-scripture.htm.

69 Tina Rasmussen may have said it best when she stated that role modeling by the leader is "the single most important lever for influencing or changing an organization's culture." See Rasmussen, Tina. 1995. "Creating a Culture of Servant Leadership: A Real Life Story." in *Reflections on Leadership*, by Larry C. Spears, ed., 282-297. New York, NY: John Wiley & Sons, Inc., p. 295.

70 Ken Blanchard and Phil Hodges. 2003. *The Servant Leader*. Nashville, TN: Thomas Nelson Inc., p. 65.

71 James "Micky" Blackwell. 2009. *When Two or More Are Gathered...in Prayer*: United Writers Press, Asheville, North Carolina. p. 3.

72 The book *Be Inspired* helps servant leaders stay inspired while serving others. This book will remind you of the many gifts God has placed in you to assist you as you serve others. Whether you need inspiration for yourself or you need words to inspire others, this book will help you fulfill your role as a Godly servant leader. See Christian and Michel Pantin. 2021. *Be Inspired: Weekly Inspirations for Servant Leaders*. Meadville, PA: Christian Faith Publishing.

Part IV:
Using the Enterprise Servant Leadership Model to Become the Best of the Best

Chapter 11
President of Lockheed Aeronautical Systems Company

The F-22 cannot be matched by any known or projected fighter...

US Air Force
F-22 Raptor Website
September 23, 2015

In Part IV, we will present examples of how Enterprise Servant Leaders, integrated product teams, lean enterprise management, integrated business systems, and Lean enterprise development tools were used under Micky's leadership at the Lockheed Aeronautical Systems Company, the Lockheed Martin Aeronautics Sector, and in the private sector in pursuit of becoming the best of the best.

In this chapter, we will focus on Micky's leadership as president of Lockheed Aeronautical Systems Company (LASC) and his activities to apply what he had learned from leading Lockheed Georgia Company Engineering and the Lockheed F-22 program to a wider range of systems, processes, and products produced by LASC.

In April 1993, after the F-22 EMD program was well underway, the president of the Lockheed Aeronautics Group, Ken Cannestra, asked Micky to become president of the Lockheed Aeronautical Systems Company (see Figure 23). Gary Riley, former program manager of the F-117 program, replaced Micky as the program manager of the F-22 Raptor.

As the new LASC president, Micky was never far away from the F-22 program since the F-22 program manager reported directly to him. He also held a seat on the F-22 Executive Committee, which included the CEOs and group presidents of Lockheed and Boeing.

Initiated Reengineering

One of the first things that Micky committed to do as president of LASC was reengineering the Lockheed Aeronautical Systems Company. In many ways, Micky acknowledged, it was much like starting over. Two to five percent improvements were no longer good enough. What Micky was interested in was 50 percent to 70 percent changes for the better. Collectively, these represented radical changes in cost, schedule, performance, and quality.

They also led to changes in the work culture. Work went from individuals to teams and from managers to coaches. It also meant empowering people at all levels of the organization.

When asked about the reason for reengineering, Micky said the primary reason was survival. Costs of all kinds had to be reduced, management had to be flattened, capital spending had to be lowered, and decisions had to be made concurrently. All these things had to be done so that Lockheed could continue to be the best of the best.

Corporate Management Memo

Date	April 28, 1993	Serial No. 747
From	Dan Tellep	

Subject	James A. Blackwell, Jr., Elected President, Lockheed Aeronautical Systems Company

I'm pleased to announce that our Board of Directors has elected James A. (Micky) Blackwell, Jr., President of Lockheed Aeronautical Systems Company (LASC) and a Vice President of Lockheed Corporation, effective immediately. Micky, currently LASC's F-22 Program Vice President and General Manager, will continue to report to Aeronautical Systems Group President Ken Cannestra.

Expansion of the Aeronautical Systems Group (ASG) business base has made it increasingly demanding for Group President Ken Cannestra to manage both LASC's day-to-day operations and the activities of the other ASG companies, which he has done since 1988. With Micky's appointment as LASC President, Ken now will be able to devote his full attention to major ASG issues including successful integration of the Lockheed Fort Worth Company.

Micky Blackwell brings to his new assignment the combination of technical expertise, managerial know-how, and leadership skills required to effectively direct LASC through challenging times. Micky joined Lockheed as a senior aerospace engineer at our Georgia Company in 1969 after seven years as an engineer with the National Aeronautics & Space Administration's Langley Research Center. He advanced through the technical ranks in increasingly responsible positions and in 1989 was named Vice President and Assistant General Manager of the Advanced Tactical Fighter (ATF) program.

Micky received his bachelor's degree in aerospace engineering from the University of Alabama, where he was named an Engineering Fellow, and earned a master's degree in the same discipline from the University of Virginia. He has participated in a number of Lockheed Institute development programs and completed the three-month Advanced Management Program at Harvard University.

Please join me in congratulating Micky on his promotion and in lending your full support as he assumes his new responsibilities. We are confident that, under Micky's leadership, LASC will strengthen its market position and solidify Lockheed's standing as the world's most widely capable military aircraft designer and producer.

Dan Tellep

Figure 23. Memo Announcing Micky's Promotion to president, Lockheed Aeronautical Systems Company.
(Image courtesy of Micky Blackwell)

New C-5M Opportunity

During Micky's first week as LASC president, the Vice President of Marketing informed him that the firm had prepared an unsolicited proposal to restart production of the C-5 Galaxy for a second time (see Figure 24). The proposed C-5D that several years later became C-5M (for "Modernized")included new commercial engines, new strengthened wings, and new avionics for the cockpit. It was a fine proposal, and the VP of Marketing and his team were ready to present it to Congress and the Air Force.

After reviewing the proposal, Micky became concerned. There were two issues that got his attention. First, it was clear that the "new" C-5M was going to be a hot airplane, and the price they were proposing was a good deal for the Air Force. Micky's second concern was about all the work Lockheed had done to cultivate Air Force goodwill on the F-22. Micky feared it might be lost if Lockheed went forward with the unsolicited proposal at that time.

There was still bad blood between Air Force Air Mobility Command and the firm after Lockheed presented an unsolicited proposal to restart the C-5 line to Congress several years earlier. The proposal, which became the C-5B that Congress funded, delayed the start of the C-17 program, which, at that time, was having developmental difficulties.

Even though the upgraded C-5 was a good deal for the Air Force, what they really wanted was the C-17 Globemaster III. Micky felt like he could not afford to let earlier bad feelings over the C-5B spill over onto the F-22 and C-130J which were still under development. Both programs were vital to Lockheed's future. As a result, Micky requested a private meeting with Gen. Ron Fogelman, who was the four-star general in charge of the Air Mobility Command.

When they met, Micky told Gen. Fogelman about the new unsolicited proposal for the C-5M, and the fact that he needed the Air Force's support for the F-22 and C-130J development. Micky also told the general he would lock the unsolicited proposal in his safe until the Air Force called and said

Figure 24. A C-5M Super Galaxy assigned to the 60th Air Mobility Wing, Travis Air Force Base, Calif. sits on the flight line at Yokota Air Base, Japan, Sept. 14, 2021. Airmen from the 730th Air Mobility Squadron participated in different training exercises including maintenance, inspections and loading capabilities in order to maintain mission readiness. (Photo courtesy of the USAF)

they wanted to see it. Gen. Fogelman greatly appreciated Micky's actions, and that was the beginning of a warm relationship that lasted through the time the general became Chief of Staff of the Air Force.[1]

C-130H Ethical Challenges

Another surprise occurred soon after Micky became Lockheed Aeronautical Systems Company president. The US government opened an ethics case against Lockheed. The case was based on alleged unethical practices that occurred during the 1989 sale of three C-130Hs to Egypt. The government claimed Lockheed used a long-term consultant and official in the Egyptian Parliament as an agent to sell C-130Hs to Egypt. Micky knew it was serious when certain agencies threatened to shut down the Lockheed Corporation's ability to sell to the US government.

According to an article in the *New York Times*, Lockheed acknowledged that certain employees had taken actions that were a direct violation of company policy. The article also stated that "by pleading guilty, Lockheed avoided a trial," and "prosecutors dropped the remaining charges against Lockheed."[2]

Micky and his staff, along with a team of lawyers, put together a multiyear ethics training program that required everyone's participation. Micky explained the situation to the entire LASC workforce. Starting with himself, everyone had to demonstrate their ethical conduct by example. Words were not enough. The employees responded well, and after a time, DOD and other agencies gave Lockheed a clean bill of health.

C-130J Super Hercules Opportunities

Gen. Fogelman had suggested to Micky's predecessor, Ken Cannestra, that he consider developing the C-130J tactical transport on Lockheed's dime. Gen. Fogelman stated that after it was developed, the US Air Force would consider it to replace their current C-130 transport fleet, as well as the National Guard and Air Force Reserve's aging C-130 inventory.

The C-130J is a modern version of the C-130H with new engines, new composite 6-bladed props, new avionics, and a two-pilot digital cockpit. Many of the technologies that were tested on the C- 130 High Technology Test Bed found their way into the C-130J.

Lockheed needed a new tactical entry into the military transport market, so Lockheed Corporate approved the use of company money to develop the C-130J Super Hercules. Because of Micky's meeting with Gen. Fogelman (see Figure 25), the Air Force began working in partnership with Lockheed engineers to make the C-130J tactical transport an airplane the Air Force really wanted.

When the design had matured, Lockheed went back to the Air Force to talk about procurement. "We like the airplane," the leadership said, "but at the present time, we don't have the budget."[3]

At that point, Lockheed began to focus its marketing and sales efforts on the US Marine Corps, the National Guard, US Air Force Reserve units, and US allies that needed to upgrade their existing C-130 fleets.

Lockheed's hottest prospect for the C-130J in 1992 was the Royal Air Force (RAF) in the United Kingdom (UK). The UK government had agreed with other European countries to help build the Airbus A400M tactical transport. However, the A400M program had already experienced several schedule

Figure 25. Micky discussing issues with Gen. Ron Fogleman.
(Photo courtesy of Micky Blackwell)

delays. They urgently needed a replacement aircraft until the A400M became available.

Micky personally made more than ten trips to the United Kingdom between 1993 and 1995 to encourage the RAF and UK government to buy the C-130J. This included bi-annual trips to the Farnborough Air Show and annual trips to the Royal International Air Tattoo at RAF Fairford, Hampshire.

During this time period, Lockheed also sponsored a number of official RAF functions which Micky attended to continue marketing the C-130J. He was fortunate to meet and entertain Prince Philip (see Figure 26), husband of Queen Elizabeth II, and their second son, Prince Andrew. In October 1995, the UK signed a contract to purchase twenty-five C-130J aircraft.

Lockheed's second customer was the Royal Australian Air Force (RAAF). Micky made several sales trips to Canberra. In December 1995, the RAAF ordered 12 C-130J Super Hercules aircraft.

Finally, Congress was able to program funds in the US defense budget to enable the Marines to purchase KC-130J tankers and the Air Force to procure C-130J transports for the National Guard and Reserve units spread around the United States.

With the growing backlog from these purchases, Lockheed knew the C-130J was going to be successful, continuing the longest continuous military aircraft production line in history.

Micky also initiated C-130J sales campaigns to other countries, including Israel. Like other sales initiatives in international countries, selling the C-130J to Israel was a long marketing campaign.

Figure 26. Micky with Prince Philip at an Air Tattoo Show in England.
(Photo courtesy of Micky Blackwell)

Israel signed a Foreign Military Sales (FMS) contract to purchase the C-130J in June 2008. Norway, Canada, India, Iraq, Qatar, and others soon joined the list making the C-130J one of the most popular military transports ever produced.

Cash Training and Other Actions

As Micky continued to look for ways to reduce company costs, he had the LASC management team undergo "cash" training. Micky shared one example that he will never forget. The director of Facilities stood up in a "cash" training session and stated that this was the first time he understood that his warehouse full of toilet paper was actually a warehouse full of "cash."

Once the team started, they found all kinds of cash hordes located throughout the plant. One example was they wanted to go to "just-in-time" management for managing materials to build the aircraft, they quickly realized they could not do that since they had more than six months of material (cash) on hand.

Other actions Micky took included directing the company's fitness center to remain open for spouses during work hours. He also directed a move to make the plant a non-smoking campus. Not only were these actions good for the employees and their families, but they were also a good way to control the firm's increasing health insurance costs. If one wanted to smoke, they had to go to a designated area of the plant, and union employees could only go at break time and at lunch. Micky also implemented a policy that Lockheed would send every employee that smoked to smoke cessation training at the company's expense. In response, he received many letters from employees, thanking him for encouraging them to give up smoking. Micky also implemented a policy that Lockheed would no longer hire a person who used tobacco products. This was legal in Georgia, but it got plenty of attention in *USA Today*.

> ### Positioning the Firm for a Positive Future
>
> *When I was president of LASC, it became apparent to me that our costs were too high. At about the same time, radical reengineering began to surface. Downsizing in the military and stiff competition in aerospace made it certain that if a company wanted to survive, they had to make deep changes.*
>
> *Reengineering was about making radical changes to the activities you were performing. The first thing we had to do is decide what business we were in. We then had to establish a survival state of mind.*
>
> *As the company reengineered and became "Leaner", we knew our operations were becoming more efficient and our people more productive—we were positioning the firm for a positive future.*
>
> **Micky Blackwell**

Another tool Micky used to help him communicate his concerns was an "Un-Quality" stamp he had made for him personally. Micky would wander around after the employees had gone home and leave notes with "Un-quality" stamped on them. The purpose was to let people know he expected them to take better care of their workspaces.[4] During one tour of the plant, Micky saw unused or obsolete electronic equipment piled everywhere on the floor. They were also in closets, on top of filing cabinets, and other places where they weren't meant to be stored. When they were finally collected, they covered an area half the size of a football field. Micky immediately directed workers to remove the unwanted equipment and come up with a better plan for storing or removing equipment that was no longer needed. The surplus equipment was later sold for scrap.

Because of these initiatives and other actions taken by his cost reduction teams, Micky saw overhead rates and material costs go down substantially.

Representing Lockheed

As president of LASC, part of Micky's job was to represent Lockheed at various functions to support the company's marketing efforts to win new business. Many of these were conferences or professional events. Others were air shows or sales campaigns.

Air Shows and Sales Campaigns

As stated previously, in July 1993 Micky started attending the Farnborough Air Shows and the International Air Tattoo in England. He also attended the Paris Air Shows, which were held in alternate years in Farnborough so they would not compete with one another. They were wonderful places to meet prospective buyers.

In October 1993, Micky made a trip to Canberra and Sydney, Australia to present a proposal to the Royal Australian Air Force (RAAF) for an updated version of the Lockheed P-3 Airborne Early Warning (AEW) aircraft. He knew it was a long shot, but at least he tried. Even though Boeing won the AEW program, in the process of making the trip, Micky got to know the RAAF leadership.

Later that month, Micky took the C-130J campaign to Saudi Arabia. The Saudis had historically been one of Lockheed's best customers.

Figure 27. Micky with Prince Sultan in tent in Saudi Arabia. (Photo courtesy of Micky Blackwell)

While Micky was visiting Saudi Arabia, he enjoyed an incredible lunch with Prince Sultan bin Abdulaziz Al Saud, the defense minister. The lunch was held in the desert in the Crown Prince's tent. The tent was filled with beautiful carpets and furniture for the prince (see Figure 27).

In November 1993, Micky accompanied by his wife, Billie, made his first trip to Israel. It was the first of many trips and became their favorite place to visit.

In the summer of 1994, Micky and Billie met the King and Queen of Jordan at the International Air Tattoo in England. See Figure 28.

In January 1995, Lockheed Martin sponsored a black-tie event for the Canadian Royal Air Force at the Royal Ottawa Golf Club. The Canadians were prime customers for the C-130J, so Billie and Micky went to Ottawa, to host the event.

Figure 28. Micky with King and Queen of Jordan at an International Air Tattoo in England.

Professional Organizations and Military Events

Another one of Micky's duties was to represent Lockheed at professional events. One of the most prestigious organizations associated with aerospace is the American Institute of Aeronautics and Astronautics (AIAA).

In 1994, Micky was named a Fellow of AIAA. Fellows are persons of distinction in aeronautics or astronautics who have made notable contributions to science, technology, and the aerospace community. Figure 29 is a picture of Micky being recognized at an AIAA Fellow Award dinner.

Micky attended numerous military functions. One of these involved lunch with Secretary of Defense Rumsfeld (see Figure 30). Another was from the Secretary of the Air Force acknowledging Micky as a "Captain of Industry" (see Figure 31).

Figure 29. Micky recognized as AIAA Fellow. (Courtesy of Bill Petros)

Figure 32 is a picture of Billie and Micky attending one of many black-tie events in Washington.

Figure 30. Micky (right) at lunch with Ken Cannestra (left) and Donald Rumsfeld (center). (Photo courtesy of Micky Blackwell)

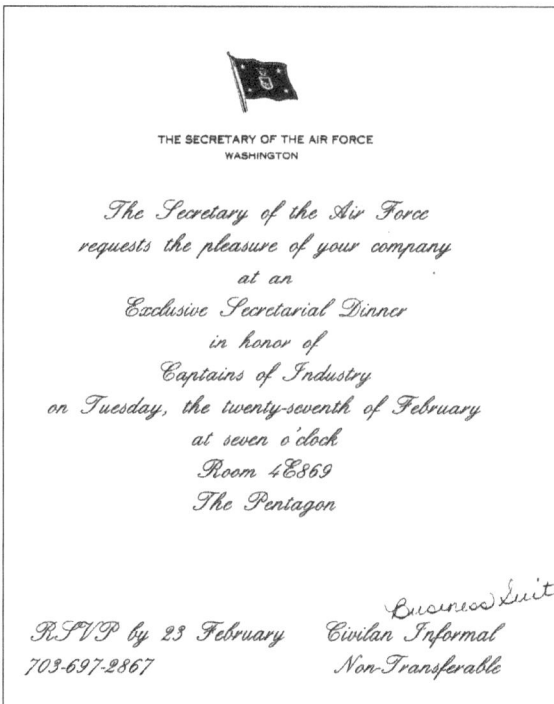

THE SECRETARY OF THE AIR FORCE
WASHINGTON

The Secretary of the Air Force
requests the pleasure of your company
at an
Exclusive Secretarial Dinner
in honor of
Captains of Industry
on Tuesday, the twenty-seventh of February
at seven o'clock
Room 4E869
The Pentagon

RSVP by 23 February   Civilan Informal
703-697-2867   Non-Transferable

Business Suit

Figure 31. Invitation to event acknowledging Micky as a "Captain of Industry."

Figure 32. Billie and Micky at a black-tie event in Washington, D.C. (Photo courtesy of Micky Blackwell)

Merger between Lockheed and Martin Marietta

In August 1994, Lockheed Chairman and CEO Dan Tellep, and Martin Marietta Chairman and CEO Norm Augustine, jointly agreed to merge the two corporations. There was great synergy between the two organizations. Both had excellent leaders who got along well, and both corporations had similar processes and cultures. Fortunately, there was little overlap between product lines, which made the merger even more attractive to investors.

When the merger was complete in 1995, the new company was called Lockheed Martin Corporation. The corporate offices were located at Martin Marietta's headquarters in Bethesda, Maryland. This put the firm close to its major customer, the US government. After the merger, Lockheed Martin's new CEO was Dan Tellep. It was also determined that Dan Tellep would retire a year after the merger was complete, and Norm Augustine would become CEO. The new corporation would be divided into five sectors, each headed by a president and COO.

The new sector executives would all be in Bethesda to maximize the synergy between the two previous competitors. That meant that the president of the Lockheed Aeronautical Systems Group (later renamed Sector) had to move to Bethesda. Ken Cannestra, the current group president did not want to make the move, so the new Lockheed Martin chairman and CEO asked Micky if he would take the job—to which he said "yes." Taking on the new role of president and COO of the Lockheed Martin Aeronautics Sector meant Micky and Billie would be leaving Marietta once again.

Lessons Learned and Important Points

Important points include:

- **As president of LASC, Micky continued to reengineer the firm to make LASC the best of the best.**
- **He continued to find ways to cut company costs.**
- **Micky tabled selling the upgraded C-5M until the USAF was receptive.**
- **As president of LASC, Micky attended air shows and sales campaigns to market the C-130J which became very successful.**
- **Micky put together a muti-year ethics program for LASC that required everyone's participation.**
- **Micky was named a Fellow of AIAA—a person of distinction in aeronautics or astronautics who made notable contributions to science, technology, and the aerospace community.**
- **The Secretary of the Air Force designated Micky as a "Captain of Industry."**
- **In March 1995, Lockheed Corporation and Martin Marietta Corporation merged to create the Lockheed Martin Corporation with corporate headquarters located in Bethesda, Maryland.**
- **Micky was promoted to lead Lockheed Martin's Aeronautics Sector as president and COO in Bethesda, Maryland.**

Chapter Notes

1 James "Micky" Blackwell. 2021. *All the Days of Our Lives: The Heritage and History of Billie and James Blackwell*. Asheville, NC: United Writers Press, p. 123.

2 Reuters. January 28, 1995. "$24.8 Million Penalty Paid by Lockheed." *The New York Times*. Accessed January 7, 2019. https://www.nytimes.com/1995/01/28/business/company-news-831095.html

3 James "Micky" Blackwell. 2021. All the Days of Our Lives: The Heritage and History of Billie and James Blackwell. Asheville, NC: United Writers Press, p. 124.

4 Ibid, p. 161.

Chapter 12

Final Years at Lockheed Martin

An individual striving to be ethical in business, must be wise, trusting, accepting, open to new ideas—and possess humor and the ability to laugh.

Anne T. Fraker
Robert K. Greenleaf and Business Ethics:
There is No Code

In this chapter, we will focus on Micky's promotion to president and chief operating officer of the Lockheed Martin Aeronautics Sector and his activities applying what he had learned on the F-22 program and as president of LASC to a wider range of corporate products and services.

President and COO of Lockheed Martin Aeronautics Sector

As noted before, when Lockheed and Martin Marietta merged, Micky was promoted to Lockheed Martin president and COO of the Aeronautics Sector, effective March 15, 1995. For Micky, this meant he was now responsible for six operating companies at Lockheed Martin:[1]

- **Lockheed Martin Aeronautical Systems in Marietta, Georgia.**
- **Lockheed Martin Tactical Aircraft Systems in Fort Worth, Texas.**
- **Lockheed Martin Aero & Naval Systems in Baltimore, Maryland.**
- **Lockheed Martin Skunk Works in Palmdale, California.[2]**
- **Lockheed Martin Aircraft and Logistics Center in Greenville, South Carolina.**
- **Lockheed Martin Logistics Management in Arlington, Texas.**

Micky's new responsibilities included oversight of the F-22 fighter, the still-going-strong F-16, and coming F-35 fighters, the F-117 stealth attack fighter, the C-130J transport, the C-5 transport, the C-27J transport, the U-2 reconnaissance aircraft, the X-33 space plane, the Joint Air to Surface Standoff Missile, and other classified and unclassified services and programs.[3]

When Micky took over as Aeronautics Sector president, annual sales exceeded $7 billion, driven by 36,000 employees. Micky rapidly established Lockheed Martin as the best military aircraft manufacturer in the world. During his time as president, with only one or two exceptions, the sector won every major US government military aircraft award and international program for which it bid.

As sector president, Micky continued the work he had already started as president of LASC in Marietta, Georgia. Using his skills as a servant leader, he expanded major initiatives throughout the Sector. These included team-led Lean Thinking, Enterprise Resource Planning, the use of IPTs, 6 Sigma, 6S, Concurrent Engineering, and TQM—all of which changed the culture of the organization.

Implementing Change Management

Micky and other Lockheed Martin senior executives recognized the challenges of bringing Martin Marietta and Lockheed together. Key steps identified by Lockheed Martin for successfully implementing and managing change included:[4]

- **Understanding and accepting the need for change while committing to the new organization's mission. This step also addressed the vision and core values of the new company, as well as strategies for successfully working through the steps of the merger.**
- **Converting the new organization's mission into action plans that could be implemented. Key elements included defining clear roles and responsibilities, identifying issues, and the need for team interventions.**
- **Establishing goals and milestones and developing criteria for measuring the success of the merger.**
- **Working in teams to execute action plans, developing measures to evaluate outcomes, and targeting strengths and weaknesses for continuing realignment and improvement.**

Merging the Lockheed and Martin Marietta corporations made great sense. Some of the reasons:

- **Declining defense budgets and increasing competition.**
- **Technologies and other resources could be leveraged to take advantage of synergies.**
- **Costs could be reduced, and capabilities could be preserved.**
- **Jobs could be kept while the company repositioned itself.**
- **Greater financial strength and flexibility with additional options to improve shareholder value.**

Lockheed Martin executives developed a vison that would unite and excite the people across the merged corporation. The following is a copy of their initial vision statement:

> "Our vision is for Lockheed Martin to be recognized as the world's premier systems engineering and technology enterprise. Our mission is to build on our aerospace heritage to meet the needs of our customers with high quality products and services and in so doing produce superior returns for our shareholders and foster growth and achievement for employees."

Characteristics of that vision included:

- **Being a global leader in defense and aerospace.**
- **Achieving mission success.**
- **Growing their non-defense portfolio.**
- **Growing a broad base of products and services.**
- **Developing premier technologies.**
- **Outstanding financial performance and flexibility.**

Combined Sales in Billions of Dollars

Combined Lockheed Martin sales in 1994 totaled $23 billion. Sales by sector in billions of dollars were as indicated in Figure 33.

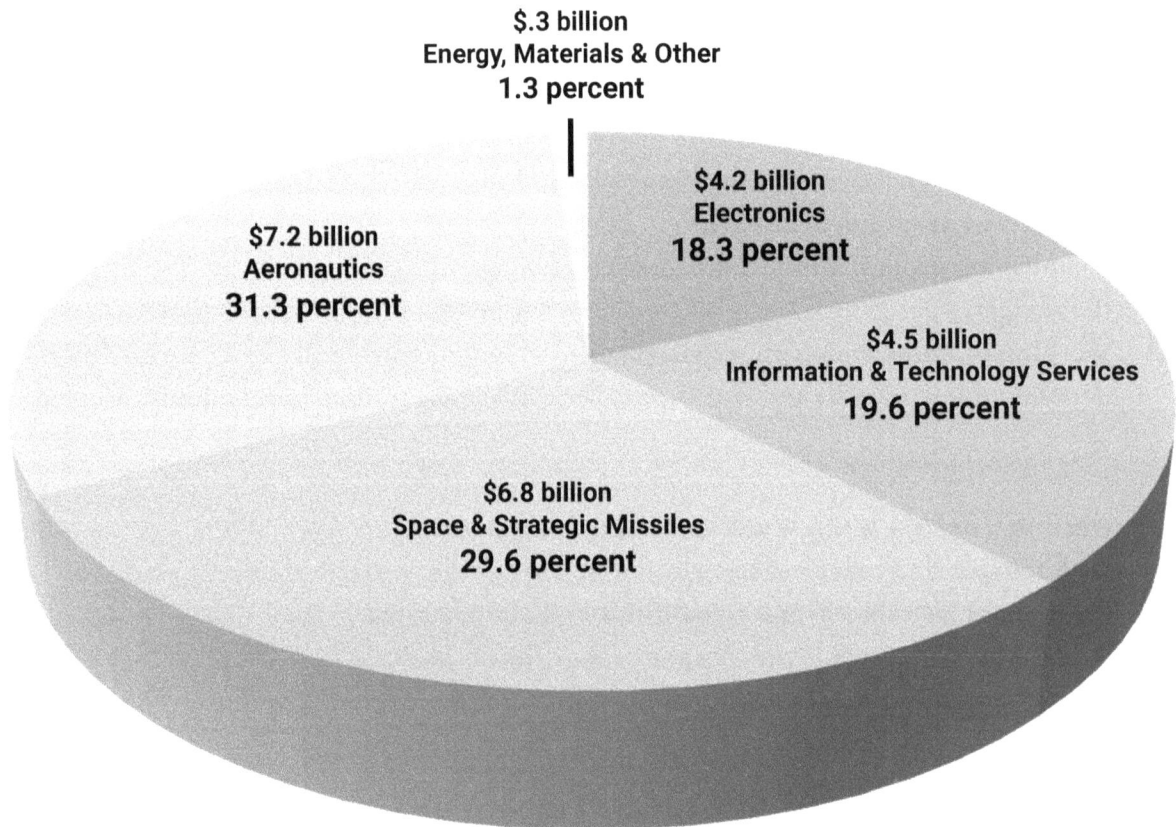

Figure 33. Lockheed Martin Sales by Sector, 1994.

Diversified Customer Base

The combined Lockheed Martin Corporation had major facilities in more than 20 states. Broken down by customer, 1994 sales were:

- **Department of Defense: 52 percent**
- **NASA and Civil government, including DOE equivalent sales: 24 percent**
- **International: 15 percent**
- **Commercial: 9 percent**

At the time of the merger, the ratio of defense to non-defense businesses was 52:48. The five-year goal was to shift that to 40:60. Penetrating commercial markets was a strategic thrust for the new corporation.

In addition to the above details, Micky sent the following information out to all Aeronautics Sector employees.[5]

> With initial annual sales of approximately $7.2 billion, our Aeronautics Sector is a leading domestic and international supplier of tactical, transport, reconnaissance, surveillance, and airborne early warning aircraft. Our products are state-of-the-art in aircraft design and systems integration. As a result, Lockheed Martin is the only corporation able to provide a "system of systems" for tomorrow's military aircraft, including advanced off-board sensors, rapid communications and data transmission, on-board integrated avionics, and advanced weapons systems. And we are the industry leader in low-cost, Lean aircraft manufacturing and integrated product development. In addition, the Aeronautics Sector is capable of "cradle-to-grave" service for any aircraft through contractor logistics support capabilities, advanced modification and maintenance facilities, depot maintenance capabilities, and contractor field teams.

There is a lot of information in the paragraph above, and it gave the Aeronautics Sector employees a good sense of where Micky wanted to go.

Servant leaders have a clear, compelling vision that excites passion in the leader and commitment in those who follow him or her. The next section builds on Micky's vision for the Aeronautics Sector and provides a glimpse of the many activities that required his attention.

Representing Lockheed Martin

As expected, Micky's new role expanded his exposure in the aerospace industry. He now represented Lockheed Martin's interests in a variety of places and ways. Some examples are as follows:

Attendance at Air Shows and Sales Campaigns

Micky continued to attend air shows at Farnborough, Paris, and other venues. There were at least three reasons why he thought it was important. First, he already had a reputation as a forward-thinking servant leader, so he wanted to show his support for employees outside the US. Second, as sector president, part of his role was to promote and help sell aerospace products and services. What better place than the world's leading airshows? Third, it gave Micky a chance to meet other leaders who shared his views about industry consolidation and opportunities to cooperate at some point in the future.[6]

Roll-out and First Flight of F-22

Even though Micky was no longer managing the day-to-day activities of the F-22 program, as aeronautics sector president, he was responsible for the Raptor, the coming JSF, the F-16 multirole fighter plus other programs that were critical to America's national defense. Roll-out of the first F-22 occurred on April 9, 1997, at the Lockheed Martin plant in Marietta, Georgia. The unveiling of the F-22 was managed like a major Hollywood event. Lee Greenwood sang the song "God Bless the USA," accompanied by the Air Force Band, as the curtain was drawn back and the Raptor was revealed. A statement from the White House called the F-22 a "catalyst for a revolution in air power."[7]

Dignitaries included Newt Gingrich, Speaker of the US House of Representatives, along with Senators Paul Coverdell and Max Cleland of Georgia. Secretary of the Air Force Sheila E. Widnall also attended along with the Air Force Chief of Staff, Gen. Ron Fogleman. The Commander of Air Force Combat Command, Gen. Richard Hawley, participated along with Brig. Gen. Mike Mushala, Director of the Air Force F-22 SPO. Lockheed Martin was represented by Norm Augustine, Chairman and CEO, along with Micky and other executives who had played a role in developing the fighter and managing the program. Retired CEO Dan Tellep, attended as well.

The first flight of the Raptor occurred on September 7, 1997. Paul Metz, Lockheed Martin's chief test pilot, was at the controls. Micky still gets emotional when he thinks back to the moment he watched the F-22 take off for the first time (see Figure 34).

Figure 34 a, b, and c. Preparing for First Flight of the Raptor. (Photos courtesy of Micky Blackwell)

Pursued International Partners

Vance Coffman, who became Chairman and CEO of Lockheed Martin on August 1, 1997, observed that Lockheed Martin's international programs were not fantasies. They were "real programs, working in "real" partnerships, with "world-class" corporations.[8] Micky emphasized that such partnerships could make a difference.

At the Farnborough Air Show in September 1998, he described why Lockheed Martin was the "partner of choice" for firms that shared their vision and were willing to share their resources. One of the reasons Micky said that was because Lockheed Martin was committed to working with international partners. They had a long history of exports and were ready to go to the next level.

In 1998, Lockheed Martin had 125 major partners from around the world working with the corporation. There were 48 partners on the C-130J in the UK alone. Lockheed Martin also had UK partners working with them on the advanced radar/night vision system on the UK Longbow Apache Program. The corporation was already working with the British to help produce the new Merlin helicopter and were working with a UK company on Air Traffic Control systems.

Partnered with Russians

At one point in the mid-1990s, Lockheed Martin became involved with Russian aircraft producer Yakovlev Design Group. According to reports, Yakovlev and Lockheed Martin agreed to explore building a multipurpose fighter.[9] One of the reasons Lockheed Martin was interested in discussing such possibilities with Yakovlev, was because one of the variants of the next fighter for the US Government had to be able to take off and land vertically. The Russians had developed a relatively simple way to do this, but officials were slow to approve the transfer of technology. In the end, Lockheed Martin reached an agreement with Yakovlev and was able to obtain their data.[10] It turns out that one of the reasons the Russians were so willing to work together was because their economy was in turmoil. Decision-makers at many levels were afraid of losing their talent because they could not pay them.

The final fighter design from this joint effort used thrust augmentation from a remote shaft-driven lift-fan located just behind the pilot. The concept was pioneered by the Russians and refined later by the Skunk Works. Years later, the Joint Strike Fighter, then designated the F-35, was awarded the Collier Trophy for its work on the development of the Integrated Lift Fan Propulsion System.

Participated with Northrop Grumman in Merger Negotiations

Micky was also involved in merger negotiations with Northrop Grumman that were ultimately unsuccessful. The title of an article in a Northrop Grumman newsletter said it all: a merger between these two giants would have forged "a new legacy of excellence."

More details about these discussions are presented later in the chapter, which is focused on the state of the sector prior to Micky's departure.

Supported NASA Space Day

Figure 35 is a photograph of Micky with NASA Director, Dan Goldin. Dan and Micky had gotten to know each other during the development of the X-33 VentureStar, an unmanned subscale spaceplane technology demonstrator.

This picture was taken on Space Day (May 22, 1997), which was established to raise awareness of US achievements in space. The day was chosen to coincide with the anniversary of President John F. Kennedy's speech which committed America to land a man on the moon.[11] Space Day was one of many activities Micky and Lockheed Martin supported at NASA. Space Day supports plans for human space exploration and encourages students to take courses that focus on Science, Technology, Engineering and Math (STEM).

Figure 35. Micky with Dan Goldin, Director of NASA, on Space Day, 1997. (Photo courtesy of Micky Blackwell)

Recipient of Awards

Throughout his career, Micky excelled in many things. Many of his accomplishments over his extraordinary career are listed in Appendix F, but two deserve to be highlighted.

Reed Aeronautics Award

The Reed Aeronautics Award is the highest award an Aerospace Engineer can receive in the United States of America. The award is given annually by the American Institute of Aeronautics and Astronautics. As presented to Micky on May 5, 1999, it reads:

> For distinguished contributions and advancements in the engineering development and management of aeronautical systems through the use of the IPT/Concurrent Engineering concepts and for leading the design and development of the F-22 Raptor Program.[12]

Collier Trophy

The Robert J. Collier Trophy, presented by the National Aeronautics Association, is the top trophy in the field of aviation, awarded each year for:

> The greatest achievement in aeronautics or astronautics in America, with respect to improving the performance, efficiency, and safety of air or space vehicles, the value of which has been thoroughly demonstrated by actual use during the preceding year.[13]

In 1998, Lockheed Martin Aeronautics Sector and its government/industry partners won the Collier Trophy for designing, manufacturing, and operating the U-2S/ER-2 high altitude, all-weather, multi-functional data collection aircraft, which serves as America's Sentinel of Peace around the world. In 2001, Lockheed Martin Aeronautics Sector and its partners won the Collier Trophy for producing the unique Joint Strike Fighter Lift Fan Propulsion System. The 2006 Collier Trophy was won by Lockheed Martin Aeronautics Sector for producing the revolutionary F-22 Raptor.[14] The last two Collier awards were made after Micky's retirement in 2000; however, the reader is now well aware of the contributions Micky made to these programs.

Joined the Conquistadores del Cielo

It is an honor to be invited to join the *Conquistadores del Cielo*. Many aerospace professionals don't even know the organization exists. When translated into English, the name means "Conquerors of the Sky." The Conquistadores are a very select group of executives from around the world, who have distinguished themselves in one or more ways in aviation or space.

The group was formed in 1938, to promote interest in aerospace and carry on the pioneering spirit of the original conquistador, Francisco Vazquez de Coronado. Their annual meetings take place at a private dude ranch in Wyoming. Being invited to join is a solemn occasion, but the meetings are reported to be fun for all who participate. The games vary from year-to-year, but usually include marksmanship, fishing, rodeo, and other activities that appeal to Type A personalities.

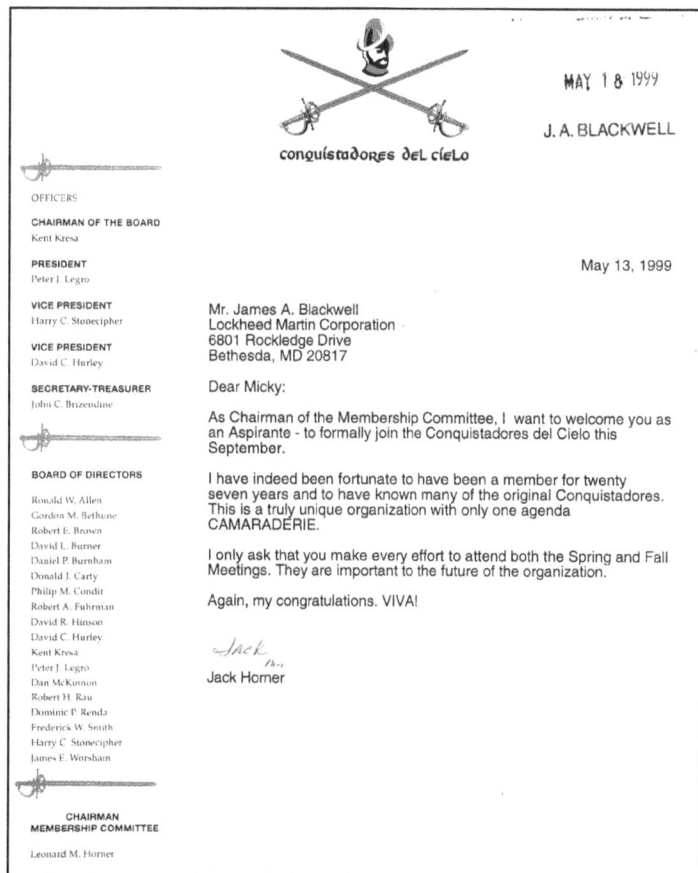

Figure 36. Invitation to Join Conquistadores del Cielo.

Micky attended his first meeting in September 1995, as a guest of Norm Augustine, Chairman and CEO of Lockheed Martin. He was inducted as a full member in September 1999.

Figure 37 is a picture of Micky with Carl Kotchian, a former president of Lockheed Corporation, at a Conquistadores del Cielo meeting.[15] Both men had to deal with alleged scandals and corruption. Some say Mr. Kotchian's activities led to the Foreign Corrupt Practices Act of 1977. More than twenty years later, Micky and his lawyers set a new standard for preventing corruption at Lockheed Martin.

Figure 37. Micky with Carl Kotchian discussing the past and the future of Lockheed Martin Corporation. (Photo courtesy of Micky Blackwell)

Difficult Times for Aerospace and Defense

In a way, the merger of Lockheed Corporation and Martin Marietta Corporation in 1995 was the product of an industry in trouble. A continuous decline in US defense budgets since the Berlin Wall came down in 1989 had affected the defense industry. By 1996, the defense budget was at its lowest level in modern history. The cuts to the Department of Defense budgets led the agency in 1993 to apply intense pressure to the defense industry contractors to get them to consolidate.[16]

The DOD outlays for military aircraft procurement for the decade spanning 1993 to 2003 which include Micky's tenure as Lockheed Martin Aeronautics Sector president are shown in Figure 38 below. The Lockheed Martin Aeronautics Sector sales over this same period are also shown. When DOD military aircraft procurement did start to rise again in 1997, it took a while for DOD's increase in outlays to be reflected in the sales of the Lockheed Martin Aeronautics Sector and the defense industry.

In the period between 1995 and 1999, the US DOD simply did not have the money to buy all that it needed. In addition, much of the US defense industry in 1995 was still operating inefficiently with old processes and support systems which made new DOD procurements cost more than they should. It was not a pretty picture for the agency or the defense industry during this period.

As a result, when Micky in 1995 was asked to take over the Aeronautics Sector of the largest defense contractor in the world, he knew he was walking into a difficult time for the industry and Lockheed Martin as military budgets continued to decrease. When Micky moved to the corporate headquarters in Maryland and transitioned into his new role, his responsibilities expanded. He was now managing six companies and was accountable for them all.

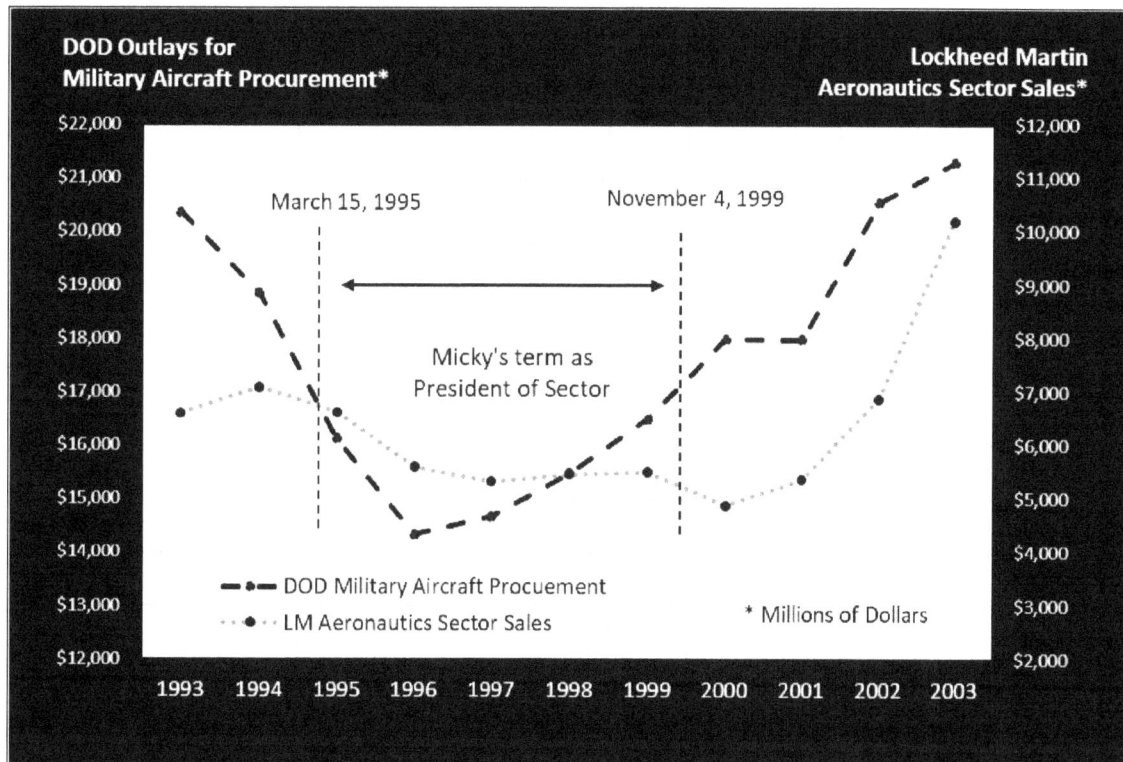

Figure 38. Lockheed Martin Aeronautical sales and DoD's military procurement.

Living in Difficult Times

Living through the difficult times of reduced military aircraft procurement from 1995 through 1999, the Lockheed Martin Aeronautics Sector continued to work to become the best of the best. Examples of their achievements are given below and will be elaborated on in the next chapter. The Aeronautics Sector:

- **Reengineered all its systems and processes to make the sector an efficient Lean Enterprise. By the end of 1999, major efficiency improvements had been made resulting in substantial cost reductions in every business area.**
- **Completed the C-130J Super Hercules tactical transport development, delivered the first 30 C-130J aircraft in 1999, and signed up several new customers.[17]**
- **Completed the Engineering and Manufacturing phase of the F-22 Raptor stealth fighter program and prepared to move the F-22 to the production phase.[18]**

- Was selected to lead one of the two competitive teams in 1997 to compete for the Joint Strike Fighter, which Lockheed Martin eventually won in 2001.
- Won the NASA contract in 1996 to design, develop, build, and fly a subscale unmanned, suborbital, reusable, single stage to orbit launch vehicle called the X-33.
- Continued to enhance and sell the F-16 Fighting Falcon as a staple front-line fighter to international air forces around the world.
- Won the Joint Air to Surface Standoff Missile (JASSM) contract in 1998 teamed with Lockheed Martin Orlando as the lead contractor to provide a high-precision, stealthy missile for use on a wide variety of aircraft.
- Won a sole-source contract in 1998 for upgrading the C-5B Galaxy with new avionics followed by a sole-source contract to upgrade the C-5B with commercial engines that were more reliable, maintainable, and powerful, along with 70 other improvements.
- Won the contract to take over engine maintenance, repair and overhaul of the C-5 engine and several other aircraft types in San Antonio, Texas.

Leadership, Accountability, Teamwork, and Performance

Even though military procurement had been decreasing since 1995, the Aeronautics Sector achieved its Lockheed Martin financial targets for 1997 and 1998 and contributed to making the corporate financial objectives by pulling forward a substantial amount from planned 1998 and 1999 cash advances, milestones, and deliveries. This made it more difficult to manage around any major difficulties the Aeronautics Sector might encounter going into 1999.

To make matters worse, the Aeronautics Sector's financial targets for 1999 were increased four times during 1998. In December 1998, Micky informed the corporation stating that, in his assessment, the Aeronautics Sector had no more than a 10 percent chance of meeting the 1999 corporate-directed financial targets. Despite this incredible financial challenge, Micky and his leadership team were still determined that the Aeronautics Sector would do everything humanly possible to try to achieve the targets.

Going into the third quarter of 1999, the Air Force, as feared, delayed the purchase of several F-22 and C-130J aircraft until 2000, and the $8 billion UAE F-16E/F Block 60 buy of 80 aircraft slipped into 2000 as well.

Finally, in a review of the C-130J program early in 1999, it was determined that the program was overrunning its development budget and needed additional funds from the corporation to complete development. The corporation was not happy with this financial hit but approved the additional funding. The increased development cost produced a negative impact of $210 million on the 1999 Aeronautics Sector operating profit.[19] From that point forward, Micky watched the C-130J program performance through weekly on-site program reviews each Saturday. There were no more serious technical or financial issues with the program. (The C-130J has gone on to be a huge money maker for Lockheed Martin Corporation.)

Recognizing in August 1999 that the Aeronautics Sector was not going to make its financial targets for the year, Micky went to each sector company and spoke to their executives on "Leadership, Accountability, Teamwork, and Performance." The following is a summary of his major points.

Leadership

"I know we take a lot of pride in the work that we do. Many are top performers and leaders in your field. Nevertheless, on the JSF, and other programs, the company is in trouble. There is no other way to say it — we are simply not performing. What I am talking about is leadership, accountability, and the management of major programs. The customer has already told us, they can't handle any more surprises. From where I sit, it looks like a burning platform. From where they sit, we have 18 months left."

Accountability

"We cannot miss any more budgets. We must hire good people and train them to be accountable. Many program managers are not well trained. I know what that is like. I survived as a program manager, but it should not have been so difficult. Program managers, IPT members, and functional managers know they are responsible. They must now begin to realize they are also accountable."

Teamwork

The third point he made was people had to work in teams. "It is really quite simple. Since we are all in the same boat, we have to learn to swim together. The people who use our products, know how to work in teams. We need to show our customers we know what that means."

Performance

"If I had to characterize our sector, I would say we have a cost problem. Every program seems to be in trouble, and we need to solve the problem together."

Micky closed with the following comments.

"There is no one in our business that is doing what we are doing. We are being 'out PR'd' by our competitors. I know we can make our numbers, but we must prove it to our shareholders. Finally, I need your help. There is no more grace left. We have had many casualties, and I will probably be next. We must show them we can win. Since I know you all personally, I have no doubt we can do it."

Micky's second difficult issue in 1999 involved the Joint Strike Fighter. Because of the importance of the JSF to Lockheed Martin, Micky knew that the corporation had to have a good relationship with the Air Force. After assessing the situation, Micky made it his mission to please Ms. Darleen Druyun, the Principal Undersecretary of Acquisition. His goal was to do whatever was possible to put the Aeronautics Sector in a favorable position to win.

Early in 1999, Micky asked Druyun if they could meet monthly. The purpose of the meeting was to review Aeronautics Sector programs. Secretary Druyun agreed and started to meet with Micky on a regular basis. All the meetings were constructive, and the discussions were frank on both sides. Micky felt they were making great progress, so he asked Druyun if she would meet with the Aeronautics Sector company presidents. She agreed to meet in Washington, but off-the-record.

The meeting was held and went just as planned. The discussions were open, and nothing was held back. The Aeronautics Sector review went well. Druyun also made "do better" comments on other Lockheed Martin programs not in the Aeronautics Sector. Micky took notes and shared them with his CEO, Vance Coffman. He was directed by Coffman to send his notes to the other sector presidents and select corporate staff. Unfortunately, no one on his staff marked them "Lockheed Martin Proprietary Data," and they quickly made their way to *Aviation Week*, a widely-read publication in the aerospace industry. Furthermore, the notes were erroneously attributed to Peter Teets, Lockheed Martin's president and COO. This was a huge embarrassment to the corporation.

Lockheed Martin's CEO called Micky into his office and expressed his deep displeasure at the disclosures. In retrospect, Micky acknowledges that it was a mistake to allow distribution of his notes without the proper "Private Data" markings. Even though they were never meant to be distributed beyond Lockheed Martin executives, he knew he was responsible for the actions of his employees and should have made sure his notes were handled differently.

As an addendum to this story, Druyun ended up being the very antithesis of servant leadership. In a story in *Air Force Magazine* in November 2004, editor John Tirpak wrote: "Darleen A. Druyun, the Air Force's top career civilian acquisition official from 1993-2002, was sentenced Oct. 1 [2004] to prison time and later probation after she admitted that, while in her USAF position, she gave Boeing preferential treatment on numerous contracts.

"Druyun confessed that she performed the favors to 'ingratiate' herself with the company in order to win a high-paying executive position for herself after retiring from the Air Force and to secure employment with the company for her daughter and son-in-law. She received a sentence of nine months in prison, followed by additional undetermined detention or house arrest, and three years' probation. The sentence and the confessions shocked the Air Force."

Retirements Announced

At the end of 1998, Lockheed Martin replaced Dr. Melvin Brashears as president and COO of the Space and Strategic Missiles Sector. On October 1, 1999, Thomas Corcoran, who had been president and COO of the Electronics Sector and headed the Space and Strategic Missiles Sector for a short period, also left the corporation.

As the end of 1999 approached, rumors were rife that Dr. Vance Coffman was about to be replaced by the Board of Directors.[20] However, on October 29, 1999, Coffman announced Peter Teets (Lockheed Martin COO) and Micky Blackwell (president and COO of the Aeronautics Sector) would instead retire.[21]

With the Aeronautics Sector missing its 1999 financial objectives, combined with the public disclosure of Druyun's "do better" comments on Lockheed Martin programs in other Lockheed Martin sectors, it was essentially game over for Micky.

Industry observers were shaken by Micky's retirement, as he was considered to be the company's third leading executive, after COO Teets and CEO Coffman.[22] Noted and highly respected aviation consultant Richard Aboulafia said, if there was anyone who could have claimed to be "Mr. American Aerospace," it would have been Micky Blackwell. He was well known for his work on the F-22 Raptor and for representing Lockheed Martin abroad.

Figure 38 (page 170) shows that Lockheed Martin Aeronautics Sector's sales beginning to rebound in 2001 as the DOD budget began to increase and the Aeronautics Sector began to book the new contracts it had won. Similarly, the sector's profit began to increase after 2000 due to increased sales and the Lean Enterprise changes Micky had implemented.

It usually takes years to develop and build new aircraft. One of the reasons it takes so long is because most new designs incorporate leading-edge technology and require rigorous testing. Increases in development costs for new aircraft are the rule rather than the exception. Figure 38 shows how long it took to turn Lockheed Martin's sales around. Unfortunately, Micky didn't hold the position long enough to reap the benefits of changes he was making and the new contracts he had won. Micky had the respect of his customers and colleagues and was well positioned to grow the Aeronautics Sector in the immediate future—if he had continued to be its leader.

In the same article that reported that Micky would be leaving his position at Lockheed Martin, David Fulghum observed that "the worst may be over for Lockheed Martin." He stated that "the bottom has been reached and now it's going to get better."[23] How true this was is discussed in the next chapter.

Micky's Thoughts about Retirement

During Micky's tenure as the head of the Aeronautics Sector, the major contracts they had won set the stage for the Aeronautics Sector to become the dominant military aircraft manufacturer in the world. He had hired people he trusted to continue the work he had started. Lockheed Martin had been good to Micky, and Micky had given his best to Lockheed Martin.

As Micky thought about retirement, he knew no one was indispensable. He also knew that things don't always turn out the way you would like them to turn out, even for servant leaders. He was 59 years old and a highly respected business executive. New horizons beckoned, and he was ready for the challenge. He was comforted by Jeremiah 29:11, because he knew God had a plan for good to give him a future and hope.

Based on Romans 8:28, Godly servant leaders trust that God is always looking out for their good.

For I know the plans I have for you, says the Lord. They are plans for good and not for evil, to give you a future and a hope.

Jeremiah 29:11 (TLB)

We know that all things work together for good to those who love God, to those who are the called according to His purpose.

Romans 8:28 (MEV)

It is because of Micky's trust in God, that he began to eagerly look forward to what God had in store for him.

Toast to the Blackwells

On January 14, 2000, Billie and Micky were honored at a retirement ceremony in Washington D.C. Dr. Vance Coffman was the host and presented a tribute to Micky. Dain Hancock was Micky's Aeronautics Sector replacement, so he talked about Micky's many achievements. Both Vance's and Dain's comments were highly complimentary.

At the end of Micky's retirement dinner, Coffman toasted Micky and Billie. The toast honored the Blackwells and wished them well in their retirement (see Figure 39).

With the audience standing and their glasses lifted, the audience honored Micky and Billie with the following words:

May the skies be clear and blue above you.
May the wind be always at your six o'clock.
May the wings of friendship bring us together again many times in the years ahead.
And may you always bask in the love and admiration of a nation, a company and
your colleagues, who owe you both so much.
To Micky and Billie Blackwell, good luck and God bless you both as you enter this
new phase of life's journey called Retirement!

Figure 39. Micky with Vance Coffman at Micky's retirement dinner in Washington, D.C. (Photo Courtesy of Micky Blackwell)

Lessons Learned and Important Points

In this chapter, we looked at Micky's final years with Lockheed Martin. Lessons learned and important points include:

- As a member of the senior executive team in the newly formed Lockheed Martin Corporation, Micky was involved in a significant management change program.
- When Micky was promoted to be the Lockheed Martin president and COO of the Aeronautics Sector, he knew he was walking into a difficult defense budget situation.
- The first flight of the F-22 Raptor occurred on September 7, 1997.
- In 1998, Lockheed Martin had 125 major partners around the world working with the corporation. They had 48 partners on the C-130J in the UK alone.
- In the mid-1990s, Lockheed Martin entered a partnership with the Yakovlev Design Group to explore the joint development of technology that would allow an aircraft to take off and land vertically.
- Micky participated in the Northop Grumman and Lockheed Martin merger negotiations, that ultimately were not successful, but, in retrospect, would have been a blockbuster transaction.
- He was active in supporting NASA Space programs.
- The Reed Aeronautics Award is the highest award an Aerospace Engineer can receive in the USA. The award was presented to Micky on May 5, 1999.
- It was an honor to be invited to join the Conquistadores del Cielo. Micky attended his first meeting in September 1995 and was inducted as a full member in September 1999.
- Nearly four years after becoming president and COO of the Aeronautics Sector, the C-130J development costs were greater than budgeted; and 1999 C-130J, F-16, and F-22 purchases were being delayed by the Department of Defense until 2000, which caused the Aeronautics Sector to miss the 1999 financial targets established by the corporation.
- Lockheed Martin's CEO announced on October 29, 1999, that Micky would retire at the end of 1999.
- Micky had hired people he trusted and loved, and he knew they would continue the work he had started.
- He knew that things don't always turn out the way you would like them to turn out, even for servant leaders.
- Micky had set the stage for Lockheed Martin to become the world's dominant military aircraft manufacturer.
- Micky, trusting in God, looked forward to his next challenge.

Chapter Notes

1 Lockheed Martin Corporation. 1995. *Annual Report*. Bethesda, MD: Lockheed Martin Corporation, pp. 10-11.

2 Initially, the official name of the "Skunk Works" was the "Advanced Development Projects" (ADP) division of Lockheed California Company. Sometimes this was abbreviated as "LADP. In 1990, the Skunk Works transitioned from being a division to an independent company under the Lockheed conglomerate, the Lockheed Advanced Development Company (LADC). In 1995, Martin Marietta merged with Lockheed to form the Lockheed Martin Corporation. The Skunk Works was still its own company and became the "Lockheed Martin Skunk Works" (LMSW). At this time the term "Skunk Works" changed from being a nickname to the official name of the organization and is a registered trademark.

3 James "Micky" Blackwell. November 8, 2011. "Lecture on Leadership and Management." Kennesaw State University, Georgia.

4 Based on materials developed by Michael Hopp and Harold Manger. March 15, 1995. "Dealing With and Managing Change." *Change Management Presentation Developed for Merger Between Lockheed and Martin Marietta*. Bethesda, Maryland: Lockheed Martin Corporation.

5 Letter from Micky to all sector employees. See Micky Blackwell. March 16, 1995. "Memo to Lockheed Martin Aeronautics Sector." Bethesda, Maryland: Lockheed Martin.

6 Almost a decade earlier Perlmutter and Heenan published a popular paper on this topic. See Howard V. Perlmutter and David A. Heenan. 1986. "Cooperate to Compete Globally." *Harvard Business Review* 64 (2), pp. 136-152.

7 John A. Tirpak., 1997. "Raptor 01." *Air Force Magazine*, p. 48.

8 Lockheed Martin. September 8, 1998. "Real Partnerships Really In-Place." *News Line Daily, Farnborough International*. London: Lockheed Martin International.

9 Luke Johnson. 1995. "Lockheed, Russia Co-Design New Fighter." *Marietta Daily Journal*, Marietta, Georgia, pp. 1A, 3A.

10 John G. Roos. January, 1997. "From the Boardroom "Micky" Blackwell, president & COO, Aeronautics Sector." *Armed Forces Journal International*, p. 54.

11 Susan Miles, ed. March 6, 1997. "Lockheed Martin backs nation's first Space Day, set for May 22." *Lockheed Martin Aeronautical Systems Star*, p. 3.

12 American Institute of Aeronautics and Astronautics. 2018. Reed Aeronautics Award Recipients. Accessed June 13, 2018. https://www.aiaa.org/HonorsAndAwardsRecipientsList. aspx?awardId=10ba0453-cdb4- 4fb3-a055-e0687427901c.

13 Collier Trophy. n.d. *National Aeronautic Association*. Accessed November 1, 2020. https://naa.aero/awards/awards-and-trophies/collier-trophy

14 Ibid.

15 Mr. Kotchian was a colorful leader. As described by the *New York Times*, he was "a central figure in a bribery scandal that rocked Japan and the Netherlands during the 1970s." Mr. Kotchian passed away in 2008. To his death, Carl maintained that his actions "simply reflected the methods of the times." See Kate Galbraith. 2008. "A. Carl Kotchian, Lockheed Executive, Dies at 94." *New York Times*. December 22. Accessed January 28, 2019. https://www.nytimes.com/2008/12/23/business/23kotchian.html.

16 Norman R. Augustine. May-June 1997. "Reshaping an Industry: Lockheed Martin's Survival Story." *Harvard Business Review*, (75) 3, pp. 83-94.

17 Lockheed Martin Corporation. 1999. *Annual Report*. Bethesda, MD: Lockheed Martin Corporation, p. 9.

18 Ibid, p. 10.

19 Ibid, p. 24.

20 Reference for Business. Vance D. Coffman, 1944- Accessed January 27, 2020. https://www. referenceforbusiness.com/biography/A-E/Coffman-Vance-D- 1944.html#:~:text=Coffman.&text=%E2 %96%A0-,Vance%20D.,America's%20early%2Dwarning%20defense%20system.

21 Vance Coffman. October 29,1999. "Micky Blackwell to Retire." Bethesda, MD: Lockheed Martin Corporation.

22 Greg Schneider. October 30, 1999. "Lockheed chief resigns as bad news worsens; No. 3 executive also steps down; profit outlook grim." *The Baltimore Sun.* Accessed August 10, 2021. https://www. baltimoresun.com/news/bs-xpm-1999-10-30-9910300147- story.html

23 Chris Joyner. October 30,1999. "Poor earnings report rocks Lockheed." *Marietta Daily Journal,* Marietta, Georgia, pp. 1A; 6A.

Chapter 13

State of Aeronautics Prior to Micky's Departure

I am one of the few that believe in loyalty to the company. I loved Lockheed Martin—just about more than anything else.

Micky Blackwell
President & COO Aeronautics Sector (Retired)
Lockheed Martin Corporation

The sad thing about Micky's retirement was that because of the actions Micky had taken, the Aeronautics Sector was poised for growth. Subsequent years showed that Micky was on the right track. Almost everything he touched was successful. This chapter provides more insight into the state of the Lockheed Martin Aeronautics Sector prior to Micky's departure.

People

Sector Staff

The ability to win new business is a function of how good your talent is and how motivated employees are to sell the products you are marketing. Micky was fortunate to be able to surround himself with highly talented and motivated people. In fact, he often stated that his biggest contribution was to just point them in the right direction and let them do their work. His sector staff consisted of both former Lockheed and Martin Marietta people as well as several new hires. His right-hand executive assistant was his best friend from California, Jim Summers.

Lockheed Martin – Northrop Grumman Merger

In 1993, the US Secretary of Defense Les Aspin called all the defense industry executives to Washington, D.C. Once gathered, they told them that the US government supported the consolidation of the nation's military industries. This meeting became known as the "Last Supper." The rationale on the part of the government was there was not enough defense work to support the current state of the industry. As a result, the defense industry underwent a substantial transition for the next several years with several corporate mergers and companies being bought and sold. In the years following the "Last Supper" both Lockheed Martin and Northrop Grumman had been active in the defense industry consolidation.

In early 1997, in the spirit of consolidation when it seemed to make sense, Norm Augustine, Chairman and CEO of Lockheed-Martin, and Kent Kresa, chairman and CEO of Northrop Grumman, agreed to merge the Lockheed Martin and Northrop Grumman Corporations.

There was no initial objection by the US government when the proposed merger of Northrop Grumman and Lockheed Martin was announced. The government had recently allowed Boeing to purchase the Rockwell Defense and Aerospace business in 1996 and McDonnell Douglas in 1997.

As part of the Lockheed Martin and Northrop Grumman merger, the Lockheed Martin Aeronautics Sector would combine with the Northrop Grumman Aerospace Systems Sector. The two sector's programs meshed almost perfectly.

In 1997, the Aeronautics Sectors of both Lockheed Martin and Northrop Grumman were both financially strong. Unfortunately, the manufacturing facilities of both sectors were still far from full. The upshot of combining the two sectors would be to fill up the best facilities and sell the rest. This was a great deal for the US government since the overhead rates of the companies receiving the merged assets would drop significantly, reducing overall costs. This was particularly important for the future bid price for the Joint Strike Fighter and for reducing the cost to the US government of ongoing aircraft programs. Further, merging the assets of the two Aeronautics Sectors was good for the two corporations, because selling unneeded facilities would yield substantial returns.

For over a year, the management at Northrop Grumman and Lockheed Martin briefed each other on their capabilities and toured each other's facilities. They introduced each other to several business opportunities.

In 1997, Jacques Gansler became the DOD Undersecretary for Acquisition, Technology, and Logistics. This made him the number three person in charge of the Department of Defense, and the DOD head of acquisition policy. Gansler announced he was against the Lockheed Martin and Northrop Grumman merger. He believed that the merger would create an unacceptable level of "vertical integration" for one company. He was supported in his view by Air Force Principal Deputy Undersecretary for Acquisition, Darleen Druyun, and Joel Klein, who was head of the Justice Department's antitrust division.

Lockheed Martin and Northrop Grumman executives tried for several months to work out a solution with the government. In a final meeting between the Pentagon, Justice Department, Lockheed Martin, and Northrop Grumman, the Pentagon and Department of Justice turned down the merger. After spending a great deal of time and resources evaluating the possibilities, the government said "no" and the two corporations terminated the proposed merger.

Missile Launch Systems and Aerostructures in Baltimore, Maryland

As part of the Lockheed and Martin Marietta merger in 1995, the Martin Marietta Missile Launch Systems and Aerostructures Company located in Baltimore, Maryland, was moved into the Lockheed Martin Aeronautics Sector.

The former Martin company in Baltimore was having a difficult time executing a contract to manufacture composite engine nacelles for Airbus. Micky asked Ray Roquemore, a manufacturing expert at Lockheed in Marietta, to take over manufacturing at the Missile Launch Systems and Aerostructures Company in Baltimore. Ray was close to retirement, and the new challenge was just what he needed. He identified the problems, came up with solutions, and quickly returned the company to profitability. A short time later, he was promoted to president of the Lockheed Martin Missile Launch Systems and Aerostructures Company. On November 3, 1997, Lockheed Martin sold the company to General Electric.

Programs

C-5M Galaxy

Micky had not been sector president long when he got a call from Gen. Ronald Fogelman, who was now the Chief of Staff of the Air Force. He inquired about the C-5 proposal that Micky had briefed him on a few years earlier. Micky told him the proposal was still in his safe. Gen. Fogelman told him to dust it off and submit it to the US Air Force Principal Deputy Undersecretary for Acquisition, Darleen Druyun. Micky reminded him that the upgraded C-5M, with commercial engines and new avionics, was a great airplane for the Air Force at a great price. He then told Gen. Fogelman that he would submit the unsolicited proposal as requested and would not present it to the media or Congress until Lockheed Martin heard back from the general that the Air Force was interested. True to his word, Micky did not allow Lockheed Martin to market the upgraded C-5M proposal, which turned out to be a good strategy that paid off.

About a year after submitting the unsolicited C-5M proposal to the Air Force, Micky got a call from Druyun. She wanted to talk about modifying the existing C-5B and selected C-5A and C-5C aircraft by replacing the existing engines with the new commercial engines described in the Lockheed Martin proposal. The commercial engines were substantially more reliable, maintainable, and powerful than what was used before. The Air Force had indeed read Lockheed Martin's proposal. Shortly thereafter, Lockheed Martin was awarded a sole-source contract for upgrading the aircraft's avionics (called the Avionics

Figure 40. Modified C-5M Galaxy. (Photo courtesy of the USAF)

Modernization Program-AMP). Several years later, contracts were awarded to Lockheed Martin to re-engine the C-5M with new commercial engines and improve aircraft reliability (called the Reliability Enhancement and Reengining Program-RERP). The reengineering of the C-5M (see Figure 40) was a very successful program for the Air Force.

Sometime later, Lockheed Martin also won the contract to take over the C-5 engine Maintenance, Repair, and Overhaul (MRO) work at the Air Force's logistics center at San Antonio, Texas. The Air Force C-5 MRO base at San Antonio was a casualty of the 1995 Base Realignment and Closure (BRAC) program. After more than a decade of operation, that business was sold off.[1]

F-35 Joint Strike Fighter

A series of multirole and/or short takeoff/vertical landing fighter technology demonstrator programs were conducted in the late 1980s that led to the opening of the Joint Advanced Strike Technology (JAST) office by the Department of Defense (DoD) in 1994. The purpose of the JAST office was to develop aircraft, weapons, and sensor technology with the aim of replacing several disparate U.S. aircraft with a single family of aircraft.

Lockheed Martin Tactical Systems Company and Lockheed Martin Advanced Development Company (the Skunk Works) won contracts from the Air Force and DARPA respectively to develop the technology required to build a Joint Strike Fighter (JSF) that could be flown by the Air Force, Marine Corps, and the Navy. The JSF would use a mostly common structure and common systems to reduce the cost of developing replacements for the Air Force F-16 and A-10, the early model Navy/Marine F/A-18s, and the Marine vertical takeoff and landing AV-8B.

On March 22, 1996, the DoD issued a request for proposal (RFP) to Lockheed Martin, Boeing, McDonnell Douglas, and Northrop Grumman to build Joint Strike Fighter concept demonstrators. The number of production aircraft projected to be purchased by the government from the eventual winner of this competition was staggering—more than 3,000.

On November 16, 1996, the Air Force, as the lead service, eliminated two of the four competitors (Northrop Grumman and McDonnell Douglas) and awarded JSF concept demonstrator contracts to Lockheed Martin and Boeing.

Micky was at Lockheed Martin's Headquarters in Bethesda, Maryland on November 16, 1996, when he heard the Secretary of Defense, Bill Perry, make the announcement that Lockheed Martin and Boeing had won the contracts to build the JSF concept demonstrators. There was a tremendous celebration throughout Lockheed Martin that day.

Micky directed the Lockheed Tactical Systems Company in Fort Worth to be the lead Lockheed Martin company for the JSF program. The Skunk Works was directed to provide engineering support to Fort Worth, and to build the concept demonstrator aircraft at the Skunk Works' plant in Palmdale, California. With additional support from the F-22 team in Marietta, Georgia, Lockheed Martin was able to field a "dream team" to compete for the JSF program.

On December 16, 1996, a few weeks after the winners of the JSF concept demonstrator contracts were announced, Boeing broke the news that they were buying McDonnell Douglas. This added substantial fighter experience and resources to the Boeing JSF team and potentially enhanced their competitiveness.

Lockheed Martin and Boeing's individual JSF contract values were around $750,000,000[2] to develop and build their JSF concept demonstrators and to define their preferred weapon system concept. Both Lockheed Martin and Boeing, under terms of the contract, would produce two aircraft each to demonstrate a conventional carrier takeoff and landing (CTOL) version, which would later be modified into a short takeoff and vertical landing (STOVL) version, and a carrier-based (CV) version. Boeing's JSF would carry the X-32 designation, and Lockheed Martin's JSF would be designated the X-35.

Lockheed Martin's X-35 vertical-lift concept for the Marine version of the JSF used thrust augmentation from a remote shaft-driven lift fan located just behind the pilot. The lift-fan vertical-lift concept was pioneered by Yakolev, a Russian company. The Skunk Works purchased the Russian technical data and further refined it to develop the unique shaft-driven lift-fan concept.

The STOVL vertical-lift concept being used by Boeing for the Marine version of the X-32, was pioneered by British Aerospace (BAE) decades before with the Harrier. McDonnell Douglas built the

AV-8B version of the Harrier under license from BAE. If BAE became their partner on the X-32, they could potentially bring a wealth of vertical-lift experience to Boeing.

The JSF competitors, Lockheed Martin and Boeing, were teammates (along with General Dynamics) on the F-22 program. In the F-22 competition, they were required to invest a substantial amount of their own money during the Dem/Val phase of the program. A cost-share arrangement with the Air Force on the F-22 was required because the Air Force did not have sufficient budget to fund both the aircraft and engine development programs. Unfortunately, the contractors never saw the expected return-on-investment on their cost-share, because the number of F-22s to be purchased was drastically reduced by the U.S. government.

Furthermore, DoD decreed that because of the need to safeguard stealth technology, the U.S. could not sell the F-22 to friendly countries. This substantially reduced the number of F-22s to be built and further reduced the contractor's return-on-investment. In the past, less-capable versions of front-line fighters were often sold to U.S. allies. This allowed contractors to keep their production lines open for future US sales and enabled coordination between the US and its friends who were using the same equipment.

Based on the F-22 contractors cost-share experience, both Lockheed Martin and Boeing asked the government to limit what could be spent on the concept demonstrator phase of the JSF contract to only government funding. That is, no prime contractor could do work on the JSF contract with their internal research and development funds and incorporate the results into the final JSF System Development and Demonstration (SDD) proposal. Each prime contractor had to be a good steward of the money given to them under the concept development contract, and they would be evaluated on how well they did with the funds they were provided.

For the next several years, the competition to win the JSF System Development and Demonstration phase was hotly contested. To enhance Lockheed Martin's JSF proposal for SDD, the company spent substantial time and resources wooing British Aerospace (BAE) to join Lockheed Martin's JSF team. As noted above, BAE had a long relationship with McDonnell Douglas (its AV-8B Harrier partner) which was now part of Boeing. Lockheed Martin was thrilled when British Aerospace announced they would partner with them on the JSF instead of with Boeing. In addition, having BAE as part of the JSF program enhanced the possibility that the United Kingdom would purchase a significant number of airplanes.

The Boeing JSF design for the X-32 concept demonstrator had a delta wing, no horizontal tails, and 2-D engine nozzle that could deflect to augment pitch control. Boeing refined their X-32 design to better meet government requirements by changing to a trapezoidal wing and adding a full horizontal tail. By the time the redesign was done, it was too late to incorporate the design changes into the X-32 concept demonstrator.

Lockheed Martin's X-35 design had a full horizontal tail, a vertical tail, and an engine nozzle that could deflect in any direction giving the airplane tremendous maneuverability.

On the Lockheed Martin F-22, the engine nozzles could deflect up and down enhancing airplane maneuverability. However, the Air Force was adamant that if both engines flamed out, they wanted enough horizontal tail to land the airplane safely. Lockheed Martin engineers could not figure out how the Boeing X-32, with no horizontal tail, could have sufficient control to land the airplane with the engine out. The puzzle was solved when Boeing notified the Air Force that they wanted to internally fund the redesign of their X-32 concept demonstrator. To do this, Boeing and Lockheed Martin would have to agree to change their contracts with the Air Force and shift to cost-sharing agreements.

Lockheed Martin was adamant that they did not want to reopen the concept demonstrator contracts. Doing so would have allowed Boeing to use their own money and spend more than the value of the contract, which violated the terms of the original agreement. While it was not necessarily easy, Lockheed Martin was able to execute its concept development contract within contract funding. This put Boeing in a very bad spot. The result was Boeing did not get to include in their System Development and Demonstration (SDD) proposal any data from tests of their X-32 concept demonstrator with a revised wing design concept and conventional stabilators that was paid for with their internal funds.

In Micky's heart, he truly believed that Lockheed Martin's X-35 was, in general, superior to Boeing's X-32. All the company's technology and experience on the F-16, F-117, and F-22 was available to the X-35 team during its development. Also, the vertical-lift concept for the Marine version of the fighter developed by the Skunk Works was felt to be superior to Boeing's vertical takeoff and landing approach.

In late 1999, Micky was confident that Lockheed Martin was going to win the JSF competition, unless a last-minute hiccup derailed the process. The financial reward for winning the production contract was huge. According to a recent Congressional Research Service (CRS) report, the U.S. Air Force, Marine Corps, and Navy are acquiring 2,456 F-35 Lightning II aircraft of different varieties, and our allies around the world are planning to buy hundreds more (see Figure 41).[3]

Because of the magnitude of what became the F-35 Lightning II program, the Lockheed Martin team determined that they needed an additional industrial partner to produce the required number of airplanes. Bill Lawler, one of Micky's classmates from the University of Alabama aerospace engineering school, was head of Northrop Grumman's (NG) aeronautical sector and had previously headed their B-2 Spirit stealth bomber program. Bill approached Micky

Figure 41. US Navy F-35Cs aboard the USS Abraham Lincoln. This was the first time F-35Cs participated in operations with F/A-18 Super Hornets, E-2D Hawkeyes, and EA-18G Growlers. August 28, 2018. (Photo JSF Program Office)

about Northrop Grumman becoming a Lockheed Martin subcontractor on the next phase of the JSF program. Bill and Micky agreed, and Northrop Grumman became a major subcontractor to Lockheed Martin on the F-35 along with BAE.

C-130J Super Hercules

True to the agreement between Gen. Ron Fogelman and Micky, in early 1993, the Air Force began helping Lockheed Martin make changes to the C-130J design so it would meet the requirements the Air Force said it needed.

The rollout ceremony for the first C-130J for the United Kingdom RAF was on October 18, 1995. Air Marshall Sir John Allison was on hand for the ceremony, as well as the RAF Pipes and Drummers. The first C-130J flight occurred on April 5, 1996. Watching the C-130J take off for the first time, was a lot like watching the F-22 on its first flight. It was also thrilling to be part of a new era for the C-130—one of the most successful tactical transport aircraft ever produced (see Figure 42).

Since Lockheed Martin sold the C-130J to the United Kingdom prior to selling it to the US Government, the aircraft had to be certified by the Federal Aviation Administration (FAA). Usually, the US Government supplies the certification for new military aircraft built in the US, but it was not the lead customer for the C-130J. Lockheed Martin successfully obtained its commercial flight certification and began deliveries of the C-130J to the United Kingdom.

Figure 42. Micky with Prince Philip inspecting C-130J. (Photo courtesy of Micky Blackwell)

After a long struggle with Congress, Lockheed Martin was successful in helping the services program funds for the National Guard and Air Force Reserve C-130Js into the Congressional budget. Lockheed Martin was also successful in helping add KC-130J tankers to the budget for the US Marines to replace the current KC-130 tankers that were nearing the end of their service life. The Marines loved the new aircraft.

To acquaint potential customers with the C-130J, Lockheed Martin flew the aircraft on a demonstration tour around the world. Following the trip, a number of new C-130J customers began to come on board. One was the Italian Air Force. To land the C-130J sale to Italy, Lockheed Martin agreed to help Alenia Aircraft modernize its tactical two-engine cargo aircraft called the C-27J Spartan.[4] Lockheed Martin and Alenia modified the C-27J to add new Rolls Royce AE2100D3 turboprop engines and other features borrowed from the C-130J.[5] In addition to signing the United Kingdom, Australia, and Italy as C-130J customers, Micky participated in marketing the C-130J to Israel, Japan, Saudi Arabia, Canada, and Norway all of which eventually purchased the C-130J.

Some of the best venues for contacting senior Air Force personnel and foreign government officials were the annual and bi-annual air shows at Farnborough, England; Paris, France; and the Royal International Air Tattoo, in Fairford, England. Micky also attended the Berlin Air Show, the UAE Air Show, and the Singapore Air Show. The C-130J was generally the major topic of discussion.

After working through the typical growing pains associated with the launch of a new aircraft, the C-130J has matured into a spectacularly successful program. The program is still going strong with more than 550 aircraft having been produced as of June 2024 for the US and more than 18 other operators around the world.

F-22 Raptor

In late 1995, Micky received an invitation to meet with Darleen Druyun, the Acquisition Executive of the Air Force. During the meeting, Micky was told that the Lockheed Martin F-22 contractor team was going to have to reduce their previously negotiated price for the program, which was now well underway. The message from the Acquisition Executive was not a pleasant one to receive. It was definitely not good news and threatened the future of the fighter.

With the cuts to the Pentagon budget proposed by the President that year, there was simply not enough money to fund the program. Micky said he will never forget Lockheed Martin's CEO Norm Augustine's comment when he said, "The budget cuts sustained by the Department of Defense are like living through two major depressions at the same time." In fact, the USAF said that if the Lockheed Martin team did not lower its price, the Air Force would have to cancel the program.

The Air Force was in anguish. The F-22 was an aircraft the Air Force was willing to give its first-born child to have. They really needed Lockheed Martin to help them. The Air Force offered to help the Lockheed Martin F-22 contractor team by showing them the "Lean Thinking" principles (discussed in Chapter 8) that Pratt & Whitney was using to reduce production costs on the F119 engine—the engine that powered the F-22. The US Air Force felt the Lockheed Martin contractor team could apply the same *Lean* principles and substantially reduce the cost of producing the F-22 airframe and equipment. They were absolutely correct.

The US Air Force took the Lockheed Martin F-22 contractor team to the Pratt & Whitney facility in Connecticut to see the work they were doing on "Lean." To be honest, Micky was not hopeful that the team would walk away with much since they had been working to cut costs and implement total quality management for several years. That turned out to not be the case. When Micky saw what they were doing, he was blown away. It was the ultimate application of good old common sense. Once you understood Lean, you absolutely had to have it—and Micky immediately made plans to fully implement Lean throughout the entire Lockheed Martin Aeronautics Sector.

The implementation of Lean Thinking resulted in major cost reductions for the F-22 program, just as the Air Force had hoped. For example, the final assembly of the F-22 in Marietta originally required two production assembly lines. By applying Lean principles, only one assembly line was needed to produce the same number of airplanes. This was an incredible achievement and a huge cost savings.

From that point forward, the F-22 program proceeded smoothly to produce the 187 aircraft approved by Congress. The Lockheed Martin F-22 contractor team and the US Air Force gave the

Figure 43. F-22 in Flight. (Photo courtesy of the US Air Force)

USAF fighting men and women an air dominance fighter that was superior to any existing aircraft by any measure. The advances in technology incorporated into the F-22 design were numerous and groundbreaking.

The F-22 program spawned planning, design, development, production, and business processes that would change forever how US military aircraft are conceived and built. Everyone associated with the F-22 program, from inception to completion, can be incredibly proud to have been involved in designing and producing this state-of-the-art fighter (see Figure 43).

The F-16 Falcon

The Lockheed Martin F-16 Fighting Falcon (unofficially referred to by pilots as "Viper") was built in Fort Worth, Texas for decades and is an extraordinary program. Not only was it a great airplane for the US Air Force, but it also became a staple for air forces around the world. The F-16 was extremely profitable and well run. The application of Lean Thinking enhanced an already great product.

Micky's activities on the F-16 during June 1995 to the fall of 1999 were primarily in helping Lockheed Martin sell the aircraft around the world. Micky worked with campaigns to market the airplane to Norway, Greece, Israel, Egypt, Jordan, Poland, Singapore, Denmark, and the United Arab

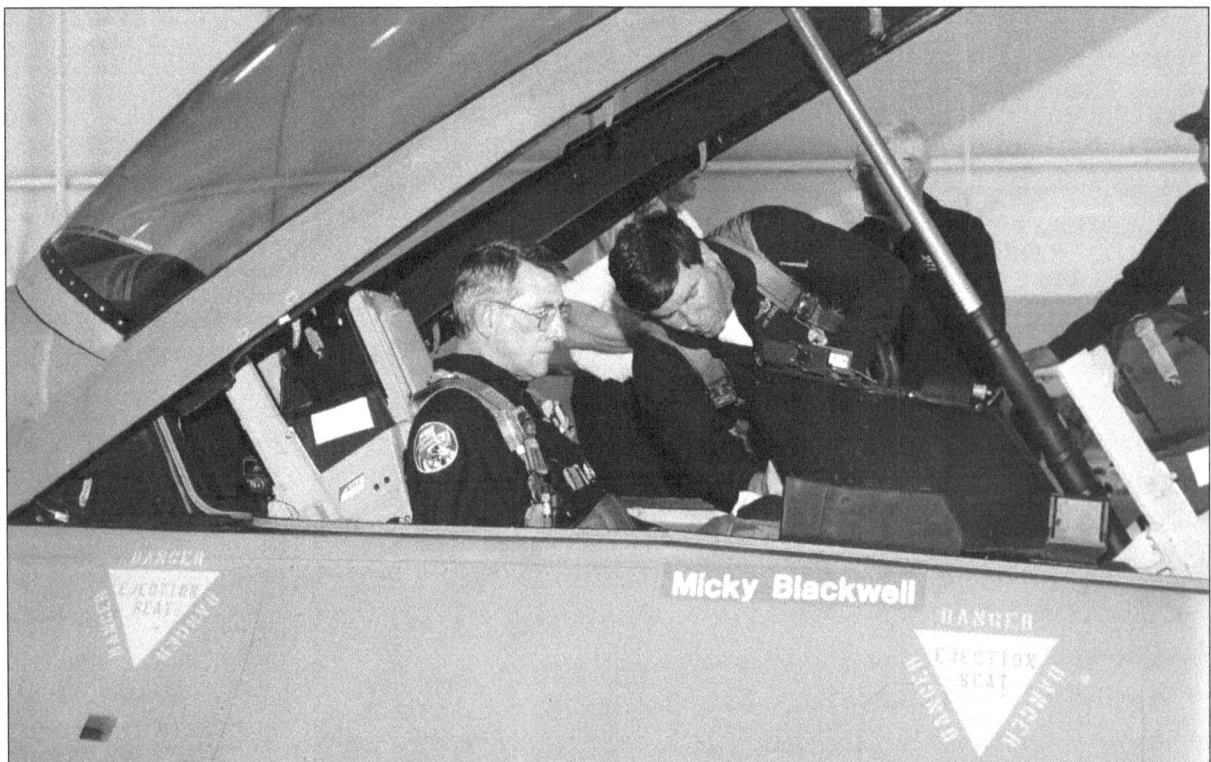

Figure 44. Micky preparing for flight in F-16 fighter at Lockheed Martin plant in Fort Worth, Texas. (Photo courtesy of Micky Blackwell)

Emirates. Lockheed Martin was successful in selling F-16s to nearly all these countries. In the last few years, the F-16 has seen a resurgence in sales. It is currently being manufactured at the Lockheed Martin plant in Greenville, South Carolina.

One of the best days of Micky's life, was the day he spent flying an F-16 fighter (see Figure 44). He put on a flight suit, climbed into the back seat, and headed straight up into the sky like a rocket. The pilot let Micky fly the jet for a while. When they landed, Micky was hosed down with water—just like all newbies who have taken their first flight in a fighter.

X-33 VentureStar Technology Demonstrator

In the 1990s, the Lockheed Martin Skunk Works was working on technologies to build a reusable single-stage-to-orbit launch vehicle. NASA planned to issue a request for a proposal to design, develop, build, and demonstrate an unmanned subscale technology demonstrator suborbital spaceplane called the X-33. The X-33 would flight test a range of technologies needed to enable the development of a next-generation single-stage-to-orbit reusable launch vehicle called VentureStar.

The Lockheed Skunk Works submitted the winning bid to NASA and was awarded the contract on July 2, 1996. They were also supported by the Lockheed Martin Missiles and Space Sector. Micky hired former astronaut Ken Mattingly of Apollo 13 fame to assist him and the Aeronautics Sector with NASA and other government interfaces.

Figure 45. The X-33 Advanced Technology Demonstrator was an unpiloted reuseable vehicle designed to launch like a rocket to 50 miles above the Earth, and land like an airplane when its mission was complete. (Image courtesy of NASA)

There were several technologies that had to be developed for the X-33 to be successful. Some of these included metallic thermal protection systems, composite cryogenic fuel tanks for liquid hydrogen, the aerospike engine, and lifting body aerodynamics.[6]

The Skunk Works was about one miracle away from making the X-33 an incredible success (see Figure 45). At that time, Lockheed Martin engineers were unable to develop a composite material fuel tank that would not leak under operational pressures. This turned out to be the program's undoing. The X-33 was ultimately canceled in 2001, however, the research on single-stage-to-orbit reusable vehicles continues.

The Joint Air-to-Surface Standoff Missile

The Joint Air-to-Surface Standoff Missile-Extended Range (JASSM-ER) is a conventional, stealthy, air-launched ground attack cruise missile designed for the US Air Force and its international partners (see Figure 46).

Initial contracts for competing designs were awarded to Lockheed Martin and McDonnell Douglas in 1996. The Skunk Works teamed with the lead contractor, Lockheed Martin Orlando. The Skunk Works

Figure 46. A JASSM-ER missile is released from a B-1 bomber. Eglin AFB's Joint Air-to-Surface Standoff Missile program office recently reached a milestone with the first delivery of the newest JASSM variant. (Photo courtesy of the USAF)

provided aerodynamic support and was responsible for the flight test portion of the program.

With a lot of great engineering, Lockheed Martin won the JASSM competition. A contract for further development was awarded in 1998.

Today, JASSM is integrated into several top-of-the-line bombers and fighters. Future integration will include the Lockheed Martin F-35 Lightning II and other international platforms.

Argentine A-4 Refurbishment Services

Using capabilities from several of the Lockheed Martin Aeronautics Sector companies, the Lockheed Skunk Works won a contract for the refurbishment of A-4s for the Argentine Air Force. Between 1996 and 1999, thirty-six A-4 Skyhawks were converted to the newer A-4AR "Fightinghawks." The program moved forward with few technical problems.

The Lockheed Martin Skunk Works also bid for and won a contract to take over the Argentine Military Aircraft Center production facilities and operate them for Argentina.

Lessons Learned and Important Points

Some of the lessons learned and important points in this chapter include:

- **Micky put the Lockheed Martin Aeronautics Sector on the right track to be successful. Almost everything he touched became a success.**
- **Lockheed Martin was awarded a sole-source contract for upgrading the C-5M with new commercial engines. The reengining of the C-5M was a very successful program.**
- **After working through the typical growing pains associated with a new aircraft, the C-130J matured into a spectacularly successful program. The program is still going strong with 500 units having been produced as of March 2022 for the US and other nations around the world.**
- **The Lockheed Martin F-16 Fighting Falcon is an extraordinary program. Not only was it a great airplane for the USAF, but it also became a staple for international air forces around the world. The F-16 was extremely profitable and well run. The application of Lean Thinking enhanced what was already a great program. The program is still going strong today.**
- **The implementation of Lean Thinking resulted in major cost reductions for the F-22 program. The F-22 Raptor was superior to any existing aircraft by any measure.**
- **Because of the magnitude of the F-35 Lightning II program, Lockheed Martin determined that they needed additional partners to produce the required number of airplanes. Northrop Grumman and BAE became major subcontractors to Lockheed Martin on the F-35.**

- The Skunk Works was about one miracle away from making the X-33 an incredible success. Research on single-stage-to-orbit reusable vehicles continues to this day.
- The Skunk Works teamed with the lead contractor, Lockheed Martin Orlando, to win the Joint Air-to-Surface Standoff Missile program. JASSM is a conventional, stealthy, air-launched ground attack cruise missile designed for the US Air Force and its international partners. Today, JASSM is integrated into several top-of-the-line bombers and fighters. Future integration will include the F-35 Lightning II and other international platforms.
- The Lockheed Martin Skunk Works supported by other sector companies won a contract for the refurbishment of A-4s for the Argentine Air Force. Between 1996 and 1999, thirty-six A-4 Skyhawks were converted to the newer A-4AR "Fightinghawks."
- The Lockheed Martin Skunk Works bid and won a contract to take over the Argentine Military Aircraft Center production facilities and operate them for Argentina.

Chapter Notes

1 James "Micky" Blackwell. 2021. *All the Days of Our Lives. The Heritage and History of Billie and James Blackwell.* Asheville, NC: United Writers Press, p. 134.

2. "Joint Strike Fighter program." n.d. *Wikipedia.* Accessed July 19, 2024. https://en.wikipedia.org/wiki/Joint_Strike_Fighter_program#JSF_competition.

3 Jeremiah Gertler. (2020). *F-35 Joint Strike Fighter (JSF) Program.* Washington D.C.: Congressional Research Service. Summary. Accessed June 6, 2020. https://crsreports.congress.gov/product/pdf/RL/RL30563.

4 In 2007, the C-27J Spartan Joint Cargo Aircraft (JCA) was purchased by the U.S. Air Force where it was deployed to meet the time-sensitive needs of the warfighter. In 2012, the JCA was retired by the U.S. Air Force due to budget restraints. These aircraft were later reassigned for use by the U.S. Coast Guard and Air Force Special Operations. See Lockheed Martin Alenia Tactical Transport Systems. n.d. *C-27J Spartan Tactical Transport Aircraft.* Accessed April 21, 2019. https://www.airforce- technology.com/projects/spartan/.

5 The Lockheed Martin C-130J Super Hercules is a four-engine turboprop military transport aircraft. The C-130J is a comprehensive update of the Lockheed C-130 Hercules, with new engines, flight deck, and other systems.

6 One of unique characteristics of the aerospike engine is its ability to use thrust vectoring as opposed to other rocket control techniques. Thrust vectoring eliminates weight and operates more efficiently in flight. For more information on the aerospike engine see NASA Dryden Flight Research Center, U.S. Air Force Flight Test Center, and Blacksky Corporation. April 19, 2004. *Aerospike Engine Flight Test Successful.* Accessed February 19, 2019. https://www.nasa.gov/centers/dryden/news/NewsReleases/2004/04- 23_pf.html.

Chapter 14

A Servant Leader's Legacy

I hope that when others look back on everything I have done, my actions will meet the highest ethical standards possible.

Micky Blackwell
President & COO Aeronautics Sector (Retired)
Lockheed Martin Corporation

When Micky retired from Lockheed Martin, he left more than just having been an executive at a large defense contractor. He left a legacy from his life and work that will be difficult to match. This chapter addresses Micky's legacy as a servant leader.

One of the more obvious benefits of his work was his contribution to America's security. The direct and indirect jobs created by the contracts won while he led the Lockheed Martin Aeronautics Sector is high on his legacy list. In addition, Micky's legacy includes the way he successfully applied the Enterprise Servant Leadership Model discussed in this book to business. His Lean Enterprise contributions to aerospace and industry are a legacy that have been recognized for the superior value they produced.

From his early days at NASA Langley to his final days at Lockheed Martin, Micky's life and work are good examples for a new leader who wants to become the best of the best. The examples he gave us are invaluable. In many ways, he helped set the standard for others to follow. He showed us what it meant to be a servant leader who served his people.

Micky's work was so pervasive that his legacy is presented in two parts. It begins by describing his activities that are known to the public. It ends with some of his more personal activities.

Legacy from Public Activities

Micky Impacted the Success of the F-22 Program

Calling Micky the "Father of the Raptor" was not a title he sought or wanted. In many ways, it went against the very culture he was trying to build. His goal was to serve others. He did his job well, but his influence was pervasive as the Raptor evolved. The Enterprise Servant Leadership Management Model and the Integrated Product Team Concept that were developed on the F-22 program helped him select employees and leaders that collaboratively worked together in high-performance teams.

The Enterprise Servant Leader "guidelines" derived from Micky's life and work (presented in Chapter 6) were developed and successfully used on the F-22 and on all projects that followed the F-22. These guidelines will provide future leaders directions on how to implement the Enterprise Servant Leadership Model in their organizations.

The general timeline for Micky's leadership of the F-22 Program is shown in Figure 47. Even though he was only directly in charge of the program from 1991 to 1993, his influence went far beyond that brief period extending in both directions.

Like any new sophisticated high-performance system, the F-22 had a few birthing problems as it entered initial production in 2001. Cost increases were a major issue, and a small number of design changes had to be made. Despite these concerns, the best fighter pilots in the world consider themselves lucky when they get to fly this fifth-generation fighter.

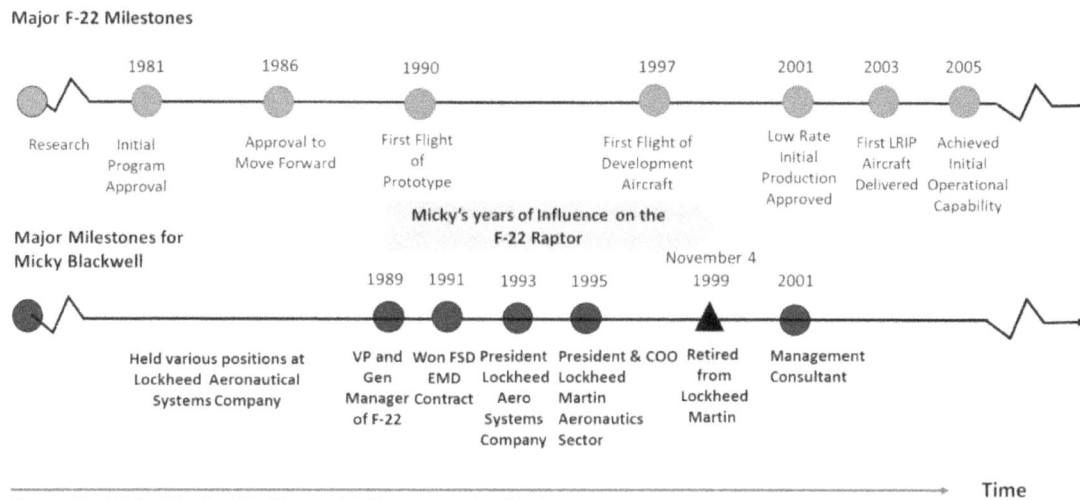

Major F-22 Milestones

1981	1986	1990	1997	2001	2003	2005

Research | Initial Program Approval | Approval to Move Forward | First Flight of Prototype | First Flight of Development Aircraft | Low Rate Initial Production Approved | First LRIP Aircraft Delivered | Achieved Initial Operational Capability

Micky's years of Influence on the F-22 Raptor

Major Milestones for Micky Blackwell

November 4

1989	1991	1993	1995	1999	2001

Held various positions at Lockheed Aeronautical Systems Company | VP and Gen Manager of F-22 | Won FSD EMD Contract | President Lockheed Aero Systems Company | President & COO Lockheed Martin Aeronautics Sector | Retired from Lockheed Martin | Management Consultant

Time

Figure 47. Micky Blackwell's Years of Influence on the Raptor.

F-22 Exponentially Improved National Defense

A key part of Micky's legacy is the F-22 Raptor—the world's best air superiority fighter (see Figure 48 for a picture of the last Raptor produced). It is stealthy, highly maneuverable, packed with integrated avionics, and capable of sustained high-speed flight without the use of afterburners. It represents "an exponential leap" in America's warfighting capabilities and performs both air-to-air and air-to-ground missions in support of national defense.[1]

According to the US Air Force, "the F-22 cannot be matched by any known or projected fighter aircraft."[2] According to Lockheed Martin, the F-22 provides the US and its allies with unparalleled air superiority and the freedom to maneuver and remain free from

Figure 48. The Last F-22 Raptor in Production at Marietta, Georgia. (Photo provided by Jeff Rhodes, Lockheed Martin)

attack.[3] In 2015, the F-22 program received the Air Force Association's John R. Alison Award for outstanding contributions by industrial leadership to national defense.[4]

Testimony to Micky's Leadership

A book was recently published by Robert A. Retsch who worked for Micky on the ATF program. Mr. Retsch was in charge of building a RCS pole model for the ATF DEM/VAL program. His team was seriously over budget. He was concerned about what to do, so he made an appointment to go see Micky who was leading the internal Lockheed ATF program. After briefly describing the problem, Micky asked him to schedule an appointment with his team for the next day.

Micky showed up on time and Retsch introduced him to each of his people. Retsch explained there was a significant budget overrun due to requirements creep, inadequate staffing, and having to work scattered inefficiently throughout the plant.

Micky left without saying too much, and Retsch wondered if he understood the issue. The next day Retsch was scheduled to present the project's budget status to his managers. Retsch had attended the review that came before his, and it had not been pleasant to watch. The managers were primed and ready to really grill him on his budget overrun. As he stood to address the first slide, he could tell that they were not happy. The tone of their questions in the previous review had been demanding and angry.

Then Micky entered the room and quietly began to speak. Immediately the tone changed, and the frenzy disappeared. Micky calmly described how he had visited Bob Retsch's department, and he understood Retsch's problems. He said "we, as a program, have done a poor job in supplying the tools that Bob needs to build our pole model. His current budget status is not all his fault." I was a little stunned that this upper-level manager would find the time to come to a lower-level meeting and defend me.

The room at once went silent. One of the managers in the room said "Yes, you're right, Micky, we haven't been supportive." The tone of the discussion had changed—and changed for the better. The interrogation was still important, but it was less about being over budget, and more about how to fix it, Mr. Retsch never had to report on his budget status again.

Retsch stated in his book "I owed my reputation, and possibly my job, to Micky. One helluva valuable lesson on leadership was on display, between his demeanor and his willingness to admit to the program's failings. It was another great example for me to emulate, and I stored it away with the others."

It was a valuable lesson in leadership, and a great example for others to follow. Micky proved, once again, that he was committed to caring for and serving his people.

Source: Robert A. Retsch. 2020. Luckiest Engineer: From Farm Boy to Skunk Works and Beyond. Self-published memoir by Robert A. Retsch.

F-22 Helped Generate Thousands of Jobs

When the F-22 Lockheed, Boeing, and General Dynamics team and the F-119 Pratt & Whitney team won their respective contracts for designing and building the F-22, those agreements generated thousands of jobs in Georgia, Texas, Washington, California, Florida and elsewhere. According to a report published by the Congressional Research Service in 2009, the F-22 program supported 8,800 direct jobs at these three contractors.[5] Lockheed estimates that the F–22 supported an additional 16,200 people working for suppliers in 44 states. When these figures are combined, the F–22 supported a total of about 25,000 direct jobs. Using a multiplier of 2.8 to estimate indirect jobs elsewhere in the economy, Lockheed estimates that an additional 70,000 jobs were indirectly supported by the F-22. When these figures are combined, Lockheed Martin projects that in 2009, a total of 95,000 jobs were directly or indirectly supported by the F–22 program.

Micky Impacted How Future Programs Will Be Led

Micky's initiatives used in the development of the F-22 and in reengineering several major Lockheed Martin organizations had a long–term impact on the industry. He showed the world the power of

Enterprise Servant Leadership when it is used to lead programs of any size. Nothing says it better than what Micky did—he used what he learned to lead the development of the world's most sophisticated aircraft. See insert "Testimony to Micky's Leadership."

Micky introduced Integrated Product Teams to streamline and improve decision-making. He implemented Enterprise Lean Thinking to increase throughput and reduce costs. He transferred knowledge and technologies from the F-22 into the JSF program resulting in billions of dollars in cost avoidance.

> *The words "servant" and "leader" describe opposite ends of the spectrum, but when you put them together, miracles can happen.*
>
> Micky Blackwell

Comments from Colleagues and Competitors

As word of Micky's retirement and departure from Lockheed Martin spread through the government, the military, and industry, letters from all over the world began to pile up on Micky's desk. Cards and letters from some of Micky's friends and colleagues are listed in Figure 49. Comments from others follow.

Figure 49. Notes and letters sent to Micky Blackwell from (a) Congressman Saxby Chambliss, Deputy Secretary of Defense John Hamre, (b) USAF Gen. Ralph Eberhart, and (c) US Senator Paul Coverdell after the announcement of his departure from Lockheed Martin.

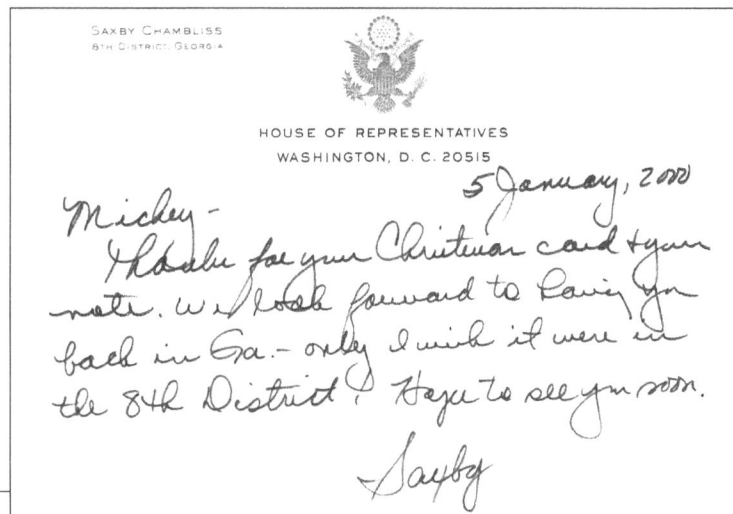

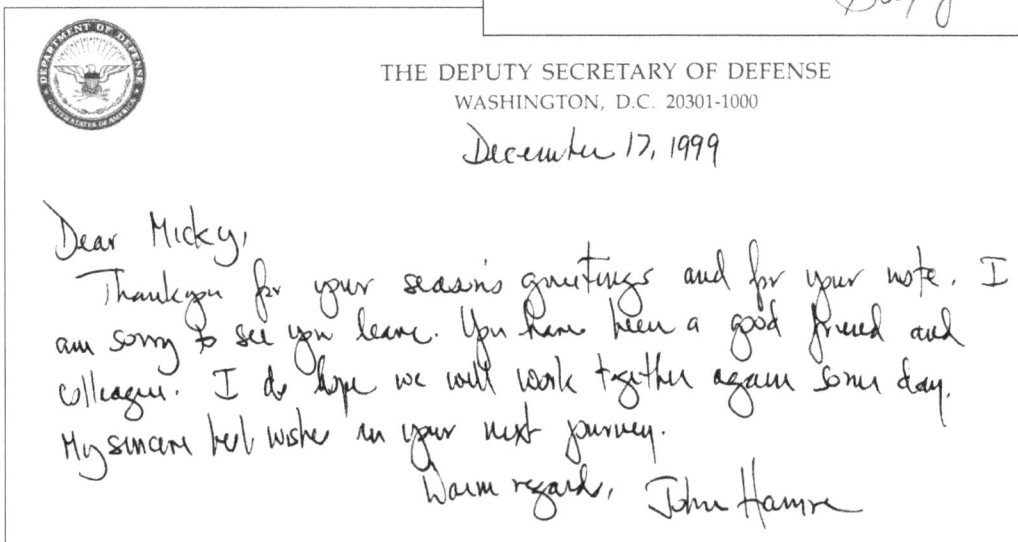

Figure 49a. Letters from US Representative Saxby Chambliss (top) and Deputy Secretary of Defense John Hamre (bottom).

AIR COMBAT COMMAND
OFFICE OF THE COMMANDER
LANGLEY AIR FORCE BASE, VIRGINIA 23665-2788

3 November 1999

Mr James A. Blackwell
Mail Point 380
Lockheed Martin Corporation
6801 Rockledge Drive
Bethesda, MD 20817

Dear Micky

The men and women of Air Combat Command join me in congratulating you on the occasion of your retirement after 30 years of oustanding service. Thanks for your superb work in the development of the F-22 fighter and the many other Air Force programs you supported as well. We wish you much happiness and success in the years ahead.

Sincerely

RALPH E. EBERHART
General, USAF
Commander

Come see us in C-Springs. All the best

Figure 49b. Letter from USAF Gen. Ralph Eberhart.

UNITED STATES SENATE

PAUL COVERDELL
GEORGIA

November 4, 1999

Mr. James A. Blackwell, Jr.
President and Chief Operating Officer
Lockhead Martin
6801 Rockledge Drive
Bethesda, Maryland 20817

Dear Micky:

Word has reached us that you have announced your retirement. Projects developed under your leadership, such as the F-22, are a critical part of America's defense strategy. Your hard work and dedication over more than thirty years of service is an example to all.

Please accept my congratulations on your many years of achievement, and my best wishes on your future endeavors as you embark on this new course in life.

Sincerely,

Paul D. Coverdell
United States Senator

Figure 49c. Letter from US Senator Paul Coverdell (R-Ga.).

Dr. Vance Coffman, Chairman and CEO, Lockheed Martin

After 30 years of service to Lockheed Martin by Micky, Dr. Coffman, Chairman and CEO of Lockheed Martin Corporation, described Micky as a legend so great, his reputation preceded him wherever he went.[6] He also said that Micky made innumerable contributions to the company. One of the most prominent was the development of the F-22 fighter.[7]

Mr. Robert Elrod, President, Lockheed Martin Skunk Works

As president of the Skunk Works, Bob Elrod wrote a note signed by 21 people from the Skunk Works who loved and respected Micky. The note said "All of us at the Skunk Works want to extend our very best wishes for your retirement and commend you for your many years of distinguished service to Lockheed Martin Corporation."

Mr. Ian R. Stopps, President of Lockheed Martin UK LTD

Mr. Stopps, president of Lockheed Martin in London wrote, "I, along with many others, were very surprised to hear of your recent retirement. You will be sorely missed in Lockheed Martin and by our customers, for you helped to project a very positive image of the Aeronautics business and our corporation."

Mr. Colin Green, Director of Operations, Rolls-Royce

Mr. Green, Director of Operations and a member of the Board of Directors for Rolls-Royce PLC, sent a personal note to Micky saying, "I read with sadness that you were leaving Lockheed after a long and distinguished career. No words of mine can possibly provide any kind of solace but suffice it to say how sorry I am to see you go."

Dr. James Roche, Northrop Grumman Executive and soon-to-be Secretary of the Air Force

Dr. Roche was the 20th Secretary of the US Air Force. Prior to serving as the Air Force Secretary, he served in the US Navy and as an executive with Northrop Grumman Corporation. In his note to Micky, Dr. Roche stated, "I'm shocked! You should not have retired. There are many reasons why this industry is in a mess today, but you are not one of them! . . . Rather, this business needs thinkers and you are one of the best."

Mr. John Weston, Chief Executive of BAE Systems

In a letter to Micky, John Weston, Chief Executive of BAE Systems said, "We shall be sorry to see you go, and we are all very sympathetic about the challenges facing Lockheed Martin... I wish you all the best in establishing yourself in Atlanta."

Mr. Moshe Keret, President of Israel Aircraft Industries, Ltd.

Mr. Keret, president of Israel Aircraft Industries Ltd., also wrote a letter to Micky. In his letter he said, "I was extremely surprised by your unexpected retirement... I would like to wish you the best in whatever you are going to do!"

Brig. Gen. Joshua Shani (Retired), Lockheed Martin Israel

Gen. Shani wrote, "[T]here is a big disappointment in the IAF (Israeli Air Force) and MOD (Ministry of Defense) because of your departure…they see you here as a real friend and as a super professional officer."

Lt. Gen. Frederick McCorkle, US Marine Corps

In an e-mail to Micky, Gen. McCorkle said, "This breaks my heart. I appreciate everything you have done for me and for our Corps. God speed to you, my friend."

Mr. Gregory H. Bradford, President of Aerospatiale Matra

Mr. Bradford, president of Aerospatiale Matra, stated "I was very surprised – and saddened – to hear the news of your retirement from Lockheed Martin. We will all miss you. We…would not be where we are today without your persistence and determination."

Yuan-Shi Peng, Ph.D. Vice Chairman of Aerospace Industrial Development Corporation

Dr. Peng, Vice Chairman of Taiwan's Aerospace Industrial Development Corporation, wrote "Being such a dedicated and outstanding leader in Lockheed Martin, your contributions are exceptional to the company and your retirement from Lockheed Martin must have been a difficult decision for the company to agree on. Please accept our best wishes and best of luck to you in your future endeavors."

Mr. Giorgio Zappa, President of Alenia Aerospazio

Mr. Zappa, president of Alenia Aerospazio, in a letter to Micky, wrote, "When I heard about your retirement, it was with a great regret for me and for all the other colleagues in the company, who had the pleasure to work with you, experiencing your high commitment and professional competence."

Mr. William H. Swanson, Chairman and CEO, Raytheon Company

Mr. Bill Swanson, Chairman and CEO of Raytheon Company, sent an e-mail to Micky stating, "I wanted to let you know you will be missed. I enjoyed our dealings together and respected what you stood for in your day-to-day business relationships."

Sir Robert Walmsley, UK Ministry of Defence

Vice Admiral Sir Robert Walmsley Chief of Defence Procurement, UK Ministry of Defence wrote, "It has been a long road, but like many tough journeys, it will have been worth the trouble. Very many thanks for all your valuable contributions…"

Mr. David Fulghum, Aviation Week

Micky also received a nice compliment from David Fulghum, a senior reporter from *Aviation Week & Space Technology*. On October 30, 1999, in the *Marietta Daily Journal*, Fulghum said, "Although the company had been criticized by the Air Force, Blackwell had been seen as a bright spot. They liked Micky Blackwell, which made me surprised he got the ax."[8]

Fulghum continued by saying "the company was not able to make enough improvements in the third quarter to save the jobs of even popular executives like Blackwell…I think they just felt they had to do something, and that's what those guys are there for," he said. "I personally thought that Micky Blackwell was terrific…I think he was a victim of circumstance."[9] In an ironic twist of fate, Mr. Fulghum was the person who wrote the *Aviation Week* article that many believe contributed to Micky Blackwell and Peter Teet's ouster from the ranks of Lockheed Martin.[10]

Ms. Marillyn Hewson, future CEO and Chairman of Lockheed Martin Corporation

Ms. Marillyn Hewson, who became CEO and Chairman of the Lockheed Martin Corporation in 2013, wrote a hand-written note to Micky. Ms. Hewson said, "I am fortunate to have had your coaching, encouragement, and support. You have made a very positive impact on me and my career—and I thank you."[11] During Hewson's tenure at Lockheed Martin, she was named "The Most Powerful Woman in Business" by *Fortune* and "CEO of the Year" by *Chief Executive* magazine. In 2019, she was awarded *TIME* magazine's list of "100 Most Influential People in the World."[12]

Legacy from Personal Activities

Micky's legacy from his personal activities includes his business related activities, public service related activities, church related activities, and family related activities.

Business Related Activities

To say that Micky Blackwell had an impact on people and organizations is insufficient to describe his influence on the City of Marietta, the State of Georgia, and industry in general. His influence on co–workers, friends, and the community was enormous. It also extended well beyond the boundaries of Lockheed Martin and the aerospace industry.

After his retirement from Lockheed Martin, he turned down employment opportunities such as becoming an executive at other aerospace related companies; working with leveraged buyout funds; and becoming Chairperson of the Mechanical and Aerospace Engineering Department of a major university. He respectfully declined these offers, because he and Billie had decided to make their home in Georgia.

Cobb County School Board

Once Micky and Billie were back in Marietta, Georgia, Micky was approached by the Cobb County School Board to learn his interest in becoming Superintendent. This was one of the largest school systems in the state of Georgia. They were looking for someone who had "real world" experience. That the School Board would consider Micky as superintendent was a major honor. However, this was too far from Micky's experience base, and he declined.

JAB Consultants

In 2001, Micky decided to form his own one-man consulting firm. His focus was on organizational leadership, aerospace products, and aerospace marketing. His clients included Lockheed Martin Aeronautics; Lockheed Martin Electronics; Ball Aerospace; IBM Aerospace and Defense; Raytheon; KPMG and other well-known companies. Although he enjoyed aerospace work, after four decades in aerospace he was ready to do something different.

Chairman of ScanTech LLC

In 2003, Micky was asked to join the Board of an emerging company—ScanTech LLC. Their focus was on using electron beam technology to scan large items such as ship containers, rail cars, and trucks for explosives. The technology was derived from Russian research. To diversify their products, ScanTech also developed systems for screening airline baggage. The same technologies could also be used to pasteurize and disinfect global food products being shipped to America.[13] After joining the Board of Directors, Micky was elected Chairman of ScanTech, and remained Chairman until 2009. ScanTech recently announced a merger with Mars Acquisition Corporation.

Chairman of Alpha Bank and Trust

Micky and a group of men in 2005 decided to start a local bank called Alpha Bank and Trust. The focus of the Bank was primarily on real estate loans. Branches were set up in two of Georgia's fastest growing markets—Marietta and Alpharetta. Micky was elected Chairman in June 2005. Working together, Micky and the Board instituted policies that were born out of servant leadership and made customer service a trademark of the organization.

Bank regulators applauded their performance for the first two years of operation. However, with the Wall Street financial crisis in 2007, the economy descended into the "Great Recession." The drop was so fast and long, Alpha Bank and Trust was no longer able to raise capital.

The bank was closed by the FDIC on October 24, 2008. As he notes in his memoirs, the board and bank staff did everything they could to keep the bank alive. After doing everything possible to save the bank, it was time to move on.

Public Service Activities

When Micky retired, he became involved in a substantial number of public service activities. This was one way he felt like he could give back to the community.

Considered for Key US Government Position

After he retired from Lockheed Martin, Micky was asked to consider a position at the US Department of Defense. He would be part of President Bush's new administration. The two positions most frequently mentioned were the Secretary of the Navy and the Secretary of the Air Force. To that end, Micky worked with Paul Wolfowitz, Jim Roche, Steve Hadley, and Andy Marshall to put together a plan for improving the Department of Defense.

Micky had supporters in Georgia, Texas, Alabama, and many other places. The head of Georgia's Republican Party wrote a letter to Donald Rumsfeld, the Secretary of Defense, to encourage Secretary Rumsfeld to ask the President to appoint Micky as the next Secretary of the Air Force (see Figure 50).

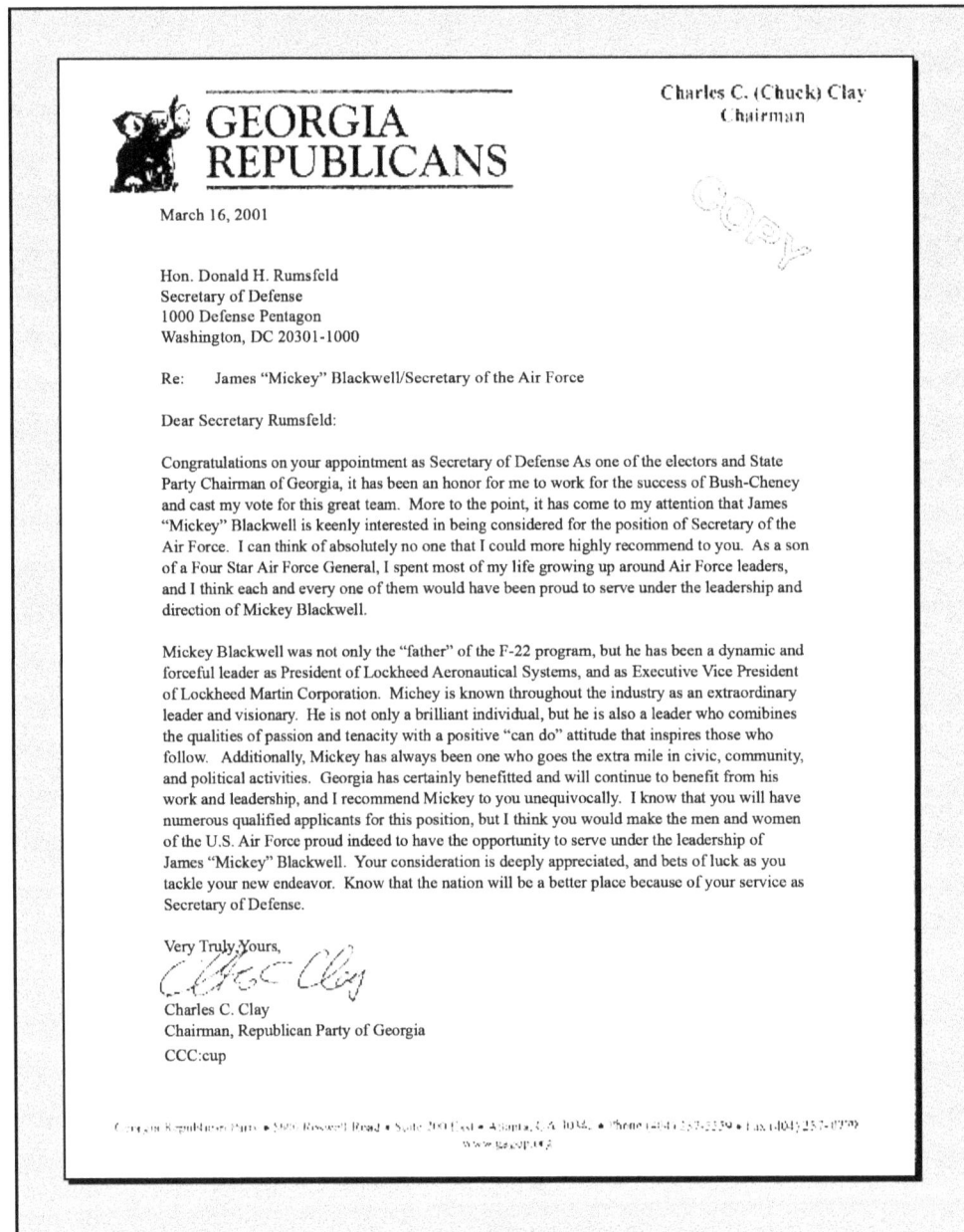

GEORGIA REPUBLICANS

Charles C. (Chuck) Clay
Chairman

March 16, 2001

Hon. Donald H. Rumsfeld
Secretary of Defense
1000 Defense Pentagon
Washington, DC 20301-1000

Re: James "Mickey" Blackwell/Secretary of the Air Force

Dear Secretary Rumsfeld:

Congratulations on your appointment as Secretary of Defense As one of the electors and State Party Chairman of Georgia, it has been an honor for me to work for the success of Bush-Cheney and cast my vote for this great team. More to the point, it has come to my attention that James "Mickey" Blackwell is keenly interested in being considered for the position of Secretary of the Air Force. I can think of absolutely no one that I could more highly recommend to you. As a son of a Four Star Air Force General, I spent most of my life growing up around Air Force leaders, and I think each and every one of them would have been proud to serve under the leadership and direction of Mickey Blackwell.

Mickey Blackwell was not only the "father" of the F-22 program, but he has been a dynamic and forceful leader as President of Lockheed Aeronautical Systems, and as Executive Vice President of Lockheed Martin Corporation. Michey is known throughout the industry as an extraordinary leader and visionary. He is not only a brilliant individual, but he is also a leader who comibines the qualities of passion and tenacity with a positive "can do" attitude that inspires those who follow. Additionally, Mickey has always been one who goes the extra mile in civic, community, and political activities. Georgia has certainly benefitted and will continue to benefit from his work and leadership, and I recommend Mickey to you unequivocally. I know that you will have numerous qualified applicants for this position, but I think you would make the men and women of the U.S. Air Force proud indeed to have the opportunity to serve under the leadership of James "Mickey" Blackwell. Your consideration is deeply appreciated, and bets of luck as you tackle your new endeavor. Know that the nation will be a better place because of your service as Secretary of Defense.

Very Truly Yours,

Charles C. Clay
Chairman, Republican Party of Georgia
CCC:cup

Figure 50. Letter from Senator Clay nominating Micky for Secretary of the Air Force.

Unfortunately, the timing and other details did not work out. When the phone call finally came asking Micky to start the interview process, Micky said "no." He had already moved from Washington

D.C. and had started his "second half" in Georgia. He decided not to return to Washington.[14] Micky and Billie wanted to spend more time with their family, use their talents in public service, and enjoy retirement. He built their dream house in Marietta which is surrounded by southern pines, clean streams, walking trails, and a national park. His home is not far from where the world's best air superiority fighter is built.[15]

Chairman of Georgia Military Affairs Committee

The first of his public service activities involved the Georgia Military Affairs Committee (GMAC). Shortly after Micky and Billie returned to Marietta, Georgia, Governor Roy Barnes, approached Micky about chairing the GMAC. The chairman of GMAC was a pro-bono public service job whose role was to oversee military bases in Georgia and advise the Governor on military affairs. Micky accepted the position and was sworn in on November 27, 2000, by Governor Barnes.

Because of his experience at Lockheed Martin, Micky was nearly certain that the US government was planning to authorize a Base Realignment and Closure (BRAC) Commission. The findings of the commission would result in closing bases in the continental US. The Department of Defense was desperate to save money, so realigning the infrastructure to match the size of our armed forces appealed to many and seemed to make sense. As a result, Georgia knew it should be prepared for a visit by the BRAC Commission.

Georgia had many military installations that were fair game for cost cutters. Micky was in the position of knowing many of the key players in BRAC. With excellent contacts and a good head start, Micky felt they could "BRAC-proof" many of Georgia's military installations. They would accomplish this by modernizing every military base in Georgia and help the US government realize that the Georgia military bases were indispensable to the nation's defense.

There was one problem. The BRAC Commission would evaluate the status of a base "as it was." Any improvements to the base had to have been already funded and implementation begun before the Commission's visit. Beginning in 2000, Micky worked with US Army Brig. Gen. Phil Browning (Retd) who was employed by the state Chamber of Commerce to work with GMAC. Their job was to put together a plan to modernize Georgia's bases, so the US government would not shut them down through their realignment and closure efforts. They were assisted by the local communities representing each military base in the state.

The GMAC toured every military base in Georgia, looking at each base's strengths and weaknesses. Gen. Browning put together a mock BRAC exercise and had the local military identify issues that needed to be resolved. Finally, they developed a multi-year action plan for modernizing each base. Enterprise Servant Leadership was used to get all participants working in a collaborative effort.

Representing the Governor, Micky asked all of Georgia's Senators and Representatives, along with their defense staffs, to meet with him in Washington, D.C. Micky wanted to brief them on what he found. Three examples follow: Micky reported on the paint peeling off the walls of soldier housing at Fort Benning. He also told them about potential water damage to the Army's central communication node at Fort Gordon. The communication node was in a concrete block building with a very bad roof and was in a dangerous flood plain. A third example was the automotive maintenance buildings at Fort

Stewart which were reported to be literally falling down. Air had to be let out of the tires to get the vehicles through the building doors.

Georgia's politicians enthusiastically supported the state's military base modernization plans. Action items were assigned, and funds were appropriated by the Congress to ensure a DOD budget sufficient to fix the problems cited. As a result, approximately $500,000,000 was added to the DOD budget to modernize Georgia military bases. Over the next several years, this money was used to implement most of the needed improvements cited in Micky's report.

After the base improvements were well underway, Micky accompanied Georgia's Governor Barnes on a goodwill visit to DOD executives in Washington, D.C. His message was "Georgia loves the military!" The trip was a huge success.

Figure 51. Micky with Gen. Myers, Chairman of the Joint Chiefs of Staff. (Photo courtesy of Micky Blackwell)

Based on the success of the first visit to Washington, D.C., Micky organized a second goodwill visit just before the BRAC hearings. This time he accompanied Georgia's new governor, Sonny Perdue, to meet Gen. Richard B. Myers, Chairman of the Joint Chiefs of Staff and Jim Roche, Secretary of the Air Force, both friends of his (see Figure 51).

One of the Governor's chief concerns was the Air Force maintenance facilities in central Georgia. If Warner-Robins AFB was closed, many people in central Georgia would lose their jobs.

Recognizing this was a serious threat to the Georgia economy, Micky introduced the Air Force's Warner Robins Air Logistics Center (ALC) to the principles of Lean Enterprise that he had implemented at Lockheed Martin. He invited the ALC Commander and his staff to visit Lockheed Martin's plant in Marietta to witness Lean in action. Micky also provided them with the names of consultants who could help them implement Lean at Warner-Robins AFB. They immediately saw its merits, and quickly implemented Lean with startling results. Later, the Air Force propagated the work they had done at Warner Robins to Air Force maintenance facilities around the world. Lean was also implemented at the Marine Corps Logistics base in Albany, Georgia. Like others before them, they had great results.

As a result of these initiatives, Georgia was prepared when the BRAC visit was announced for 2005. The GMAC orchestrated the presentation on each military base that was given to the BRAC committee in Atlanta. The Committee visited each military base where they were greeted by local representatives and an enthusiastic public. Everywhere they went, they saw people foot-stomping the theme, "We love the military!" to great effect.

Georgia came out of the BRAC process smelling like a rose. They lost a small Navy school in Athens, which has since become a University of Georgia facility. They also lost the Naval Air Station in Marietta, which is now the home of the Georgia National Guard. In terms of net jobs, Georgia gained over 8,000 jobs! Another successful accomplishment by the servant leader from Georgia.

Micky continued as chairman of the GMAC reporting to the governor until 2008.

Chairman of Marietta Redevelopment Task Force

In late 2001, Micky received a phone call from Bill Dunaway who was running for mayor of Marietta, Georgia. Bill had been a longtime drug store owner in Marietta and was the owner of "The 1848 House," a fine-dining restaurant also located in Marietta. Bill asked Micky to support him in his run for mayor. At that point, Micky did not know Bill very well, so he asked him what his strategic plan was for developing the city. Bill's response was honest. He said he didn't have one right now, but when he was elected mayor, he promised to build a strategic plan. Micky said he would support him and sent him a check.

Bill Dunaway was elected mayor in November 2001. One of the first things he did was call Micky and tell him it was time to build that strategic plan, and he wanted Micky to do it. He also told Micky he wanted him to chair a new task force to look at redeveloping the city. After thinking about it for a few moments, Micky accepted the appointment.

Micky became Chairman of the Marietta Redevelopment Task Force (MRTF), reporting directly to the mayor. The purpose of the citizen task force was to determine what redevelopment issues were facing the City of Marietta and to recommend to the Mayor and Council action plans to fix the issues. In his new job, Micky interviewed many Marietta citizens and formed a task force of 13 people representing various aspects of the city. Once again, Micky's servant leadership came into play as he put together task force members that wanted to make Marietta the best of the best.

The first meeting of the MRTF was on February 18, 2002. The Task Force conducted over 60 interviews with people from the Marietta School System, Marietta City government, prominent Marietta citizens, city-planning consultants, other Cobb County City Mayors, real estate developers, investors, public-safety officials, HUD officials, Federal Home Loan Bank executives, and the Atlanta Regional Commission.

Based on what the Task Force heard from the above interviews, the team put together its findings and recommendations concerning the issues surrounding the redevelopment of the City of Marietta. Micky presented the findings and recommendations to the Marietta Mayor and City Council on May 30, 2002.

The Task Force strongly believed that the recommended actions, if taken by the City Council, would greatly improve the redevelopment process, attract new investors, improve the quality of life, and stimulate Marietta redevelopment.

Micky's PowerPoint presentation to the City Council was over 100 slides long and went into considerable depth on each of the major issues. To this day, Micky still thinks it was the longest presentation he has ever given. At the end of his remarks, the Task Force was given a standing ovation by the City Council and the members of the public who were in attendance.

An incredible amount of redevelopment was accomplished over the next several years. A strategic plan for the city of Marietta was developed. Historic districts were instituted, new zoning rules were implemented, old HUD housing was torn down, city ordinances were revised, the Marietta Historic Board of Review was overhauled, blighted areas of the city were identified, plans were made for redevelopment, and new redevelopment projects were begun.

The Marietta Redevelopment Corporation (MRC) was constituted in 2003. The MRC was funded by the City of Marietta for the purpose of buying blighted real estate and transforming it into a productive part of the city.

In late 2007 and 2008, redevelopment in Marietta severely slowed down. No one had planned on the length and depth of the recession, so Micky retired from the MRC in 2008. As the economy improved, redevelopment in Marietta included starting new housing developments replacing substandard housing, building a thriving downtown city square with new restaurants and stores, reopening of the Strand movie theater, building new parks, and starting roadway and sidewalk improvements.

Strategic Plans for Non-profits

Based on his experience with strategic planning at Lockheed Martin, several non-profit community leaders approached Micky to see if he could help them develop a strategic plan for their organizations. Historically, many plans are too long or did not have the right level of detail to be of use, so Micky created a process that was helpful to many organizations.[16] In short, he found a way to put strategic plans together that culminated in concise track-able tactical objectives. Some of the organizations he was able to help included:

- **City of Marietta, Georgia.**
- **Cobb Family Resources in Marietta, Georgia.**
- **The Strand Theater in Marietta, Georgia.**
- **Aircraft Museum and Discovery Center in Marietta, Georgia.**
- **Atlanta Horticultural Society in Atlanta, Georgia.**
- **Marietta Museum of History in Marietta, Georgia.**
- **First United Methodist Church in Marietta, Georgia,**
- **St. John Neumann Catholic School in Lilburn, Georgia.**

Micky was very pleased with the results of the strategic planning sessions. Each organization ended up with a clear vision statement, mission statement, and measurable objectives.[17]

Strand Theater Board

In 2002, Mayor Dunaway and other community leaders were exploring the possibility of restoring the Strand Theater on the Marietta Square. Over time, the movie theater building continued to deteriorate. It had stopped showing movies and had been empty for years. A group of concerned citizens known as the "Friends of the Strand" asked Micky to join the theater's Board of Directors.

Restoring the Strand Theater was a key part of revitalizing Marietta. The theater was located on one of the corners of Marietta's Square. As any developer will tell you, having control over a main corner is the key to success, but it still took six years to complete the restoration. In addition to improving the appearance of the facility, they were able to procure a Mighty Allen theater organ. The Strand Theater reopened in December 2008. Micky served on the Board from 2003 to 2008.[18]

Aviation Museum and Discovery Center Vice-Chairman

The Aviation Museum and Discovery Center (AMDC) was conceived in 2003 by a group of Marietta citizens who were interested in preserving Marietta's aviation heritage. The goal was to pass on Marietta's knowledge and experience to children interested in Science, Engineering, Technology, and Mathematics (STEM).

The Board of Directors of AMDC consisted of 30 civic-minded citizens of Marietta and Cobb County. Micky's old boss at Lockheed, Bob Ormsby, was elected Chairman, and Micky was elected Vice Chairman. The Aviation Museum and Discovery Center leased 15.5 acres from the USAF through Cobb County. The site is located close to Lockheed Martin in Marietta, Georgia. The first aircraft that was donated was a Lockheed Jetstar executive jet. The date was June 7, 2006. Other aircraft were added later and put on display, including several that were built at Lockheed Martin's Marietta aircraft production facilities during and after WWII.

Today, the Aviation Museum and Discovery Center continues to fulfill its primary objectives—preserving the history of aviation in Marietta, Georgia and being used for STEM education.

Chairman Kiwanis' Business and Public Affairs Committee

Micky was elected Chairman of the Kiwanis Business and Public Affairs Committee of the Marietta, Georgia Kiwanis Club and served from October 1, 2004, through September 30, 2005. During his time as chairman, he led the development of Flournoy Park in downtown Marietta. He also raised money to study the potential of a downtown trolley. Micky visited Chattanooga, Tennessee; Denver, Colorado; and Savannah, Georgia to look at how they operated their downtown trolley systems. Although the City of Marietta was fully supportive, some officials in the Cobb County Government were not, and they stonewalled attempts to make it happen. Fortunately, a private concern took the committee's work and launched a commercial trolley system in downtown Marietta. After several years of operation without government funding, the trolley system ceased operation due to economic reasons.

University Advisory Boards

During the early part of Micky's retirement, he continued to serve on several university advisory boards. These included:

- **Mercer University Board of Trustees, Mercer Engineering Advisory Board, and Chairman Mercer Engineering Capital Campaign, 1986-2004.**
- **University of Alabama Engineering Advisory Board, 1997-2006.**
- **Founding member of Kennesaw State University Advisory Board on Leadership, Character, and Ethics, 2001-2008.**

Foundations and Scholarships

Micky and Billie have endowed scholarships at both Mercer University and the University of Alabama. The scholarships were established in their parents' names as well as their own. They also established a Blackwell Family Foundation at the Cobb Community Foundation. Their daughters are Directors of the Blackwell Foundation. The interest on the Blackwell Foundation funds can be given to any philanthropic cause they choose. Micky and Billie have used it as an example to teach their children how to bless others when you and your family have been greatly blessed. It has been a tremendous success. The gifts that have been given have all gone to good causes.

Billie and Micky also gave a major gift to MUST ministries.[19] MUST is a religious-based organization that helps care for the homeless. The endowment provides MUST a rainy-day fund for hard economic times.

Christian-Related Activities

Bible Teacher at Marietta First United Methodist Church

After retiring from Lockheed Martin, one of the first things the Blackwells did upon their return to Georgia, was rejoin the Marietta First United Methodist Church (MFUMC). After a year, they were asked to start a new Sunday School class to attract young adults in the community. Billie was the chief organizer of the new class, and Micky agreed to be the full-time Bible teacher. That began a 14-year odyssey that was extremely rewarding.

Over the years, the class experienced tremendous numerical and spiritual growth. Many of the single adults got married, and Micky and Billie attended their weddings. They were also there when their children were born. At the end of 2014, Micky relinquished his fulltime teaching role with Kindred Spirits. The group had grown so much spiritually that they could teach themselves. The class had expanded to over 80 people—a great legacy for a servant leader who loves his people.

In 2015, Micky and Billie started attending a Sunday School class at MFUMC for senior adults. The class has over 150 members. Micky currently teaches this class on a rotational basis. Micky is in great demand as a Bible teacher throughout his church and his community.

Board Member, "Lead Like Jesus"

In 2002, Micky was asked by Ken Blanchard to join the Board of Directors of a new organization called "*Lead Like Jesus.*" Ken is the author of the best-selling book, "*One Minute Manager*" and is one of the foremost authorities on servant leadership. Micky remained on the Board until 2011. The board included high-profile people such as Rosie Greer (pro football player); Dan Cathy (Chairman of Chick-Fil-A); William Pollard (Chairman of Service Master); Don Soderquist (Senior Vice Chairman of Walmart); and Bob Buford (noted author and entrepreneur).

Today, *Lead Like Je*sus is a vibrant organization that has spread the "servant leadership" message all over the world. Micky has used Blanchard's work in classes, lectures, and retreats he has delivered on "Godly Servant Leadership" over the past 20 years.

"When Two or More are Gathered...in Prayer"

While Micky was rising in the Lockheed organization, he and Billie joined fellow Christians in lay revivals around the south. The purpose of the meetings was to tell other Christians about their spiritual renewal.

Micky first experienced "corporate prayer" when he met and prayed with the lay people before their activities. Corporate prayer is defined as "prayer to God the Father by two or more people gathered together as one united body for the purpose of making intercessory prayer regarding a shared burden." Corporate prayer is a servant-led approach to team prayer.

In 2008, Micky felt God was calling him to write a book on what he had learned about corporate prayer. He self-published the book in 2009 by the title, "*When Two or More are Gathered ...in Prayer.*"[20] It has been used by many churches and organizations that want to study corporate prayer.

Family-Related Activities

Being a servant leader starts in the home. Micky and Billie have been happily married 63 years. Micky is still deeply in love with Billie. They have two children, Kaye and Kelley, and four grandchildren of which they are extremely proud. He has written his and Billie's memoirs in a self-published book titled "*All the Days of Our Lives: The Heritage and History of Billie and James Blackwell.*"[21]

Honors and Awards

A summary of Micky's honors, awards, achievements, and recognition is presented in Appendix F.

Lessons Learned and Important Points

Micky left a public and private legacy that will be difficult to match. Some of the reasons are as follows:

- As stated by his CEO, Micky's reputation was so great it preceded him wherever he went.
- Micky was a leader who understood the needs of people.
- His goal was to serve others. He did his job well, and his influence got more pervasive as the Raptor evolved.
- Lockheed directly or indirectly supported a total of 95,000 jobs in 2009 with the F-22 program.
- The F-22 program received the Air Force Association's John R. Alison Award for outstanding contributions by industrial leadership to national defense.
- Micky implemented Lean Thinking to increase throughput and reduce costs.
- He transferred knowledge and technologies from the F-22 into the JSF program, resulting in billions of dollars in cost avoidance.

- Micky received many kind notes from friends and competitors when his retirement was announced. But perhaps a note from David Fulghum at *Aviation Week* said it best, "Although the company was criticized by the Air Force, Micky was seen as a bright spot. Almost everyone was surprised when Micky got the ax."
- In addition to his other accomplishments, Micky was seriously considered for a senior position in President Bush's administration.
- Micky supported several university boards following retirement. He also supported a number of foundations and established scholarships at many of the same schools.
- He led a statewide group of Georgia citizens in preparation for the BRAC process. Not only did Georgia not lose any jobs, but the state also gained 8,000 new jobs.
- In addition to helping the Strand Theater do renovation and strategic planning, Micky was able to help a series of non-profits in and around Marietta conduct similar strategic planning efforts.
- He was also involved in leading the Marietta Redevelopment Task Force.
- Micky helped start the Marietta Aviation and Discovery Center to capture the history of aviation in Marietta and help students who are interested in STEM.
- Micky participates in many church-related activities such as teaching Bible studies and lecturing on servant leadership.
- He is a self-published author of a book on corporate prayer titled *When Two or More are Gathered...in Prayer.*
- He has self-published his memoirs in a book titled *All the Days of Our Lives: The Heritage and History of Billie and James Blackwell.*

Chapter Notes

1 It should be noted that the Air Force recently announced plans for upgrading the F-22 to ensure that it can sustain its combat role until 2060. As stated in one article, the USAF is "vigorously pursuing new avionics, radar, targeting sensors, weapons, glass cockpit displays and Artificial Intelligence for its F-22 stealth fighter to try to sustain air supremacy." These upgrades are being made in response to Russian and Chinese 5th-generation stealth fighter threats. See Kris Osborn. February 8, 2018. "The Air Force is upgrading the F-22 to keep it combat ready until 2060." *Business Insider.* Accessed March 18, 2018. http://www.businessinsider.com/air-force-upgrading-f-22-2018-2.

2 U.S. Air Force. 2015. *F-22 Raptor Fact Sheet.* September 22. Accessed January 22, 2018. http://www.af.mil/About-Us/Fact-Sheets/Display/Article/104506/f-22-raptor/.

3 Lockheed Martin. n.d. *F-22 Raptor Capabilities.* Accessed October 14, 2017. http://www.lockheedmartin.com/us/products/f22/f-22-capabilities.html.

4 Lockheed Martin. n.d. *F-22 Raptor: Mission Ready Statement.* Accessed March 17, 2018. https://lockheedmartin.com/us/products/f22.html

5 Jeremiah Gertler. 2009. *Air Force F-22* Fighter *Program: Background and Issues for Congress.* Washington, D.C.: Congressional Research Service, pp. 4-5.

6 Vance D. Coffman. Chairman, Chief Executive Officer and president, Lockheed Martin Corporation. January 14, 2000. *"Retirement speech for James A. Blackwell Jr."* Washington, D.C.: Lockheed Martin Corporation.

7 Ibid.

8 James "Micky" Blackwell. 2021. *All the Days of Our Lives. The Heritage and History of Billie and James Blackwell*. Asheville, NC: United Writers Press, p. 144.

9 Chris Joyner. October 30,1999. "Poor Earnings Report Rocks Lockheed." *Marietta Daily Journal*. Marietta, GA, pp. 1A, 6A.

10 David A. Fulghum. October 25, 1999. "USAF Official Skewers Lockheed Martin." *Aviation Week & Space Technology*, p. 35.

11 Money, Inc. described Ms. Hewson as "one of the most influential businesswomen in the entire world." See Berman, Nat. 2018. "10 Things You Didn't Know about Lockheed Martin CEO Marillyn Hewson." *Money Inc.* Accessed December 29, 2019 at https://moneyinc.com/ lockheed-martin-ceo-marillyn-hewson/.

12 Jeanne Sahadi, 2020. CNN Business. Accessed May 1, 2021. https://www.cnn.com/2020/06/15/ success/women-ceos-fortune-500-marillyn- hewson/index.html

13 For a more in-depth discussion on ScanTech's capabilities, see ScanTech Holdings at http://www. scantechholdings.com.

14 The "second-half" refers to Bob Buford's book about self-renewal. See Robert P. Buford. 2008. *Halftime, updated*. Grand Rapids, MI: Zondervan.

15 Ibid, p. 213.

16 Micky used guidelines published by Dr. Terry van der Werft. See James "Micky" Blackwell. 2021. *All the Days of Our Lives*, p. 166.

17 Ibid, p. 167.

18 Ibid.

19 MUST stands for "Ministries United in Service and Training."

20 James "Micky" Blackwell. 2009. *When Two or More are Gathered …in Prayer*. Asheville, NC: United Writers Press.

21 James "Micky" Blackwell. 2021. *All the Days of Our Lives. The Heritage and History of Billie and James Blackwell*. Asheville, NC: United Writers Press.

Chapter 15
Concluding Remarks

Servant leadership is rare in the modern business world. Most people will tell you it's all about money; nothing else matters. Morals, ethics, and values don't seem to mean much anymore—unless you work for a servant leader who knows they mean everything in the world.

Micky Blackwell
President & COO Aeronautics Sector (Retired)
Lockheed Martin Corporation

I would like to conclude this book with some final remarks.

The purpose of this book was to describe in detail a new way of doing business called the "Enterprise Servant Leadership Management Model" (ESLMM), which is superior to traditional management models. The ESLMM is based on the life and work of James "Micky" Blackwell and his teams.

Specifically, I showed how applying the new Enterprise Servant Leadership Management Model will help future leaders and their organizations become the best of the best, create maximum value for their customers, and fully engage the company employees to attain maximum performance in every area of the business enterprise.

Servant Leadership is Different

Servant Leadership is different. Putting others before self is not usually the standard management practice, and focusing on serving others is distinctly different from traditional leadership practices. We have shown in this book that servant leadership is a superior way to lead people. But if the book stopped here, it would be a sad ending to the story I have tried to share with you.

The good news is that servant leadership is growing. It is now being applied across a wide range of industries and various sizes of programs. Its success is causing many to reflect on where the concept came from. Regardless of your views about the origins of servant leadership, it appeals to many who are weary of traditional management thinking. Jesus showed us the way over 2,000 years ago. The results should not surprise us. People are attracted to leaders who are committed to serving others first.

Body of Knowledge Expanded

In the Introduction, I noted that that the body of knowledge on servant leadership needed further development. It was observed that there were few guidelines on how to implement servant leadership in a large program that involved the entire enterprise. To respond to this need, we included guidelines in the book based primarily on how closely Micky and Lockheed Martin worked with its primary customer, the US Air Force, on the development of the F-22 Raptor. This was especially true in the use of Integrated Product Teams. Knowledge-driven value generation was also a new idea, as was the six-step example for building a Servant-Led Business Model. A new way of leading called Enterprise Servant Leadership was also introduced. Numerous examples were included to illustrate how the new concepts worked.

A major contribution to the body of knowledge on servant leadership was the description of the Enterprise Servant Leadership Management Model that provides a map for the way forward. It starts with leading by example and concludes by praying for people and inspiring others with Christian core values learned from the Bible.

As mentioned previously, many textbooks, tools, and articles have been written since 1970, when Greenleaf published his first essay, *The Servant as Leader*. When a search for the term "servant leadership" is entered on the Internet, 44-million hits now show up on Google.

To say there is interest in servant leadership is to understate the obvious. Today, interest ranges from the heart of a servant leader to the art of servant leadership. Others stress the principles and practices that will make you successful. There are also many references to servant leadership in the Bible, which takes the subject to an entirely new level. The bottom line is that the success of servant leadership cannot be disputed.

What *can* be disputed, however, is the way it is implemented. From "Leading by Example" to "Leading Across the Value Network," the five levels of servant leadership shown earlier in Chapter 5 tend to correlate with business impact. Micky's experience at Lockheed Martin is just one example. The benefits to the Raptor were huge and significant—but when Micky moved to Lockheed Martin Corporation as Aeronautics Sector President and COO, his influence was even greater.

Many researchers have studied the topic of servant leadership. A 2013 review of 39 such studies found that "servant leadership is a viable leadership theory that helps organizations and improves the well-being of followers."[1] These findings bode well for the future of servant leadership, and this book should add to the body of knowledge on the topic.

Final Image of Micky

Today, there are many pictures of Micky Blackwell available to the public (see Figure 52), but there is one image of this leader I will never forget. It is a picture of Micky teaching a community-wide men's Bible study in Marietta, Georgia. The title of his lesson was "Names for God the Father." The message he delivered was inspiring. When Micky finished his comments, we all watched as he did something different. He closed his Bible and, all by himself, in a quiet, but strong voice, sang the hymn "Holy, Holy, Holy" *a cappella*.

The response was spontaneous. There were seventy men in the room that morning. Every one of them stood, clapped, and shouted affirmations. Some raised their arms in an act of praise.

But deep in his heart, Micky knew it wasn't about him. It was about the King of Kings and Lord of Lords, the great I AM.

Summary

If you are interested in servant leadership, this book can help. It doesn't answer every question, but it does provide a framework for managing enterprise-level programs with a servant leader's heart.

Figure 52. James "Micky" Blackwell. (Photo courtesy of Micky Blackwell)

I close this book with a comment by Robert Vanourek:

> I see our institutions changing, from hierarchical chain of command groups with rigid rules led by superior, elitist bosses who direct the activities of subordinates seen as inferior to a whole new approach. I see an open, participative, entrepreneurial environment with loose flexible teams. I see a core set of values being well understood by everyone. I see a common venture with clear linkages to a shared vision, where value is created for people, where people see how they are connected, where they can grow and realize more of their innate potential. I see organizations with trust and caring, where work is a meaningful part of your life experience. And, most of all, I see servant leaders guiding these institutions, servant leaders at all levels throughout them.[2]

What Vanourek saw and described in 1995 was the "Enterprise Servant Leadership Management Model" described in this book, which uses servant leaders throughout the enterprise to plan and manage operations.

As Micky has frequently said, "If you know the way forward, do not hesitate to act."

If you can help aspiring leaders find their way, that is even better. Reach out and point them in the right direction. Hopefully, I have done that.

For who is greater, he who sits at the table, or he who serves? Is it not he who sits at the table? Yet I am among you as the One who serves.

Luke 22:27 (NKJV)

There is only one thing important in life and that is loving God and your fellow man. We need to get this right. It is all part of being the best of the best.

Chapter Notes

1 D. L. Parris and J. W. Peachy. 2013. "A Systematic Literature Review of Servant Leadership Theory in Organizational Contexts." *Journal of Business Ethics*, 113, pp. 377–393.

2 Robert A. Vanourck. 1995. "Servant Leadership and the Future." In *Reflections on Leadership: How Robert K. Greenleaf's Theory of Servant Leadership Influenced Today's Top Management Thinkers*, by Larry C. Spears. New York: John Wiley & Sons, p. 307.

Acknowledgments

Victorious warriors win first and then go to war.

Sun Tzu
The Art of War

In the spirit of servant leadership, I would like to thank Micky Blackwell himself. When he collected material for this book, he didn't do it for himself; he did it for those who wanted to know more about why this subject is important. In a never-ending quest for names, dates, times and places, Micky responded promptly to all requests for information — materials that included personal notes, pictures, work files, summaries of events, and in-depth interviews with other leaders and news commentators. He showed me, once again, what it means to be a servant leader—he went out of his way to provide details most never knew existed.

One of the best things about working with the Blackwells was hearing the stories behind the facts. If a hallmark of a good leader is the ability to tell a good story, Micky and Billie Blackwell are among the best. They have stories that will charm you and stories that will break your heart. For that, I will forever be grateful. It was a pleasure to work with you both.

I would also like to thank Tom Gray for writing the foreword for the book. As a father of three, a pastor in a growing church, an active member in the mission field, and a large community Bible study leader, I know your time is valuable and your words are even more so. Thank you for taking the time to share your thoughts about our mutual friend.

I want to say thanks to Roy Barnes, Ken Blanchard, Phil Hodges, Ron Fogelman, and Neely Young. Your endorsements were insightful and appreciated by all.

Published author Ken Kirk reviewed early drafts of the manuscript and made many suggestions for improving the book. Jim Summers and Marty Phillips, former senior executives at Lockheed Martin's Aeronautics Sector and close colleagues of Micky Blackwell, reviewed early versions of the book and also made significant recommendations for improvement. The contribution of these reviewers was much appreciated.

Many thanks to Lockheed Martin Aeronautics Historian, Jeff Rhodes, for providing Lockheed Martin photos and for the many hours he spent editing the book to ensure historical and factual accuracy.

When I became ill, Micky Blackwell stepped in to help do the final editing of the book and arrange for its publication. For this, I will ever be grateful.

Finally, I would like to acknowledge the incredible contributions of Vally Sharpe to the editing of the book and getting the book ready for publication.

Robert Materna

Appendices, Bibliography,
and
Information about the Author

Appendix A: Micky Blackwell's Professional Articles and Books

Articles

Loving, Donald and Blackwell, James A., Jr. *Low-Speed Aerodynamic Characteristics of a Modified Arrow-Wing Supersonic Transport Configuration with High-Lift Devices*. NASA TM X-961, February 1964.

Blackwell, James A., Jr. and Kelly, Thomas C. *Effects of Configuration Geometry on the Transonic Aerodynamic Characteristics of Canard Airplane Configurations*. NASA TN D-2465, July 1964.

Blackwell, James A., Jr. and Kelly, Thomas C. *Aerodynamic Loading Characteristics of a Reentry- Glider and Launch-Vehicle Model at Transonic Speeds*. NASA TM X-1090, 1964.

Blackwell, James A., Jr. *Transonic Pressure Distributions Over Protuberances and Adjacent Areas in Proximity to the Nose of a Launch Vehicle*. NASA TN D-3216, November 1965.

Whitcomb, Richard T. and Blackwell, James A., Jr. *Status of Research on a Supercritical Wing*.

Paper presented to "Confidential" Conference on Aircraft Aerodynamics held at Langley Research Center, May 23-25, 1966, and published in NASA SP-124.

Blackwell, James A., Jr. *Supersonic Investigation of Effects of Configuration Geometry on Pressure-Coefficient and Section Normal-Force Coefficient Distributions for a Two-Stage Launch Vehicle*. NASA TN D-3408, June 1966.

Blackwell, James A., Jr. *Numerical Method for the Design of Warped Surfaces for Subsonic Wings with Arbitrary Planform*. Thesis presented to the University of Virginia for degree of Master of Aerospace Engineering, August 1966. NASA TM X-57857.

Samuels, Richard D. and Blackwell, James A., Jr. *Effects of Configuration Geometry on the Supersonic Aerodynamic Characteristics of a Simulated Launch Vehicle*. NASA TN D-3755, October 1966.

Brooks, Eugene, N., Decker, John P. and Blackwell, James A. Jr. *Static Aerodynamic Characteristics of a Model of a Typical Subsonic Jet-Transport Airplane at Mach Numbers from 0.40 to 1.20*. NASA TM X-1345, December 1966.

Blackwell, James A., Jr. *Effect of Reynolds Number and Boundary-Layer Transition Location on Shock-Induced Separation*. Paper presented at the AGARD Specialists' Meeting on "Transonic Aerodynamics" held at Paris, France, September 18-20, 1968, and published in AGARD Conference Proceedings No. 35.

Blackwell, James A., Jr. *Preliminary Study of Effects of Reynolds Number and Boundary-Layer Transition Location on Shock-Induced Separation*. NASA TN D-5003, January 1969.

Blackwell, James A., Jr. *A Finite Step Method for the Calculation of Theoretical Load Distributions for Arbitrary Lifting Surface Arrangements*. NASA TN-5335, February 1969.

Blackwell, James A., Jr. and Kelly, Thomas C. *Transonic Investigation of Effects of Configuration Geometry on Pressure Coefficient and Section Normal-Force Coefficient Distributions for a Two Stage Launch Vehicle*. NASA LWP-753, May 1969.

Blackwell, James A., Jr. *Aerodynamic Characteristics of an 11-Percent-Thick Symmetrical Supercritical Airfoil at Mach Numbers between 0.30 and 0.85*. NASA TM X-1831, 1969.

Blackwell, James A., Jr. *Transonic Airplane Design Based on NASA Supercritical Design Concepts*.

Lockheed-Georgia ER-10273, September 1969.

Blackwell, James A., Jr. *High Reynolds Number Simulation*. Lockheed-Georgia ER-10249, July 1969.

Blackwell, James A., Jr. *Analysis of Experimental Results for Gelac Wing Design W43 for L-1011- 8,* Lockheed-Georgia, October 1969.

Blackwell, James A., Jr. and Bennett, J.A. *A subsonic Viscous Flow Method for Analysis of Two-Dimensional Airfoils and Swept Wings.* Lockheed-Georgia ER-10706, May 1970.

Puckett, T. C. and Blackwell, James A., Jr. *Theoretical Method for Calculating the Symmetrical Airfoil Shape for a Prescribed Velocity Distribution at Zero Angle of Attack - DCT Program WINV.* Lockheed-Georgia ER-10897, August 1970.

Bennett, J. A., Davis, R. C., and Blackwell, James A., Jr. *A Method for Calculation of Approximate Airfoil Section Pressure Distributions on Tapered Swept Wings.* Lockheed-Georgia ER- 10864, December 1970.

Blackwell, James, A., Jr. *Simplified Method for Estimating Drag-Rise Mach Number and Post Drag-Rise Characteristics for Advanced Technology Wings.* Lockheed-Georgia ER-11144, July 1971.

Blackwell, James A., Jr. *Correlation of Experimental and Analytical Aerodynamic Data on a Supercritical Airfoil, Body and Aircraft.* Lockheed-Georgia ER-11073, December 1971. (Confidential)

Harris, Charles D. and Blackwell, James A., Jr. *Wind-Tunnel Investigation of Effects of Rear Upper Surface Modification and a NASA Supercritical Airfoil.* NASA TM X-2454, 1972.

Blackwell, James A., Jr. *A Study of Transonic Wave Drag Due to Lift and Transonic Lift Equivalent Area Concepts.* Lockheed-Georgia Company LG73ER0088, September 1972.

Blackwell, James A., Jr. *Aerodynamic Design, Test and Analysis of the Lockheed-Georgia/NASA ATT-95 Aircraft.* Lockheed-Georgia Company LG72ER0041, November 1972.

Blackwell, James A., Jr., Stevens, W. A., and Nash, J. F. *Three-Dimensional, Compressible Turbulent Boundary Layer Program for Aircraft Wings.* Lockheed-Georgia Company LG74ER0103, August 1974.

Burdges, Kenneth P., Micky Blackwell, James A., Jr., and Pounds, Gerald A. *High Reynolds Number Test of a NACA 651213, a = 0.5 Airfoil Section at Transonic Speeds.* NASA CR- 2499, 1975.

Burdges, Kenneth P., Blackwell, James A., Jr., and Pounds, Gerald A. *High Reynolds Number Test of a NASA 10% Thick Supercritical Airfoil at Transonic Speeds.* NASA CR-132468, 1975. (Title unclassified, paper classified)

Blackwell, James A., Jr. Burdges, Kenneth P. and Hinson, B. L. *Effect of Wind-Tunnel Wall Porosity on a 10% Thick Supercritical Airfoil at Transonic Speeds.* NASA CR-132712, 1975. (Title unclassified, paper classified)

Blackwell, James A., Jr. *Numerical Method to Calculate the Induced Drag or Optimum Loading for Arbitrary Non-Planar Aircraft.* NASA SP-405, May 1976.

Blackwell, James A., Jr. and Pounds, G. A. *Wind-Tunnel Wall Interference Effects on a Supercritical Airfoil at Transonic Speeds.* AIAA 9th Aerodynamic Testing Conference, June 7-9, 1976.

Hinson, B. L. and Blackwell, James A., Jr. *Design and Wind-Tunnel Test of a 20% Thick Supercritical Airfoil at Transonic Speeds.* NASA CR-145118, 1977. (Title unclassified, paper classified)

Blackwell, James A., Jr. *Scale Effects on Advanced Aircraft Wing Designs. Reviews in Viscous Flows.* Proceedings of the Lockheed-Georgia Company Viscous Flow Symposium, pp. 1- 38, LG77ER0044, June 22-23, 1976.

Blackwell, James A., Jr. *The Aerodynamic Design of an Advanced Rotor Airfoil.* NASA CR-2961, 1977.

Blackwell, James A., Jr. *An Empirical Correction for Wind Tunnel Wall Blockage in Two- Dimensional Transonic Flow,* AIAA Paper 78-806 AIAA 10th Aerodynamic Testing Conference, April 19-21, 1978.

Blackwell, James A., Jr. *Scale Effects on Supercritical Airfoils.* 11th Congress of ICAS, Lisbon, Portugal, September 10-16, 1978.

Blackwell, James A., Jr. "Experimental Testing at Transonic Speeds," *Transonic Aerodynamics,* David Nixon, Ed., Volume 81, *Progress in Astronautics and Aeronautics,* 1981, American Institute of Aeronautics and Astronautics, Inc., New York, NY, pp. 189-238.

Books

Blackwell, James A., Jr. *When Two or More are Gathered…in Prayer.* Lilburn, GA: United Writers Press, Inc. 2009.

Blackwell, James "Micky." *All the Days of our Lives: The Heritage and History of Billie and James Blackwell.* Asheville, NC: United Writers Press. 2021.

Appendix B: Kelly Johnson's 14 Rules

The Lockheed Skunk Works for many years has demonstrated a unique ability to rapidly prototype, develop, and produce a wide range of highly advanced aircraft and products for the US armed forces and intelligence agencies.

Based on lessons learned from early Skunk Works programs, C. Kelly Johnson developed and wrote the Basic Operating Rules of the Skunk Works which have been called Kelly Johnson's 14 Rules.[*] These basic operating rules address program management, organization, contractor/customer relationships, documentation, customer reporting, specifications, engineering drawings, funding, cost control, subcontractor inspection, testing, security, and management compensation.

Even though the Skunk Works was conceived in 1943, their original operating rules are still valid and are used today. Johnson's 14 Rules for the Skunk Works are as follows:

1. The Skunk Works manager must be delegated practically complete control of his program in all aspects. He should report to a division president or higher.

2. Strong but small project offices must be provided both by the military and industry.

3. The number of people having any connection with the project must be restricted in an almost vicious manner. Use a small number of good people (10% to 25% compared to the so-called normal systems).

4. A very simple drawing and drawing release system with great flexibility for making changes must be provided.

5. There must be a minimum number of reports required, but important work must be recorded thoroughly.

6. There must be a monthly cost review covering not only what has been spent and committed but also projected costs to the conclusion of the program.

7. The contractor must be delegated and must assume more than normal responsibility to get good vendor bids for subcontract on the project. Commercial bid procedures are very often better than military ones.

8. The inspection system as currently used by the Skunk Works, which has been approved by both the Air Force and Navy, meets the intent of existing military requirements, and should be used on new projects. Push more basic inspection responsibility back to subcontractors and vendors. Don't duplicate so much inspection.

9. The contractor must be delegated the authority to test his final product in flight. He can and must test it in the initial stages. If he doesn't, he rapidly loses his competency to design other vehicles.

---

[*] Source: Jay Miller. 1993. *Lockheed's Skunk Works: The First Fifty Years.* Arlington, TX: Aerofax, Inc., 210.

10. The specifications applying to the hardware must be agreed to well in advance of contracting. The Skunk Works practice of having a specification section stating clearly which important military specification items will not knowingly be complied with and reasons therefore is highly recommended.

11. Funding a program must be timely so that the contractor doesn't have to keep running to the bank to support government projects.

12. There must be mutual trust between the military project organization and the contractor, very close cooperation, and liaison on a day-to-day basis. This cuts down misunderstanding and correspondence to an absolute minimum.

13. Access by outsiders to the project and its personnel must be strictly controlled by appropriate security measures.

14. Because only a few people will be used in engineering and most other areas, ways must be provided to reward good performance by pay not based on the number of personnel supervised.

Appendix C: F-22 Engineering, Manufacturing, and Development Contract

ᴺᴱꜰ 67X					67X

AWARD/CONTRACT			1. PAGE 1 ᴏꜰ 80

2. PROC INSTRUMENT ID NO. (PIIN)	3. EFFECTIVE DATE	4. REQUISITION/PURCHASE REQUEST/PROJECT NO.	5. CERTIFIED FOR NATIONAL DEFENSE UNDER BDC **DO-A1** REG 2/DMS REG 1 RATING
F33657-91-C-0006	0 2 AUG 1991	FY7615-91-00161	

6. ISSUED BY CODE FQ7615	7. ADMINISTERED BY CODE S1111A
USAF/AFSC Aeronautical Systems Division (ASD) Wright-Patterson AFB OH 45433-6503 BUYER: CAPT C. BRATTEN, ASD/YFK (513) 255-1695	Defense Logistics Agency DPRO Lockheed Aeronautical Systems Company 86 S. Cobb Dr Marietta GA 30063

8. CONTRACTOR NAME AND ADDRESS CODE 98897	FACILITY CODE EZ7472 IF "9" FOR MULTIPLE FACILITIES SEE SECT "G"	9. SUBMIT INVOICES (4 copies unless otherwise specified) TO ADDRESS SHOWN IN
Lockheed Corporation For It's Division Lockheed Aeronautical Systems Company 86 S. Cobb Dr Marietta GA 30063	MAILING DATE AUG 02 1991	10. DISCOUNT FOR PROMPT PAYMENT

10. DISCOUNT FOR PROMPT PAYMENT
N

11. AUTHORIZED RATE A. PROGRESS PAY B. RECOUP % %	12. CONTRACT PERCENT FEE %	13. PAYMENT WILL BE MADE BY
14. PURCHASE OFFICE POINT OF CONTACT ARN/A1E/ARN	15. SVC/AGENCY USE	HQ DFAS-CO/ALB CODE F59240 IF "9" FOR MULTIPLE DISBURSING OFFICES, SEE SECT "G" Kirtland AFB NM 87185-5850

16. TYPE CONTRACTOR A	17. SECURITY A. CLAS TS	B. DATE OF DD 254 23 Oct 90	19. (RESERVED)	20. DATE SIGNED	21. SURV CRIT	22. TOTAL AMOUNT

18. CONTRACT ADMINISTRATION DATA					
A. FAST PAY	B. CONTRACT (1) KIND (2) TYPE 3 9	C. ABSTRACT RECIP D. SPL CONT ADP POINT PROVISIONS FUNC LMT	E. CONT ADMIN		C $9,550,096,600.00

23. AUTHORITY FOR USING OTHER THAN FULL AND OPEN COMPETITION
X PURSUANT TO 10 USC 2304(C) (1) : (41 USC 253(C) ( )

24. TABLE OF CONTENTS (The following sections marked "X" are contained in the contract.)

(X)	SEC	DESCRIPTION	PAGE(S)	(X)	SEC	DESCRIPTION	PAGE(S)
		PART I - THE SCHEDULE				**PART II - CONTRACT CLAUSES**	
X	A	SOLICITATION/CONTRACT FORM	1	X	I	CONTRACT CLAUSES	65
X	B	SUPPLIES OR SERVICES AND PRICES/COSTS	3			**PART III - LIST OF DOCUMENTS, EXHIBITS AND OTHER ATTACH**	
X	C	DESCRIPTION/SPECS/WORK STATEMENT	13	X	J	LIST OF ATTACHMENTS	78
X	D	PACKAGING AND MARKING	14			**PART IV - REPRESENTATIONS AND INSTRUCTIONS**	
X	E	INSPECTION AND ACCEPTANCE	15		K	REPRESENTATIONS, CERTIFICATIONS AND OTHER STATEMENTS OF OFFERORS	
X	F	DELIVERIES OR PERFORMANCE	17				
X	G	CONTRACT ADMINISTRATION DATA	22		L	INSTRS., CONDS., AND NOTICES TO OFFER	
X	H	SPECIAL CONTRACT REQUIREMENTS	24		M	EVALUATION FACTORS FOR AWARD	

PREVIOUS EDITIONS ARE OBSOLETE

CONTRACTING OFFICER WILL COMPLETE BLOCK 25 OR 29, AS APPLICABLE

25. ☒ CONTRACTOR'S NEGOTIATED AGREEMENT (Contractor is required to sign this document and return _____ copies to issuing office.) Contractor agrees to furnish and deliver all items or perform all the services set forth or otherwise identified herein for the consideration stated herein. The rights and obligations of the parties to this contract shall be subject to and governed by the following documents: (a) this award/contract, (b) the solicitation, if any, (c) such provisions, representations, certifications, and specifications, as are attached or incorporated by reference herein. (Attachments are listed herein.)	29. ☐ AWARD (Contractor is not required to sign this document.) Your offer on Solicitation Number_____, including the additions or changes made by you which additions or changes are set forth in full above, is hereby accepted as to the items listed herein. This award consummates the contract which consists of the following documents (a) the Government's solicitation and your offer, and (b) this award/contract. No further contractual document is necessary.
26. CONTRACTOR Lockheed Corporation BY _____ (SIGNATURE OF PERSON AUTHORIZED TO SIGN)	30. UNITED STATES OF AMERICA BY _____ (SIGNATURE OF CONTRACTING OFFICER)
27. NAME AND TITLE OF SIGNER (TYPE OR PRINT) J. A. Blackwell Attorney-In-Fact	31. NAME OF CONTRACTING OFFICER (TYPE OR PRINT) DONNA L. HATFIELD Contracting Officer
28. DATE SIGNED 21 Mar 91	32. DATE SIGNED 0 2 AUG 199

AFSC Form 701, OCT 85

Appendix D: Key Dates and Events in the History of the F-22 Program

Key Dates in YF-22 Dem/Val Flight Test Schedule

Date	Event
November 3, 1990	Supercruise demonstrated with GE YF120 engines
November 15, 1990	First thrust vectoring flight
November 25, 1990	AIM-9M Sidewinder missile launch
December 10, 1990	High angle of attack testing begins
December 17, 1990	High angle of attack testing Completed 60 degrees demonstrated
December 20, 1990	AIM-120 AMRAAM launch
December 27, 1990	Supercruise demonstrated with Pratt & Whitney YF119 engines
December 28, 1990	Maximum Mach number demonstrated
Source:	Richard Abrams. 1991. YF-22A Prototype Advanced Tactical Fighter Demonstration/Validation Flight Test Program Overview. Palmdale, California: Lockheed Advanced Development Company.

Key Events in the History of the F-22 Raptor Program

Date	Event
April 23, 1991	The Air Force selected a Lockheed team for development of the world's most advanced air superiority aircraft. Air Force Secretary Donald Rice stated that the choice was based on confidence in the ability of the Lockheed team and Pratt & Whitney to produce the aircraft and its engine at projected costs. Rice emphasized the importance of the team's management and production plans and added that the choice offered better reliability and maintainability. Neither design was judged more maneuverable or stealthy.[1]
August 2, 1991	Contracts totaling $11 billion were awarded to Lockheed and Pratt & Whitney for engineering and manufacturing development of the aircraft, including 11 development/prototype aircraft.[1]
September 7, 1997	First flight of the F-22 Raptor.
December 12, 2005	Air Combat Command declared that the first squadron of F-22s had achieved Initial Operational Capability. Twelve F-22s were assigned to the 27th Fighter Squadron of the 1st Fighter Wing at Langley Air Force Base, Virginia.[1]
January 21, 2006	The F-22 flew its first operational sorties, taking part in an on-going air superiority mission over the United States.[1]
February 8, 2007	The Lockheed Martin-led F-22 Raptor team received the National Aeronautic Association 2006 Robert J. Collier Trophy. The Collier Trophy is considered to be America's most prestigious award for aeronautical and space development.
May 2, 2012	Delivery of the final Raptor to the US Air Force. The ceremony was attended by Gen. Norton Schwartz, Chief of Staff of the Air Force; Senator Johnny Isakson of Georgia; Micky Blackwell, and other distinguished guests.[1]
September 24, 2014	The F-22 Raptor successfully completed its first combat mission in Syria. The aircraft struck a single command and control building in the Islamic State of Iraq and Syria (ISIS) [2]
Sources:	[1] Jeremiah Gertler. 2009. Air Force F-22 Fighter Program: Background and Issues for Congress. December 22. Washington, D.C.: Congressional Research Service. p. 3. [2] Lee Ferran. 2014. After Years of Trouble, F-22 Raptor's 1st Combat Mission a Success. 23 September. ABC News. Retrieved at https://abcnews.go.com/ International/years-trouble-22-raptors-combat-mission-success/story?id=25709236

Delivery of Final Raptor

On May 22, 2012, senior officials involved with the F-22 program attended a ceremony at Lockheed Martin in Marietta, Georgia, the purpose of which was to celebrate delivery of the final Raptor to the US Air Force. Micky Blackwell is the fifth person from the right in Figure 53.

Figure 53. Celebrating delivery of the final F-22 Raptor at the Lockheed Marietta plant in Marietta, Georgia. (Photo courtesy of Lockheed Martin)

Appendix E: Dimensions and Characteristics of the F-22 Raptor

Basic Dimensions

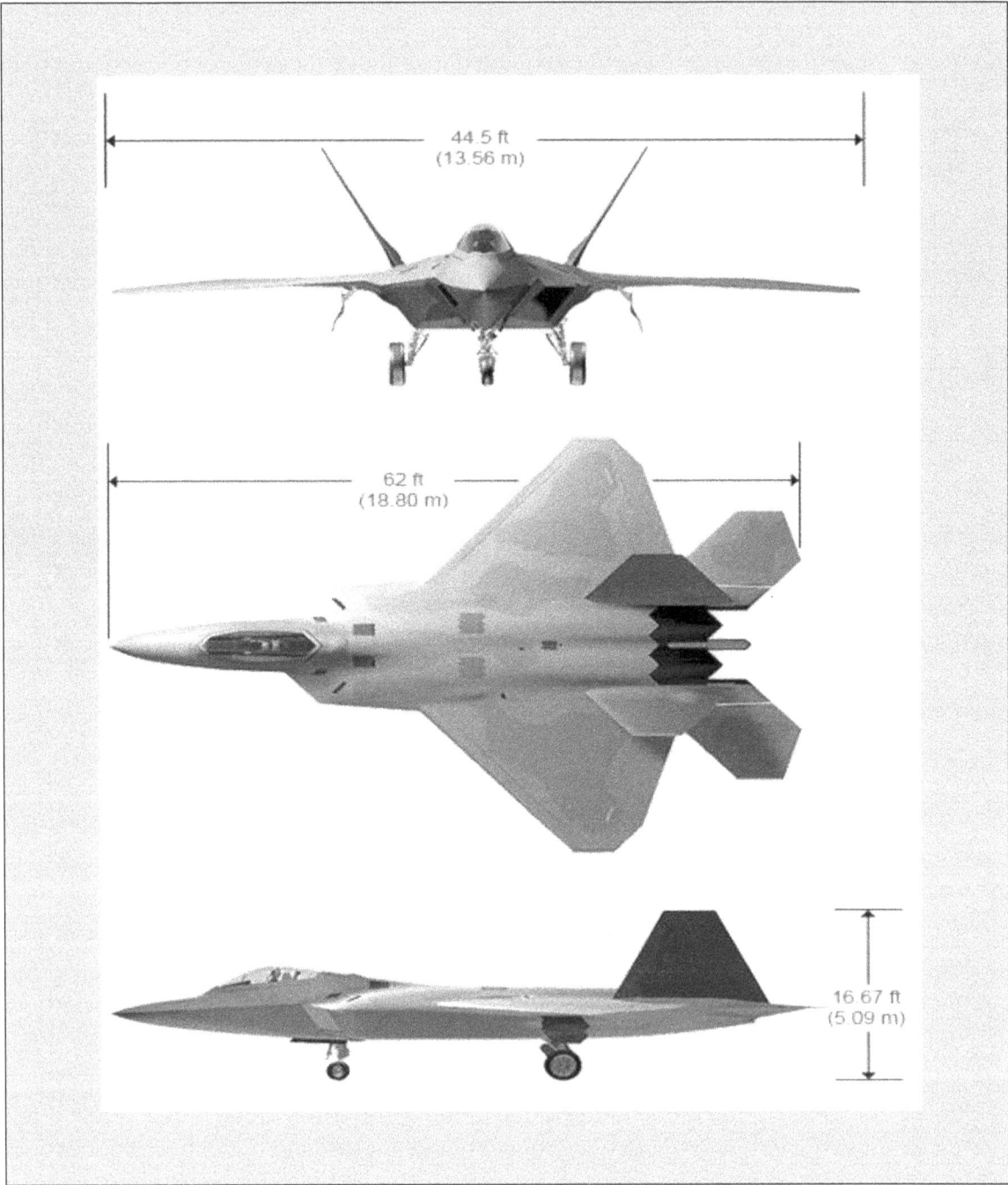

General Characteristics

PRIMARY FUNCTION	Air Dominance, Multi-role Fighter
Contractor	Lockheed-Martin, Boeing
Power plant	Two Pratt & Whitney F119-PW-100 turbofan engines with after-burners and two-dimensional thrust vectoring nozzles.
Thrust	35,000-pound class (each engine)
Wingspan	44 feet, 6 inches (13.6 meters)
Length	62 feet, 1 inch (18.9 meters)
Height	16 feet, 8 inches (5.1 meters)
Weight	43,340 pounds (19,700 kilograms)
Maximum takeoff weight	83,500 pounds (38,000 kilograms)
Fuel capacity	Internal – 18,000 pounds (8,200 kilograms); 2 external wing fuel tanks weighing 26,000 pounds (11,900 kilograms)
Payload	Same as armament air-to-air or air-to-ground loadouts, with or without two external wing fuel tanks
Speed	Mach two class with supercruise capability
Range	More than 1,850 miles ferry range with two external wing fuel tanks (1,600 nautical miles)
Ceiling	Above 50,000 feet (15 kilometers)
Armament	One M61A2 20-millimeter cannon with 480 rounds, internal side weapon bays carriage of two AIM-9 infrared (heat seeking) air-to-air missiles and internal main weapon bays carriage of six AIM-120 radar-guided air-to-air missiles (air-to-air loadout) or two 1,000-pound GBU-32 JDAMs and two AIM-120 radar-guided air-to-air missiles (air-to-ground loadout)
Crew	One
Unit cost	$143 million
Initial operating capability	December 2005 Inventory – total force, 183

Source: U.S. Air Force. 2015. F-22 Raptor Fact Sheet. September 22. Accessed January 22, 2018.
http://www.af.mil/About-Us/Fact-Sheets/Display/Article/104506/f-22-raptor/

Appendix F: Micky Blackwell's Honors, Awards, Achievements, Foundations, and Scholarships

When it comes to achievements, captains of industry are a breed unto themselves. In addition to being good leaders and communicators, they have an abundance of energy that exceeds most mortals. Some of Micky's honors, awards, achievements, and contributions to charitable causes are as follows:

Honors and Awards

- Named 150th Anniversary Distinguished Engineering Fellow, University of Alabama, College of Engineering, 1988.
- Named Engineer of the Year, American Institute of Aeronautics and Astronautics, Region II, 1992.
- Awarded Honorary Doctor of Laws, Mercer University, 1994.
- Named Fellow of the American Institute of Aeronautics and Astronautics, 1994.
- Inducted into the Alabama Engineering Hall of Fame, 1995.
- Received Reed Aeronautics Award (highest industry individual award for aeronautics), 1999.
- Named Honorary Vice President of Royal International Air Tattoo (UK), 2000.
- Named Fellow of the Mercer University National Engineering Advisory Board, 2000.
- Named Citizen of the Year, Cobb County, Georgia, for the work he did on the Marietta Redevelopment Task Force, 2002.
- Named Top 100 Most Influential Georgians by *Georgia Trends Magazine*, 2002, 2003, and 2004.
- Awarded the Hixon Medal by the Kiwanis Club International for the work he did on the Business and Public Affairs Committee, 2005.
- Named Most Influential Georgian by *Janes Magazine*, 2005-2006.

Achievements

- Member of the Mercer University Board of Trustees, 1998-1990.
- Member of Engineering Advisory Board, Mercer University, 1986-2004.
- Chairman of Mercer University Engineering Capital Campaign, 2001.
- Member of NASA Aeronautics Advisory Board, 1987–1989.
- Selected for Who's Who in America, 1990-1991.
- Member of Marietta Kiwanis Club, 1993–2021.
- Chairman of Kiwanis Business and Public Affairs Committee 2005–2006.
- Member of Kennesaw State University Board of Directors for the Michael J. Coles School of Business, Marietta, Georgia, 1994–1995.
- Steward, Trustee, and Teacher at First United Methodist Church Marietta, Georgia, 1994–present.

- Member of the University of Alabama Engineering Advisory Board, 1997–2006.
- Member of the Board of Trustees of Henry Mayo Newhall Hospital in Valencia, California, 1988–1990.
- Member of the Engineering Advisory Board, University of Virginia, 1989–1993.
- Chairman, Georgia Military Affairs Coordinating Committee reporting to Governor of Georgia, 2000–2008.
- Consultant to Lockheed Martin, 2000–2001.
- Consultant to Raytheon Aircraft, 2001.
- Member of the National Academy of Science Aerospace & Engineering Board, 2001–2005.
- Member of the Cobb County Community Foundation Board of Directors, 2001–2006.
- Founding member of the Kennesaw State University Advisory Board on Leadership, Character & Ethics, 2001–2008.
- Consultant to IBM Aerospace and Defense, 2001–2004.
- Consultant to Galileo Avionica, Italy, 2002.
- Chairman of the City of Marietta Redevelopment Task Force reporting to the Mayor of Marietta, Georgia, 2002–2003.
- Member of the "Lead Like Jesus" Board of Directors, 2002–2011.
- Vice Chairman of Marietta Redevelopment Corporation, 2003–2008.
- Vice Chairman of the Marietta Aviation Museum and Discovery Center, 2003–2009.
- Member of the Marietta Friends of the Strand Theater Restoration Board and Advisory Committee, 2003–2011.
- Chairman of the Board of Directors ScanTech LLC, 2004–2009.
- Consultant to KMPG, 2005–2006.
- Chairman of the Alpha Bank and Trust Board of Directors, 2006–2008.
- Member of the WellStar Hospital Institute for Better Health Board of Advisors in Marietta, Georgia, 2006–2007.

Foundations and Scholarships

- Micky and Billie established scholarships for helping engineering students at Mercer University and at the University of Alabama. The scholarships were established in their own names as well as the names of their parents.
- Cobb Community Foundation. The Cobb Community Foundation inspires charitable giving by building resources for the future and connecting donors who care with causes that matter. Micky and Billie established a Blackwell Family Foundation as part of the Cobb Community Foundation.

Bibliography

Abrams, Richard. 1991. *YF-22A Prototype Advanced Tactical Fighter Demonstration/Validation Flight Test Program Overview*. Palmdale, California: Lockheed Advanced Development Company.

Abrams, Richard, and Jay Miller. 1992. *Lockheed/General Dynamics/Boeing F-22: Advanced Tactical Fighter Unveiled!* Aerofax Extra 5, Arlington, Texas: Aerofax Inc.

Achieving Design-to-Cost Objectives. n.d. *NPD Solutions*. Accessed June 21, 2021. https://www.npd-solutions.com/dtc.html#:~:text=A%20design%20to%20cost%20approach%20consists%2 0of%20 the,development%20budgets%20and%20target%20costs%3B%20More%20item s...%20.

Aerospace Industries Association of America. 2010. *Aerospace Facts & Figures 2009*. 57th Edition. Arlington, Virginia.

Air Force Research Laboratories. n.d. Accessed August 27, 2001. http://www.wpafb.af.mil/ Welcome/Fact-Sheets/Di.

Alberts, David S., John j. Garstka, and Frederick P. Stein. 2003. *Network Centric Warfare: Developing and Leveraging Information Superiority*. Washington D.C.: Command and Control Research Program.

All About Truth. n.d. *The Inspiration of Scripture*. Accessed June 20, 2021. https://www.allabouttruth.org/ inspiration-of-scripture.htm.

American Institute of Aeronautics and Astronautics. 2018. *2018 Reed Aeronautics Award Recipients*. . Accessed June 13, 2018. https://www.aiaa.org/HonorsAndAwardsRecipientsList. aspx?awardId=10ba0453-cdb4- 4fb3-a055-e0687427901c.

—. 2018. *Reed Aeronautics Award Recipients*. Accessed June 13, 2018. https://www.aiaa.org/ HonorsAndAwardsRecipientsList.aspx?awardId=10ba0453-cdb4- 4fb3-a055-e0687427901c.

Anderson, David M. 2020. *Concurrent Engineering*. Accessed September 20, 2021. http:// design4manufacturability.com/concurrent-engineering.htm.

Aronstein, David C., Michael J. Hirschberg, and Albert C. Piccirillo. 1998. *Advanced Tactical Fighter to F-22 Raptor: Origins of the 21st Century Air Dominance Fighter*. Reston, VA: American Institute of Aeronautics and Astronautics.

Augustine, Norman R. May-June 1997. "Reshaping an Industry: Lockheed Martin's Survival Story." *Harvard Business Review*, 83-94.

Autry, James A. 2001. *The Servant Leader: How to Build a Creative Team, Develop Great Morale, and Improve Bottom-Line Performance*. Three Rivers Press.

Avery, Grant. 2018. *"Servant Leadership: Reducing the Risks of Complex Projects." Linked In*.

June 21. Accessed August 2, 2021. https://www.linkedin.com/pulse/servant-leadership- reducing-risks-complex-projects-grant-avery.

Balasubramanian, P., N. Kulatilaka, and J. Storck. 2000. "Managing information technology investments using a real-options approach." *Journal of Strategic Information Systems* (9): 39-62.

BCI Global. n.d. *Logistics Partner Selection*. Accessed September 28, 2021. https://bciglobal.com/en/ logistics-partner-selection.

Beckman, Kathleen . n.d. *Ephesians Six: Prayers in Spiritual Warfare*. Accessed June 17, 2019. https://www. kathleenbeckman.com/ephesians-six-prayers-in-spiritual-warfare.

Berman, Nat. 2018. "10 Things You Didn't Know about Lockheed Martin CEO Marillyn Hewson." *Money Inc.* Accessed December 29, 2019. https://moneyinc.com/lockheed-martin-ceo- marillyn-hewson/.

Bethel, Sheila Murray. 1995. "Servant Leadership and Corporate Risk Taking: When Risk Taking Makes a Difference." In *Reflections on Leadership: How Robert K. Greenleaf's Theory of Servant Leadership Influenced Today's Top Management Thinkers*, by Larry C. Spears (ed), 135-148. New York, NY: John Wiley & Sons, Inc.

Bigelow, Eric. 2015. *Continuous Improvement Requires Servant Leadership.* January 20.

Accessed September 24, 2018. https://www.industryweek.com/requires-servant- leadership.

Bika, Nikoletta. n.d. *The problems with employee integrity tests.* Accessed December 31, 2020. https://resources.workable.com/stories-and-insights/employee-integrity-tests.

Blacksky Corporation. 2004. *Aerospike Engine Flight Test Successful.* April 19. Accessed February 19, 2019. https://www.nasa.gov/centers/dryden/news/NewsReleases/2004/04- 23_pf.html.

Blackwell, James "Micky." 2021. *All the Days of Our Lives: The History and Heritage of Billie and James Blackwell.* Ashville, NC: United Writers Press.

—. 2014. "Learning to lead like Jesus: Part I." *Micky Blackwell Lecture Notes.* Marietta, GA, July 27.

—. 2014. "Learning to Lead Like Jesus: Part II." *Micky Blackwell Lecture Notes.* Marietta, GA, August 31.

—. 2014. "Learning to Lead Like Jesus: Part III." *Micky Blackwell Lecture Notes.* Marietta, GA, September 18.

—. 2011. "Lecture on Leadership and Management." Kennesaw State University, Kennesaw, GA, November 8.

—. 2003. "The Micky Blackwell Story." *Personal Notes of Micky Blackwell.* Marietta, GA, June 16.

—. 2004. "What kind of history will you make?" *Commencement Speech.* Kennesaw State University, Kennesaw, GA.

—. 2009. *When Two or More are Gathered in Prayer: How Praying Together can Change our World.* Lilburn, GA: United Writers Press, Inc.

Blackwell, Micky. December 17, 1992. "Challenges of 1990s Business Climate Equate to Some Drastic Changes for U.S. Defense Industry 1992-1993." *Lockheed Aeronautical Systems Company Star Volume 5, Number 24* (Lockheed Aeronautical Systems Company).

Blackwell, Micky. 1998. "1999 & 2000 Cash & EBIT Commitment - Aeronautics Sector." Bethesda, MD: Lockheed Martin, December 21.

Blackwell, Micky. 1994. "Like 'Humpty Dumpy' LASC processes are too fragmented." *Star* 2.

—. 1999. "Aeronautics Sector: An Overview." *Lockheed Martin Today.*, September: 3, 8.

—. 1995. "Memo to Lockheed Martin Aeronautical Sector." Bethesda, MD: Lockheed Martin, March 16.

—. 1993. "New Column to focus on issues affecting LASC team." *LASC Star.* Marietta, GA: Lockheed Aeronautical Systems Company, June 17.

—. 1992. "Challenges of 1990s Business Climate Equate to Some Drastic Changes for U.S. Defense Industry 1992-1993." *Star*, December 17: 7.

Blanchard, Benjamin S. 2004. *Logistics Engineering and Management (6th ed).* Upper Saddle River, NJ: Pearson Prentice Hall.

Blanchard, Ken. 2018. "What does servant leadership in action look like?" *Smart Brief.* March 2. Accessed August 24, 2018. https://www.smartbrief.com/original/2018/03/what-does- servant-leadership-action-look.

Blanchard, Ken, and Phil Hodges. 2005. *Lead Like Jesus: Lesson from the Greatest Leadership Role Model of All Time.* Nashville, TN: Thomas Nelson, Inc.

Blanchard, Ken, and Phil Hodges. 2003. *The Servant Leader.* Nashville, TN: Thomas Nelson Inc.

Bluestone, Barry, Peter Jordan, and Mark Sullivan. 1981. *Aircraft Industry Dynamics: An Analysis of Competition, Capital, and Labor.* Boston, MA: Auburn House Publishing Company.

Blunt, Ray. n.d. *"The Toughest Choices a Leader Must Make." GovLeaders.org.* Accessed August 20, 2021. https://govleaders.org/choices.htm.

—. n.d. *GovLeaders.org.* Accessed August 20, 2021. https://govleaders.org/choices.htm.

Bolkcom, Christopher. 2002. *F-22 Raptor Aircraft Program.* CRS Issue Brief for Congress, Foreign Affairs, Defense, and Trade Division, Washington, D.C.: Congressional Research Service.

Boulton, David. 1978. *The Grease Machine: The Inside Story of Lockheed's Dollar Diplomacy.*

New York, NY: Harper & Row Publishers Inc.

Bovee, Courtland L., John V. Thill, and Barbara R. Schatzman. 2003. *Business Communication Today.* Upper Saddle River, NJ: Prentice Hall.

Bradley, Stephen P., and Richard L. Nolan. 1998. *Sense & Respond: Capturing Value in the Network Era.* Boston, MA: Harvard Business School Press.

Breen, Bill. 2002. "High stakes, Big Bets." *Fast Company.* March 31. Accessed 10 11, 2017. https://www.fastcompany.com/44742/high-stakes-big-bets.

Brown, Bernard J. 2010. *Lessons Learned on the Way Down.* Bloomington, IN: Inspiring Voices. Brown, Daniel James. 2013. *The Boys in the Boat.* New York, NY: Penguin Books.

Buford, Robert P. 2008. *Halftime, updated.* Grand Rapids, MI: Zondervan.

Burnett, William B., and William E. Kovacic. 1989. "Reform of United States Weapon System Acquisition Policy: Competition, Teaming Agreements, and Dual-Sourcing." *Yale Journal on Regulation* 6 (2): 249-317.

Cert, Career. n.d. *4 Ways to Build Stewardship as a Servant Leader.* Accessed September 1, 2021. https://www.careercert.com/blog/ems/4-ways-to-build-stewardship-as-a- servant-leader/.

Challenges of Servant Leadership. n.d. *Penn State Leadership.* Accessed August 2, 2021. https://sites.psu.edu/leadership/2013/11/11/challenges-of-servant-leadership/.

Chamberlin, Philip. 1995. "Team Building and Servant Leadership." In *Reflections on Leadership: How Robert K. Greenleaf's Theory of Servant Leadership Influenced Today's Top Management Thinkers,* by Larry C. Spears, 169-178. New York: John Wiley & Sons.

Chambers, Joseph R. 2000. *Partners in Freedom: Contributions of the Langley Research Center to U.S. Military Aircraft of the 1990's.* Washington, D.C.: National Aeronautics and Space Administration.

Champy, James. 1995. *Reengineering Management: the Mandate for New Leadership.* New York, NY: Harper Business.

Christensen, Clayton M. 1997. *The Innovator's Dilemma: When New Technologies Cause Great Firms to Fail.* Boston, MA: Harvard Business School Press.

Circle, Vantage. n.d. *Servant Leadership, its Principles and Examples in the Workplace.* Accessed August 20, 2021. https://blog.vantagecircle.com/servant-leadership/.

CNN Money. 1999. *Lockheed's $70 M Comma: Spelling error leaves defense giant in the red after military jet sale.* June 18. Accessed July 17, 2018. https://money.cnn.com/1999/06/18/worldbiz/lockheed/.

Coan, Mona, ed. 1998. "Plan B. With merger hope ended, Executive Office eyes alternatives." *Lockheed Martin Today,* August: 1, 8.

Coffman, Vance D. Chairman, Chief Executive Officer and president, Lockheed Martin Corporation. 1999. "Micky Blackwell to Retire." Bethesda, MD: Lockheed Martin Corporation, October 29.

Coffman, Vance D. Chairman, Chief Executive Officer and president, Lockheed Martin Corporation. 2000. "Retirement speech for James A. Blackwell Jr." Bethesda, MD: Lockheed Martin Corporation, January 14.

Cole, Jeff. 1999. "Lockheed Lowers 1999 Forecast: Two More Top Officials to Leave." *Wall Street Journal*. Lockheed Martin News Watch Corporate Communications, November 1. 2.

Collins, James C., and Jerry I. Porras. 1996. "Building Your Company's Vision." *Harvard Business Review* 74 (5): 65-77.

Collins, Jim. 2001. *Good to Great.* New York, NY: Harper Business.

Communication Tips for Servant Leaders: 6 Ways That Learning Styles Help Your Listeners Hear You. n.d. Accessed June 23, 2021. http://christian-leadership.org/communication-tips- for-servant-leaders-6-ways-that-you-can-help-your-listeners-hear-you/.

Communication Tips for Servant Leaders: Do You Fail to Communicate Because You Fail to Listen? n.d. Accessed June 23, 2021. http://christian-leadership.org/communication- tips-for-servant-leaders-do-you-fail-to-communicate-because-you-fail-to-listen/.

Comptroller General of the United States. 1982. *C-5A Wing Modification: A Case Study Illustrating Problems In The Defense Weapons Acquisition Process.* Washington, DC: U.S. General Accounting Office.

Connolly, Maria. 2016. *Strong Convictions – The Secret to Becoming an Influential Leader in Your Community.* August 17. Accessed February 14, 2020. https://newayscenter.com/2016/08/17/strong-convictions-secret-becoming-influential- leader-community/.

Cooper, Brett and Evans Kerrigan. 2020. *Productive vs. Unproductive Conflict in the Workplace, HR Daily Advisor.* Accessed December 2, 2020. https://hrdailyadvisor.blr.com/2020/10/02/productive-vs-unproductive-conflict-in-the- workplace/.

Covey, Steven R. 1977. *"Forward." Servant Leadership: A Journey into the Nature of Legitimate Power & Greatness.* New York/ Mahwah, NJ: Paulist Press.

Cristea, Emilian, and Gelle Khalif Hassan. 2018. *Critical success factors of potential CPFR implementations in Sweden.* Master's Thesis, Jönköping University, Sweden.

Daniels, Jeff. 2017. *Chinese theft of sensitive US military technology is still a 'huge problem,' says defense analyst.* CNBC. November 8. Accessed July 17, 2018. https://www.cnbc.com/2017/11/08/chinese-theft-of-sensitive-us-military-technology- still-huge-problem.html.

Davenport, Thomas H., and Laurence Prusak. 1998. *Working Knowledge: How Organizations Manage What They Know.* Boston, MA: Harvard Business School Press.

Davenport, Thomas H. 1993. *Process Innovation: Reengineering Work through Information Technology.* Boston, MA: Harvard Business School Press.

Davis, Crystal J. 2015. *Servant Leadership and Handling Conflict. CID Consulting Solutions, LLC.* April 17. Accessed June 22, 2021. https://drcrystaldavis.wordpress.com/.

de Waal, Andre, Ruben Orig, and Simon van der Veer. May 2010. *The High Performance Partnership Framework as Value Chain Enhancer.* The Netherlands: The HPO Center.

Deloitte. 2017. *Manufacturing USA; a Third-Party Evaluation of Program Design and Progress.* United Kingdom: Deloitte Touche Tohmatsu Limited.

Dennis, Robert S., and Mihai Bocarnea. 2005. "Development of the servant leadership assessment instrument." *Leadership & Organization Development Journal* 26 (8): 600- 615.

Dholakia, Sameer. 2018. *Servant Leadership Is a Philosophy, Not a Checklist.* May 24. Accessed May 28, 2018. https://www.entrepreneur.com/article/313475.

Do, Doanh. 2017. "What is Continuous Improvement (Kaizen)?" *The Lean Way Blog.* August 5. Accessed November 20, 2020. https://www.linkedin.com/pulse/what-continuous- improvement-kaizen-doanh-do.

Dominik, Michael T. 2013. *Servant leadership behaviors of aerospace and defense project managers and their relation to project success.* Doctoral Dissertation, Philadelphia, PA: Eastern University.

Duffy, Grace L. Ed. 2013. *The ASQ Quality Improvement Pocket Guide: Basic History, Concepts, Tools, and Relationships.* Milwaukee, WI: ASQ Quality Press.

Ellzey, Karen, and Steve Valenziano. 2004. *Corporate Real Estate 2010: Integrated Resource and Infrastructure Solutions.* Atlanta, Ga: CoreNet Global.

Ethics and Core Values. n.d. *Lockheed Martin.* Accessed February 11, 2020. https://www. lockheedmartin. com/en-us/who-we-are/ethics.html.

Evans, James R., and William M. Lindsay. 2005. *The Management and Control of Quality (6th ed.).* Mason, OH: Thompson Southwestern.

F-22 Raptor Contractors. n.d. *Global Security.org* . Accessed August 18, 2019. https://www.globalsecurity. org/military/systems/aircraft/f-22-contract.htm.

Flight Global citing Flight International. 2000. *My View - Micky Blackwell, Former president of Lockheed Martin's Aeronautical Sector.* January 1. Accessed October 15, 2017. https://www.flightglobal.com/ news/articles/my-view-micky-blackwell-former- president-of-lockheed-martin39s-aeronautical-60472/.

Flight International. 2000. *My View: Micky Blackwell, Former president of Lockheed Martin's Aeronautics Sector.* January 1. Accessed October 15, 2017. https://www.flightglobal.com/ news/articles/my-view-micky-blackwell-former- president-of-lockheed-martin39.

Florida, Richard, and Jim Goodnight. 2005. "Managing for Creativity." *Harvard Business Review*, July-August: 125-131.

Fraker, Anne T. 1995. "Robert K. Greenleaf and Business Ethics: There is No Code." In *Reflection on Leadership*, by Larry T. Spears (ed), 37-48. New York, NY: John Wiley & Sons Inc.

Frick, Don M. n.d. *Robert K. Greenleaf Biography, Robert K. Greenleaf Center for Servant Leadership.* Accessed February 26, 2018. https://www.greenleaf.org/about-us/robert-k- greenleaf-biography/.

Frick, Don M. 1995. "Pyramids, Circles, and Gardens: Stories of Implementing Servant Leadership." In *Reflections on Leadership: How Robert K. Greenleaf's Theory of Servant Leadership Influenced Today's Top Management Thinker*, by Larry C. Spears, 257-281. New York: John Wiley & Sons.

Friedman, Alan. 1994. "Defense Cutbacks Spur Layoffs." *Marietta Daily Journal.* Marietta, GA, March 30. 3B.

Fulghum, David A. 1999. "USAF Official Skewers Lockheed Martin." *Aviation Week & Space Technology*, October 25: 35-36.

Futrell, Patti. 1995. "Lockheed Reengineers through "Lean Enterprise" in its Goal to be #1 in the Military Aircraft Market." *The Source*, Spring: 4-5, 8.

Galbraith, Kate. 2008. "A. Carl Kotchian, Lockheed Executive, Dies at 94." *New York Times.*

December 22. Accessed January 28, 2019. https://www.nytimes.com/2008/12/23/business/23kotchian. html.

Garamone, Jim. 2000. "Joint Vision 2020 Emphasizes Full-spectrum Dominance." American Forces Press Service. June 12. Accessed July 6, 2018. http://archive.defense.gov/news/newsarticle.aspx?id=45.

General Accounting Office. 1982. *C-5A Wing Modification: A Case Study Illustrating Problems In The Defense Weapons Acquisition Process.* General Accounting Office, Washington, D. C.: U.S. Government Printing Office.

George, Michael L. 2003. *Lean Six Sigma for Service. Back cover.* New York, NY.: The McGraw- Hill Companies.

George, Michael L. 2002. *Lean Six Sigma: Combining Six Sigma Quality with Lean Speed.* New York, NY: The McGraw-Hill Companies.

Gertler, Jeremiah. 2009. *Air Force F-22 Fighter Program: Background and Issues for Congress.*

Washington, D.C.: Congressional Research Service.

Gertler, Jeremiah. 2020. *F-35 Joint Strike Fighter (JSF) Program.* Washington D.C.: Congressional Research Service, Summary. Accessed June 26, 2020. https://crsreports.congress.gov/product/pdf/RL/RL30563.

Goldfein, David A. 2019. *Global power, lethality, and servant leadership: Air Force Chief of Staff addresses Airmen, cadets at Air Force Academy.* February 22. Accessed July 5, 2019. https://www.usafa.af.mil/News/Article/1766264/global-power-lethality-and-servant- leadership-air-force-chief-of-staff-addresse/.

Graham, Vickie M. 1995. "One Contractor's Viewpoint." *Airman*, February: 26-29.

—. 1995. "One Contractor's Viewpoint." *Airman*, February: 26-29.

Gray, Tom. 2018. *This Will Help: 6 Principles to Jump-Start Your Spiritual Engine.* Asheville, NC: United Writers Press.

Green, Colin H. 1999. "Personal Letter to Micky Blackwell." England: Rolls-Royce, Office of the Director of Operations, November 4.

Greenleaf, Robert K. Center for Servant Leadership. 2016. "Culture: An Unspoken Yet Powerful Force." Accessed August 24, 2018. https://www.greenleaf.org/winning- workplaces/workplace-resources/ask-an-expert/culture-an-unspoken-yet-powerful- force/.

Greenleaf, Robert K. 1970. *The Servant as Leader.* Atlanta, GA: The Greenleaf Center for Servant-Leadership.

Greenleaf, Robert K., Essays by. 2002. *Servant Leadership: A Journey into the Nature of Legitimate Power and Greatness 25th Anniversary Edition.* Edited by Larry C. Spears. New York/Mahwah, New Jersey: Paulist Press.

Haeckel, Stephan H. 1999. *Adaptive Enterprise: Creating and Leading Sense-and-Respond Organizations.* Boston, MA: Harvard Business School Press.

Hammer, Michael, and James Champy. 1993. *Reengineering the Corporation: a Manifesto for Business Revolution.* New York, NY: Harper Business.

Hansen, Morton T., and Julian Birkinshaw. June 2007. "The Innovation Value Chain." *Harvard Business Review*, pp. 121-130.

Harper, Bob. 1997. "General Richard E. Hawley." *Sky Power, The F-22: Air Dominance for the 21st Century*, Spring: 19-23.

Harrington, H. James. 1991. *Business Process Improvement: The Breakthrough Strategy for Total Quality, Productivity, and Competitiveness.* New York, NY: McGraw-Hill, Inc.

Harris, Elizabeth. n.d. "4 Steps to Profitable Revenue Growth. Resultist Consulting." Accessed November 30, 2019. https://www.resultist.com/blog/bid/256549/4-Steps-to-Profitable- Revenue-Growth.

Hartman, Amir, John Sifonis, and John Kador. 2000. *Net Ready: Strategies for Success in the E-conomy.* New York, NY: McGraw-Hill.

Herman, Rebecca. 2020. *"What is Servant Leadership?" Purdue Global.* Accessed June 18, 2021. https://www.purdueglobal.edu/blog/business/what-is-servant-leadership/.

—. 2020. *What is Servant Leadership?* Accessed February 26, 2021. https://www.purdueglobal.edu/blog/business/what-is-servant-leadership.

Hill, Derek. n.d. *What Does the Bible Say About Criticism? A Christian Study. What Christians Want to Know.* Accessed February 21, 2021. https://www.whatchristianswanttoknow.com/what-does-the-bible-say-about-criticism- a-christian-study/.

Holy Bible. n.d. *Bible Gateway, New King James Version.* Accessed October 23, 2017. https://www. biblegateway.com/passage/?search=John+13%3A1-17&version=NKJV.

Hopp, Michael, and Harold Manger. 1995. "Dealing With - and Managing - Change." *Change Management Presentation Developed for Merger Between Lockheed and Martin Marietta.* Bethesda, MD: Lockheed Martin Corporation, March 15.

Hubbard, Richard. 1991. *Your Upkeep will be Your Downfall.* Comp. Richard Hubbard.

Iarocci, Joe. n.d. *4 Reasons Humility is a Cardinal Virtue of Servant Leadership.* Accessed August 2, 2021. https://serveleadnow.com/blog-4-reasons- humility/#:~:text=These%20particular%20things%20 might%20humble%20servant- leaders%2C%20of%20course%2.

Irving, Justin A, and Gail J. Longbotham. 2007. "Team Effectiveness and Six Essential Servant Leadership Themes: A Regression Model Based on items in the Organizational Leadership Assessment." *International Journal of Leadership Studies,* (Regents University) 2 (2): 98-113.

Jennings, Kenneth R., and Heather Hyde. 2012. *The Greater Goal: Connecting Purpose and Performance.* Oakland, CA: Berrett-Koehler.

Jennings, Kenneth R., and John Stahl-Wert. 2004. *The Serving Leader: Five Powerful Actions That Will Transform Your Team, Your Business, and Your Community.* Oakland, CA: Berrett-Koehler.

John, Belinda. 2016. "Conviction: The Strength of Successful Leadership." *SW.* Accessed February 14, 2020. https://www.shulamitewomen.com/conviction-the-strength-of- successful-leadership/.

Johnson, Luke. 1995. "Lockheed, Russia Co-Design New Fighter." *Marietta Daily Journal* 1A, 3A.—. 1992. "Crash won't hurt ATF plans." *Marietta Daily Journal,* April 30: 1A, 8A.

Joyce, Michael, and Bettina Schechter. 2004. *The Lean Enterprise-A Management Philosophy at Lockheed Martin.* Fort Belvoir, VA: Office of the Under Secretary of Defense for Acquisition Technology & Logistics.

Joyner, Chris. 1999. "Poor earnings report rocks Lockheed." *Marietta Daily Journal.,* October 30: 1, 6A.

Kaetz, James P. n.d. *Encyclopedia of Alabama.* Auburn University. Accessed January 10, 2018. http://www. encyclopediaofalabama.org/article/h-2536.

Kalhorn, Renita. 2000. *"The Hidden Pitfalls of Servant Leadership." Forbes.* September 2. Accessed September 1, 2021. https://www.forbes.com/sites/renitakalhorn/2020/09/02/the-hidden-pitfalls-of-servant-leadership/.

Kandebo, Stanley W, and David Hughes. 1995. "F-22 to Counter 21st Century Threats." *Aviation Week & Space Technology,* July 24: 38-43.

Kandebo, Stanley W. 1999. "Lean Thinking Spurs Culture Shift at LMAS." *Aviation Week & Space Technology,* July 12: 56-59.

—. 1995. "F-22 Team Characterizes New Materials, Processes." *Aviation Week & Space Technology,* July 24: 46-47.

—. 1999. "Lean Thinking Prompts Line Shift for F-22." *Aviation Week & Space Technology,* July 12: 61-63.

Katzenbach, Jon R, and Douglas K Smith. 2003. *The Wisdom of Teams: Creating the High- Performance Organization.* New York, NY: McKinsey & Company.

Lee, John M. 1971. "Rolls-Royce is Bankrupt; Blames Lockheed Project." *New York Times Archives.* February 5. Accessed January 30, 2018. http://www.nytimes.com/1971/02/05/archives/rollsroyce-is-bankrupt-blames- lockheed-project-rollsroyce-enters.html.

LeFew, Donna. 1993. "Blackwell Emphasizes Dramatic Change for LASC's Future." *The Leader*, December: 5.

Leland, John W., and Kathryn A. Wilcoxson. 2003. *The Chronological History of the C 5 Galaxy*. Scott Air Force Base, IL: Office of History, Air Mobility Command.

Lencioni, Patrick M. 2002. "Make Your Values Mean Something." *Harvard Business Review* 80 (7): 113-117.

Lockheed Loan Backed. 1972. "New York Times Archives." September 7.

Lockheed Martin. n.d. *C-27J Spartan Tactical Transport Aircraft*. Alenia Tactical Transport Systems. Accessed April 21, 2019. https://www.airforce- technology.com/projects/spartan/.

Lockheed Martin Corporation. 1995. *Annual Report*. Bethesda, MD: Lockheed Martin Corporation.

Lockheed Martin Corporation. 1996. *Annual Report*. Bethesda, MD: Lockheed Martin Corporation.

Lockheed Martin Corporation. 1997. *Annual Report*. Bethesda, MD: Lockheed Martin Corporation.

Lockheed Martin Corporation. 1998. *Annual Report*. Bethesda, MD: Lockheed Martin Corporation.

Lockheed Martin Corporation. 1999. Annual Report. Bethesda, MD: Lockheed Martin Corporation.

—. n.d. *F-22 Raptor Capabilities*. Lockheed Martin Corporation. Accessed October 14, 2017. http://www. lockheedmartin.com/us/products/f22/f-22-capabilities.html.

—. n.d. *F-22 Raptor: Mission Ready Statement*. Lockheed Martin Corporation. Accessed March 17, 2018. https://lockheedmartin.com/us/products/f22.html.

—. n.d... "Full Spectrum Leadership." Lockheed Martin Corporation. Accessed February 4, 2019. https:// www.lockheedmartin.com/en-us/who-we-are/leadership-governance/full- spectrum-leadership.html.

—. 1998. "Lean Thinking is Real Too." *Newsline Daily, Farnborough International*. London, England: Lockheed Martin International. 4.

—. n.d. *Lockheed Aircraft Service Company: The Beginning of a Global Lockheed Martin*. Accessed January 25, 2018. https://www.lockheedmartin.com/us/news/features/2015/151110-lockheed-aircraft- service-company.html.

—. 1998. "Real Partnerships Really In-Place." *News Line Daily, Farnborough International*.

London, England: Lockheed Martin International, September 8.

Lockheed Martin. n.d. "Leadership and Corporate Governance Lockheed Martin: Full Spectrum Leadership." *Lockheed Martin*. Accessed February 21, 2020. https://www.lockheedmartin.com/en-us/ who-we-are/leadership-governance/full- spectrum-leadership.html.

Lockheed Martin. n.d. *Lockheed Aircraft Service Company: The Beginning of a Global Lockheed Martin*. Bethesda, MD: Lockheed Martin. Accessed January 25, 2018. https://www.lockheedmartin.com/us/ news/ features/2015/151110-lockheed-aircraft- service-company.html.

Lopez, Isabel O. 1995. "Becoming a Servant Leader: The Personal Development Path." In *Reflections on Leadership*, by Larry C. Spears (ed.), 149-160. New York, NY: John Wiley & Sons.

Lopez, Stephanie. 1994. *An Investigation of Integrated Product Development: A Case Study of an F-22 Prime Contractor*. Air Force Institute of Technology, Ohio: Wright-Patterson Air Force Base.

Managing the Finance Function in Engineering. n.d. *Course Hero*. Accessed June 21, 2021. https://www. coursehero.com/file/97642722/MANAGING-THE-FINANCE-FUNCTION-IN- ENGINEERING-1docx/.

Mason., Debbie. 2017. *Ethical Behavior Through Servant Leadership*. Accessed February 19, 2021. https:// www.businessmagazinegainesville.com/ethical-behavior-through-servant- leadership/.

Materna, Robert, Robert E. Mansfield Jr., and Frederick W. Deck III. 2013. *Aerospace Industry Report*. 3rd. Daytona Beach, FL: Aerospace Industries Association and Embry-Riddle Aeronautical University - Worldwide.

Maxwell, John C. 2007. *The 21 Irrefutable Laws of Leadership: Follow Them and People Will Follow You.* Nashville, TN: Thomas Nelson, Inc.

Maza, Vivian. 2019. "(2019, March 26). The Importance Of Establishing Company Core Values -- And How To Define Them." *Forbes.* Accessed February 13, 2020. https://www.forbes.com/sites/ forbeshumanresourcescouncil/2019/03/26/the- importance-of-establishing-company-c.

McLellan, John. 1995. "Blackwell taught us value of open communications with employees, customers." *Star*, March 30: 2.

Michel, Roberto (Senior ed.). 1999. "Lean Meets ERP." *Manufacturing Systems.* New York, NY: Cahners Business Information, Mid-November (article reprint).

Miles, Susan. 1993. "Blackwell: Radical change needed to compete in the '90s marketplace." *Star* 1,3.

—. 1994. "Lean Production's streamlined processes bring increased efficiency to Manufacturing areas." *Star*, February 10: 4.

Miles, Susan, ed. 1997. "Lockheed Martin backs nation's first Space Day, set for May 22." *Star*, March 6: 3.

Miles., Susan. 1994. "Goal in Manufacturing is to be the Best in the Business." *Star*, January 20: 1, 4.

Miller, Jay. 1993. *Lockheed's Skunk Works: The First Fifty Years.* Arlington, TX: Aerofax, Inc. Miller, W. Roger, and Jeffrey P. Miller. n.d. *"Leadership Styles for Success in Collaborative*

Work." Association of Leadership Educators. Accessed June 1, 2021. https://www.leadershipeducators. org/Resources/Documents/Conferences/FortWorth/ Miller.pdf.

Mullin, Sherman N. 1992. *The Evolution of the F-22 Advanced Tactical Fighter.* 1992 Wright Brothers Lecture AIAA Aircraft Design Systems Meeting, AIAA 92-4188, American Institute of Aeronautics and Astronautics.

Mullin, Sherman N. 2012. *Winning the ATF.* Mitchell Paper 9, Arlington, VA: Mitchell Institute Press.

NASA. n.d. *Aviation Pioneer Richard T. Whitcomb.* Accessed November 1, 2017. https://www.nasa.gov/ topics/people/features/richard_whitcomb.html.

NASA Biography. n.d. *Andrew S. W. Thomas, Ph.D. and Former NASA Astronaut.* Accessed February 28, 2018. https://www.jsc.nasa.gov/Bios/htmlbios/thomas-a.html.

NASA Dryden Flight Research Center, U.S. Air Force Flight Test Center, and Blacksky Corporation. 2004. *Aerospike Engine Flight Test Successful.* April 19. Accessed February 19, 2019. https://www.nasa.gov/ centers/dryden/news/NewsReleases/2004/04- 23_pf.html.

National Aeronautic Association. n.d. *Collier Trophy,* Accessed November 1. https://naa.aero/awards/ awards-and-trophies/collier-trophy.

National Aeronautic Association. 2018. *Collier 1980-1989 Recipients.* Accessed June 8, 2018. https://naa. aero/awards/awards-and-trophies/collier-trophy/collier-1980-1989- winners.

National Aeronautic Association. n.d. *Collier Trophy.* Accessed November 1, 2020. https://naa.aero/ awards/awards-and-trophies/collier-trophy.

National Aeronautic Association. n.d. *Collier Trophy.* Accessed September 1, 2020. https://naa.aero/ awards/awards-and-trophies/collier-trophy.

Navigate Challenges with a Resilient Business Mindset. n.d. *USPS Delivers.* Accessed August 21, 2021. https://www.uspsdelivers.com/resilient-business-start-with-flexibility/.

Neuschel, Robert P. 2005. *The Servant Leader: Unleashing the Power of Your People.* Evanston, IL: Northwestern University Press.

Nielsen, Lisa. 2018. *Role of Business Communication, Chron.* October 15. Accessed March 30, 2019. https://smallbusiness.chron.com/role-business-communication-2881.html.

Niemi, Christopher J. November–December 2012. "The F-22 Acquisition Program: Consequences for the US Air Force's Fighter Fleet." *Air & Space Power Journal* 53-82. Noah, Timothy. 2009. *The government's record on industry bailouts.* March 31. Accessed May 25, 2018. http://www.slate.com/articles/news_ and_politics/chatterbox/2009/03/the_bailout_rec ord.html.

Nunes, Paul, and Tim Breene. 2011. "Reinvent Your Business Before it's too Late." *Harvard Business Review.* January-February, 81-87.

Office of the Inspector General, Federal Deposit Insurance Corporation. 2009. *Material Loss Review of Alpha Bank and Trust, Alpharetta, Georgia, Report No. AUD-09-010.* May. Accessed April 11, 2018. https://www.fdicoig.gov/publications/reports09/09-010- 508.shtml.

Osborn, Kris. 2018. "The Air Force is upgrading the F-22 to keep it combat ready until 2060." *Business Insider.* February 8. Accessed March 18, 2018. http://www.businessinsider.com/air-force-upgrading-f-22-2018-2.

Our Mission and Vision. n.d. *Robert K. Greenleaf Center for Servant Leadership.* Accessed June 7, 2019. https://www.greenleaf.org/our-journey/.

Packard, Heather. 2011. *Lessons in Leadership: The Case of Servant Leadership in Finance.* December 9. Accessed July 31, 2018. https://blogs.cfainstitute.org/investor/2011/12/09/lessons-in-leadership-the-case-for- servant-leadership-in-finance/.

Pantin, Christian, and Michele Pantin. 2021. *Be Inspired: Weekly Inspirations for Servant Leaders.* Meadville, PA: Christian Faith Publishing.

Parris, D. L., and J. W. Peachy. 2013. *A Systematic Literature Review of Servant Leadership Theory in Organizational Contexts.* Vol. 113. Journal of Business Ethics.

Pattillo, Donald M. 2001. *Pushing the Envelope: The American Aircraft Industry.* Ann Arbor, MI: The University of Michigan Press.

Peck, Scott M. 1995. "Servant Leadership Training and Discipline in Authentic Community." In *Reflections on Leadership: How Robert K. Greenleaf's Theory of Servant Leadership Influenced Today's Top Management Thinkers*, by Larry C. Spears, 87-98. New York: John Wiley & Sons.

Perlmutter, Howard V., and David A. Heenan. 1986. "Cooperate to Compete Globally." *Harvard Business Review* 64 (2): 136=152.

Petersen, Willie. 2002. "The Mark Twain Dilemma: The Theory and Practice of Change Leadership." *Journal of Business Strategy.* September-October. Accessed June 28, 2018. http://williepietersen.com/wp-content/uploads/pdf/Mark_Twain_Dilemma.pdf.

Pinelli, Thomas E., Rebecca O. Barclay, John M. Kennedy, and Ann P. Bishop. 1997. *Knowledge Diffusion in the U.S. Aerospace Industry: Managing Knowledge for Competitive Advantage.* Greenwich, CT: Ablex Publishing Company.

Plexico, Alvin. n.d. *Leadership Communication Styles - The Pros and Cons. Purdue University.* Accessed June 22, 2021. https://www.cla.purdue.edu/academic/communication/graduate/online/leadership-communication-styles.html.

Porter, Michael E. 1980. *Competitive Strategy.* New York, NY: The Free Press.

—. 1985. *Competitive Advantage: Creating and Sustaining Superior Performance.* New York, NY: The Free Press.

Porter, Michael E., and Victor E. Millar. 1985. "How information gives you competitive advantage." In *On Competition*, by Michael E. Porter, 75-98. Boston, MA: Harvard Business School Press.

Porter, Michael. n.d. *The Value Chain from Competitive Advantage.* Accessed January 10, 2021. http://people.tamu.edu/~v-buenger/466/Value_Chain.pdf.

Pratt & Whitney: a United Technology Company. 2018. *F119-PW-100 Turbofan Engine.* Website Report, Hartford, CT: Pratt & Whitney.

Preiss, Kenneth, Steven L. Goldman, and Roger N. Nagel. 1996. *Cooperate to Compete.* New York, NY: Van Nostrand Reinhold.

Pritchett, Price. 1992. *The Team Member Handbook for Teamwork.* Dallas, TX: Price Pritchett & Associates.

Rabbolini, Omar. 2020. *How To Resolve Conflicts Like A Servant Leader.* Accessed February 10, 2021. https://medium.com/swlh/how-to-resolve-conflicts-like-a-servant-leader- 460c73707dec.

Radmacher, Earl D. et al, eds. 1997. *The Nelson Study Bible: New King James Version.* Nashville, TN: Thomas Nelson Publishers.

Rasmussen, Tina. 1995. "Creating a Culture of Servant Leadership: A Real Life Story." In *Reflections on Leadership*, by Larry C. Spears ed., 282-297. New York: John Wiley & Sons.

Ray, Greg. 2014. *World class processes begin with the "right" process owners.* January 21. Accessed February 16, 2020. https://www.industryweek.com/finance/cost- management-bpm/article/21965469/ worldclass-processes-begin-with-the-right-process.

Reed, Lora L., Deborah Vidaver-Cohen, and Scott R. Colwell. 2011. "A New Scale to Measure Executive Servant Leadership: Development, Analysis," *Journal of Business Ethics* 415– 434.

n.d. *Reference for Business. Vance D. Coffman, 1944-.* Accessed January 27, 2020. https://www.referenceforbusiness.com/biography/A-E/Coffman-Vance-D- 1944.html#:~:text=Coffman.&text=%E2%96%A0-Vance%20D.,America's%20early%2Dwarning%20defense%20system.

Reuters. 1995. "$24.8 Million Penalty Paid by Lockheed." *The New York Times Company News.* January 28. Accessed January 7, 2019. https://www.nytimes.com/1995/01/28/business/company-news-831095.html.

Rieser, Carl. 1995. "Claiming Servant Leadership as Your Heritage." In *Reflections on Leadership: How Robert K. Greenleaf 's Theory of Servant Leadership Influenced Today's Top Management Thinkers*, by Larry C. Spears (ed), 49-60. New York, NY: John Wiley & Sons, Inc.

n.d. *Robert K. Greenleaf Center website. Our Mission and Vision: Robert K. Greenleaf Center for Servant Leadership.* Accessed June 7, 2019. https://www.greenleaf.org/our-journey/.

Roberto Michel (Senior ed.). 1999. ""Lean Meets ERP." *Manufacturing Systems Cahners Business Information, Mid-November* (article reprint).

Rocco, Matt. 2020. *"Why is Effective Communication Crucial to Become a Servant Leader?" Etech.* August 5. Accessed August 3, 2021. https://www.etechgs.com/blog/effective- communication-to-become-a-servant-leader/.

Roll, Don. n.d. "An Introduction to 6S. Vital Enterprises." Accessed January 29, 2020. http://www.vitalentusa.com/learn/6s_article.php.

Roos, John G. 1997. "From the Boardroom "Micky" Blackwell, president & COO, Aeronautics Sector." *Armed Forces Journal International*, January: 54.

Sahadi, Jeanne. 2020. *CNN Business.* Accessed May 1, 2021. https://www.cnn.com/2020/06/15/success/women-ceos-fortune-500-marillyn- hewson/index.html.

Scan Tech Holdings. n.d. Accessed March 15, 2020. http://www.scantechholdings.com.

Schaeufele, John. 2004. *Enthusiasm: definitely a force multiplier.* October 5. Accessed March 26, 2019. https://www.af.mil/News/Commentaries/ display/Article/142275/enthusiasm- definitely-a-force-multiplier/.

Schermerhorn, John R. 2002. *Management, 7th ed.* New York, NY: John Wiley & Sons. Schlender, Brent. 1995. "1995. Whose Internet Is It, Anyway?" *Fortune Magazine*, December 11: 110.

Schneider, Greg. 1999. *"Lockheed chief resigns as bad news worsens; No. 3 executive also steps down; profit outlook grim." The Baltimore Sun.* October 30. Accessed August 10, 2021. https://www. baltimoresun.com/news/bs-xpm-1999-10-30-9910300147-story.html.

Section 8: Ethical Leadership. Community Tool Box. n.d. Accessed August 20, 2021. https://ctb.ku.edu/ en/table-of-contents/leadership/leadership-ideas/ethical- leadership/main.

Shoff, Dave. 2020. *"Servant Leader Principle #10 – Community." Leader as Servant.* March 2. Accessed August 30, 2021. https://leader-as-servant.com/2020/03/02/servant-leader- principle-10-community/.

—. 2020. *"Servant Leader Principle #10 – Community." Leader as Servant.* March 2. Accessed August 30, 2021. https://leader-as-servant.com/2020/03/02/servant-leader-principle- 10-community/.

Sirohi, M. N. 2016. *Military Space Force and Modern Defence.* New Delhi, India: Vij Publishing.

Six Indicators of Inefficient Work Management. n.d. Workfront. Accessed May 7, 2018. at https://www. workfront.com/blog/six-indicators-of-inefficient-work- management#:~:text=Six%20Indicators%20 of%20Inefficient%20Work%20Management.%201%20Continually,6%20B.

Spears, Larry C. 2010. "Character and Servant Leadership: Ten Characteristics of Effective, Caring Leaders." *The Journal of Virtues & Leadership* 1 (1): 25-30.

Spears, Larry C., ed. 1995. *Reflections on Leadership: How Robert K. Greenleaf's Theory of Servant Leadership Influenced Today's Top Management Thinkers.* New York, NY: John Wiley & Sons.

Special to the *New York Times*. 1972. "Lockheed Loan Backed." *The New York Times Archives.* September 7. Accessed January 24, 2018. http://www.nytimes.com/1972/09/08/archives/lockheed-loan-backed- rail-loans-voted- by-senate-body.html.

Staats, Bradley R., and David M. Upton. 2011. "Lean Knowledge Work." *Harvard Business Review*, October: 100-110.

Stetzer, Ed. 2019. *Defining Leadership: What Is It and Why Does It Matter in Church.* Accessed May 29, 2021. https://www.christianitytoday.com/edstetzer/2019/september/defining- leadership-christian- serving-god-empower-people.html.

Stevenson., Richard W. 1991. "New in Defense: Teamwork." *The New York Times*, December 22: Section 3, 3.

Stolpe, Matt. n.d. *Bonfyre: Embrace the Informal for Effective Internal Communication.* Accessed May 31, 2019. https://bonfyreapp.com/blog/embrace-informal-effective- internal-communication#contentTop.

Tan, Siang-Yang . 2006. *Full Service: Moving from Self-Service Christianity to Total Servanthood.* Grand Rapids, MI: Baker Books Publishing, 54-55.

Tarallo, Mark. 2018. *The Art of Servant Leadership. SHRM.* May 17. Accessed August 20, 2021. https:// www.shrm.org/ResourcesAndTools/hr-topics/organizational-and-employee- development/Pages/The- Art-of-Servant-Leadership.aspx.

Tarr, Dennis L. 1995. *The Strategic Toughness of Servant Leadership in Reflections on Leadership: How Robert K. Greenleaf's Theory of Servant Leadership Influenced Today's Top Management Thinkers. by Larry Spears (ed).* New York, NY: John Wiley & Sons.

Tatum, James B. 1995. *"Meditations on Servant Leadership" in Larry C. Spears, ed. 1995. Reflections on Leadership: How Robert K. Greenleaf's Theory of Servant Leadership Influenced Today's Top Management Thinkers.* New York, NY: John Wiley & Sons.

The Air Force Cadet Wing. 1965. *Contrails: The Air Force Cadet Handbook, Volume II, 1965-66.* Colorado Springs, CO: United States Air Force Academy.

The Institute for Strategy and Competitiveness. n.d. *U.S. Cluster Mapping Project*. Accessed March 4, 2019. http://clustermapping.us/cluster.

The New York Times. 1991. "Managing; General Fain, the Team Player." December 22: Section 3, 23.

Theory X and Theory Y. n.d. MSG Management Study Guide. Accessed April 12, 2021. https://www.managementstudyguide.com/theory-x-y-motivation.htm.

Thomas, Andrew S. W. n.d. , *Ph.D. and Former NASA Astronaut*. Accessed February 29, 2018. https://www.jsc.nasa.gov/Bios/htmlbios/thomas-a.html.

Thompson, Kenneth N. 2010. *Servant Leadership: An Effective Model for Project Management*. Doctoral Dissertation, Minneapolis, MN: Capella University.

Thompson, Robert. 2017. *The Study of Brokenness as a Critical Success Factor in the Effective Leadership of the Pastor*. Doctoral Dissertation, Portland, OR: George Fox Evangelical Seminary.

Tidd, Joe, and John R. Bessant. 2018. *Managing Innovation: Integrating Technological, Market and Organizational Change*. 6th ed. Hoboken, NJ: John Wiley & Sons.

Tirpak, John A. 1997. "Raptor 01." *Air Force Magazine*, July: 46-50.

Topcu, Mustafa Kemal, Ali Gursoy, and Poyraz Gurson. 2015. "The Role of the Servant Leadership on the Relation between Ethical Climate Perception and Innovative Work." *European Research Studies; Anixis 18 (1)* 18 (1): 67-79.

Tun, Lei Lei. 2020. *"Encouraging Innovation Through Servant Leadership." Udacity*. July 8. Accessed June 23, 2021. https://www.udacity.com/blog/2020/07/encouraging- innovation-through-servant-leadership.html.

Tzu, Sun. n.d. *The Art of War*. Accessed April 6, 2018. https://www.goodreads.com/work/quotes/3200649-s-nzi-b-ngf.

U.S. Air Force. 2015. *F-22 Raptor*. September 23. Accessed October 19, 2018. https://www.af.mil/About-Us/Fact-Sheets/Display/Article/104506/f-22-raptor/.

U.S. Air Force. 2015. *F-22 Raptor Fact Sheet*. September 22. Accessed January 22, 2018. http://www.af.mil/About-Us/Fact-Sheets/Display/Article/104506/f-22-raptor/.

Van Dierendonck, Dirk. 2011. *6 Key Servant Leadership Attributes." IEDP Developing Leaders*. September 26. Accessed February 1, 2018. https://www.iedp.com/articles/six-key- servant-leadership-attributes/.

Van Putten, Alexander B., and Ian C. MacMillan. 2004. "Making Real Options Really Work." *Harvard Business Review* 82 (12): 134-141.

Vanourck, Robert A. 1995. "Servant Leadership and the Future." In *Reflections on Leadership: How Robert K. Greenleaf's Theory of Servant Leadership Influenced Today's Top Management Thinkers.*, by Larry C. Spears, 298-307. New York: John Wiley & Sons.

Vantage Circle. n.d. *Servant Leadership, its Principles and Examples in the Workplace*. Accessed August 20, 2021. https://blog.vantagecircle.com/servant-leadership/.

Wagner , Gary F., and Randall White. July-August, 1995. *"F-22 Program Integrated Product Development Teams."* Program Manager.

Wagner, Gary F, and Randall White. 1993. *An Investigation of Integrated Product Development Teams on the F-22 Program*. Dayton, OH: Wright-Patterson Air Force Base, OH: Air Force Institute of Technology, 1, 2.

Walker, Sam. 2019. "One Fix for All That's Wrong: Better Managers." *The Wall Street Journal*, March 23-24: B1-B2.

Wartzman, Rick, and Andy Pasztor. 1991. "Lockheed Team Gets Air Force Contract to Build Next-Generation Fighter Plane." *The Wall Street Journal*, April 24: A3.

Warwick, Graham. 1991. "Team Player." *Flight International*, 27 November – 3 December, 21. We Empower Servant Leaders. 2020. *"Servant Leadership."* December 16. Accessed August 22, 2021. https://www.weempowerleaders.com/servant-leadership-pros/.

Weber, Jason. n.d. *"Improving Team Effectiveness through Servant Leadership." Leadership: Training Industry.* Accessed September 2, 2021. https://trainingindustry.com/magazine/mar-apr-2018/improving-team-effectiveness- through-servant-leadership/.

What is Work Breakdown Structure? n.d. Accessed August 1, 2021. https://www.visual- paradigm.com/guide/project-management/what-is-work-breakdown- structure/#:~:text=What%20is%20Work%20Breakdown%20Structure%3F%201%20Wor k%20Breakdown,5%20Other%20Use%20Cases%20of.

Wikipedia. n.d. *"Overview: Integrated Master Plan."* Accessed January 15, 2022. https://en.wikipedia.org/wiki/Integrated_master_plan.

—. n.d. *"Servant Leadership."* Accessed September 18, 2021. https://en.wikipedia.org/wiki/Servant_leadership.

Williams, Del. 2012. "Servant Leadership Sustains Competitive US Manufacturing Advantage." *Industry Today.* Accessed 30 June, 2018. https://industrytoday.com/article/servant- leadership-sustains-competitive-us-manufacturing-advantage/.

Williams, Michael D. 1999. *Acquisition for the 21st Century: The F-22 Development Program.* Washington D.C.: National Defense University Press.

Wisner, Joel D., Keah-Choon Tan, and G. Keong Leong. 2012. *Principles of Supply Chain Management: A Balanced Approach.* 3rd ed. Mason, OH: South-Western Cengage Learning.

Witt, David. 2014. *Ken Blanchard: 3 Enduring Truths about Leading Others.* May 5. Accessed February 1, 2018. https://leaderchat.org/2014/05/05/ken-blanchard-3-enduring-truths- about-leading-others/.

Womack, James P., and Daniel T. Jones. 2003. *Lean Thinking: Banish Waste and Create Wealth in Your Corporation.* 2nd ed. New York, N.Y.: Free Press.

Yang, Jin, Hefu Liu, and Jibao Gu. 2017. "A multi-level study of servant leadership on creativity: The roles of self-efficacy and power distance." *Leadership & Organization Development Journal,* 38 (5): 610-629.

Yeung, Bernard. 2013. "Lead a Collective Change in Attitude." *The Experts: How Should Leaders Spur Innovation.* Wall Street Journal, March 12. https://www.wsj.com/articles/SB100014241278873238267 0457835292147382531.

Zahorsky, Darrell. 2019. "Elements of a SMART Business Goal. The Balance Small Business." Accessed February 13, 2020. https://www.thebalancesmb.com/elements-of-a-smart- business-goal-2951530.

Zappos Insights. 2014. *5 Benefits of Getting to Know Your Team.* 11 5. Accessed 8 18, 2018. https://www.zapposinsights.com/blog/item/5-benefits-of-getting-to-know-your-team.

Zell, Stacy. 2014. *Lockheed Martin, Six Sigma and Corporate Sustainability.* June 20. Accessed October 7, 2014. https://www.sixsigmadaily.com/six-sigma-guides-lockheed-martin- sustainability goals/#:~:text=Six%20Sigma%20Guides%20Lockheed%20.

Micky Blackwell, President, Lockheed Aeronautical Systems Company

"WE NEVER FORGET WHY IT'S CALLED A NEXT GENERATION FIGHTER."

The only sure way to protect generations of the future is with a capable arsenal of the future. In terms of air superiority, that can only mean one aircraft. The F-22. This fighter incorporates the latest technological breakthroughs, assuring America will maintain air superiority and continued leadership in world aviation, as well as providing technological filter-down to private industry. And because it will cost 30% less to maintain, support and deploy than current fighters, the F-22 is a cost-effective solution for the Air Force of the 21st century. F-22. Because providing for the security of future generations isn't an option. It's a duty.

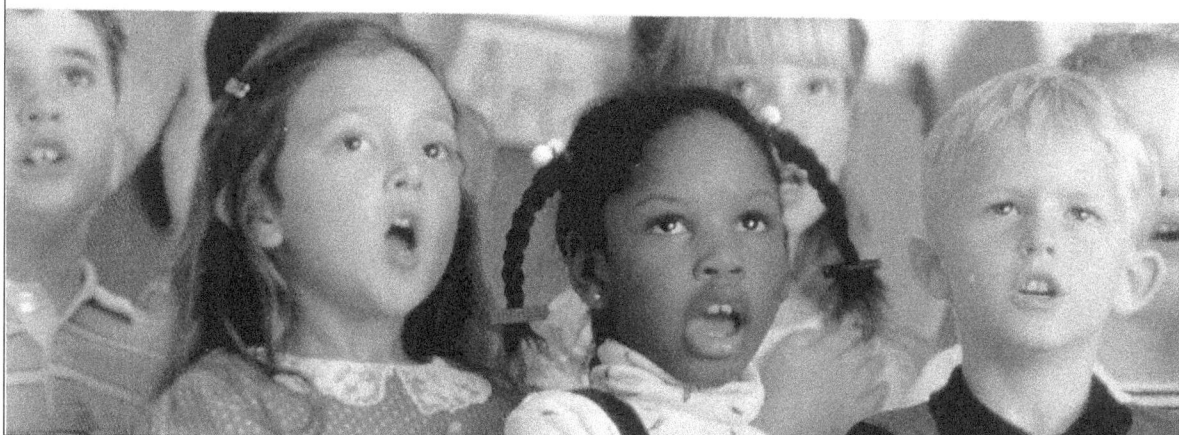

LOCKHEED · BOEING
PRATT & WHITNEY

Source: Lockheed ad as it appeared on inside back cover of Air Force magazine, June 1994.

INDEX

D

DARPA, 183
Decision-Making, 36, 41, 72, 80, 115, 131, 134, 195
Define Your Core Values, 134, 144
Denmark, 188
Department of Defense, 34, 38, 47, 86, 93-94, 104, 115, 117, 140, 154, 164, 170-171, 175, 177, 181-184, 187, 201-204
Dimensions and Characteristics of the F-22, 230
Distinguished Engineering Fellow, 232
Druyun, Darleen, 80, 174-175, 181-182, 187
Dunaway, Bill, 205-206

E

Egypt, 69, 154, 188
Elrod, Robert, 198
Empathetic, 79, 82
Engineering and Manufacturing Development, 34, 41, 115-116
Enterprise Resource Planning, 7, 46, 99, 102, 107, 110, 119-120, 162

F

F-16, 47-48, 162, 165, 172, 177, 183, 185, 188-190
F-22, 1-5, 8, 11, 16, 18, 20, 27-28, 31, 34-35, 37-48, 53, 55, 58, 60, 65-67, 71-73, 75-81, 83-84, 86, 88-89, 91-94, 99-100, 102-105, 107-110, 115-116, 118-121, 124, 129-133, 135, 139-140, 144, 151, 153, 162, 165-166, 168-169, 171-172, 175, 177, 183-184, 186-188, 190, 192-195, 198, 209-210, 212
F-22 Team Project Office, 42, 115
Fain, Gen. James, 5, 8, 35, 80, 115-116, 147
Finance, 41, 73, 87, 107, 109, 114, 116, 122-123, 131, 136, 138, 146
Financial Performance, 163
First Flight of F-22, 165
Flow, 101-102, 106, 109-110
Focus on Quality, 139, 142, 145
Foreign Corrupt Practices Act, 69, 124, 170
Form Integrated Product Teams, 135, 144
Fort Worth, 14, 42, 47-48, 80-81, 104, 106, 162, 183, 188
Foundations and Scholarships, 208
France, 186
Fulghum, David, 175, 199-200, 210-211

G

Gansler, Jacques, 181
General Electric, 35, 181
Georgia Institute of Technology, 25, 137
Georgia Military Affairs Committee, 203
Giogio Zappa, 199
Goal, 13, 25, 34, 39, 55-56, 61-62, 66, 71, 75, 87, 91, 94-95, 100, 107, 133, 145, 165, 174, 192, 207, 209
Goldin, Dan, 168
Greece, 188
Green, Colin, 198
Greenleaf, Robert K., 15, 17, 53-55, 62-64, 83-84, 136-137, 142, 146, 148, 162, 213
Group of 12, 24
Guidelines and Examples, 65

H

Hancock, Dain, 176
Heppe, Dick, 36-37, 48
Hewson, Marillyn A., 200, 211
High Reynolds Number, 19, 22, 24
High Technology Test Bed, 30, 154
High-Performance Teams, 73, 87, 192
Hodges, Phil, 17, 54, 61-63, 66, 74, 77-78, 83-84, 89, 95, 144, 148
Hyde, Heather, 62, 91, 95, 133, 145

I

IBM Aerospace and Defense, 201
India, 156
Innovation, 53, 55, 58, 71-72, 82, 92, 103, 116-119, 126, 130-131, 136, 138, 142, 146
IPT, 41, 73, 87, 89-90, 93-94, 113-114, 116, 126-128, 135, 138, 168, 173
Iraq, 156
Israel, 155-157, 186, 188, 198-199
Italy, 186

J

Jabez, 20-21
Japan, 108-109, 153, 178, 186
Jasper, Alabama, 11-13, 20
Jennings, Ken, 55, 62, 91, 95, 133, 145, 241
Johnson, Ken, 24
Joint Air-to-Surface Standoff Missile, 189-191
Joint Strike Fighter, 47, 71, 167, 169, 172, 174, 181-183, 191
Jordan, 32, 157-158, 188
JSF, 71, 80-81, 104-105, 107, 165, 173-174, 183-185, 191, 195, 209

W

Walmsley, Vice Adm. Sir Robert, 199
Warner-Robins AFB, 204
Weston, John, 198
Whitcomb, Richard "Dick", 18-19, 21, 74
White House, 166
Wolfe, Tom, 1
Work Breakdown Structure, 73, 116, 131

X

X-33, 162, 168, 172, 189, 191

Y

Yakovlev, 167, 177
Yuan-Shi Peng, 199

About the Author
ROBERT MATERNA, PH.D.

Robert Materna was born in Front Royal, Virginia on July 4, 1947. Even though he was born in the Blue Ridge Mountains, he grew up in a small town called Madison, Ohio which is east of Cleveland, Ohio.

Life was good on the shores of Lake Erie. It was far from the big cities and a nice place to raise a family. Robert's life changed in 1965, when he accepted an appointment to the United States Air Force Academy. Following graduation, he went through pilot training in Valdosta, Georgia. He spent the next three years flying C-141 Starlifters in and out of Southeast Asia. He also flew supplies into Israel during the Yom Kippur War. When the war was over, he spent another ten months flying OV-10 Broncos in northeastern Thailand.

After returning from Asia, he attended the Air Force Institute of Technology (AFIT) in Ohio. With his Master's in his hand, he held several positions in logistics. He flew T-39 Sabreliners on the weekends and obtained his airline pilot rating. Five years later, he received orders to Charleston Air

Force Base, South Carolina. Most missions involved flying C-141s to Europe, but he also was part of the plan to bring the hostages out of Iran. In addition to his duties as an Instructor and Special Operations pilot, he managed the flight schedule for all active duty and reserve forces assigned to the base north of Charleston.

After three years at Charleston, he was invited to join the faculty at AFIT. Following five years of intense academic work, he earned his Ph.D. at Georgia State University in Business Administration. He then fulfilled his commitment to the Air Force doing research, teaching, and consulting for the Department of Defense. Even though Robert enjoyed his military career, he retired after 21 years as a lieutenant colonel to pursue other interests.

His next job was at NCR, one of America's oldest multinational corporations. After three years of travel and extensive market research, he was recruited and hired by Andersen Consulting (now Accenture), the world's largest consulting firm. Following several winters in Chicago, Robert moved south to Atlanta. In addition to changing jobs, he shifted the focus of his research. He worked for a non-profit studying trends in the workplace and corporate infrastructure management.

In 2005, after decades of research and passports filled with visas, Dr. Materna returned to academia and the scholarly work he enjoyed. During the last years of his career, he leveraged his experience to build a graduate program in Logistics and Supply Chain Management for Embry-Riddle Aeronautical University – Worldwide. He also developed and managed their Industry Advisory Board; launched the Center for Aviation and Aerospace Leadership; delivered symposiums on aerospace manufacturing; and published books and reports on the aerospace industry. Some of his publications include:

Materna, R., Mansfield, R. E., Walton, R. O. (2015). *Aerospace industry report: facts, figures & outlook for the aviation and aerospace manufacturing industry (4th ed.).* Daytona Beach, Florida: Embry-Riddle Aeronautical Industry-Worldwide.

Materna, R., Mansfield, R. E., & Deck III, F. W. (2013). *Aerospace industry report: facts, figures & outlook for the aviation and aerospace manufacturing industry (3rd ed.).* Daytona Beach, Florida: Center for Aviation & Aerospace Leadership at Embry-Riddle Aeronautical University-Worldwide and the Aerospace Industries Association.

Materna, R. (2010). International Air Transportation, in P. David & R. Stewart (Eds.) *International logistics: The management of international trade operations* (3rd ed.) Mason, Ohio: Thomson, pp. 290-311.

Materna, R. & Mansfield, R. (2010, July-September). Preserving a crown jewel: Strengthening the U.S. aerospace supply base. *Logistics Spectrum,* 44 (3), pp. 19-24. This paper won the Best Paper Award for the annual 2010 SOLE Symposium and was subsequently published in the *Logistics Spectrum.*

Professor Materna retired from Embry-Riddle Aeronautical University in 2015.

In 1978, Robert joined an organization called Officer's Christian Fellowship. Through his exposure to other Christian officers and, with the help of his wife Sharyn, he became a Christian later that year. His life would never be the same.

In 1995, when Micky and Billie moved to Maryland when he became the new president of Lockheed Martin's Aeronautics Sector, Robert and Sharyn bought the house that Micky and Billie built in Marietta when Micky ran the F-22 program and was president of Lockheed Aeronautical Systems Company.

While putting the final touches on this book, Robert passed away on New Years Day 2023 from complications relating to a courageous battle with Parkinson's disease. With the publication of this edition of *Enterprise Servant Leadership*, his beloved wife Sharyn completes his final mission.